The Politics of Motherhood

THE POLITICS OF

edited by

Alexis Jetter,

Annelise Orleck,

and Diana Taylor

DARTMOUTH COLLEGE

MOTHERHOOD

Activist

Voices

from

Left to Right

Published by University Press of New England : Hanover and London

Dartmouth College

Published by University Press of New England, Hanover, NH 03755

© 1997 by The Trustees of Dartmouth College

"Waiting in the Wings: Reflections on a Radical Motherhood" © 1996 by Cherríe Moraga

Printed in the United States of America   5   4   3   2   1

CIP data appear at the end of the book

This volume is dedicated to the memory of Patsy Ruth Oliver, environmentalist, storyteller, hell-raiser and mother. She touched and inspired so many. Her personal motto makes an apt epigram for this book:

So many people don't think that one person can make a difference. But really, it has to start somewhere, so let it start with me.

Contents

Mothers' Resistance Against the State

Nationalist Motherhood

Redefining Motherhood: Technologies and Sexualities

Reflections on Feminism and Motherhood

Preface

From the Kitchen Table

This all began in October 1992 at Diana Taylor's kitchen table. We were casually discussing our work—mine on militant housewives and welfare mothers, hers on the Argentine Mothers of the Plaza de Mayo. Maybe it was the espresso, but before the afternoon was out we were planning a conference that would bring together scholars interested in motherhood with mother-activists from around the world. The conference took place in May 1993, and it was an unforgettable experience. Many of the women represented in this volume participated in that remarkable weekend during which we all learned to listen and to speak across disciplinary as well as cultural boundaries. There was a spirit of openness and deep engagement during those three days that we hope is at least partially reproduced in this volume.

We want to express our gratitude to all of the women whose names appear in this book, as well as to Susan Ackerman, Ivy Schweitzer, Susanne Zantop, Alice Ip, Dagmar Thorpe, Grace Thorpe, Patricia Green, Marguerite Bouvard, Julie Peteet and Marilyn Young, who helped to make the Redefining Motherhood conference happen.

We would like to thank Gail Vernazza for the superhuman effort she put into organizing that conference and for her assistance in putting together this volume. Special thanks to Teresa Thurston, Rebecca Slisz, Heidi Gamer, Shannon Sullivan, Marisol Negrón, Jacqueline Lazú and many others who have contributed time and energy to the conference and the book.

The most difficult part of putting together any collection, especially one that brings together activists in a variety of causes, scholars from diverse disciplines, journalists and fiction writers, and women from around the globe, is figuring out how to make the pieces fit together in a readable whole. If this book hangs together, it is largely because of the tireless and impeccable editorial work done by Alexis Jetter. Virtually every piece in this book bears her imprint.

A.O.

INTRODUCTION

Tradition Unbound

Radical Mothers in International Perspective

Annelise Orleck

Since everyone has, or has had, a mother, most people have strong feelings and opinions about the institution of motherhood. Perhaps the most deeply rooted of these is the notion that mothers are by definition apolitical, isolated with their children in a world of pure emotion, far removed from the welter of politics and social struggle. Underlying this static image of the mutually absorbed madonna and child is the unstated belief that bearing and raising children alters a woman's consciousness in an essentially conservative way, quieting and grounding even the most rebellious of women. The essays, interviews, articles and stories collected in this volume offer an alternative perspective: For the women whose lives are described here, motherhood is not an isolating or individualized experience, but rather the basis for inclusion in an activist community, the inspiration for and the foundation of visions of large-scale social change.

There is little discussion in the pages that follow of the themes usually associated with examinations of motherhood: biology versus social construction; nature versus nurture; balancing career and child rearing; whether or not there is some sort of inborn "maternal" instinct. Nor will there be essays about child psychology, mothering techniques, breastfeeding or mother–child bonding. Those topics have been explored in other kinds of books. Our concern here is with the many ways that motherhood has been politicized, both as a means to control women—through state regulation, medical intervention, and brutal military assault—and as a means by which women have sought to regain control over their lives and the lives of their children.

Some of the women whose voices appear in this book were formerly apolitical housewives, first moved to take political action by concern for their own children. For them, the radicalizing process involved a series of crucial leaps from caring about their own children, to caring about other mothers and children, to engaging with pressing social and political issues of national and even international import. Becoming politically active changed these women's understanding of themselves as mothers and as individual adult women, affirming in them a sense of collective power, entitlement and moral authority. Other mothers whose stories are told in this collection were involved in political work long before their children were born. These women found that becoming mothers transformed them in new and profound ways, challenging and reshaping their perceptions of themselves as activists. Previously, these veteran activists had approached social change from a macroscopic perspective; through mothering, they developed a visceral sense of how large-scale political issues affect the lives of individual children.

The women in this book were radicalized at different stages of the mothering experience: for some, a change in consciousness came with pregnancy; for others, it came through the process of caring for children. For a few it came even before conception. Alarmed by their experiences with those who control the new reproductive technologies, these women felt compelled to defy an industry that objectifies and commercializes conception, childbirth and the maternal body. Once politically active, some of these women used their motherhood strategically, aware that speaking out as mothers would give them more credibility in sexist societies than they would have as individual women. But others sincerely believed that motherhood conferred upon them special insights and responsibilities to solve the problems plaguing their families and communities.

The activists, scholars, journalists and writers whose voices are gathered together in this volume explore the politicization of motherhood in vastly different social and cultural contexts. Here we meet mother-activists from blue-collar upstate New York neighborhoods and rural Kenyan villages, from the broad avenues of Buenos Aires and the dusty alleys of the Gaza Strip, from the expanses of the White Earth Reservation in Minnesota and the stifling sweatshops of New York's Chinatown. Besides class, race, nationality, and culture, these activist mothers are divided by social status and political ideology. They are single and married mothers, lesbian and heterosexual mothers, militarist and anti-militarist mothers, racist and anti-racist mothers. Indeed, they have few commonalities but for the fact that they all have found in motherhood a spark of radical change. We have included essays by and interviews with activists as well as descriptive and analytic essays by journalists and scholars. We hope in this way both to provide context, and to reveal hidden dimensions of the vital dialogue between scholarship, journalism and activism.

We recognize the importance of contextualizing the differences noted here. Instead of talking about "mothers" generally we ask "which mothers?" It would be a distortion to pretend that conceptions or meanings of motherhood carry across national, cultural, political and religious boundaries, that they could be the same for women of different races, ethnicities, classes, ages, or sexual preferences. As sociologists Evelyn Nakano Glenn and Patricia Hill Collins have pointed out in their writings about mothers of color, much theorizing about motherhood—even some feminist theorizing—has assumed a universality of experience based on the lives of white, middle-class women. The experiences, identities and concerns of mothers of color, as well as poor and working-class mothers, have been ignored or obscured. That is equally true of mothers from other nations and cultures. Listening to their voices, focusing on the concerns of mothers who are so rarely heard, cracks open and then recasts popular understandings of motherhood.[1]

Personally, socially and politically, it is impossible to speak about motherhood without speaking of social systems of power and domination. For, while motherhood is an individual and highly personal experience, it is also a social institution, shaped by and tied to the ideology of the nuclear family. Looked at in that way, motherhood is always a politicized role, especially in its most romantic and idealized portrayals. Notions of "good motherhood"—underscored by popular images of maternal devotion and self-sacrifice—serve to regulate not only who becomes a mother but what it means to be a mother in a particular milieu. The institution of Motherhood with a capital M regulates acceptable behavior, restricts expression, and designates appropriate spaces for action. Women are controlled and pitted against one another through their relationship to motherhood. Substantial privileges await those who perform their roles properly. Punishment awaits those "bad mothers" who don't. It is against this nexus of power relations that mother-activism must be assessed.

Just as we must take complex systems of power relations into account when we speak of motherhood, so must we when we discuss "motherist" politics. Given dramatic differences in the class, race, ethnicity, culture, sexual and political orientation of mother-activists, it is impossible to describe a single, coherent "motherist" politics. Nevertheless, there are characteristics that carry across lines of difference. Philosopher Sara Ruddick and political theorist Nancy Hartsock, long-time analysts of the link between mothering and politics, have argued that the work done by individual mothers in caring for and nurturing their own children gives them a particular political viewpoint from which they can work to change the world for all children. That maternalist perspective, with its emphasis on giving and nurturing life, has been associated with many different kinds of mother-activism: from environmental justice to subsistence, anti-militarist, and even nationalist struggles.[2] There are also contradictions and conflicts that transcend the differences between mothers' movements. Perhaps the most profound is that activism often takes mothers away from their children—sometimes simply because the mothers must spend long hours doing political work, but at other times because the mothers risk imprisonment or even death in trying to create a better world for their children.

Despite the risks, there is clearly a political strength that comes from claiming mother politics. The women represented in this volume strike out angrily at romantic images of family life that obscure real families and their very real problems. Many of them recognize no separation between motherhood and activism. They see caring for children as a way of caring for the future. But recognizing the interconnections between their roles as mothers and activists does not spare these women the painful contradictions inherent in turning motherhood into the basis for activism. Two particularly poignant reflections on that theme come from mother-activists whose stories appear in this volume. Argentine radical Alicia Partnoy made the wrenching decision to stop breastfeeding her daughter in the late 1970s because she knew that arrest and imprisonment were inevitable if she continued to fight the military junta. She wanted to wean her baby gently, if too early, before she was torn away from her. Kenyan environmentalist Wangari Maathai remembers struggling for years with her children's anger. What cause, they asked her, could be worth risking a beating or arrest that might take her from them? Only as adults were Partnoy and Maathai's children able to assure their mothers that they understood the reasons for the sacrifices they were all forced to make.[3]

Fully aware of these painful contradictions, women activists around the world continue to embrace politicized motherhood as an empowering identity. Burning through the mists of biological and emotional essentialism that shroud the reality of motherhood, women are reclaiming and reshaping the role that has so long been used to control them. But this does not mean that they are necessarily embracing feminism, egalitarianism or peace. The strategies that mother-activists have chosen, the goals they strive toward, the visions of motherly responsibility they espouse, the ideologies they subscribe to are as varied as women themselves. Romantic assertions about the "natural" idealism, selflessness or moral superiority of mothers fall apart quickly when we examine actual mothers' movements close up.

RADICAL MOTHERS: A RECENT HISTORY

In 1995, newscasts were filled with angry mothers protesting on behalf of their children. On January 20, several Massachusetts welfare mothers were removed bodily from the floor of the U.S. House of Representatives when they attempted to address a hearing on welfare reform. "We need to be here," one woman boomed as she was carried out. "We need to testify." On Valentine's Day, poor mothers in more than 70 U.S. cities staged "have-a-heart" demonstrations protesting budget cuts that they feared would leave their children hungry and without medical care. Later the same spring, mothers of children killed by gunfire marched on Washington, D.C., carrying pictures of their dead. They had come to call for stricter gun control and to express their outrage at those in Congress who were working to repeal the ban on assault weapons. Mothers also marched that year through housing projects across the United States, in self-created mothers' crime patrols—out to spot and report drug dealers.[4]

Such protests have by no means been limited to the United States. In Russia, mothers of boys sent by Boris Yeltsin to invade Chechnya organized a movement to get their sons to desert. They traveled to besieged Grozny to retrieve their children from prisoner-of-war camps, and then stood behind their shaken teenaged sons, urging them to explain to reporters why they could no longer serve in a fratricidal war.[5] In Argentina, the now-greying Mothers of the Plaza de Mayo continue to march on the streets of Buenos Aires, bearing photos of their long-dead children. In the wake of the army chief's public confession that the military had tortured and murdered civilians during the Dirty War of the late 1970s and early 1980s, the Mothers demanded that the government bring the murderers to justice.[6]

These are but a few examples of the political mobilization of mothers around the world during the last two years. How do we understand the anger and the activism of these women? Are these completely separate movements or are there common threads that bind them? How does our sense both of politics and of motherhood change if we accept the idea that, for many women in cultures around the world, motherhood is a powerful political identity around which they have galvanized broad-based and influential grassroots movements for social change?

Maternalism has not always, or only, been espoused by mothers. In the women's social reform movements that swept the United States at the turn of the twentieth century, many of the most visible activists were single women activists who argued a special role for women in "cleaning up" the worst abuses of industrial capitalism. These women used the language of maternal morality and purity to open up a space for activism by single women. Progressive reformer Jane Addams, the best known figure in the settlement house movement, argued that the growth of cities necessitated an extension of mothers' responsibilities beyond the home, to the city street, the neighborhood, and ultimately to the nation. The settlement house and women's social reform movements channeled such maternal sentiments into a broad vision of reform politics that generated sympathy across gender and class lines for the idea of a benevolent state that cared for those who could not care for themselves. Many married middle- and upper-class women, who were reluctant to challenge accepted norms of feminine behavior, could now justify their involvement in political activism by arguing that they were merely taking up their maternal responsibility for "social housekeeping." This welling up of politicized maternalist sentiment sparked a re-envisioning of the very idea of the United States, which began to look to many citizens less like a sea of atomized, competitive individuals than a family bound by notions of collective responsibility. This was not strictly a United States-based phenomenon. Women's social reform movements and maternalist politics also fueled the emergence of gendered social welfare states in early twentieth-century France, Germany and Great Britain.[7]

Women's peace movements have adopted an even more explicitly maternalist rhetoric. Indeed, peace activism is sometimes seen as the archetypal "motherist" movement. That image has arisen in large part because of the language of maternal protectiveness employed by women in various peace movements. From the European Women's Peace League of the mid-nineteenth century to the U.S. Women's Peace Party of the 1910s, Women Strike for Peace (WSP) in the 1960s, and the movement of Oxford Mothers for Nuclear Disarmament (who occupied England's Greenham Common) in the 1980s, women have claimed that they are compelled to fight for peace because they are humanity's "custodians of life."[8] One WSP leaflet from 1961 offered an explanation for women's anti-nuclear activism that exemplified this mode of "motherist" political thinking: "Women spend years of their lives bringing up children to be healthy individuals and good citizens. Now, in the nuclear age all women—not only mothers—have an . . . urgent duty to work for peace in order that our children may have a future."[9]

Such linkages between women, maternal instinct and pacifism have not gone uncontested. Feminist activists and theorists have challenged them as both reductive and essentialist—forcing all women into an idealized relationship with maternity and children that reflects neither the diversity of women's experiences nor the diversity of women's desires. Also, as several of the essays in this volume vividly illustrate, the notion that mothers are automatically drawn to pacifism ignores numerous historical and contemporary examples of mothers who support violent racist movements in the name of protecting their children. Even more numerous have been those who argue that it is the responsibility of "good" (read, patriotic) mothers to raise their children to become soldiers, in either nationalist revolutions or service to the nation-state.[10]

Essays in this volume by Diana Taylor and Simona Sharoni trace mothers' anti-militarist activism in Argentina and Israel, examining an archetypal motherist organization—the Mothers of the Plaza de Mayo—and two of its offspring, Parents Against Silence and Women in Black. These authors take a critical view of the conflation of women with motherhood and of the notion that mothers are innately more concerned with peace than are nonmothers. However, neither Taylor nor Sharoni are willing to write these movements off as hopelessly essentialist or conservative.

Sharoni argues that women anti-war activists have been keenly aware of "the available space for women to voice dissent in a particular context, at a particular historical moment." While U.S. anti-Vietnam War activists, the Argentine Mothers of the Plaza de Mayo and Israel's Parents Against Silence employed the imagery of traditional motherhood in their demonstrations, they did not necessarily believe that all mothers were peaceful or that all women acted out of an instinct to preserve the lives of children. Instead, Sharoni writes, we must at least entertain the possibility that these women used their motherhood strategically, to maximize the effectiveness of their movements. Their use of the language of nurturing and care may then be understood as an attempt to galvanize broad-based support and to fend off attacks in a repressive, wartime political climate.

In her book, *Women Strike for Peace: Traditional Motherhood and Radical Politics in the 1960s*, historian Amy Swerdlow admits that she and other mother-activists employed their motherhood to gain credibility and deflect charges of subversion in the heyday of the Cold War. But this was far from a cynical act. Swerdlow insists that members of Women Strike for Peace acted out of a deep and very real maternalist world view. "The image WSP projected of concerned, understandably emotional, middle-class matrons was not merely a ruse perpetrated by women to disguise deeper political motives. I recall that I stressed my maternal interests rather than my radical politics, when I spoke and wrote for WSP, because I believed that my genuine motherly concerns would be received and understood by non-political women, the media and public officials."[11]

Grace Paley, a colleague of Swerdlow's and an equally committed peace activist, has often expressed discomfort with the peace movement's invocation of the sanctity of motherhood. In her essay for this volume, recalling the six days she spent in prison for sitting down in the middle of New York's Fifth Avenue to block a military parade, Paley describes an encounter between a middle-class pacifist mother and a group of poor mothers jailed for prostitution. With characteristic humor and candor, Paley skewers notions of good and bad motherhood by injecting the explosive issues of class and race into the safe, middle-class precincts of pacifist mothers' movements.

In a starkly different prison tale in this volume, Alicia Partnoy describes the dangers inherent in singling women out for special treatment as mothers. Partnoy's remembrance of her imprisonment in the 1970s by Argentina's military junta makes devastatingly clear how the motherhood of women political prisoners has been manipulated by state-sponsored torturers. Denying mothers the ability to touch their children during prison visits—a restriction not placed on fathers—and electroshocking the breasts of young mothers were punishments designed to break down the bonds of mothers and their children, exacting a psychological as well as a physical toll. The final act of severing that bond came when prison officials stole the babies of female political prisoners and gave them to military families to raise. In such ways were "bad mothers" punished and "good mothers" given control over the next generation.

Partnoy's experience illustrates the danger of rallying women behind the banner of "good motherhood." Notions of what constitutes good motherhood vary dramatically from culture to culture and according to political belief. So do women's understandings of how to protect their children. The idea that motherhood entitles women to speak to and for entire societies has moved women to organize courageous movements against military dictatorships, and to confront poverty, environmental degradation and racial inequality. But it can also move mothers, in their capacity as nurturers of "the future of the race," to espouse violent racist ideologies.

As a result, the very idea of "motherist" politics becomes dangerously slippery, as the essays in this volume by Claudia Koonz, Kathleen Blee and Kathy Dobie make clear. These authors introduce us to Bosnian Serb women who believe that they are protecting their children by blocking trucks bearing relief supplies for Muslim women's children, and to white supremacist women in the United States who believe that they are fulfilling their motherly responsibilities by beating up "race-mixers." Claudia Koonz identifies two types of right-wing mothers active in the 1990s: "backlash conservatives" in democracies like the United States and Italy, where influential feminist movements have empowered women on the right as well as the left to take political action; and women in former Communist countries, where the rhetoric of gender equality has covered over a reality in which women find little space to organize independent political movements. Here the politicization of motherhood takes a more sinister form, as images of traditional motherhood are mobilized in the service of genocidal nationalism.

But Eastern Europe has no monopoly on murderous, right-wing mothers' politics. As Kathy Dobie and Kathleen Blee illustrate, the violent, racist ideology of skinhead and Klan mothers resides comfortably within a framework of maternal care. Blee describes advertisements for toddler car seats and Aryan cookbooks that appear alongside militant calls to arms in White Power newsletters. Dobie's skinhead mothers trace an evolution, from beating up integrationists to nurturing racist children, as a logical continuum in the maturation of a white supremacist woman. These movements, too, embrace a politics of motherhood, though in a form that most would find chilling.

The Italian Housewives' Federation, profiled in this volume, offers a different model for right-wing mothers' activism — eschewing scapegoating in favor of savvy electoral and economic maneuvering. The self-proclaimed goal of Federcasalinghe is to force the state to pay salaries to "good mothers" — women who perform the socially useful tasks of nurturing children, husbands and elderly relatives. While feminists charge Federcasalinghe with trying to push women back into the home, and warn that the group's vision of state-sponsored motherhood is uncomfortably close to that of Mussolini's Italy, leaders of this contemporary Catholic housewives' movement insist that they are only interested in bringing recognition to women who work in the home. Few in Italian politics believe that the state will ever pay salaries to housewives, but they acknowledge that Federcasalinghe has successfully used maternalist politics to forge a powerful national voting bloc with the visibility and economic clout to reward its allies and punish its enemies. Politicians of all stripes have come to court; after all, who wants to be seen as disrespectful to mama?

Recently, housewives in many countries have begun to demand political and economic recognition. In October 1995, housewife activists from 14 European and Latin American nations, members of the newly formed Inter-Continental Union of Housewives, gathered in Buenos Aires, Argentina, for a conference entitled "Housewives: Citizens of the World." Although the delegates disagreed on moral questions, including birth control and sex education in public schools, they resolved as a group that housewives should be paid for the labor they do caring for children, husbands and the elderly. Some delegates demanded state-funded salaries for housewives, and others wanted laws guaranteeing wives a set percentage of their husbands' earnings. But all wanted both political and economic recognition. "The mother, the housewife, is the basis for the family, the society and the nation," said Siglinde Porsche, president of the German Housewives' Federation. "They must receive honor, and not only with words but with money."[12]

Understanding the power of that "good mother" image, some mother-activists in the United States have brazenly manipulated the emotions of a vulnerable public for the most cynical of purposes. Take for example Mothers Against Drunk Driving (MADD), the group that brought the iconography of concerned motherhood to television screens, highway billboards, editorial columns and the floor of Congress during the 1980s. Founded by Candy Lightner, who lost a child to a drunken driver, MADD raised national consciousness about the dangers of driving drunk. In riveting televised hearings during the mid-1980s, Lightner and other MADD mothers testified before Congress about children killed by drunk drivers and about teenagers killed while driving inebriated. MADD was the force behind many states' decisions to increase penalties for drunk driving and for those who sell alcohol to teens. All this publicity enabled Candy Lightner to cash in on her "good mother" credentials.

In 1994, she took a well-paid job as lobbyist for a consortium of the nation's brewers. Her assignment was to convince members of Congress to ease restrictions on the sale of alcohol. Few Americans could lay claim to greater moral authority on the subject. The lesson: Once it is reduced to a logo, "good motherhood" can be bought and sold for all sorts of purposes.[13]

There are other complexities that must be factored into any analysis of "motherist" politics. In this country, ideas about what is and isn't "good motherhood" break down quickly along class and racial lines. Only the middle and upper classes have the luxury even to think about whether or not they will be "full-time, stay-at-home" mothers. For poor and working-class women, such choices are not available. As the essays in this volume by Mary Childers and Xiaolan Bao and the interview with Ruby Duncan graphically illustrate, poor mothers in the United States are consumed with issues of daily survival: hunger, violence, inadequate housing and health care. These concerns shatter divisions between private and public spheres. To be "good" mothers, to protect and nurture their children, they are forced to leave their homes, to labor for wages (often caring for the children of wealthier working women), and to organize politically as mothers.[14]

Poor mothers are assaulted, too, by the politics of blame. Far from being idealized as mothers, these women are held accountable for all manner of social ills. Poor women and children live at the bleak crossroads where racism and sexism meet this culture's hatred of the poor. Caught in the myth of class mobility and the ideology of individualism, poor mothers are failures if they ask for public assistance, and social outcasts if they try to raise their children without a man.

Stigmatized as a group, some poor mothers learn to respond politically, as is illustrated by my study of a twenty-year movement by welfare mothers in Las Vegas. In trying to protect their children from the very real deprivations caused by politically motivated social welfare cuts, these women schooled themselves in the workings of local, state and federal government agencies. Dealing with the welfare bureaucracy is usually a deeply humiliating experience for poor mothers. But when the women of West Las Vegas organized during the 1970s and 1980s, it became a process of empowerment. These poorly educated former cotton pickers moved beyond the limitations of maternal politics and ultimately demanded a future for themselves as well as for their children.

In mobilizing poor white mothers and mothers of color, the cries of poisoned children have been just as powerful as those of hungry children. In an era of "risk assessment," tens of thousands of women have found that the health of their children has been deemed an acceptable risk by corporate polluters looking for places to dump hazardous waste. The essays by Dollie Burwell and Alexis Jetter, and interviews with Lois Gibbs and Patsy Ruth

Oliver, describe the struggles of U.S. mothers who were transformed, to use Oliver's words, from "hysterical housewives to committed environmentalists" to protect their children from toxic waste in their homes, streets and schools. These women have sparked a nationwide grassroots rebellion, called the environmental justice movement, that has forced the nation's biggest environmental organizations to broaden their focus from trees and animals to include people. "It's mostly women—mothers and housewives—who get involved to protect family, home and community," says sociologist Robert Bullard. "These are not traditional environmentalists. These are people talking about survival."[15]

The relationship between environmental protection, cultural preservation and physical survival is a central concern for two other mother-activists interviewed in this volume, Wangari Maathai and Winona LaDuke. Maathai, a world-renowned Kenyan environmentalist and political dissident, links deforestation to malnutrition. By the late 1970s, the cutting of Kenya's once lush forests had led to severe erosion—even desertification—and had devastated communities that had lived sustainably for generations. Without firewood or sufficient water, mothers found it nearly impossible to cook traditional foods for their children, resulting in widespread malnutrition.

Alarmed, Maathai in 1977 created the Green Belt Movement, which paid traditional women to plant and maintain rows of trees around their villages, schools and churches. The women committed themselves to reclaiming for future generations "the bounty which is the birthright and property of all." Within a decade, the movement had spread to include 50,000 traditional mothers in a dozen countries across Africa. As with other mother-led movements chronicled in this book, concern for children has generated a form of collective action that has ultimately moved beyond familial concerns. The Green Belt Movement has emboldened mothers to challenge authoritarian rulers and to assert the rights of women in every sphere: social, economic and political.[16]

Working out of northern Minnesota, Anishinabe leader Winona LaDuke also links environmental restoration with cultural preservation and economic independence. Embedded in traditional native cultures, LaDuke argues, is a model for social, spiritual and economic sustainability that has worked for thousands of years. But that model is dependent on living in balance with the earth, and teaching one's children to respect that balance. LaDuke, who was arrested in 1995 for blocking the entrance to a GTE telephone book plant that uses paper from old-growth trees, sees herself less an activist than as "a responsible parent." She explains, "It would be wrong for me to talk to my children about opposing cultural destruction without opposing clear cutting, because then they will not have forests when they grow up."[17]

Sustainability is a central theme in LaDuke's protests and in what she calls her "rebuilding" work. She has established the White Earth Land Recovery Project to help Anishinabe people buy back their lands, which have shrunk to one-tenth their 1867 acreage. Anishinabe women and men have now set up rice processing facilities, a maple sugaring project, and marketing collectives to garner fairer prices for their handicrafts and wild rice.

For these Native American women, like others profiled in this book, concern for their children's future is a powerful galvanizing force. LaDuke writes: "Throughout North America, native women, joined with families and the men of their communities, both resist environmentally and culturally destructive projects and engage in rebuilding efforts . . . Many women are positive that the best security for themselves and their families isn't in the context of the modern industrial world but in a self-defined context of our own cultures and ways of living."[18]

The fight against cultural destruction has been at the heart of many mothers' movements, in particular those created to resist occupation by a foreign military power. Mother-activists have propelled themselves to the center of nationalist struggles by emphasizing their role as the preservers and transmitters of culture, and by rejecting the notion that the capacity to bear children makes a woman innately pacifistic. Women have served nationalist causes by raising and sacrificing soldier sons, by becoming combatants themselves, and by "mothering" the nation: providing nurturing and care for other mothers' sons, who become "their" children under the siege conditions created by guerilla war and state-sponsored violence.

Anthropologist Julie Peteet, whose work has strongly influenced scholars studying Palestinian women, has written searing accounts of life and death in Palestinian refugee camps. Describing the Tel al-Zaater refugee camp in Beirut, where thousands of Palestinians died at the hands of the right-wing Christian Falange, Peteet writes:

An unknown number of women died trying to provide water for their children in the besieged camp where water and food were scarce resources obtained only under gunfire or shelling. A survivor of the siege told me: "We couldn't get water or food, and children were dehydrated. But women would go out of the shelters to get water. Ten women would go out for water; only two or three would come back. They died—there was no solution: either their children died of thirst or their mothers died under the shells and bullets."[19]

In this volume, Carol Bardenstein and Rema Hammami explore the ways that the Palestinian nationalist struggle has engaged and transformed conceptions of good motherhood. As Hammami notes, the nationalist movement has actively sought "to use the identity of motherhood to mobilize women politically." Mothers whose sons die fighting against Israel earn the title "mothers of martyrs." They hold places of honor at nationalist rallies and at the funerals of other mothers' sons. However, as Hammami notes, women who actually engage in combat find it difficult to reintegrate into traditional Palestinian communities and gender roles. Hammami, who is both a nationalist and a feminist, believes that unless ways are found to reconcile the two, women will not be liberated by Palestinian nationalism. Palestinian feminists who are active in the *intifada* are attacked both by Israeli military authorities, who are anxious to quash all nationalist activity, and by Palestinian Islamic fundamentalists, for whom mother-activism is the only acceptable political role for women. Bardenstein argues that even this limited, socially sanctioned form of activism has proven empowering for Palestinian women. The role of mothers as providers of food and shelter "has been significantly expanded in scope and politicized as Palestinian mothers have come to consider themselves, and to be considered by others, as actors in the resistance."

The willingness of mothers to politicize their familial responsibilities in times of crisis is not new, nor is it restricted to a nationalist context. Mothers' activism around subsistence issues has occurred for at least two hundred years, and in various cultural and political settings. Mobilizing around their traditional roles as providers of food and shelter, Mothers in the U.S. and French revolutions, in turn-of-the-century and Depression-era U.S. immigrant neighborhoods, staged demonstrations and boycotts to demand lower food and housing costs.[20]

In her pioneering 1982 article about the activism of Barcelona housewives in the 1910s, Temma Kaplan identified a sense of group identity that she labeled "female consciousness." Distinguished from feminist consciousness by its embrace of traditional gender roles, female consciousness moves apolitical women to take collective action when they find themselves unable to provide adequate food and shelter for their families. Kaplan's analysis alerted historians of working-class, environmental and nationalist politics to the important contributions of mothers and housewives. It also offered scholars a way of understanding a form of women's protest that is often unaffiliated or only loosely affiliated with larger political movements.[21]

Kaplan's essay in this volume, on the Aba Women's War of 1929, raises another issue that is central to motherist politics: the ambivalence of authorities when faced with rebellious mother-activists. The idealization of motherhood in many societies creates a taboo around using physical force against women in general and mothers in particular. Women political activists have used this taboo, as well as others surrounding motherhood, to expand their political maneuvering room in repressive situations.

This strategy was employed in the United States, during the first decades of this century, when mothers mobilized in neighborhood networks to support striking husbands, sons and daughters by creating human chains to block factory entrances so that manufacturers could not bring in replacement labor.

Women also placed themselves at the front of predominantly male labor protests, daring police to shoot the mothers of small children. Often, the police backed down. But in Cleveland, Ohio, in 1911, and in Lawrence, Massachusetts, in 1912, police took the lives of women protestors who thought their motherhood would protect them.[22]

Just as these immigrant women's motherhood was overshadowed in the minds of policemen by differences in class and ethnicity, in the Aba Women's War that Kaplan describes, white British soldiers were unmoved by the African women who asked whether they would really "shoot your mothers." Claudia Koonz's essay describes a much more recent confrontation, in which women in the former Yugoslavia challenged soldiers with signs that commanded, "Soldiers, do not shoot mothers!" But these women's status as mothers did not protect them in the face of intense hatred of difference. In Serbia and Croatia in the 1990s, as in Eastern Nigeria in 1929, Cleveland in 1911, and Lawrence in 1912, soldiers fired on unarmed women because racial, ethnic or class differences made it impossible for them to see these women as mothers like their own.

As we approach the twenty-first century, additional questions of difference have entered the debate over who is and who isn't allowed to claim the mantle of motherhood. Across the United States, lesbians are embroiled in court battles to determine their right to adopt or to raise their own biological children. In the 1995 Sharon Bottoms case, the Virginia Supreme Court awarded custody of Bottoms' natural son to the boy's grandmother and the grandmother's physically abusive husband. The court removed all visitation rights from Bottoms' female partner and granted only limited visitation to Bottoms herself. The decision was cheered by the Christian Right and mourned by the rapidly growing number of lesbian mothers across the United States, all of whom felt a little less secure about the safety of their own families.[23]

The fear and loathing of alternative families, stirred up during the last decade by social conservatives, makes any lesbian seeking motherhood radical by definition. In this volume, playwright Cherríe Moraga and educator Linda Mulley explore the politics surrounding alternative insemination, lesbian pregnancy and child raising in a homophobic society. For Moraga, the experience of pregnancy began a radical redefinition both of her self-image as a Chicana lesbian activist and of her understanding of who a mother is. Moraga describes her evolution in a lyrical series of journal entries and dreams. She takes the reader through a transformation in consciousness that recasts two decades of activism in the new light of motherhood.

For Mulley, a rural lesbian who works with disabled children, it was not the act of bearing a child but of adopting and raising one that politicized her. Here she recounts the painful process of watching her twelve-year-old daughter tormented by homophobic schoolmates. Mulley found herself fundamentally changed by this experience, radicalized in an even more profound way than she was by her initial coming out in an era of gay rights marches and protests, nearly twenty years earlier. Watching her daughter's suffering forced Mulley out of the closet for a second time—this time as an "amazon mother." Like many of the mothers in this volume, Mulley moved from "kitchen-table activism" on behalf of her own child into a broader political engagement on behalf of other children. An educator, Mulley helped organize a statewide movement to improve the climate in Vermont schools both for gay and lesbian youth and for the children of gay and lesbian parents.

Over the past thirty years, dramatic advances in reproductive technologies have radicalized conceptions of motherhood for women of all sexual orientations. New reproductive technologies have enabled lesbians, older women, and women who are infertile for various reasons to have the children they could not otherwise have. But, as the frightening essays by Rita Arditti and Madhu Kishwar make clear, technology does not erode prejudices or reorder existing hierarchies.

Technology simply reflects and reinforces existing power relations, in invidious fashion and with sweeping effect, tightening control over who gets to be a mother and under what circumstances. Poor women have not been able to afford the exorbitantly priced technologies now available in infertility clinics. Technology has more often been used against the poor, particularly women of color, than in support of them. The shameful histories of forced sterilization programs in the U.S. South, on Native-American reservations and in Puerto Rico are nightmare reminders of the many ways that new technologies can be used as weapons against women. Women without men have not always been welcome to take advantage of the new technologies either, regardless of ability to pay. The vast majority of sperm banks in the United States refuse to sell sperm to lesbian women. And while men in their sixties and seventies may father children without attracting much notice, the news that new technologies have enabled women in their fifties to conceive children has set off heated ethical and moral debates. Unless we remove motherhood from the realm of the ideal and ground it in the very real and complex world that the essays in this book describe, the new reproductive technologies will become just a more refined tool of social control as poor women become surrogates for the rich, and amniocentesis is used to enable prospective parents to abort unwanted girls.[24]

The final essays by Sara Ruddick and Marianne Hirsch offer the reflections of scholars who have struggled with the contradictions between motherhood, political activism and feminism for more than twenty years. Though concerned about the sentimentalization of motherhood and the use of that ideal to further militarist or racist ends, Ruddick concludes that there is a place for maternal politics in pursuit of peace, caring and justice for all children. At the end of a diary chronicling her long struggle to reconcile feminism and motherhood, Marianne Hirsch concludes that, although the relationship between the two may never be easy, mothers need feminism and feminism needs mothers. What shape the new maternal politics will take, and what form the future alliance between mothers and feminism will assume, remain elusive.

In the end, this collection seeks not to simplify but to complicate understandings of motherhood. It seeks to illuminate, not resolve, contradictions. The essays and interviews that follow are really a conversation among diverse women from around the globe who speak a multitude of languages: activists fighting a wide range of battles, scholars from varied disciplines, and a host of different writers—journalists and educators, short story writers and playwrights. There has been no attempt made to homogenize these voices or to create facile political agreement. We hope that the reader will enjoy, as we did, grappling with the divergent languages, styles and politics presented in this book. Our purpose here is to explode static portraits of idealized motherhood, and to replace them with fresh images of women who, faced with a host of challenges, found in their motherhood the tools and inspiration to fight for radical change.

NOTES

1. See Evelyn Nakano Glenn, "Social Constructions of Mothering: A Thematic Overview," and Patricia Hill Collins, "Shifting the Center: Race, Class and Feminist Theorizing About Motherhood," in *Mothering: Ideology, Experience and Agency*, ed. Evelyn Nakano Glenn, Grace Chang and Linda Rennie Forcey (New York: Routledge, 1994).

2. Sara Ruddick, *Maternal Thinking: Toward a Politics of Peace* (New York: Ballantine Books, 1989), pp. 127–139.

3. Wangari Maathai and Alicia Partnoy, dialogue at the Redefining Motherhood Conference, Darmouth College, Hanover, N.H., May 15, 1993.

4. *Los Angeles Times*, January 21, 1995; *New York Times*, February 19, 1995; *Boston Globe*, May 16, 1995; *New York Times*, October 18, 1994.

5. *New York Times*, Allesandra Stanley, "Mothers Act to Save Their Sons from War," February 11, 1995. According to Stanley, many of the Russian mothers went to Chechnya at the public invitation of the Chechen separatist leader, Dzhokar Dudayev, who said that he would release Russian prisoners of war only into the custody of their mothers. Both print journalists and CNN reporters referred to the prior organization of Russian mothers against the Afghanistan war. And it was on CNN that mothers urged their sons to explain why they would no longer serve in the Chechen incursion.

6. Calvin Sims, "Army Chief's Admission of 'Dirty War' Rips Veil from Dark Era," *New York Times*, April 27, 1995.

7. The term "social housekeeping" came from Women's Christian Temperance Union founder Frances Willard, who argued that government is just "housekeeping on the broadest scale." Maternalist arguments suffused everything Jane

Addams wrote. Two particularly clear expressions were "Utilization of Women in City Government," a chapter of *Newer Ideals of Peace* (New York: Macmillan, 1907), and "Why Women Should Vote," *Ladies Home Journal*, January 1910, both reprinted in *Jane Addams: A Centennial Reader*, ed. Emily Cooper Johnson (New York: Macmillan, 1960). For a comparative analysis, see Sonya Michel and Seth Koven, "Womanly Duties: Maternalist Politics and the Origin of Welfare States in France, Germany, Great Britain and the United States, 1880–1920," *American Historical Review* 95 (October 1990):1076–1114.

8. For an overview of the history of maternalism and pacifism, see Carolyn Strange, "Mothers on the March: Maternalism in Women's Protest for Peace in North America and Western Europe, 1900–1985," in *Women and Social Protest*, ed. Guida West and Rhoda Lois Blumberg (New York: Oxford University Press, 1990), pp. 209–224. For a history of U.S. women and essentialist arguments for pacifism, see Harriet Hyman Alonso, *Peace as a Women's Issue: A History of the U.S. Movement for World Peace and Women's Rights* (Syracuse: Syracuse University Press, 1993), and Alonso, *The Women's Peace Union and the Outlawry of War, 1921–1942* (Knoxville: University of Tennessee Press, 1989).

9. Amy Swerdlow, *Women Strike for Peace: Traditional Motherhood and Radical Politics in the 1960s* (Chicago: University of Chicago Press, 1993), p. 27.

10. For an overview of the feminist debate about maternalism and militarism, see Micaela di Leonardo, "Morals, Mothers and Militarism: Anti-Militarism and Feminist Theory," review essay in *Feminist Studies*, vol. 11, Fall 1985:599–617. For a historical perspective on "difference feminism," see Karen Offen, "Defining Feminism: A Comparative Historical Approach," *Signs* 14, (autumn 1988):119–157.

11. Swerdlow, *Women Strike for Peace*, p. 236.

12. Jason Webb for Reuters, "Housewives Unite to Get Some Respect," "Housewives Call For Pay at World Congress," "World Housewives Call for Cash to Stay at Home," October 25, 26, 28, 1995.

13. Margie Bonnett Sellinger, "Already the Conscience of a Nation," *People Weekly* 22 (July 9, 1984):102; Tamar Lewin, "Founder of Anti-Drunk Driving Group Now Lobbies for Breweries," *New York Times*, January 15, 1994.

14. There are relatively few accounts of poverty or welfare policy that incorporate the perspectives of poor women. See Theresa Funiciello, *Tyranny of Kindness: Dismantling the Welfare System to End Poverty in America* (New York: Atlantic Monthly Press, 1993), for an inside-out perspective on public assistance; see too Danny Seifer, *Nobody Speaks for Me: Self-Portraits of American Working-Class Women* (New York: Simon and Schuster, 1976); Xiaolan Bao, *Holding Up More Than Half the Sky: Women Garment Workers in New York Chinatown, 1949–1990* (Urbana: University of Illinois Press, forthcoming); and Alexis Jetter, Annelise Orleck and Diana Taylor, "Mothers at Risk: The War on Poor Women and Children," in George Demko and Michael Jackson, *Populations At Risk in America: Vulnerable Groups at the End of the 20th Century* (Boulder, Colo.: Westview Press, 1995), pp. 104–128.

15. Besides Lois Gibbs' interview in this volume, see Lois Gibbs, *Love Canal: My Story* as told to Murray Levine (Albany: State University of New York Press, 1982). For general information on the grassroots environmental justice movement, see *Confronting Environmental Racism: Voices from the Grassroots*, ed. Robert Bullard (Boston: South End Press, 1993).

16. Besides the Maathai interview in this volume, see *San Francisco Chronicle*, October 1, 1990, January 14, 1992; *Christian Science Monitor*, May 2, 1991, August

26, 1991; *New York Times*, March 5, 1992; *National Catholic Reporter*, March 20, 1992; *Time*, April 27, 1992; and *Washington Post*, June 2, 1992.

17. Besides LaDuke's interview in this volume, see Winona LaDuke, *Learning from Native Peoples* (Great Barrington, Mass.: E. F. Schumacher Society, 1994).

18. Winona LaDuke, "Minobimaatisiiwin: The Good Life," *Cultural Survival Quarterly* (winter 1992) 71.

19. Julie Peteet, "Cultural Politics of Motherhood: Discourse, Ritual and Practice Among Palestinians," pp. 9–10. Paper presented at the Redefining Motherhood Conference, Dartmouth College, Hanover, N.H., May 14–16, 1993.

20. See Barbara Clark Smith, "Food Rioters and the American Revolution," *William and Mary Quarterly* s3 51 (January 1994):3–38; Judith A. Miller, "Politics and Urban Provisioning Crises: Bakers, Police and Parlements in France, 1750–1793, *Journal of Modern History* 24 (June 1992):227–62. See also Paula Hyman "Immigrant Women and Consumer Protest: The New York City Kosher Meat Boycott of 1902," *American Jewish History* 70 (September 1980):91–105; Dana Frank, "Housewives, Socialists, and the Politics of Food: The 1917 New York Cost-of-Living Protests," *Feminist Studies* 11 (summer 1985):255–285; Annelise Orleck, " 'We Are That Mythical Thing Called the Public:' Militant Housewives During the Great Depression," *Feminist Studies* 19 (spring 1993):147–172.

21. Temma Kaplan, "Female Consciousness and Collective Action: The Case of Barcelona, 1910–1918," *Signs* 7 (spring 1982):545–566.

22. See Ardis Cameron, *Radicals of the Worst Sort: Laboring Women in Lawrence, Massachusetts, 1860–1912* (Urbana: University of Illinois Press, 1993), pp. 117–170; and Pauline Newman, "From the Battlefield—Some Phases of the Cloakmakers' Strike in Cleveland," *Life and Labor*, October 1911. An interesting contrast to the situations described here, in which the soldiers do shoot, is the scene during the 1937 Flint, Michigan, sit-down auto strike, where Genora Dollinger brings her Women's Emergency Brigade in front of the police and challenges them, "If you'll shoot into the bellies of unarmed men, then you'll shoot the mothers of small children." In that case the police did back down. (See Lyn Goldfarb and Lorraine Gray's 1978 documentary on the strike, *With Babies and Banners*.) In this situation, it is likely that the police and the women were mostly of the same race and ethnicity.

23. "Virginia Supreme Court Rejects Lesbian's Custody Bid," *New York Times*, April 22, 1995.

24. Alexis Jetter, interview with Jennifer Firestone, Director of Alternative Insemination Program, Fenway Community Health Center, March 23, 1995; see too Janice Raymond, "Women as Wombs: International Traffic in Reproduction," *Ms* 1, no. 6 (May–June 1991):9–23.

ENVIRONMENTAL ACTIVISM

Overview

Environmental Justice

Annelise Orleck

The environmental justice movement was galvanized by mothers—
mostly poor, and mostly women of color—who were horrified at the
effects that toxic waste dumping, pesticide runoff and deforestation
were having on their children and families. This grassroots protest movement
powerfully illustrates the ways that mothers, working from a maternalist
perspective, have broadened the focus of established political groups to embrace the concerns of women and children. Since the late 1970s, when mothers first began protesting against corporate and governmental policies that
turned their communities into "sacrifice zones," the environmental justice
movement has forced the world's largest environmental, civil rights and human rights organizations to grapple with the human costs of environmental
degradation.

Lois Gibbs, interviewed here, was a twenty-seven-year-old housewife in
Niagara Falls, New York, in 1978, when she learned that her children were
attending elementary school atop a massive toxic waste dump. Her discovery,
and her response, shocked and riveted the country. For two years, Gibbs led
the citizens of Love Canal in a battle for relocation. She also fought to force the
government to investigate the high incidence of cancer in her community and
to assess possible links with the 20,000 tons of toxic chemicals that had been
dumped below it. President Jimmy Carter finally delivered an emergency
declaration in 1980, enabling the residents to relocate.

In the process of her struggle, Gibbs was transformed from a mother who focused primarily on her own children to a political activist concerned with other mother's children as well. She began by going door to door in her community, talking with other parents—primarily mothers—about the dangers of toxic waste. Later she formed a network of parents. After she left Love Canal, a phone call from a mother whose son died from diseases related to toxic exposure convinced Gibbs that she needed to share her expertise with endangered families throughout the country. In 1983, Gibbs established the Citizen's Clearinghouse for Hazardous Waste to provide technical and organizational support to other communities fighting corporate polluters.

One year before Gibbs founded Citizen's Clearinghouse, an African-American mother and organizer from North Carolina led a dramatic mothers' and childrens' protest against hazardous waste dumping in their community. If any one organizer or group can be credited with forcing both civil rights and environmental organizations to take the mothers' environmental movement seriously, it was Dollie Burwell and the mothers of Warren County, North Carolina. When they and their children laid their bodies in front of trucks carrying highly toxic PCBs in 1982, the protest made newscasts across the country. Their struggle moved environmental and civil rights leaders, as well as the federal government, to acknowledge the correlation between race, class and exposure to hazardous wastes in the United States. Burwell was one of the key organizers of the first People of Color Environmental Summit in Washington, D.C., in 1991. That conference generated a national network that campaigned for and ultimately won the creation of an environmental equity office within the Environmental Protection Agency.

Burwell, like Gibbs, both transformed and was transformed by the environmental justice struggle. The battle over the landfill was just the beginning. Burwell now coordinates a network of grassroots organizations across the South that are trying to stop officials from targeting poor Black communities when siting incinerators and toxic waste facilities. And she has spearheaded a political mobilization in North Carolina that elected significant numbers of mothers of color to local, state and federal posts for the first time in 1992. Burwell was one of those elected. Since that time she has served as registrar of deeds for Warren County. That way, she says, no land can be bought or sold without her knowing about it.

Patsy Ruth Oliver of Texarkana, Texas, was one of many concerned mothers across the nation who picked up the banner of the environmental justice movement. Like Gibbs, Oliver had watched her family and neighbors suffer the horrific effects of toxic dumping: headaches, skin rashes, nausea, miscarriages, and serious respiratory diseases. Finding that her working-class African-American neighborhood was built on a deadly creosote dump, Oliver tried to get the Environmental Protection Agency (EPA) to act. For eight years, while the EPA stalled, the residents of Carver Terrace sickened and died. Oliver says that her experience with the EPA turned her from "a hysterical housewife" to a "true believer in the environmental movement." When Lois Gibbs visited Texarkana in 1980, Oliver knew she had to act. "If they would do that to a white community," she thought, "they surely will not care about poisoning a black one."

Between 1980 and 1993, Oliver hectored, charmed and dogged her friends, neighbors, and local environmentalists to demand that the federal government buy out the residents of Carver Terrace so that they could leave what she called "the toxic twilight zone." She also offered her whirlwind energy to other devastated communities in the Southwest. She joined the struggle to force *maquiladoras*—U.S.-owned factories—on the Texas–Mexican border to clean up their hazardous waste dumps. Particularly hard hit are the twin border towns of Brownsville, Texas, and Matamoros, Mexico, hellish landscapes where pregnant women bear malformed children with frightening frequency. Holding a horribly afflicted baby in her arms, Oliver promised herself that she would take on that struggle as her own. Oliver's campaign attracted the attention of Friends of the Earth, which made her one of the first African-American women on the board of a Big Ten Environmental organization.

Oliver's premature death, like those of her mother and daughter, are reminders that mother-environmentalists are fighting life-and-death battles. Patsy Ruth Oliver's journey illustrates the incredible distance that mother-activism has taken some women: from an assembly-line munitions worker and single mother to an international symbol for the environmental justice movement—chosen as part of the official U.S. delegation to the World Environmental Summit in Rio de Janeiro. Oliver embodies both the great achievements and terrible costs of radical motherhood. Journalist Alexis Jetter has contributed two portraits for this section: one in Oliver's own words, culled from a series of interviews, and the other an article that traces Oliver's history as an activist mother and sets her movement in context.

The struggle against environmental degradation is not unique to the United States. Women across the continent of Africa have organized to combat the devastation, drought, and erosion caused by deforestation. Wangari Maathai, interviewed here, is the founder of that movement. Maathai is an opposition leader, environmentalist, human rights activist, and former anatomy professor in her native Kenya. In 1977, she learned that rural children were suffering from malnutrition because their mothers had no firewood with which to cook. In response, Maathai founded the Green Belt Movement, which has trained more than 50,000 women—many of them traditional mothers—to plant more than 10 million trees. The mothers' movement has four goals: to stop soil erosion, create cooking fuel, create green belts around schools and villages, and provide income for the women planters.

Today, the Green Belt Movement, which has spread to a dozen other African countries, has become a force for democratization as well: Kenya's rural women are demanding greater political freedom for themselves and their children. But that transformation is threatening to the authoritarian regime of Kenyan president Daniel arap Moi, who has repeatedly had Maathai arrested, attacked, and forced into hiding. In a country where dissent is synonymous with treason, she and her mothers' movement walk a fine line.

The final piece in this section is an interview with Winona LaDuke, a writer, lecturer, environmental activist and mother who in recent years has created the White Earth Land Recovery Project to help her Anishinabe people buy back lost tribal lands in northern Minnesota. The White Earth Reservation, where she lives with her two children, is less than one-tenth its 1867 size. LaDuke's organization has bought back 1,000 acres so far and she hopes over the next fifteen years to buy back another 30,000. LaDuke also directs the Environment Program of the Seventh Generation Fund, a Native foundation that supports grassroots Native initiatives in environmental justice and community restoration. She cofounded the Indigenous Women's Network, a consortium of grassroots indigenous women organizers, and is a board member of Greenpeace.

The narratives that follow illuminate the varied processes of radicalization experienced by mothers facing environmental devastation. They also highlight the conflicts that arise out of mother-activism, and the ways that women who may not initially be concerned with upending gender roles may nevertheless do so just by virtue of their activism. Gibbs recalls that, although the women in her community had the complete support of their husbands in their struggle to relocate, tensions arose as apolitical housewives were transformed into activists. There were basic issues of contention: someone had to do the household chores, someone had to watch the children. If the women were off at night attending meetings, that meant the men had to pick up the slack. Many were unwilling. Gibbs estimates that half of the women most active in the Love Canal struggle were divorced within a few years. Wangari Maathai, too, addresses the hostility that faces women who violate accepted gender norms by leaving their homes and speaking out against the existing political and social order. Not only did Maathai's husband divorce her but he did it very publicly, reviling her in Parliament and the press as an example to other Kenyan women of what befalls a "bad wife and mother."

Mother-activism creates conflicts with children as well. Dollie Burwell recounts feeling deeply torn when her young daughter announced that she intended to get arrested in a community protest against hazardous waste dumping. It is one thing, Burwell writes, for a mother to put her life on the line, another for her to contemplate endangering the safety of her child. Still, Burwell and other mothers knew that their children faced far greater risks from exposure to toxics than from a night or two in jail. Many mother-activists in the environmental justice movement, including Gibbs and Oliver, had seen their own children afflicted by diseases related to toxic waste. Protest and organizing could not always heal their family members. Sometimes all that they could hope for was to prevent other mothers' children from suffering the same fate.

"What Is Your Wife Trying to Do—Shut Down the Chemical Industry?"

The Housewives of Love Canal

An interview with Lois Gibbs

Conducted and edited by Alexis Jetter

I'll start from the beginning. I grew up on Grand Island, between Niagara Falls and Buffalo. My father was a bricklayer; I was one of six children. We were taught to believe that if there was a problem, the government would protect you. It was your basic civics class sort of teaching that said: We have a structure in this country. And if you go through the structure and you are right then you will receive relief.

I believed in the American Dream, too. After high school, I envisioned doing what my mother had done: I would be a full-time homemaker and raise my children. So I got married, and in 1973 my husband and I bought our home in Niagara Falls. It was a three-bedroom, single-family ranch, a nice little white house with a white picket fence. We had the stereotypical American life—complete with station wagon.

We didn't know about Love Canal. There was nothing in our deed. None of our papers spoke about it. There was just nothing known about it. And it was three blocks from my home.

When we moved into the house my son Michael was one year old and healthy. There was nothing wrong with him. But during the time that we lived there, Michael started to get really ill. First he had ear infections, then colds, flu and pneumonia. Every week I was taking Michael to the doctor for an ear infection. It just didn't make sense. When I talked to my pediatrician about it, he said, "Some kids are just more sickly than others and you have one of those. You'll just have to give him more love."

But then he started developing more severe effects. He developed epilepsy, with petite mal and then grand mal seizures. He developed a liver disorder; his liver enzymes were all confused and nobody knew exactly what that meant. He developed asthma, and then a urinary tract disorder where he couldn't urinate and he had to have two operations. He developed an immune system disorder. He had no immune system left. They discharged him from the hospital and sent him home because it was safer for him to be home than at the hospital where he was exposed to infection.

And, as all of this stuff was going on, I kept saying to my pediatrician, "So what is this?" I thought I was doing everything right. I taught Sunday school, so I did the religious right thing. Every day we went to the playground or the zoo, so he was outdoors. He was getting fresh air and good food. He had a mama who certainly cared about him. And yet he was just so sick. It just didn't make any sense.

And then I gave birth to Melissa who was perfectly healthy—at first. She didn't develop all those chronic illnesses. But she did develop a blood disease called ITP (Idiopathic Thrombocytopenic Purpura). Her platelets, which clot the blood, were being eaten by the body itself. She looked like a child abuse case. Everywhere on her body were bruises or what appeared to be bruises. Sometimes they were just little red dots. Some bruises were the size of a coffee cup. Both of her cheeks were huge red bruises. I thought: "What is going on? What is the matter with this child?"

So then I took her in to Dr. McMann's office and he said he thought she had leukemia. A normal platelet count for a child her age was about 250,000–450,000. Hers was 1,000. It was a matter of: "Take your child to Buffalo Children's Hospital now. Don't pick her up. Don't put a seatbelt on her. Don't squeeze her. Any bump or bruise, especially to the head, could create an internal hemorrhage and kill her." So there was this anxiousness on my part that I'm sure fed into her fear. Even though I tried to be as calm and collected as possible, I was a basket case. She was three years old.

And I took her to Buffalo Children's Hospital. As a result of just moving her to the hospital, and her screaming, and the intensity of her screams, her nose was bleeding, her mouth was bleeding. Most of the blood vessels underneath the skin just burst. So all over her face was more of those little red bruises.

She was afraid. There was no time for preparation. There was no time to say this is what is going to happen, this is why it is going to happen. When we got to the hospital they began doing all of these tests, because her blood count was so low they didn't want to introduce any chemicals into her body—including an anesthetic. So they were going to have to do these tests by holding her down. When you held her down you could see your fingerprints on her skin. It would bruise there. You could see your handprint on her. It was just terrible.

They were going to do a bone marrow test in her hip. And because they couldn't give her any anesthetic, the doctor wanted me to stay in the room to see if I could calm her—and help hold her down. Because they didn't want to use straps for fear of causing a hemorrhage. So I stood there and I held her down and tried to calm her. But I just got really sick when I saw this guy preparing this little tray. They had the syringes and the needles. And I realized, "I can't handle this." I knew that I was going to create more problems than she was if I stayed.

My three-year-old daughter was screaming and crying and begging me to stop them. She kept saying: "I won't be bad anymore. I promise." It was as if she was somehow being punished for something she did. And we kept saying: "You didn't do anything wrong. You're sick. Something happened to you and we need to find out what it is." We kept trying to explain but she was too young to understand.

It turned out to be ITP and not leukemia. She was hospitalized for several days while they tried different drugs to stop the internal hemorrhage. But they weren't able to bring her blood back to the normal level. So, now the child couldn't ride her tricycle and she couldn't go outdoors without a guard adult. Our house was carpeted from the floor to three feet up the wall so that she wouldn't bump herself on anything. The stairs had three inches of foam on top, and all our tables and things that had edges had foam taped around them. Our house looked like a battle zone.

But the really sad part is that, while all of this was happening to Michael and Melissa, there *were* people who knew why they were sick. The city knew, and the county knew, and the state knew, and the federal government knew. They all knew that homes around Love Canal had levels of toxic chemicals that exceeded workplace standards. They knew that people were at great risk in the Love Canal community and they never said anything. Not to us and not to our doctors. My pediatrician had no clue. Michael's pediatric urologist saw five children on the same block in Love Canal who had to have exactly the same surgery. The doctors didn't inquire. They thought it was a fluke. The state knew and they made a decision not to say a word, to us, to our doctors, to our families. And that's the part that's really outrageous.

In the spring of 1978, Michael was in kindergarten and I still had no clue why all this was happening. That's when I read in the *Niagara Gazette* about Love Canal, a toxic chemical dump between 97th and 99th Streets. The reporter discussed the various chemicals that were in Love Canal, and he talked about the known effects from exposure to those chemicals. And I looked at that article and I saw seizures. I saw skin rashes. Michael had terrible psoriasis as well. (By the way, he's twenty-three now and totally gray.) The article talked about blood disorders. It talked about leukemia. It was a list of all the diseases that my children were developing.

And that's when I realized that what was wrong with my children was not just that I was unlucky enough to have children who were sick. It was related to the dump site. And every day, except in the dead of winter and rainy days, we went over to play at the school playground with the children for at least an hour. And the playground of the 99th Street school, where Michael was in kindergarten, was located right over the toxic dump. And often we saw different colors in the dirt. But you don't think about that being dangerous. You think about it being weird. It never occurred to me or my neighbors that there was a problem here.

When you walked out of the door in the morning and smelled the chemicals, you thought: "Mmmm. Good economy." So many of the people there were chemical operators and Goodyear Chemical workers. As long as you smelled the chemicals you knew you could pay the mortgage. My husband, Harry, got paid $10,000 a year as a chemical worker. So on that money we had to pay the mortgage, buy the station wagon and pay these tremendous medical bills.

Prior to all of this I was a very shy, introverted person. I was afraid to talk. I wouldn't even teach church classes to adults. I would do it for children but not for adults. At school I had few friends. I wasn't into sports or clubs of any sort. So it was really difficult for me to move out of that personality into a more aggressive, confrontational and articulate person who could speak to other people.

So when I read about the Love Canal thing, and Michael was in school, the thing I thought about was that I had to move Michael to another school. Because Michael was special. He was more susceptible than the other children. So I went to see Dr. Long, the head of the school board. I brought the newspaper article with me and I said: "I believe that this school is hurting my child and here are the reasons why." And he said to me, "Ms. Gibbs, if you can get two doctors' statements that say that Michael's health is at risk from being in that school, then we'll transfer him."

I had no clue at that time how difficult that would be. Michael's doctor said: "I'd give it to you in a minute except that I have a real problem. If I get called into court to testify that Michael is having problems from these chemicals, I have no real basis for that. That's why Dr. Long asked you to do that. He knew that I have no knowledge of toxicology. You want my gut reaction. I think that you're absolutely right and I think that you should take Michael out of that school but I can't sign that statement." All he could sign was a statement that said that Michael's illness could be possibly aggravated by these chemicals. So he really wasn't saying anything definitive.

But I got his statement and one from my family practitioner and I went back to Dr. Long after jumping through those damn hoops. And I said, "Here's your statements. Move my child." He said that he wasn't going to do it. If he moved Michael Gibbs based on these statements then he would set a precedent. If it was dangerous for Michael Gibbs then it was dangerous for all 407 children who attend the 99th Street School. And he was not about to move all of those children because of one irate, hysterical housewife.

I just sat there and he never looked me in the eye. I burst out crying. And I said, "Michael's got to go to school. And he can't go to this school." And Dr. Long talked about the number of private schools, and Catholic schools in the community that he could go to. You know, my husband made $10,000 a year. There was no way that we could afford private school. Any amount extra would put us over the edge. He said, "I'm sorry but there's nothing I can do for you." I think that I was in some weird state of shock because I didn't move. I didn't say anything. I just sat there and stared at him. And he said, "Ms. Gibbs, you have to leave now. Sitting here is not going to change my mind."

So I talked to my brother-in-law who worked at Syracuse University as a biologist. I asked him what could I do. We decided to do what we had seen other people do, which was to go door to door with a petition to close the school, and see how many people we could get to sign onto it.

So I wrote the petition. And I practiced with my mother and my dog Fearless: "Hi, I'm Lois Gibbs." I asked my mother to watch the kids. And I went out with my little clipboard to the first door and stood there. I knocked so lightly that their dog didn't even bark. I was so scared. My legs were shaking. I felt like I had to go to the bathroom. I thought, they're going to think I'm crazy. It was the most frightening moment of my life because it was the beginning of coming from this shy, quiet, well-behaved young woman into something that was very unknown to me and very frightening to me. And I literally ran all the way home.

Michael developed pneumonia very soon after that, in a matter of days. We took him into the hospital. In those days they used to have that plastic sheeting that went over the cribs. He had this little white face, with these freckles sticking out, and he's on this white bed, with white sheets. And I thought, the reason that he's there is not because of Occidental Petroleum, or Hooker Chemical, or the state of New York, or the Board of Education. The reason he was in the hospital that day, I felt, was because I didn't do anything. I didn't knock on that first door.

For many years I had honestly taken pride in being the best mom on the block. My kids had the right sweaters for the right temperature. Their faces weren't dirty. I prided myself on being a responsible mother. And yet when it came to doing something to protect my children that was not within my norm, I was afraid. And, as a result of being afraid, I helped to put Michael into that bed, I contributed to his sickness. So at that moment I made a decision that, when he got well, I would go back to that first door. And I would talk to people. And I would figure out how to do this. Because nobody else was going to protect my baby but me.

So after Michael got well, I went back out to that same door and I knocked, this time loud enough that the dog heard me. And someone came to the door. And I just blurted out what I had to say. And the person said, "I agree. My kid is really sick too. And I'd like to talk to you about it." And it went on. And each house was equally friendly and equally concerned. People didn't know what to do themselves. They were in the same state I was in, maybe a week before. And they began to share their stories.

They talked about things relating to their children. But they also talked about how their wives had babies that were malformed, how a thirteen-year-old had a hysterectomy due to cancer, how a twenty-one-year-old died of "crib death," according to her death certificate. And then we had three women in a row with children who had to have surgery so that their skulls could grow normally. And I realized, this is not about the school. This is about the whole neighborhood.

And folks would also talk about things that they knew, especially the older residents, about the holes in the "impermeable" clay covering the dump. Love Canal was like a basin of water filled with chemicals. And the earth that covered it was like the crust of a pie. Sometimes that crust would break. You'd have a hole and if you stuck a stick in it there'd be all this black soup on it. Each time the city came out to dump dirt on the hole, but one time a back hoe just fell into the hole and was gone. People would talk about stuff coming up in their basements. They would talk about sump pumps they used to control the water, how they had to replace those every year.

It was at that point that we realized we needed to do some further testing. We needed to go beyond the school. Meanwhile, the state saw the writing on the wall. They saw the news articles. They saw me going door to door. So in the spring of 1978 they came to test the school grounds.

They had a couple of meetings to talk about the preliminary results. And I said: "If you have all these chemicals on the school grounds, should we allow our children to remain in school?" And they would say stupid things like: "If you were a good mother you would make sure that your child stayed on the sidewalk. As long as your child stays on the sidewalk your child will be perfectly safe. It's only if they go and put their hands in the dirt that there's a problem." And then they started talking to us about hygiene habits. If they drop their apples or their lollipops in the dirt that they shouldn't put them back in their mouths. And I said, "Excuse me? I'm confused. This doesn't make any sense to me." So these informational meetings were essentially to pacify us. But all they did was enrage me even more. Because I thought, how can I send my child off to school in the morning and say: "Only walk on the sidewalk. Don't put your hands in your mouth. If you drop something don't pick it up." It was just insane.

So I continued to collect my petitions and all this other health data on what people had experienced. I told the state people: When I finish I want to bring this data to Albany and meet with you. So we set up a time, August 2, 1978, to meet with the state health authorities to talk about what we'd found and to talk about not reopening the school in September.

And so Debbie Cerillo and myself and my husband all drove to Albany. Mind you, we didn't have any money. So the three of us all slept in the same room. We ate McDonald's or something on the way. My husband had to take off work. Debbie had to pay for a baby-sitter. Anyhow, we get to Albany and the meeting is first thing in the morning. So we go to the office where we're supposed to meet with the Health Department official. They told us the Love Canal meeting is in the auditorium. We said, "There's only three of us. We don't need an auditorium."

So we walk down to the auditorium and it's a circus. There are cameras and TV people and lighting and a stage and a podium and people buzzing all over with suits on and little name tags. We thought: This can't be the right meeting. So we asked a guy: "Is this the Love Canal meeting?" And he said yes. So we asked: "Who is meeting here?" And he said, "The Health Commissioner is meeting with a couple of Love Canal residents and then he's going to do a press conference. Are you the Love Canal residents? Can I talk to you?" I said: "No." We were trying to figure out what was going on. I had no clue. I had never been to the state capital before.

So we sit ourselves down in the first row of this huge auditorium with seats for 200 people. All of these media people kept coming over and wanting to talk to me. Commissioner Whalen gets up and says that he is going to order preg-nant women and children under the age of two, in the first two rows of houses that circle Love Canal, to evacuate. And the reason for evacuation was because children under the age of two haven't completed their brain development. Their blood filtration system, the kidneys and liver, have not been fully devel-oped. So the chemicals go directly to their brains.

Debbie and I looked at each other. We had come to talk about our petition and all of a sudden there's this health emergency. So Debbie stands up and says in the middle of Whalen's talk: "My child is two years and one month. What does that mean? What has happened to her? Is it already done? Is she poi-soned?" I don't even remember what I said but I know that it had so many cuss words in it—and I don't curse—that on the nightly news that night they bleeped me six times. I was so angry, because here I had the mayor of Niagara Falls who had said to me: "Don't worry. We're testing. We'll let you know." We had the state health department field researchers saying, "Don't worry." We had Dr. Long who said there's no problem.

And all of a sudden Whalen is saying that there's a health emergency here and people need to be moved. So we literally didn't shut up for the next half hour. When Debbie stopped talking, I talked. When I stopped, she talked. We were screaming. We were hysterical. So they asked for a break. And Whalen left and never came back. The rest of the meeting was run by their staff people. It was so shocking that we didn't have enough rational thinking to ask: Who is going to pay for the move? We weren't thinking. We were in a literal state of shock.

We got back in our car and drove five hours home. When we got there my mother came running out and said: "Don't worry about the kids. The kids are fine. Go to 99th Street. They need you over there." I said: "But I have to go to the bathroom." And she said, "You don't have time. Go there right now." It was only about two blocks away. We pull up and there are all these people milling in the streets. One of the neighbors has a barrel in which he's got a fire and he's telling people to bring their mortgages and burn them because they're worthless. There was someone else on a makeshift microphone asking: "Has Lois Gibbs come back yet? Has anyone seen Lois Gibbs? She met with the health authorities. She'll have some answers." I was hiding behind a tree. They kept mentioning my name like I'll have some magical answers. I didn't have anything to say to these folks. And to this date, I had never spoke with more than people in their houses. I had never spoken to a crowd of people. Pregnant women were just hysterical, crying "Oh my god. What's going to happen to my baby?"

So finally someone saw me hiding behind this tree. They dragged me up to this makeshift microphone and they applauded me. And I thought, "Please don't applaud me. I don't have anything to give you." And I thought, "What am I going to say to these people?" So I grabbed hold of the microphone. And it's one of those microphones that when you grab it lets out a screech. And finally I say, "I don't know what to say. I don't have any answers. I am in shock, just as you are. I can't believe that they never sent anybody from the Department of Health to Love Canal to talk to people about these moves." So they started shouting at me: "Who's going to pay for our moves? And where are we going to go? And what about my wife? She's pregnant. And what is going to happen to our child?" They were all looking for answers which I didn't have. And this made me realize that I was so angry I had forgotten to ask some of the basic questions. I said, "I'll get on the phone and call Whalen's office and ask some of these things." I said, "Go to a relative's house. Go to friends. Go wherever you can. But pregnant women really should leave. And we'll get together and see if we can pool our limited resources to pay for those who really have no place to go so that they can stay at hotels. How many of you know churches? Let's talk to the churches."

And then I went home and I just sat there and cried. It's like what you read in a book, or see in a movie. It had no reference to anything in my reality. The following day the state came down. They sent the Department of Transportation, which was used to building roads (this had never happened in New York State before). They set up a makeshift office in the 99th St. School and began to process people who were pregnant or who had children under the age of two, giving them vouchers for local hotels or motels on a temporary basis.

We had the first meeting of the Love Canal Homeowners' Association at the Fire Hall down the street. We said we really need to call ourselves something. We need to elect people who can speak on our behalf. We need people to raise money so that we don't have to go to Albany out of our own pockets. I was elected President and Debbie Cerillo was Vice-President.

In the meantime we still believed that the Health Department would do the right thing. So we were talking to the health authorities about doing future tests, to find out what was really going on. We clearly believed that the entire two rows of homes should be evacuated. We hadn't moved yet to the ten-block neighborhood. And the Health Department said, "If you cooperate with our health study and if you do this, and if you do that." And we said, "No. We understand that these people are like canaries in the mine. We know that. We work in the plants. We work in the mines. We understand that moving pregnant women and children is removing our indicators."

We could relate. Most of our relatives worked in the factories. And they knew about these indicator people. So the health officials gave us these forms to fill out. We went to the health survey, and it was the most disgusting thing I ever saw. They didn't put anything about your children. The health survey was focused on adults and the number of pregnancies you had. And my children were sick. There was no place to put that Michael had all of these problems or that Melissa did. There was no place for that. So we said that we weren't going to participate in their health study because their health study was inadequate. We were doing this for our kids and we want to know how many other children have epilepsy. How many other children have ITP? How many other children have leukemia? We weren't able to pronounce the word epidemiology or all of those big fancy words that they used. But we were able to understand that the questionnaire did not include children.

So we did a lot of press work. And the governor, Hugh Carey, would get really upset when we talked about these things. We said, "All right. If he's upset then maybe we should stop mucking around with these health people and work on Governor Hugh Carey." What we also realized was that Carey was up for reelection. We decided we would go after Hugh Carey because he could give us what we wanted.

So the Homeowners' Association, formed right after the street event, focused all of our energy on Hugh Carey. Now we demanded that he come to Love Canal to talk to the people. He was the governor of the state. He had the power and the resources to do something. So we demanded that he do something. So we decided that whenever we spoke to the press, whatever they asked us we would answer, and we would say that we want Governor Carey to come to Love Canal.

You see we looked at the news articles that we were collecting in our scrapbooks and we realized that every time we said something about Governor Hugh Carey, somebody then asked Carey about it. It was clear to us from reading those articles that he could do something. And he was running in a campaign. And even if we didn't talk to every media representative that media representative might still ask Carey on the campaign trail, "What's happening at Love Canal, Governor?" We had the ability with him running for election to put pressure on him.

So he came and he agreed to meet with myself, my brother-in-law and Debbie Cerillo. He was the most intimidating, outrageous person I ever met in my life. He's got those beady eyes that stare right through you. By this time, it was August. I'd been doing this since spring. Here is this big, powerful man who is sitting across the table from me saying: "So tell me what you want, Lois." I let him call me Lois, but later I started calling him Hugh. And I couldn't speak. I was literally frozen in place. And he was just staring at me, growing impatient because I wasn't speaking. My mind just went blank. Then my brother-in-law saved me. He said, "It's really clear what they want, Governor. They want relocation." He then went outside, he made a short speech, but then he didn't take questions from the crowd. Then he went to the Niagara Falls airport and flew away. We were sick when we saw the coverage he got, about what a caring governor he was.

So we thought, we've got to do something. We can't let him use this as a platform for his re-election. So we did the same thing to badger him to come back. And this time we were organized. We told his staff person that, this time, we want the governor to take some questions from the people. If he's such a good caring governor, he should speak to us. So he agreed to take two questions. And so then we organized our folks and over two bottles of wine we came up with a question, and we had to delegate someone to ask the question. And I was delegated because I was always delegated to do these things, though I think that day any woman could have asked the question.

So the governor comes. He has the small group meeting with the leadership. It was this meeting where, when he called me Lois, I called him Hugh. I felt very proud of that. I thought, yes, I have guts. After the last meeting my brother told me to think of Carey on the toilet with his pants down and then he would be less scary. So when he came into this meeting, I sort of smirked because all I could think of was him sitting there with his pants down. And Carey looked at me like: "What are you smiling about?" So this meeting was absolutely useless. My agenda was that he was going to allow two people from the audience to speak.

So he makes this whole speech about how much he cares and that he's considering closing the school. "Blah, Blah, Blah." And then after he gets done talking I raise my hand to ask a question. And Carey's looking for someone else to raise their hand. Now he's looking like a fool because the media is looking at him and looking at me and wondering why he refuses to call on me. So he calls on me and while I give this long introduction to the question we are sending three-, four- and five-year-olds marching down to the front of the auditorium and looking up at the governor. These little girls with little red ribbons in their hair. And little boys all dressed in their Sunday best. And when they all got there I said, "Governor Carey, I have only one question for you. Are you going to allow these three-, four- and five-year-olds standing in front of you to remain at Love Canal and die?" It wasn't something where he could say "We're going to do a study." The answer was yes or no. And he's looking at these little kids and the flashes are going off and the cameras are going off making him real nervous. And finally he said, "No, of course I'm not. I care about these little youngsters." And he agreed to evacuate all 239 families. You could hear his people behind stage yelling and moaning. "What did he do that for? We don't have appropriations for that." They were totally unprepared to do that. It was his setting that forced his hand during an election year.

So then everyone in the audience asked: "Well how are we going to do that Governor? How are we going to get our money?" And the governor introduced Tom Frye who was going to "explain all the details."

What it taught us was that politicians are moved by public images. They were moved by the fact that there were these kids there, and he's in the middle of a hot reelection campaign, and the media is focusing on these little girls with ponytails and what the governor is going to do for these children. They had faces. They were not abstract anymore. They were real. We continued to struggle using that same sort of method. We then went to Jimmy Carter. And in 1980 we got full evacuation.

But all that we did, we did because we had to do it for our kids. There was no way out. There was no financial way out. What could we do? Up and leave? We owned a $40,000 house. You literally were trapped there. We could see our children deteriorating. That's how we found the courage to do these things.

By May of 1980, they had said that the first two rows of homes were totally evacuated. Pregnant women and children under the age of two from the first ten blocks were evacuated. So you had houses that were boarded up and houses that were being lived in. We were told not to go into our basements. And if women insisted on doing laundry they should run down quickly, throw the laundry in and run back up. (I don't remember any women who "insisted" on doing laundry.) We were told not to go into our backyards. We were told not to plant a garden. Both elementary schools by this time had been closed. Our children were being bused outside the community. We had standby buses for immediate evacuation in case of explosion or release.

Around that time they came down and said that they had done a chromosome test and they said that there was chromosome damage in the Love Canal residents that they tested. They said that "we don't know what that means for the individuals but for the population as a whole it means that you have more risk of cancer, birth defects and genetic damage, not only to yourself but in your children." When they said in your children, that's when the community lost it. It's one thing to have a sick child. It's another thing to say that your kids are going to be genetically damaged. And once again they released all this to the media without meeting with the people. They met with the twelve individuals who were tested and then they did a press release.

So the next day in *The Buffalo News* it said there will be no more evacuations for the Love Canal people. So all of these people started coming to the Love Canal Homeowners' Association and saying, "Lois, what are you going to do?" They were getting angry. They were yelling at each other and they were yelling at me. Well, there were two EPA representatives in town now but they had failed to give us their phone numbers or to tell us how to contact them. So Marie, one of our key leadership people, got on the phone and called every hotel in town to find out where they were. And then she said, "I want you to come and talk to the people who are gathering right now on the front lawn. They're really angry and someone needs to talk to them."

So this guy came over who was the EPA public relations person. We said, "We don't want you. We want someone who understands this study and who can talk to these people about what to do." So he calls up Dr. Lucas and Lucas comes over. And after he hung up the phone with Dr. Lucas, we said, "By the way Frank, we want you to know that we're holding you hostage. Because we cannot leave this area, you cannot leave this area. When we get evacuated, you'll get evacuated. So have a nice seat." He said, "Are you serious?" I said, "Yes." So here comes Dr. Lucas and the crowd says, "We're holding you hostage."

It really was a spontaneous decision. We had been told too many times that there was nothing we could do. I was opposed to it, knowing that this could really hurt us. Some of us could go to jail. But one thing Love Canal taught us was that we were always very democratic. So if the majority agreed on x then we would do x, even if we thought it was wrong.

So Dr. Lucas comes in. We tell him we're going to hold him hostage. Dr. Lucas is a cytogeneticist. He was the most nervous person I'd ever seen in my entire life. So we put him in this room and say, "We've got to tell someone that we're holding hostages." So I call up the White House because I had Rosalynn's phone number. And I said, "We're holding hostages and I would like to talk to

President Carter about it." And so the secretary, who knows me by first name because I called every single day, said: "You'll have to hold Lois." Then she comes back and says, "Nobody can speak to you right now because they're all in a meeting." And then she goes on to say that Love Canal is not as bad as we're making it out to be. People are dying everywhere of cancer. I said, "Lady, I'm holding hostages. If I had a gun I could shoot them. What the hell are you giving me this lecture for? I really don't need it right now, thank you."

So I hang up the phone. And of course what happens is that they take out the domestic hostage holding book. What do you do? So the FBI comes and they're on the roof across from us with sharpshooters. And their agents infiltrated the crowd with their suits and sunglasses. They're supposed to fit in. Our people wear jean jackets and nylon windbreakers. And these guys are running around with these fancy jackets. Anyway, I called the White House and the FBI got on the phone, and the EPA got on the phone. And I said, "If I let them out in this crowd, this crowd is going to kill them." They said, "No they're not. You're overstating it." So I get Frank, the EPA PR guy, and tell him to hold the phone out the window. And I went on the porch and I said, "I've got the FBI and the EPA on the phone and I told them if I let these guys go, you all are going to kill them. Is that right?" And they scream, "Yeah." So I said, "I'm not really holding them hostage. I'm detaining them for their own health and safety."

So this went on for about five hours. They kept putting all these big shots on the phone who said I was doing the wrong thing. Meanwhile women—blue collar, law-abiding women—were pouring gasoline on lawns across the street and saying that the EPA was burning them. Little old ladies, with pink, spongy rollers were rocking Volkswagens and telling them that they couldn't come through our neighborhood because it was dangerous. It was getting out of control. We didn't have any weapons or anything like that. Somebody made bologna sandwiches. Somebody else brought chocolate chip cookies. It was really kind of comical. And then after five hours, the FBI said, "You have five minutes to decide what to do. We are going to come in and take these men out of here." And I said, "Look, I don't know what to do." And they said, "We're going to rush it." And I said, "No, you're not because somebody is going to get hurt. There's children out front. There's old people out front." So I went out on the porch trying to figure out how to convince these people to let these guys go. I knew that this was going to be a real dicey situation.

So I gave this five-minute speech about how we had sent a message to the White House. We'd let them know that we were serious, that we were tired of it all. And then I said what we ought to do is to let these guys go and give Jimmy Carter until Wednesday at noon to evacuate us. And if he doesn't do that, then what we did today will look like a Sesame Street picnic compared to what we're going to do Wednesday at noon. "But we cannot do this without your permission," I said. "We need a vote." And I think we miscounted the vote slightly. But not a great deal. People were sort of in between.

So the FBI came and got their men and escorted them up. And then we had to come up with what the hell are we going to do Wednesday at noon to top this? This was an election year. Jimmy Carter was in a tight race. Everybody was waiting. Now we had the media a captive audience until Wednesday at noon. So Wednesday precisely at noon, all of these people gathered on the front lawn and I had the phone out the window and President Carter issued an evacuation order so that we could leave temporarily. Full evacuation would happen when they could get the money together in October. People lived in military housing. Some people lived in hotels. Some people found apartments.

So what role did women play? Most of our key leadership were women. There were only two men. Mostly all of the activities were done by women. Part of the reason is that most of the men worked in the chemical industry. And there was a big conflict because a lot of plants said to the workers that, if you talk about Love Canal, you have to go to your supervisor. Despite the fact that the industry had no right to do that to them, a lot of the men didn't get involved because they were afraid that they were going to lose their jobs. Some of that fear was real. And I think some of it was feigned. So mostly all of the organizing was done by the women in the community. And most of it was based on the protective nurturing sense that women have to protect their kids at any expense. And I think that why we were so successful was because women were in that leadership role. Women do things differently from men, based on our life experiences. Women are more willing to build consensus and share responsibility where men are more in a control mechanism and give direction, as opposed to building responsibility and leadership and training other people to do things. And a lot of passion for the movement was the maternal "I've got to protect my kids. I've got to do this." Most of the men were supportive. They just weren't active. And the men that were active began to feel pressure to stop.

By the end of that very first summer my husband no longer was the health and safety officer for his shift for the union. He was removed from that position. Then he was thrown off the bowling team. Then it was one of these communities where every other Friday night they would go to a bar and play pool. He couldn't go to the bar anymore because everyone would pick fights with him. "What is your wife trying to do? Shut down the chemical industry? Doesn't she understand we've got to have jobs? Who's your wife sleeping with? I heard she went to Washington." All this kind of nasty, petty crap. It really became very difficult for him to do anything in a normal social environment because of who I was. That helped to divide us.

But the other part was that the men in our community are from a culture where they are the protectors and the providers. And suddenly they were no longer protecting the families. The women were. And they couldn't provide for the family. As a result of that there were a lot of marriages that were really strained because the men felt less like men. Like their masculinity was put in question, that their authority was put in question in this cultural context. All of a sudden they were saying, "We're tired of doing diapers. It's not what we're supposed to do. That's a woman's job." All of those things changed in our family life. And a lot of the men got really jealous because the women would go to these meetings. They were just jealous because they knew their women were bright and beautiful. And there were a lot of conflicts in the marriages. Probably about 50 percent of the marriages of people who were most active broke up.

It was a liberating thing for the women but there were so many other factors that came in. I think the women were liberated but at the expense of their marriage, at the expense of the health of their children. I became a different person but all of these terrible things had to happen. So, although they were somewhat liberated they were unwilling to acknowledge it. They were unwilling to accept it because it came as a result of some very tragic events that will always be with us. Because your children are with you for the rest of your life. My nineteen-year-old daughter who was talking about having children when she grew up. How am I going to talk to her about the fact that women get their eggs when they're born and she may not have a normal child? How do I broach that conversation with her? And how does she broach it with the person that she chooses as a partner? So yes there were positive things but there were so many negatives that the positives were almost neutralized.

How did I make the leap from caring for my children to caring for all children? I think that it's a real scary leap. And the reason that I made the leap was because I was so angry at what they did to my life that I hold a grudge. And that helped me make the leap. I think that when I moved from Love Canal to Washington, I was riding a high about the ability to achieve change. And that combination overrode my fear that this would not work.

At the end of Love Canal a lot of people began calling and saying, "I have one of these dumps. How did you do that?" And the one that helped me make the decision was a call from a woman whose son had brain cancer and he was going to die in two months. And the woman said that she believed that it was related to the environment. And the woman wanted to get involved and she wanted to know, after her son passes on, how does she do it. And why isn't there somebody there, an organization that can help us.

That was the call that made me see that I needed to set up an organization to help women like her. Because I could relate immediately to what she was saying because I had the same personal experience. My children survived, but that ache in your belly wondering if they'll survive. That rage, how dare they do this, I knew. So I packed up my U-Haul and my two kids, because by that time I was divorced, and I moved to Washington to start the Clearinghouse. And I had $10,000 from the sale of the house to start it. I had no job. I had very few friends here. I had a few connections that I'd made through the Love Canal struggle. I rented a house here. I thought, "I don't know how we're going to do it. But if we could win at Love Canal, we can set up an organization to help that woman in Texas." I think it was a combination of the high that said, "You can do anything," and the sense of anger, renewed every time someone called me. Still today, when someone calls to tell me what terrible thing has happened to them, I go back to it. I know what that's like.

These people need help. That's what we started Clearinghouse to do. I want to focus on the community. I don't want to be another environmental organization that lobbies and passes regulations. I want to be an organization where, when the next Lois Gibbs calls and says, Dr. Long said this and did that, we can say, "Here's what you need to do. You need to take a petition and let me tell you that the first time you take the petition you'll be scared to death. But you'll get over it. Because this is what will happen if you don't get over it." If somebody had nudged me earlier on, Love Canal might have been won sooner. There was nobody to say, "Knock on the door, hold your breath and let it go. Nobody is going to slam the door in your face."

I think that mothers have a particular role to play because mothers are the ones who are most passionate about the future of our children. They're the ones who are willing to take those extra steps to protect the future of those children because they are the childbearers, because they are the nurturers, because they are the ones who think generation to generation. Men think about today and next year. But women think about it in a much longer vision. And I think that they're critical to the environmental justice movement and to the environmental movement in general.

A Mother's Battle For Environmental Justice

Alexis Jetter

Patsy Ruth Oliver was driving up and down her dusty Texas road, looking for the snake she'd run over the night before. "There goes the EPA and the Army Corps of Engineers all wrapped into one package," she had muttered before backing up, taking aim at the snake, and flooring her creaky old Dodge Diplomat. "Of course, the reptiles are a lot more respectable than our enemies," she said remorsefully the next morning. "The rattlesnake is a gentleman. He warns you before he strikes."

With five children and seven grandchildren, fifty-eight-year-old Patsy Ruth Oliver was a whirlwind of a woman with mischievous eyes and a devilish wit, a gripping storyteller whose language was a mixture of grit and Gospel. Unable to remain idle while her children, her mother, her husband and her friends began to sicken and die from the effects of toxic waste buried beneath their homes, Oliver organized her neighbors to fight back. For more than a decade, she did battle with the Environmental Protection Agency, corporate polluters, and the U.S. Congress to free the people of Carver Terrace from what she called their "prison of poison."

When I saw her it was summertime in Texarkana, a faded railroad town on the Texas-Arkansas border, and the brutal humidity made it difficult to breathe. In Carver Terrace, Oliver's old neighborhood, it smelled like someone was brushing hot, sticky tar onto a sun-scorched roof. But it was just the air, licking at the toxic soil of this suburban ghost town.

Dark patches of creosote seeped through the withered lawns, around rusting swing sets and down the cracked center of the street. Tiny bubbles of what locals call "migraine gas" floated in oily puddles. Before long, my head ached and my tongue was coated with a strange greasy taste.

"If it starts stinging," Patsy Ruth Oliver warned, "don't scratch. Just rub. Otherwise it will start welting." Grabbing a stick, she stabbed the ground and waited patiently for the evil-smelling muck to rise. "When it oozes up," she said almost cheerfully, "you smell it even more."

Welcome to "Toxicana," Oliver's hometown and Superfund Site No. 677, one of the worst toxic waste dumps in the country. "Every time I come back here it's like a pain in my heart," said Oliver, her voice echoing off the plywood-shuttered houses. "There's just death everywhere. There's not a house here that hasn't been affected."

In 1993, over the objections of the Environmental Protection Agency— which insisted that the carcinogens lacing Carver Terrace's water, air and soil did not pose an immediate threat—Oliver and the angry mothers of Carver Terrace finally convinced Congress to authorize a buyout so that they could leave their homes of twenty-five years. This grassroots, mother-led movement handed the EPA a rare and embarrassing defeat, enabling many families to start new lives in neighborhoods free of toxic pollutants. But the saga of what many call the "black Love Canal" did not end there.

The battle for Carver Terrace has become a rallying cry for the growing "environmental justice" movement, which charges that industrial polluters target minority neighborhoods. And it transformed Patsy Ruth Oliver from a small-time hellraiser, intent only on protecting her own family, into a formidable grassroots organizer, helping groups across the Southwest combat what they call environmental racism.

"I didn't know beans about toxics," says Oliver, her Texas drawl barely keeping pace with her words. "I was a nurse and a housewife and a mother. What did I know? But suddenly, everything I had worked for in my life was up for grabs—because of toxics. My American dream had turned into an American nightmare."

If you had half a minute, Patsy Ruth Oliver would tell you with relish that she was part Choctaw and all rebel, a bastard out of Texarkana with an unbent spirit. When her dog Terry bit her, she bit him back. As a young woman, Oliver fought segregation the same way: In the 1960s, she proudly endured being splattered with rotten eggs during sit-ins at the "whites-only" Woolworth's lunch counter, and she dodged buckshot in a "wade-in" at the town lake. "That was a hurting thing," she said. "That was a belittling thing. But it made us a stronger people."

She started work as a domestic at ten, spent years as a nurse's aide, and ultimately landed one of the best-paying jobs there was for African-Americans in Texarkana: assembling detonators on the high-explosives line at the Lone Star Army Ammunitions Plant. It was a casual irony to Oliver that she both lived and worked in places that are now Superfund sites. She jokes that one may have saved her from the other. "If I hadn't been working swingshift, graveyard shift and weekends at the plant, I might be dead by now."

By the early sixties, Oliver had five children and a failed marriage to a career military man. She moved with her children and her mother to a public housing project. It wasn't a bad place, she says, but she hated it there. She wanted a backyard for her children, a flower garden for herself, and a comfortable place for her mother to call home. And so, while she worked at Lone Star, waitressed on weekends and cooked for white families on the side, she plotted her escape. "Mama, we're going to have a house," she vowed. "I don't know how we're going to get it, but we're going to get it."

One day on the bus in 1967, Oliver heard some women talking excitedly about a new subdivision. It was named after George Washington Carver, the African-American agricultural chemist and educator. Prices were low. And for upwardly mobile blacks in segregated Texarkana, it was just about the only game in town. As the construction site swung into view, Oliver stood up, pulled the cord, and got off the bus. After chatting with developer Sam Weisman, she plunked down her cash, promised to return with $90 on payday, and walked away clutching a down-payment receipt for a brand-new, ranch-style brick home.

Oliver knew that her dream house lay atop the bulldozed remains of a wood treatment plant. As a girl, she had cut through the 62-acre Koppers Company yard when she was late for classes at segregated Dunbar High. But in 1967 few traces of the plant remained, and no one worried about toxic creosote waste. "It never crossed my mind," says Weisman, now retired and living in Shreveport, Louisiana. "I was just looking for a piece of property to develop for the colored in the area." He hit paydirt. Preachers, teachers and factory workers flocked to the neighborhood's seventy-nine modest homes, and gloried in the pride of ownership. Children raced their bicycles down Milam Street and played in the creek. And Oliver, with deep satisfaction, planted a flower garden and watched her children grow.

But over the years, odd things began to happen. After a hard rain, dark gunk would bubble up through the ground and give puddles an oily sheen. Something ate holes in the bottom of plastic swimming pools and corroded galvanized water pipes. And grass simply wouldn't grow; residents were forced to buy truckloads of topsoil to keep their lawns and gardens alive. There was no relief inside, either. The sharp, smoky smell of tar wafted from faucets, and greasy black sludge appeared in sinks and bathtubs. Cats and dogs grew listless, formed tumors, and died. And slowly, without talking to each other, without admitting it to themselves, people started to get sick.

Once robustly healthy, Oliver gradually developed a thyroid tumor and a ruptured gallbladder. Nathaniel Oliver, a sweet-tempered seaman and cook whom Patsy Ruth married in 1979, got a painful cyst on his kidney. And her mother, a vital and energetic woman, suddenly couldn't keep down any food at all. Over coffee, meeting by chance in doctors' offices or at the grocery store, the mothers of Carver Terrace started comparing notes: They'd all had upset stomachs, dizzy spells, shortness of breath and night sweats. Their daughters were having prolonged menstrual cycles and more miscarriages than anyone could remember. Small children had frequent headaches, nosebleeds and rashes. And people in nearly every house in Carver Terrace, it seemed, were having liver, heart, kidney or thyroid problems.

The death toll climbed steadily. By Oliver's count, twenty-seven people in seventy-nine homes died, many from cancer. Some were already old and sick. But often death came inexplicably and without warning. Two women in their forties died suddenly at work. One man got dizzy and fell through his living room window; another was found dead sitting in his bathroom.

At night, residents would sit out in their yards to escape the odor inside their homes. But there it would be, riding on the evening breeze. Some residents began to connect the old creosote plant with the odor in the air and the dark gunk in their backyards and sinks. Others tried to convince themselves that the smell was rising off the nearby railroad tracks, or from a leaky car engine.

The truth did not begin to emerge until 1979, one year after leaking barrels of dioxin were discovered beneath Love Canal, New York. In response, Congress ordered the nation's largest chemical firms to identify their hazardous waste sites. The Pittsburgh-based Koppers Company, which had left a string of toxic dumps across the country, placed Carver Terrace high on its list.

For Koppers knew two things that Oliver and her neighbors did not: Their pretty, landscaped yards were saturated with creosote. And prolonged exposure to the oily black liquid, a distillate of coal tar, could prove deadly. Creosote exposure can induce nausea, headaches and dizziness; cause second-degree burns and rashes; and lead to cancer, kidney failure, respiratory ailments and liver problems.

State investigators came to inspect Carver Terrace in 1980. One inspector, shocked by his readings, warned mothers that it wasn't safe for their children to play outside. The state's findings were alarming. The soil and groundwater were contaminated with arsenic, pentachlorophenol, creosote and polycyclic aromatic hydrocarbons—a potent carcinogen. But residents were told nothing about the study for four years.

In 1984, the bombshell dropped: Texas officials asked the EPA to place Carver Terrace on the Superfund list, the $9-billion trust that Congress established in 1980 to clean up toxic waste dumps. The EPA flew in a pack of scientists and administrators, armed with arcane explanations and a slide show. The site was toxic, they told residents, but not immediately hazardous to their health. Cleanup crews could reduce dangers to an "acceptable risk" level.

There was, however, one catch. More studies were needed before a cleanup could begin. "That may not sit well with a lot of folks, but you can't start removing the whole face of the earth," said Stan Hitt, chief of the Superfund Enforcement Office in EPA's Dallas office. "You have to study the problem."

"They studied us, all right," agreed Oliver. "To death." Over the next eight years, EPA and Koppers Company took turns analyzing Carver Terrace's water, soil and air—virtually everything, in fact, except its people. For reasons that EPA still cannot explain, residents were never interviewed.

Soon men arrived in protective white "moonsuits," rubber gas masks and disposable gloves to inspect the soil that scantily clad children played in every day. Why were EPA employees dressed for germ warfare, residents wanted to know, when they were being told the neighborhood was safe? "We require them to wear clothes like that to minimize potential health effects from continual exposure," explained EPA spokesman Roger Meacham.

That answer satisfied no one in Carver Terrace, where exposure was measured in decades, not days. "They couldn't answer us," said Nathaniel Oliver, a tall, gentle man who has harsh words only for the federal government. "Because they'd been lying to us for such a long, long time." And so the inspectors poked and sampled, while Patsy Ruth Oliver watched from her front porch, her curiosity turning slowly to anger.

Workers shut down the sand and gravel company next door, ringed it with a wire mesh fence and posted a warning: "SOIL CONTAMINATED WITH TOXIC WASTE: KEEP OUT." Soil on their side of the fence, residents were told, was safe. "Our toxics down here are real intelligent," drawled Oliver. "They can read. They'll stay on that side of the fence."

Neighbors erected their own sign. Leroy Davis, told by his doctor that he was too sick to stay in Carver Terrace, nailed one to a tree before leaving for a nursing home. "WELCOME TO TOXIC WASTE DEATH VALLEY," it read above a skull and crossbones. "ENTER AT YOUR OWN RISK." But residents were stuck. For as word of the contamination spread, property values plummeted; one house reportedly sold for only $7,000. "We were trapped," said Oliver, "in a prison of poison."

In 1988, the EPA finally unveiled its report. It was four volumes long and took two people to carry. And it concluded that the soil of Carver Terrace could be safely removed, mechanically washed, and replaced with fresh topsoil. What about our health, Oliver and others demanded. Those concerns had been fully addressed in the report, they were told. And so Oliver read it, "with a dictionary in one hand because I am no chemist."

But Patsy Ruth Oliver didn't need a glossary to realize that someone had made some deadly assumptions about her community. Yes, there were contaminants in the creek, the report stated. But it dismissed that danger, saying it was "difficult to imagine" that anyone would swim in such a shallow, snake-infested and murky brook. Yet Oliver knew that every child in the neighborhood had played there. No one at EPA had ever asked.

She read on. Children could easily place creosote in their mouths, the study said, but "the unfavorable taste will be enough to keep a child from ingesting soils from the seep area again." That rankled, too. Oliver knew many children in Carver Terrace who used to eat "mud pies." One, Suzette Fulce, had her thyroid removed at seventeen.

Incredulous, Oliver read further. Eating vegetables grown in contaminated soil could be harmful, the report said. "But only one residence in Carver Terrace has been observed to have a vegetable garden." That was too much. "People had gardens all around," Oliver said angrily. "But they didn't come looking." For years, her entire family had eaten the tomatoes, onions, potatoes, watermelons, beans, peas, turnips, collard, cantelope and strawberries that Nathaniel grew in their garden.

Was that why her mother was wasting away from esophageal cancer? Why her daughters had suffered miscarriages? Why her own stomach pained her so? Nathaniel was stricken by the thought that the vegetables he had so carefully grown and cooked for his family might have poisoned them. "I got scared and I got angry," he said. "Nobody told us. We had to find out for ourselves."

Oliver had had enough. If the government had evacuated residents and purchased homes in Love Canal, New York, and Times Beach, Missouri, then why must they stay in Carver Terrace? "We don't want to die out," she declared. "We want a buyout."

The EPA insisted that no buyout was warranted. "This situation is certainly no Love Canal," Meacham said. But Oliver thought she knew what distinguished Carver Terrace from Love Canal, and it wasn't the soil. "If there's one thing I know," she said, "it's racism. I have a master's degree in Jim Crow."

And so Patsy Ruth Oliver started to raise hell. Together with a local watchdog group, Friends United for a Safe Environment (FUSE), she pounded on doors, got petitions signed, organized a network of mothers who compiled notes on their families' ailments, and led marches through the neighborhood. No one was more surprised than Oliver, for she had long been a homebody. "I could have been one of the people hiding behind their curtains and watching the march go by," she said. "But here I was leading the damn thing!"

She and other residents descended on the state capitol in Austin, on EPA offices in Dallas—where officials locked their doors and sent their employees home—and on EPA headquarters in Washington, D.C. "If they can take down the Berlin Wall," she demanded, "why can't the EPA take down this invisible wall and release us?"

Soon her face was a regular feature on the front page of the Texarkana Gazette and her rapid-fire denunciations were a growing irritant to her targets. "She's a troublemaker," grumbled developer Sam Weisman. "She's a thorn in our side," groused EPA's Roger Meacham. "She's a lightning rod," chuckled Dave Hall, Texarkana's coordinator for emergency management. Patsy's family couldn't decide what they felt most: concern or pride. "She's going to get herself killed," Nathaniel fretted. "I couldn't have been prouder of her than if she was Sen. Carol Moseley-Braun talking about the Daughters of the Confederacy flag," said daughter Stephanie, forty-one.

Oliver, who had gone back to school to get her nursing degree, now turned her full attention to toxins. "Carver Terrace became a school for me," she said. "I started rubbing elbows with these rocket scientists, hoping it would rub off a little on me. Everytime they said something, I was like E. F. Hutton: I listened and was very quiet." She chuckled at the memory. "Why, I was so quiet, you could hear a rat piss on cotton!"

Still, Oliver admitted, it was a bit daunting. For the environmental movement was white, and she was a black woman from the rural South. "Sometimes I was all alone," Oliver said. "Sometimes I looked like a fly in a glass of buttermilk." But she took her allies where she found them. And toxins, she liked to say, "are equal opportunity killers—they don't discriminate."

Oliver had long prided herself on her meticulous appearance in public. Now she traded in her glamorous dresses and wigs for T-shirts and corn braids, and hit the road. Her five children mourned the lost elegance—"Patsy was like a black Auntie Mame," said Stephanie—but they cheered her on.

She flew off to address a Greenpeace summit on industrial waste in Washington, D.C., and attend Stop Toxic Polluter seminars at Tennessee's famed Highlander Center, where Martin Luther King, Jr., was once trained in community organizing. She joined several regional environmental groups that sent her to the Earth Summit in Rio de Janiero. And soon she was swapping tips with activists from across the United States, from Navajo elders fighting an asbestos dump in New Mexico to African-American women fighting a proposed PCB landfill in North Carolina. Their revolts had sewed the seeds for a new grassroots movement: environmental justice.

"Patsy typifies what's happening in the environmental justice movement in communities of color," says Robert Bullard, director of the Environmental Justice Resource Center at Clark/Atlanta University. "It's mostly women—mothers and housewives—who get involved to protect family, home and community. These are not traditional environmentalists. These are people talking about survival."

Encouraged by her new allies, Oliver took to the airwaves, starring in a flashy Greenpeace eco-video for VH-1, MTV's station for adults. "We don't have the complexion for protection!" charged Oliver, echoing a popular slogan. Even Rev. Jesse Jackson weighed in: "The people of Carver Terrace," he said, "have seen only poisonous creosote at the end of their rainbow."

Finally, in November 1990, Congress appropriated $5 million to purchase Carver Terrace and relocate its inhabitants. Residents were elated. But it took nearly three years for the Army Corps of Engineers—who residents felt woefully undervalued their homes—to complete its task. By that time Oliver's mother, who had marched with her daughter through the rain-drenched streets of Carver Terrace and accompanied her on the grueling 700-mile round trips to Austin, had died.

Patsy Ruth never really got over it. One official made the mistake of urging her to be patient during those endless delays. "Don't ever use that word with me," she snapped. "The most patient woman I knew is dead, stretched out in her grave. Keeping my mouth shut was the worst thing I ever did."

Back in Carver Terrace, Oliver stared glumly at the small house they once shared, which was nailed shut and posted with a U.S. government "NO TRESPASSING" sign. "My American dream died a long time ago," she said in a low, trembling voice. "And when my mother died, it really died. It's hard for me to respond when people ask: 'How do you like your new home?' It's just a house, and it's not on toxic soil." But her mother's death forged a resolve in Oliver. "OK, Mama, I told you I was going to get us out of here," she vowed. "I made you that promise. And I decided, once I got out, to carry on that fight."

She did. Oliver threw herself into environmental work across the Southwest. In the border towns of Brownsville, Texas, and Matamoros, Mexico, she joined the fight to curb chemical emissions by the nearby *maquiladoras*, factories built in Mexico to avoid U.S. wage and environmental regulations. Pollution in those towns was so extreme that women were giving birth to horribly malformed babies. "I know what hell looks like," Oliver said after returning from one tour of Matamoros. "Dead animals in the water, raw sewage. You can't imagine." Oliver also combatted construction of toxic waste incinerators along the Texas-Arkansas border, and rallied against operators of a Jacksonville, Arkansas, Agent Orange factory that wanted to burn dioxin-laden waste. In 1993, in recognition of her work, Oliver became one of the first two black women named to the board of Friends of the Earth.

Oliver was out of town so much she barely found time to enjoy the new house that she and Nathaniel had built just outside Texarkana. But she made sure to plant a flower garden, which she inspected like a hawk every morning. And the message on her answering machine was gleeful: "We always enjoy hearing from our friends," Oliver greeted callers. "And, thank God, we're out of the Toxic Twilight Zone."

But tragically, not for long. "We're out of Carver Terrace," Oliver used to say, "but it's not out of us." Just a few months after Oliver moved to her new home, her eldest daughter, Stephanie, died suddenly from a brain aneurism.

And on December 15, 1993, the day that the Army Corps of Engineers finally arrived in Texarkana to bulldoze her old house in Carver Terrace, Patsy Ruth Oliver died in her sleep.

"Friends, Neighbors Mourn Carver Terrace Leader," the Texarkana Gazette said the next day. "An Environmentalist Passes," noted the Texas Observer in a full-page obituary. The writer, a fellow Texarkana environmentalist, recalled Oliver's first speech: "We're not going to let our dreams die," she had said. "We want to leave our children a legacy of clean air, clean water and clean land on which to live. And not only in Texarkana, but throughout this United States of America. We want our voices heard so loud that we'll ring from the mountaintops, and from shore to shore."

Her children have vowed to continue the work that she left off. And at the funeral, as her sons and daughters stepped forward to recall their mother's spirit, humor and fire, they read from a program inscribed with a simple message. "So many people don't think one person can make a difference," Oliver had told her children. "But really, it has to start someplace. So let it start with me."

So Let It Start With Me

An Interview with Patsy Ruth Oliver

Conducted and edited by Alexis Jetter

I was a nurse and a housewife and a mother—what did I know? Then I went to a meeting one Sunday and it just blew me out of the water. I could've stayed one of the people hiding behind the curtains and watching the march go by. But before long I was leading the damn thing!

When you are a mother, and you intend to survive, your instincts take over. And you become a fighter. You become a warrior for your cause. And you fight to survive. Being a black woman born in the South, that came very easily to me. Because I had come through the civil rights struggles, where I had to fight to eat lunch at a lunch counter, downtown. I've had eggs thrown on me. I've had dogs sicked on me. And I rode that Freedom Bus. And I came to the decision that if I could take that to make this world better for my children, if I could fight to integrate schools for a better education for them—then I was really going to fight now. For a better way of life for my neighbors, my children and myself.

I used to be just a homebody. If it wasn't for my children and my mother, I wouldn't be involved. But everything I had worked for was up for grabs—because of toxics. My American dream had turned into an American nightmare. It totally consumed my whole life. And it has ever since. If something needs to be done, I just stop what I'm doing, even if I'm in the middle of making dinner. If you want to clean things up, you have to be an agitator. An agitator like in a washing machine—you have to stay in constant motion.

I was born on a stormy day, and I've been stormy ever since! [Laughs] I was what Southern people call a bastard. But I've been called worse. I was reared in the home of my aunt, because my mother had me at sixteen and out of wedlock. My aunt let me be wild, let me be free and let me be me. She was always telling me about our Choctaw heritage and black heritage. She let me know I was somebody. And that, regardless of the color of the skin you're wrapped in, God made us all. That he instilled in you a brain—and that the only color that matters is gray.

Segregated schools just made me stronger. They made me a rebel. I've always dreamed of being a person of intelligence. I lost myself in books. Teachers motivated us to dream dreams. But it was hard to not have the the tools to achieve, the books to read, to keep pace with the white children.

When I was seven or eight, a black man was lynched by the cotton mill. We weren't allowed to watch. We just knew that they were coming through. It was the Klan. It was said that he raped a white woman; it was never proven. Just to speak to a white woman, you could be lynched. They stormed the jail and took him out, and they hung him. And then, a few days later, they cut him down from the tree. And then, our parents made an issue of driving by, some that had cars, or in a wagon, or walking by, to take the children over to that tree. To let us know what had happened there.

It put fear in your heart. It put anger in your heart. Sometimes it made you want to fight. It angered me to the point of wanting to fight a fight against the unjust, for that man. But then I thought, this will not bring him back. It will not prove anything. It's like Maya Angelou's book: *I Know Why the Caged Bird Sings*. I felt like I was caged into a system that only worked for white people. It made me a rebel within.

I've always lived right there by the railroad tracks. They always say that poor people, people of color, lesser-class people—they always place them by the railroad tracks. That's good. Cause it motivates you to always want to get out. I crossed those tracks when I moved into Carver Terrace. I was moving away from the ghetto and the projects into a middle-class neighborhood. In 1968, with the civil rights movement, there was a great wind blowing for righteousness and justice. It meant something to me to be able to cross that track, because I was crossing a boundary in my life. I felt like I was on my way, and that I was giving my children the chance to get even further away.

I really didn't like living in the projects because we never owned anything. You couldn't have the flowers that you wanted. My children couldn't have the swings and sandboxes that I wanted for them. We couldn't have gardens, we couldn't have dogs, we couldn't have cats. I wanted that for my children, the whole American Dream. And I wanted something better for my mama.

I said, "Mama, we're going to have a house. I don't know how I'm going to get it but we're going to get it." So I started working at the bullet factory, the

Lone Star Ammunition Depot. I would work five days a week in high explosives, then waitressed at the officers' club on weekends and babysat for the colonel.

I worked on the E-line: that's the high explosives line. Any munitions plant has its dangers. And a lot of stuff we did by hand. But it paid a lot better than most jobs in Texarkana. I took that job to keep my children fed and bread on the table—yeah, I took a chance. I never knew if my kids were going to greet me as a corpse or as a person.

Then one day I was making a small detonator that sets off a hand grenade. A steel projectile hit me with such force, it just knocked the whole skin off my thumb, and the blood was spurting. I had sense enough to make a tourniquet with my right hand to stop the flow of blood. My forelady came around sand said: "Patsy, why did you stop the line?" I says: "I'm hurting." She says: "You're not hurt." This white woman was talking down to me. I said: "Oh really?" And I just held it in front of her and let go the tourniquet, and blood just went all over her face. She screamed: "Call the ambulance!"

I nearly lost my thumb and all the ligaments were torn. They had to make me another thumb. The graphite and particles are still beneath the skin. That will bother me forever. But I went back to work there shortly afterward. You have to do what you have to do. I worked my way up from high explosive operator to union steward. I had to be the head of something so I could raise hell! [Laughs] And help other people raise hell.

I first heard about Carver Terrace in 1967. I was on the bus, coming from downtown, when I was cooking for people. I heard the ladies on the bus talking: "You know that's going to be a black neighborhood, a subdivision for black people." And I thought: Wow. I like that idea. I'm going to get out of Stephens Court. My children have a chance. I'm going to risk it.

I reached up for the cord on the bus and got off. Believe it or not, I only had $10 to my name. I walked across the tracks and I prayed: Oh God, please be with me. Let this be my chance. I told the developer, a white man, that I was a mother and I had five children and I wanted to move to Carver Terrace. He said the house would cost $10,000. My auntie's voice came in my ear: Always tell the truth. I told him I had only $10 for a downpayment. I thought he was going to say no. But he said "I'll take your $10 and you can pay me the remaining $90 on your next payday."

Well, I literally took wing. It was eight blocks to Stephens Court. I walked, I strutted. I got home and said, "Mom, honey, you better get to packing this junk up, because we're getting out of here." She knew not to say 'no.' "Where are we going?" she asked. I said, "We're buying a house. We're getting the hell out of here. I'm not living in a ghetto no more." She said, "Girl, what have you gone and done?" I said, "God has worked this deal. Just believe in me a little while. Here's the receipt!"

There were a lot of doubting Thomases. "Oh she'll never do it. She's single. She hasn't got a husband. She's got all those kids. She'll never make it." But that didn't stop me. Something in my mind said I could. So I did it.

I could have my friends over for holiday barbecues. I could sit in my yard, enjoy the pride of ownership and set an example for my children. They did not have to bring their friends to the projects. They could bring them home with them, they could spend the night, have slumber parties, pajama parties. You could set up Kool-Aid in the backyard, and watch them play basketball there in their own backyard, watch them ride a bicycle for the first time. These things meant a lot to me.

The thing that made me the happiest was my mother: It gave her a lot of energy. She marveled at the idea of ownership. This was a first for us. That I was able to make this dream come true. A lot of black people were desperate for decent houses. They lived in dustbowls, shotgun apartments and shantytowns. They lived in projects. They were just starting to come into wage-earning situations. If you didn't teach or preach, you were a domestic. And back then, there was no choice about where blacks could live in Texarkana. We lived where we were told. Filthy ghettos with unpaved roads, where everything was second class.

Let me tell you, the prospect of being able to own our own homes in a community with paved roads, water and sewer service, a neighborhood playground— well, hearts just beat faster. This was the real American dream, a dream that we could just begin to dream. We were so consumed with the happiness, wrapped up in it, that in 1985, when we first started getting word about the contamination, we just couldn't believe it. But then the word came down that we were living on a Superfund site. And our dream became a nightmare.

One Sunday when we were having lunch, two white men came into the neighborhood. And they were at my neighbor's house. She called me. "Patsy, drop what you're doing and come down here. I have something I want to tell you." I knew it must be something very, very important for Francis to call, because she never missed her Sunday afternoon on TV. So I rushed down.

She said: "I want to introduce you to two white men." I looked at her. "What you want to introduce me to two white men for on a Sunday afternoon?" I was very suspicious. Because in the South, black people are suspicious when white people come—like Greeks with Trojan horses. So she said, "They want to tell you about this toxic neighborhood you're living in."

I said, "Toxic neighborhood I'm living in?" Middle-class citizen, Carver Terrace? She said, "Yes, because they haven't told you the full story. They haven't printed it in the paper. You're living on a Superfund site. These toxics will kill you, literally."

What is Superfund? I knew nothing about this. They told us that we had toxic chemicals out there from the old creosote plant. I asked Jim Presley,

"Well, how do you know all this, and what are your affiliations, and what do you do here in Texarkana, and what have you come here for?" And he said, "It's time to come and tell you people the truth. I could not sit idly by and watch the toxics consume you." He belonged to an organization called Friends United for a Safe Environment. And this is when we started to really dialogue.

Then, after a week or more, EPA came into our neighborhood. They gathered at the neighborhood church—which was also in a toxic situation. So, we went to church to see this film by EPA about how they could come in and wash the soil and clean it up and there really wasn't anything wrong with it that couldn't be straightened out by EPA. They said that they were really on top of it and we were going to be safe.

That didn't set too well. But most neighbors believed this. Because they really thought that the Environmental Protection Agency was the one to do the job. We were naive enough to believe, even in the rural South, that they were going to take care of us.

But as time rolled on, it wasn't happening. And then, I'm nosy by nature, being a woman. I started noticing my friends and my children and their friends were having ailments. Usually when my daughter Bess was out of school, some of her friends were out of school. It was the same symptoms. And if I got sick, the neighbor next door was sick.

So the mothers started visiting over coffee, and then going from door to door. I'd say, "Well you know I woke up with a terrible headache and sweats last night, and it wasn't hot. And I couldn't breathe and I had shortness of breath." And she says, "I did too, and I went to the doctor, and he just said it was bronchitis." And on and on. "Oh. My child had a nosebleed last night." And "my child was sick last night." And "my child was nauseous last night." And "oh, my child has a terrible rash" and it goes on and on, repeating itself. And "oh, what are we going to do? Where do you think it's coming from?"

And we began to really question EPA. And then we began to form a network of women in the neighborhood, from block to block, seeing what their symptoms were. We were all feeling it. At night you would wake up with a headache. It felt like a hangover, but you knew you didn't drink anything stronger than water. You came out of the shower and you had a burning sensation: it stung and burned and itched. And when you towelled it off, it felt like you were rubbing your flesh raw. I tried to put soda in my bath to make it soothing. I went through a lot of boxes of Arm & Hammer baking soda.

You'd go off on vacation, and the whole time you were away, you felt light-headed and energized. But the minute you came back, you didn't have any energy. You couldn't breathe. The tearing of the eyes came back. The hair falling out came back—and you didn't know whether it was the air or us pulling out our hair. Because it was so stressful—just knowing that two or three people were in the hospital every month.

But we thought: Maybe I slept wrong, maybe there was a gas leak, maybe I worked too hard on the yard, I was tired when I came in from work. You just tried to place the blame everywhere but on your dream. For a long time, we thought this was the way it was supposed to smell, because we were nearby the creek and the railroad tracks. I suppose when you're trying to be happy, I think when you're feeling successful for the first time, you don't want to ask questions. You don't really want to know.

And then, suddenly, we started to get young people dying. We had one woman, she had two sons and a lovely daughter and she went to work and said she had a headache. It just got fierce. But before she got to the hospital, she had a rupture. She didn't make it. We had another young woman, in her late forties. She was working in the school cafeteria. She took sick on the job and they were trying to rush her to the hospital and she went into a coma. Her children and her mother buried her.

LaVerne Williams came home one night and found her husband in her bathroom, sitting on the stool, dead. That was a very shocking thing. He was in his late fifties, early sixties and still going to work. Then a flock of young men were getting sick.

It was getting worse. It got to the place where the hearse was out there more than Yellow Cabs. There was always death or damn near dead or "I'm dying" or "I've got to have surgery," or "I've had surgery" or "I spent some time in the Emergency Room." That's all we ever heard. It was constant. And meanwhile the EPA was saying it was not hazardous to our health.

But one inspector told the mothers that we shouldn't let our children play in the dirt. So you won't see too many swingsets in Carver Terrace. And the ones that are here weren't ever used. They told us that the children couldn't play in the soil. You tell me what parent can keep an eye on children twenty-four hours a day! Both parents were working in those days. Mothers were nervous to have their children even go outside in Carver Terrace. One woman was so fearful that she just kept her children jailed inside all day long.

So I started questioning the EPA: You said this land is contaminated. Don't you know that concrete is porous? How are you going to raise the houses up and sweep out under them? How are you going to clean the acquifers? I started asking: Why? How? When? How can you assure us that it's going to work? How did we get on the Superfund list in the first place if it wasn't dangerous to our health? And if it weren't so easily absorbed, why did those EPA people come out in their moonsuits when we had only our street clothes on all day? They just told us they were studying us. And they studied us all right—to death.

I was getting scared of the water in Carver Terrace. I had a pipe burst. I had a plumber come out and dig up the waterpipe. That galvanized pipe was rusted. And it started to crumble just like a soda cracker in your hand. And there were holes up and down that pipe. So I knew that chemicals from the ground had seeped into the drinking water coming into my house. And I said: If the chemicals can do this to a galvanized iron pipe, what can it do to a human stomach?

And then we started seeing this gunk start coming up in our facebowls and bathtubs. You could flush the toilet, and all this goop would come up in your sink. It wasn't sewage, but this oily, blackish, greenish, tarry looking substance. And it had a very, very foul odor to it. It let off a smoky air about it. You could see it coming up just like fumes. And you could smell it as soon as you could see it.

Those EPA people refused to take a drink of water from my hydrant. They came out in their moonsuits one July, and I was sitting watching one of them take soil samples outside my house. This man was literally just wringing wet, just like he had walked out of a rainstorm. And I knew he was thirsty. So I went in and got a can of cold 7-Up, poured it over some ice, and said: "Here, have a cold glass of—." But he didn't see anything but looked like water.

He jumped up, raised up his two little hands like I'd pulled a gun on him. "No, ma'am, No ma'am, I'm not thirsty." And sweat was pouring off of this stiff! That made my day! Here I was offering this man a drink of water, and you would've thought I'd pulled a .38 magnum on him.

We asked the fire department about coming down there. Their response to us was they were not equipped to put out chemical fires. We asked them what to do if there was a fire. They said: Run like hell. We were literally locked into a prison of poisons. Get this one idea in mind: Once EPA found out that these homes were in a toxic area, it really drove our prices down to nil. So we had no value on our property. We could not sell our property to get out, because no one wanted in to a toxic situation.

We wanted a buy-out, but many of our residents had to die out instead. EPA said they had to study us first. And they sure did. They studied us for eight years. They literally studied us to death. They made lab rats out of us. They made us walking, talking specimens. Living in the South, we know we're an endangered species. Why not show us the same kindness Greenpeace shows whales?

You tried sitting out in your yard anytime in the evening, and this is what you have to inhale. For twenty-five years, we had to live with it. If this had been Spring Lake Park [a white neighborhood]—damn! They would have had those people out in a minute. But instead they came out here and watched us. It's sickening.

So we went to the preachers, to Friends United for a Safe Environment, and we literally walked in the rain. We went to the media, we got the media on our side. And I was constantly screaming "environmental racism!" We shouldn't have to live like this.

So then, I got my neighbors together and we organized. We became the Carver Terrace Community Action Group. And we did something for the first time in Texarkana, that black people had never done: we took on City Hall. Then I went to the state capital in Austin, and I took my plea to them. And a representative down there from Dekalb, Texas, a southerner, heard my cry. And he contacted Congressman Jim Chapman, who heard our cry.

We had one black City Councilman that we elected that year—these mothers of Carver Terrace and other friends—and we got him to propose that we should be relocated from this toxic situation. And that passed. And then we heard from the Rev. Jesse Jackson, who wrote a letter stating that he thought we should be able to get out. And we carried that to the media. And the next thing I knew, I had met up with another national organizer, John O'Connor from National Toxics Campaign in Boston, and I was asked to go on the board.

And finally Greenpeace got the news. So I went up and talked to Greenpeace. And I didn't even know who Greenpeace was. I found out that it was a prominent, very popular anti-toxic organization. We started networking and bringing people in that had been affected by these chemicals, and saw the same identical patterns.

And when Lois Gibbs came in from Love Canal, that really put the wrench on it. That was really an education. That drove it home. She came to the church. Told us about Love Canal, and how they fought the battle and won. How the children and women were affected. She told us that EPA was going to lie, like they did, and they weren't going to help us. And that they were in bed with the polluters. They weren't enforcing any of the laws that were already on the books.

And what was scary about that was, here was this lily-white town in the middle of New York! And I said, if this is how they treat white people in liberal New York, if this is how they treat their own, we don't have a chance. Here we are, all black in the rural South. We don't have a chance of a snowball in hell. Because if there's one thing I know, it's racism. I have a master's degree in Jim Crow.

The worse I felt, the angrier I got. And when I lost my mother, I was the angriest of all. She was my buddy and my closest friend. She was my copilot when I drove cross-country. And when she died, I said: OK mama, I told you I was going to get us out of here. You walked this way with me. You fought this fight with me. I made her that promise. And I decided once I got out of here, to carry on the fight. Someone had to come in from the outside to rescue us. So it's only natural that I want to give back, and to carry on the fight.

We're out of Carver Terrace now. But it's not out of us. Every time I come here it's like a pain in your heart. Everybody's had a death or something in their house. Carver Terrace drove home a message for me: that we were suffering and people were making profits off of our misery. And it took people from outside Texarkana to care enough to say: This wasn't right and this wasn't just. To hell with the system. It's wrong! Where's your justice? Where's your conscience?

They did it for the all-mighty American dollar. And I don't say this often: but whoever profited off the miseries of the people of Carver Terrace, I truly hope there is a hell for them. I sure do. Because they have made a hell on earth for us here. We didn't die and have to go to hell. We lived in a hell. And I mean—our children and our parents, and our husbands and our babies, and some of the babies we wished we could have had—we paid a high cost.

But it seems like the longer I stay out of Carver Terrace, I'm starting to get a new zest for life. I have more energy. It used to be, I'd get out four or five sentences and then I'd have to catch my breath. Now it seems like my shortness of breath is going away. My lungs are clearing up, I don't have the drippy nose I used to have, I don't have the burning of the face when I wash my face in the morning, the color's coming back in my skin. I don't itch anymore. I was just clawing myself to death. The grandkids are not sick.

I lived there twenty-five years, and the saddest part in leaving was knowing that some people didn't make it out. The doubting Thomases, some of them didn't make it out. And I think: What a waste of life. Those people may have had four, five, ten—maybe fifteen or twenty—more years of life if they were in another place. I hope they never reincarnate again in another place like Carver Terrace.

I believe in reincarnation. I see death as a friend. I see it as a journey. I see it as sleeping the long sleep, where you don't have too many worries about tomorrow. And when I come back, I don't want to be an environmentalist! I don't want to fight for my rights. I want to have some justice and some peace of mind. I want to be Jane Doe Citizen. I swear. I don't want to have to go through any more of this the next time around!

But what I want to tell you today is, the truth of it all is, that no matter what the color of your skin, the toxic situation that we are in makes us kindreds. Because it is no disgrace to be a member of the human race—and toxics do not discriminate.

Sometimes the Road Gets Lonely

Dollie Burwell

You called me an agitator. If you don't believe that that's a compliment, the next time you wash your clothes you must take the agitator out of your washer and see if you don't have just a bunch of wet dirty clothes. And you are right. What I'm going to do is get all the dirt out and leave this county clean.

It is not easy being a mother and an activist. It is even more difficult for a mother to be an activist in a small rural community in North Carolina, especially a small rural county like Warren County, where 65 percent of the 18,000 population are African-Americans. Many times being an activist can cause you to be called names that are not pleasant to be called. You are often labeled a "troublemaker." Mothers are often asked why aren't they home taking care of the children instead of out causing trouble. Sometimes when you are labeled a troublemaker in a small rural community, it can really cause problems for you.

When you are a mother and an activist in a small community, sometimes the road gets lonely and it gets difficult. Sometimes you can feel like you are not making a difference. Sometimes you can really feel like giving up the struggle. So the Dartmouth Motherhood Conference provided for me another wave of encouragement, motivation and inspiration that I desperately needed.

As an environmental activist in my community, I am constantly struggling to educate people about the danger of hazardous and toxic waste landfills and incinerators. Many times I am disliked by government officials and by waste management companies officials because I tell people the truth. I tell them that jobs and prosperity and economic growth do not come with hazardous and toxic waste landfills and incinerators. That people living in areas where these facilities are located do not get high-paying jobs; what they get are strange diseases and health problems. I tell them that these waste management companies prey on poor and minority communities when they locate these facilities because they know that they are vulnerable and sometimes lack education and knowledge. I tell them that the government officials in these communities are just looking for a way to increase the tax base and provide jobs.

Of course, this does not make me popular with the powers that be. Especially when these waste management companies promise so much—shopping centers, jobs, economic and industrial growth. To a small county with double-digit unemployment, these promises sound like the best thing since sliced bread!

This happened a few years ago in Northampton County, North Carolina, a county adjacent to where I live. A waste management company promised county government officials a shopping center, lots of jobs and a few other goodies. Since Northampton County is one of the state's poorest counties, these promises sounded to county government officials like they were God-sent. They believed that the county could really benefit from having a hazardous and toxic waste incinerator. They were convinced that this facility would provide hundreds of jobs for people, and people would look upon them as real leaders for having made this move for the county. Northampton County is also about 70 percent African-American.

One night at a hearing, one of the officials called me a troublemaker. He told the people that I didn't know what I was talking about. The incinerator was going to be safe, he said, and all I did was go around the state talking to people and discouraging economic development by instilling fear in the people of the community. I was just an outside agitator. When I got up to speak I thanked him for the compliment. Of course he looked at me like, "What is this fool talking about? I know I'm not crazy. I did not compliment her."

So I said, "Mr. Clark, I know you are wondering what kind of compliment you gave me. But you called me an agitator. If you don't believe that that's a compliment, the next time you wash your clothes you just take the agitator out of your washer and see if you don't have just a bunch of wet dirty clothes. I want to thank you for calling me an agitator because you are right, what I'm going to do for Northampton County is get all the dirt out and leave this county clean." I don't think Mr. Clark called any other activist an agitator.

For a very long time a myth existed that environmental problems were only the concern of white, middle-class males. But from native lands to urban ghettos, from welfare rolls to university rolls, mothers and minorities are fighting back against toxic siege and impacting the environmental justice movement. I feel that I can best explain how mothers have played a role in environmental activism and how mothers are fighting back against toxic siege by telling the 1982 story of how mothers of predominantly black, rural, mostly poor Warren County, North Carolina, struggled against the state's siting of a polychlorinated biphenyl (PCB) landfill resulting in more than five hundred arrests of mostly women and children.

Before the Warren County demonstrations, racial and ethnic communities had been only marginally involved with issues of hazardous and toxic wastes. In the fall of 1982, mothers and daughters, fathers and sons of Warren County launched one of the largest civil rights demonstrations since the 1960s. But let me back up a bit. During the summer of 1978, a transformer company illegally and deliberately sprayed 31 gallons of PCB fluid along 240 miles of roadside in 14 counties of North Carolina. In some areas concentrations were as high as 10,000 parts per million, 200 times above the level the Environmental Protection Agency designates as safe.

After examining 90 potential sites, the state of North Carolina officially announced its intention to bury 40 cubic yards of this PCB-laced soil in the town of Afton. Citizens of the community felt deeply that the state's decision to bury the PCBs in Warren County was based solely on the fact that the Afton was 85 percent African-American. Citizens felt this way because in choosing this site, the Environmental Protection Agency had to waive two of its very important requirements. One of their requirements was that the bottom of the landfill had to be at least 50 feet above the groundwater table. At the Warren County site, the landfill would be only 7 feet above the groundwater. The second important requirement that they waived was that a site had to have a thick and permeable soil formation such as large clay pans. Warren County's soil samples showed only small amounts or no clay presence. But in spite of that, on June 4, 1979, the Environmental Protection Agency waived these requirements and gave the state of North Carolina final approval to construct the landfill on the Afton site. The citizens of Warren County felt that their civil rights had been violated.

Many people in the community believed that EPA and the government would, in fact, protect them. They firmly believed that if there had to be a landfill, it would have to meet all the requirements. When the EPA waived these requirements, people were infuriated. Some people were ready to resort to violence. Once the landfill was constructed, someone cut up the plastic liner that the state had put in. Many people were ready to actually shoot anyone who drove a truck bringing PCB-laced soil into the county. This is where I believe the church was extremely helpful in our struggle. The church played a major role by encouraging people to pray and put their faith into action. This prevented people from becoming violent. Though our community is poor, its people are very proud. We have a lot of working-class people whose lands were inherited from generations past. People did not want to see their land destroyed.

My affiliation with the Southern Christian Leadership Conference (SCLC) and the United Church of Christ Commission for Racial Justice had taught me what nonviolent civil disobedience could accomplish. So I immediately gathered people together and told them that there were other ways to prevent the state and EPA from destroying our community. I told them that I believed that we could save our community though nonviolent struggle. So we began to meet at church and pray and march and protest. We invited other civil rights organizations and churches to join us in our struggle. Spirituality was a major part of the movement.

Mothers argued vigorously that the state's decision to put the landfill in Warren County was based on racial and political grounds. The fact that Warren County had the highest percentage of African-Americans of any county in the state, the fact that the county was rural, mostly poor, had very little voting power and almost no economic power were the reasons why the state was putting the landfill in Warren County. Scientific data indicated that the Warren County site was not the best site. Mothers in Warren County joined other citizens in filing a lawsuit to prevent the state from hauling toxic and hazardous waste to the Warren County landfill. This suit was dismissed by the state court. Mothers then joined other citizens in persuading the Warren County Board of Commissioners to file a second lawsuit. But the Commissioners got a lot of pressure from the state, and they later withdrew the lawsuit. But that didn't stop the mothers of Warren County.

Mothers came out to public hearings, bringing their children and letting the state know that they would not stand by and let them dump poison on their children. Many mothers knew that they were fighting more than just a one-time PCB dump. Because by that time, Governor James B. Hunt was saying that the state needed a permanent hazardous and toxic waste facility. The state had purchased a 100-acre tract of land and had an option to purchase an additional 240-acre tract in the Afton community.

By 1982, when the trucks began to roll into Warren County, headed for the landfill, we knew we had to act. From September 15 to October 27, 1982, over five hundred people were arrested. Hundreds of mothers in Warren County literally laid their bodies in front of trucks filled with PCB-contaminated soil to stop the unjust dumping of toxic waste in their community. We knew that laying our bodies in front of those trucks was risky, but we were willing to put our lives on the line for justice.

For six weeks, more than two hundred mothers marched from three to four miles every day, many engaging in civil disobedience, and many were arrested. We prayed, we sang, we met every day at the church. We asked God to bless us and protect us, but we knew we had to continue the struggle. During that six-week period, I was arrested and jailed five times. On one occasion I spent three days in jail with four other mothers including Mrs. Evelyn Lowery, convener of the SCLC women and the wife of Joseph Lowery, who was then president of the Southern Christian Leadership Conference. We spent our time in jail writing a statement on behalf of the children. But many of our children wanted to speak for themselves. They participated in the demonstrations and marches and many were also arrested.

I remember, on the very first day of the demonstrations, I was getting my ten-year-old daughter all ready to go to school—or so I thought. I had made breakfast and laid out her clothes so that she could get dressed and catch the bus for school when she informed me that she was not going to school but was going to the march. I told her that in all probability I would be arrested and that it would really be better if she went on to school. She said, "Well, Mom, I have my aunt's telephone numbers. I am probably going to get arrested too, so if you get arrested I will call my aunt. They will give me one phone call, won't they?"

Now, I was willing to put my life on the line. But when it came right down to it, as a mother, I just didn't know whether I wanted my ten-year-old daughter to put her life on the line. Though it was a difficult decision for me to say "yes" to her, I had to do it. I could not in good conscience be hypocritical. I couldn't let her believe that justice was important enough for me to fight for but that it was not important enough for her to fight for.

So as expected, both of us were arrested that day. Just as I was being taken to jail I saw her being taken to another paddy wagon. Then I saw her being stopped by all these reporters. I saw tears running down her face as she talked to the reporters. I panicked—I tried to get out of the paddy wagon but they wouldn't let me. I could see her talking but I couldn't hear what she was saying. I was by this time crying myself. I had to stay in jail for the rest of the day wondering why she was crying. I thought perhaps she had become frightened.

But, as it turned out, she did get her telephone call from juvenile hall and called my sister to pick her up. And later that day when I got out, I saw her on television. I heard her say to the anchor person that she was not afraid of going to jail. She said, "I'm afraid of what this waste is going to do to my family and to the people." She had actually believed that we were going to keep the trucks from dumping the soil. And when she saw the trucks going in after they had started taking us away she became hurt because she believed that the people were really going to die from this waste and she was devastated. People who saw her on the national news all over the country called; they sent funds and some of them came to participate. The children played a major role in helping to get the attention of the media and other support. I think people could have seen me or some other adult crying and not been so moved to action, but seeing a ten-year-old crying, they came to our aid.

I believe that without the mothers of Warren County there would not have been an environmental justice movement. The environmental justice movement is just emerging and the old environmental movement is being redefined. While I was talking to Patsy Ruth Oliver, I indicated to her that I was featured in the Audubon Society magazine as activist of the month and I also expressed how overwhelmed I was at being featured. She said, "Well if you think that's something, I was featured in *Sierra*." So the environmental justice movement is emerging and we really have mothers to thank for that because out of that struggle in Warren County, North Carolina, came a whole new environmental justice movement.

"We haven't told you why the Commission for Racial Justice got involved in environmental justice," Dr. Benjamin F. Chavis, Jr., told the audience at the 1991 First National People of Color Environmental Leadership Summit held in Washington, D.C. Dr. Chavis, the former Executive Director of the United Church of Christ Commission for Racial Justice and the NAACP [National Association for the Advancement of Colored People], is also the publisher of one of the nation's leading environmental studies, "Toxic Waste and Race in the United States." "God did not whisper," he told the crowd. "God spoke to us through an African-American woman, a woman who led her children and her community to jail. This woman started this leadership summit. If it had not been for her, the Commission for Racial Justice would not have gotten involved. A lot of accolades have gone toward our organization, but I want to give credit where credit is due. It was Dollie Burwell and other African-American sisters like her that caused us to take seriously the life and the consequence of the environmental struggle."[1]

The mothers who struggled for environmental justice in Warren County, North Carolina, struggled in the same tradition and in the same spirit as their foremothers who cooked, fed their children, washed and ironed their clothes, cleaned their house, went to work on their jobs, and still had the commitment and found the time to fight for justice and freedom. As the mothers laid their bodies in front of trucks, as they were hauled off to jail by more than two hundred state troopers, they knew that they were neither politically nor economically powerfully enough to stop the trucks. But they knew that they had to take a stand for their children's sake. They knew that the media would not do them justice in telling the story of the struggle, but it did not matter because they knew in their hearts that they were doing the right thing.

We may not have stopped that one dump, but we stopped others. Mothers in Warren County forced the state of North Carolina to give back to the county 95 of the 100 acres of land that it had purchased. The state did not exercise its option to purchase the 240 additional acres. The governor called a moratorium on landfills in North Carolina. Mothers also lobbied to get legislation passed that prevented any other hazardous or toxic waste facility from being located within a 100-mile radius of the county.[2]

Mothers in Warren County continue to struggle for empowerment, both politically and economically. In 1982, following the demonstrations, Eva M. Clayton, an African-American woman and mother, was elected to the Warren County Board of Commissioners and then elected by her colleagues to chair the board, becoming the first African-American woman in the state to chair a Board of Commissioners. In 1992, this same woman and mother became the first African-American woman to be elected to the U.S. House of Representatives from North Carolina. She was also the first African-American to be elected president of the Democratic freshman class. In 1988 another mother, Patsy Hargrove, became the second African-American woman and mother to be elected to the Warren County Board of Commissioners. That same year, a Native American mother and an African-American mother were also elected to the Warren County Board of Education.

Wanting to be sure that if any other large tracts of land were sold to anybody I would be in a position to find out who they were and why were they buying the land, I ran for Register of Deeds, and as a result of winning the election I became the first African-American woman to manage all of the county's real property and vital records. All of these mothers ran very vigorous and well-managed campaigns and were reelected for second terms in 1992.

There are many mothers of all races in our communities who are struggling for environmental justice and fighting back against the toxic siege. Many of you have heard of Lois Gibbs, the white mother who led the struggle of Love Canal, New York, and is now the Director of the Citizen's Clearinghouse for Hazardous Waste. You may also have heard of Joanna Guthierez, a Hispanic mother, and her four-hundred-member "Mothers of East Los Angeles." This woman gave lectures and circulated petitions to churchgoers after Sunday Mass and organized weekly marches and successfully stopped a toxic waste incinerator that was slated for the mostly poor and Hispanic community of Vernon, California, where she lived.

But you probably have not heard of Janice Dickerson, an African-American mother and organizer working every day with families along an 80-mile strip between New Orleans and Baton Rouge, Louisiana, known as Cancer Alley, to stop the toxic siege and environmental racism. You probably have not heard of Jesse Dearwater, a Native American mother and founder of Native Americans for a Clean Environment, who lost her job as a hairdresser because she dared to spread the word in her community of Iron, Oklahoma, about the town's largest industry that was also the town's largest hazardous waste producing industry, and who organized and struggled daily against toxic aggression and environmental racism.

Within our communities the voices of women really must be acknowledged. Environmental racism deals a double blow to women because women are the ones who usually wind up caring for the sick babies and families. Mothers are playing very important roles in social and political change in the country. As this new movement for environmental justice emerges, it will be even more important that the role of mothers be lifted up and their voices heard.

NOTES

1. Editor's note: Other environmental leaders credit the Warren County demonstrations with pressuring the EPA to issue the 1992 landmark report, *Environmental Equity: Reducing Risk for All Communities*, which correlated race and income level with hazardous waste dump sites nationwide. Says Robert Bullard, former University of California Riverside sociologist and editor of *Confronting Environmental Racism*, "This study was only initiated after massive civil disobedience protests in predominantly African-American Warren County." See Bullard, ed., *Confronting Environmental Racism: Voices from the Grassroots* (Boston: South End Press, 1993).

2. In 1992, the state of North Carolina announced that it was going to transfer contaminated water from the Warren County dump to Emille, Alabama. Burwell led her community in protest, saying that "environmental justice is not taking contamination from one poor black community to another poor black community." The protesters forced the state to set up a commission, chaired by Burwell, to find a suitable technology to detoxify the Warren County landfill. They are still searching for answers.

"The River Has Been Crossed"

Wangari Maathai and the Mothers of the Green Belt Movement

An Interview with Wangari Maathai

Conducted and edited by Alexis Jetter

The wind swept me. That seems to be my way of life. I stand somewhere and the wind sweeps me. But wherever I'm swept, I try to germinate . . . Something triggered in my mind, a good idea at the right time. "Why don't we plant trees? . . . And now women come and say: "We never buy firewood anymore. We have shade. Even the birds have come back.

A MEMORY OF GREEN

I grew up in Nyeri up on the mountains, very green mountains. My people are farmers, and they always farmed the highlands, and [took shade] under the trees. My earliest memories are of a spring where we had arrowroots. Now arrowroots are plants that grow where there is plenty of water. They are very green and they can grow very tall—certainly taller than a six-year-old! They have very broad leaves, which we used to get water to drink when we went to work in the field. The leaves have oil on top, so when you put clear water on the leaves, the water dances. It looks silvery against the green, and it is very, very, very beautiful. And it was as clean as clean could be.

Now that's my image of the early years when I could say the land was green. And it's not as if my own grandmothers had not worked in the same field. But there was a way they had with the soil; the soil was not disappearing. But when I went back after several years, that stream was gone. It had dried up, and so had many others like it. Several places, where there had been marshy wetlands, had dried up.

And I remembered that, about the time when I was enjoying the little stream, the forests that were very close to us went up in flames. Those flames will live with me; they went up many feet above the forest. The British government was cutting down the indigenous forest so that they could establish plantations. Later I connected the fact that they had cut down the forest and put in northern trees and some southern trees—like the eucalyptus from Australia—and that perhaps these trees had taken too much water from the ground.

Something else I noticed. There used to be these huge fig trees. Fig trees are kind of holy trees to us. Our ancestors would offer sacrifices there. That was their cathedral. That's where they went to communicate with their God. These trees too have been cut down. I now think that there may be a link, that these fig trees were part of a water system that kept this part of the country watered and forested. And rich, so rich. One of the first missionaries that came to this part of the country told the local people that they should be grateful to God because he had given them land with plenty of food, plenty of forest and plenty of water. We knew that.

But now that we look back—and we are hungry, and we have no forests, and we have no water—we remember these words. We can now see what we have done in the name of development. So my childhood experience reinforces my conviction that something has gone wrong, seriously wrong in the name of development.

THE SEEDS OF AN IDEA

The wind that swept me into environmentalism and politics came when I was at the University of Nairobi. A group of women in the university linked up with the National Council of Women of Kenya, and it was there that we met our rural sisters and started to listen to each other's problems. I already knew that rural women had very little income, low social status, and had to go long distances to get fresh water. But I also got the message that, in the rural areas, children were suffering from malnutrition and assorted diseases.

It turned out we had cut trees and planted cash crops for international markets and that by doing so we had forced the women to change the diet of their families. This community now grows cash crops instead of traditional food. [In addition, to save on firewood, Kenyan mothers were feeding their children processed white bread, refined rice, margarine and sweetened tea.]

That triggered my thinking about so-called development. We appeared to be moving toward affluence. But in fact we were killing our future by having children who were suffering from malnutrition.

Something triggered in my mind, a good idea at the right time. "Why don't we plant trees?" I said to the women at the National Council. "Sounds like a good idea," they said. "Why don't you do it?"

THE GREEN BELT MOVEMENT

There is no doubt that where the program has been successful, the countryside has changed. Women come and say: "We never buy firewood anymore. The lorries that used to come and bring firewood to us are gone. We have shade. Even the birds have come back. Soil erosion has been curtailed."

Thousands of women have been in the forefront of environmental conservation through the Green Belt Movement. In areas where women have received the message, they have transformed themselves into barefoot foresters and have provided themselves with firewood, building materials, and fruits. They have transformed the countryside. They have protected and restored biological diversity and brought back the beauty of the land. Even the birds and other forms of life have been brought back by the women working on the land day and night to heal it and make it more fertile.

It's almost like a revolution when you go to areas where the whole community has been changed. Recently I was taking some guests from Norway for a tour, and we had not told the women we were coming. We met some men along the road and we started asking them, "Have you heard of the Green Belt Movement?" Yes, he had. "And do you know who is doing it?" Yes, proudly he said, "It is the women. The women have done wonderful work." And we said, "Have you heard of the leader of the Green Belt Movement?" And he said, "Yes I've heard of Wangari. I don't know her. But she has helped the women here. They have done a wonderful job. Yes, we are very happy about the leadership of women." He didn't even know he was talking to me!

It is the women who work on the land. I would not have thought of going to organize men. First of all, I don't think they would have listened to me anyway. But interestingly, once we started planting trees with the women, the men became involved. They didn't see this as a women's job. They saw this as a way of improving their lot. Because they own the land, so they saw it as a long-term economic investment. It was good to see the men working, anyway! [She laughs] In the field at least. And then we tried to go to the children, to schools.

One of the best things about this movement is that it's a development project. It's an environmental project. It's an empowering project. It's an income-generating project. It affects everybody in the community, and everybody in the community participates. And I think this is where its power is. And if we can manage to sustain it, it could easily become a custom, a culture. The women have the techniques. They don't have to wait for anyone. We're putting the foresters out of a job, which I think is good. They can go and do something else.

In the end I think it's been a very positive program for the women because they have shown—without shouting—that they can provide good leadership, that they can change the community positively, that they don't have to engage in a fight with the men, that they are just doing what needs to be done. They gain a lot of self-confidence, especially when they gain these techniques. To discover that there is no magic to reforestation. That a person who cannot read or write can plant trees that grow with the same dignity as those planted by persons who have a diploma.

And also, I think it makes them feel very good because they link up with the women who are educated. I think there has been a tendency, certainly in our part of the world, to set up the educated women as a different breed from their sisters in the rural areas. And there was an effort to try to say that women like us, who are educated, have nothing to offer to the rural sisters. I think that myth now has been killed. I see them trusting and believing that indeed we can work as one.

A PERCEIVED THREAT TO POWER

But when you have a constituency that runs into thousands of women, who have the support of their men who see this as a good project, and therefore identify this as good leadership—that provides a threat to politicians who are used to just declaring themselves leaders without providing any leadership. And so they tried to discredit me.

They said that I was the wrong person to lead, that I am a bad example because I am too educated, that I have Western values—values like equality between women and men—that in many ways I am a white woman in a black skin. I knew that it was a game they were playing to discourage women from participating. They would say, "Don't follow her. She's the wrong kind of a person. And you know, she doesn't even have a husband!" So they ridiculed me and took any opportunity to chastise me in public.

For a very long time I became the whipping girl. Anybody who wanted to whip women could use me. And every time I made a move that was progressive, whether I was attacking or presenting an idea, or if I was being honored or recognized for something, they always reminded women and men, "Whatever she does, don't forget that this woman was divorced by her husband because she's not a good woman. She's not a good example. She doesn't have morals. She just isn't right. She's not a good African woman."

Because when I challenge the government over national issues, the whole movement identifies with the challenge. And they feel that they too are participating in whatever I'm doing. This is a bit threatening. I can understand. That is what power is all about. Women are looking for power. And that's power.

A BLUEPRINT FOR CHANGE

When we started the Green Belt Movement, we were confronting the fuel-wood crisis for the rural woman. And we saw that, by planting trees, she could solve that. That's been solved; that's easy. It makes me wonder why [this technique] is not more applied, because the fuel-wood crisis can be solved very easily. We were thinking about preventing soil erosion, and that too can be done quite easily. And we were trying to provide food, because, you know, Africa is considered a hungry continent.

There are very many reasons why Africa is hungry. One of course is political. Another is that the land is allowed to degenerate so much that it does not produce any more food. Then there is also the cash crop. We were dealing with a community that had traditionally fed itself, and was [once] very healthy. Almost too healthy to the amazement of the first missionaries that came! They lived on the mountains so they didn't even suffer from malaria. But this community now grows cash crops instead of traditional food. We saw that the children were suffering from malnutrition and diseases associated with malnutrition because they changed their diet.

So the original idea was to address basic needs of a community. But as we approached these needs, we recognized that there were political reasons for their problems. Now, if you find that there is a political reason, do you abandon it? Do you ignore it? Or do you address it? My tendency is to address it.

The women we are dealing with grow cash crops; they are growing coffee. They should be paid for their coffee. They work so hard on the coffee. But at the end of the month they cannot receive payment, because the government officials have misappropriated the coffee money. They have used it for something else—maybe for themselves. And there is no reason why the women growing coffee should use herbicides and pesticides. The government must inform them that these chemicals will destroy the soil and their water system. If they don't, they are exploiting the people. Because the people can hardly read the labels on the containers. They need to be trained to protect themselves.

Now degradation of the soil and the water system is an extremely serious health problem. But it is a symptom of development and international trade.

The women need to link their health and the need for money. They may decide: We don't want any money anymore. We are not going to grow coffee. We are going to grow food. We are not going to starve. However, until very recently, you could not uproot coffee once you planted it, because the government would not let you grow any food crops inside the coffee plantation. Now if the government does not pay you, and you are not allowed to grow food crops, what are you supposed to eat?

So these women are being exploited from all angles. It is impossible to go to that community, and just tell them: Let us plant trees. You realize once you get there that there are so many other issues you need to address. But you don't lose track of what you went there to do: You went there to reclaim the environment. But you reclaim it from all these different things—including, therefore, demanding that these people must be free. These people must be informed. These people must be allowed to move. These people must be allowed to exchange. These people must be allowed to assemble! Because in our country, if you assemble nine people, and if you don't have a license, you will be arrested. Now how can you plant trees with groups if they do not have the freedom to assemble?

So this is why, when we talk about the trees, we are constantly addressing other issues. That's why we say the tree-planting campaign, the environmental agenda, is a vehicle for the other agendas that need to be addressed. It is much easier for us to use the environmental agenda as our vehicle. Otherwise, we wouldn't be making any of these other inroads. Once you start making these linkages, you can no longer just do tree planting. When you start working with the environment seriously, the whole arena comes: human rights, women's rights, environmental rights, children's rights—everybody's rights.

[In 1992, Wangari and a group of rural mothers held a hunger strike in a downtown Nairobi park, which drew thousands of supporters.] These were rural women, whose sons had been incarcerated by the dictatorial authorities. They challenged the authority that had charged their sons with treason, which is punishable by death. The mothers argued that, because their sons had been jailed for demanding political changes that had since been granted, they should be released.

When the authorities turned on the women with beatings and tear gas, the women used an old tradition to ward off the attackers: Some of them stripped naked and shocked the oppressors and onlookers alike! Women decided to use their bodies to fight the injustices against their children. [Wangari and several others had to be hospitalized after police teargassed them and beat them unconscious.] It took one year before all the prisoners were released, but they were finally all released alive.

The current political [regime] in my country considers me and others like me a real disgrace to the rest of our sisters. We are publicly abused and ridiculed as women and mothers, and the other women have been advised not to follow in our footsteps. But there are many women who are faithful and who know that they and their mothers had to break barriers, too, and embrace new values and new rules.

My grandmother would have no words for this revolution, but I think that she would be impressed at the way her daughter and granddaughter have embraced the challenges of their times and successfully redefined their original roles and values.

I hope I live long enough for girls in this country not to be afraid to be educated, to be successful. I don't want to be an example to the girls that they cannot aspire to become Ph.D.s, that they cannot aspire to become university professors, because they will be divorced and humiliated. I have three children. They're now all in college. And I know that they suffered along with me.

But now they can look back and almost admire the fact that we persevered together. And many girls in Kenya now are inspired by the fact that the valley has been deep but it also has been crossed. The river has been crossed. [She smiles radiantly] Now I can see girls say, "I want to be like her." And that's good.

Reclaiming Culture and the Land

Motherhood and the Politics of Sustaining Community

An interview with Winona LaDuke

Conducted and edited by Annelise Orleck and Alexis Jetter

I get called a Native American activist, which I think is kind of ludicrous. I mostly consider myself a responsible parent. I think that not letting others say what you are is important. I want my children to think that it's normal to do what I do.

In the Native community, and my community at White Earth, we parent through extended families and clan relations. That's the essence of it. So parenting is not done by you. It's done by everybody, though I'm obviously the most active of the parent people in my kids' lives. My kids spend a lot of time with me, but so do a lot of other children. That practice is an essential piece of our culture.

This came up recently because I had an intern working with me at White Earth who was really conservative. He told me, "I'm really concerned about your son. He's not with you enough." Now, in reality, he's with me plenty. My kids travel with me a lot, although right now they're off hunting with their father. They had a choice and I said, "Fine. Go spend two weeks in the bush with your dad."

What I realized was that this intern was really concerned with the absence of a nuclear family. What he hadn't grasped yet, even though he's entirely immersed in our community, what he has not fathomed, is that we do not largely operate in nuclear families. We operate in extended families. And that's how we parent.

But I do think that it's real important for a politically active parent, as with any other parent, to illustrate to children the values that you're trying to instill in them. And those lessons have to be experiential. You don't tell them how to live. It's how you live your life. That's how children learn. At least that's my experience. And so I try to practice the cultural traditions and values that I want them to absorb.

In our community, our cultural practice is that your daily life is guided by ritual. The significance is in everything that you do: how you cook, what you cook, how you prepare food, how you prepare clothing for your children, how you look, how you walk outside. In our way of living there is ceremony in everything. So for instance, a couple of weeks ago someone gave me a beaver that they had shot. They knew that I like to eat beaver meat. This was a neighbor who is part of our extended system. He and his son brought me the beaver and asked if I wanted it. And I said, "Yeah, that would be great."

And so my children and I butchered the beaver. Now there are certain things you do when you butcher an animal. You talk to it. You put tobacco out. In the case of a beaver, you don't let a dog eat its bones. And when you butcher it, you undress it. That's how you talk to it. You undress it. So what my children learn from that is a whole set of things that they can't learn from just hearing about it. They only learn from experiencing it and seeing it as a common thing, not an unusual thing.

I think that the separation of political and cultural and spiritual is an artificial separation that's articulated by industrial society. But that split doesn't actually exist. Because cultural practices are political practices. And how you live your life is political. We spend our time trying to pretend that it's all separate but it isn't. In our community, we view it differently. For me, whether it's opposing cultural destruction or opposing clear-cutting, it's the same. Opposing clear-cutting is opposing cultural destruction. It would be wrong for me to talk about cultural preservation to my children and not oppose clear-cutting because they won't have forests if I don't oppose clear-cutting. So a lot of my thinking is around that.

I get called a Native American activist, which I think is kind of ludicrous. I mostly consider myself a responsible parent. I think that not letting others say what you are is important. I want my children to think that it's normal to do what I do. My children do have the sense that what I do is not necessarily common. Recently my daughter started asking me if I'm famous. I don't know where she got that. She's six. I don't know how they know what is famous and what isn't. I said, "No." She said, "Then how come everybody knows who you are?" So I don't know if they consider the things I do totally normal. But, at the same time, that's the only way they've ever known me to be. So they don't balk at the things that I do.

They have had to deal with my being arrested. We've had a lot of talks about who the police are and where they are. They don't have a sense of good police. They have experiences of going through Customs and having the person they're with pulled out. And they had some terrible experiences with cops. So they don't have a sense of cops as good guys. There are a lot of people who go in and out of jail in our community. But when I got arrested I explained to them why and they thought it was okay.

At the same time, if the kids were asked, I'm sure they'd say, "I wish mommy stayed home more." As a politically active parent, you need to strike a balance. I have seen children of politically active Native people walk away for a period of time because their parents did not attend to them as a primary part of their lives. It usually was a male parent who, not unlike my father, was not present in their lives. I think they felt that there was a competition and they resented it.

And so I try to not repeat that with my children, which is hard. I travel a lot. I cannot get a foundation to fund my social change work but I can get a college to pay me to come and talk. So I take my children with me whenever I can—but I make sure that they have a lot of fun.

Like my children, I was raised in a context in which being "responsible" for others was normal. I come from a biracial family. My mother is Jewish and my father is Ojibwe. And they're both very political. They did different things. My father, ever since I was little, was active in the Native community. My mother was active in the civil rights movement. I spent a lot of time in the anti-war movement when I was a kid. And my maternal grandmother was active in the International Ladies' Garment Workers' Union.

I was raised with the belief that "bearing witness to wrong" or engaging in more active resistance was the right thing to do. My whole upbringing was based on that. My mother instilled in me a broad sense of social justice that I hear myself repeating to my children. I am thankful in many ways for my upbringing. My mother likes to travel and she took me to Europe and I saw these churches and I was so awed. And I remember my mother's refrain: "You know how they built those churches? They didn't pay union wages. They exploited everyone to build those churches."

But I think the part of my upbringing that has stuck with me the most is that I was raised as an outsider. I think I gave up trying to be cool or an insider by about the fifth grade. There were no Jews or Indian people in our town. My mom used to get letters from the John Birch Society when I was little. And because I was the darkest kid in my school, my primary experience was being socialized as a dark kid. You get centered on your own when you're not based on affirmation by others.

Being different was valued in my home. My mother was an artist so she thought it was important not to conform. She is very earth based in her cultural practice. She writes books on Third World women and art. So she always raised me with a great appreciation for a lot of cultures and very little appreciation for American culture. Consumerism was really frowned on in our house. Because it's part of cultural destruction.

A lot of the struggle we have as parents is created by the deculturalizing of people. The taking away of people's culture is a very American thing to do—to everyone. And then that culture is replaced with a monochrome American culture. That causes a lot of psychological and social problems for people. That's largely why we have the level of consumption we have. Because it's conditioned: To become "American"—whatever that is—you shop and you buy and you wear. That same thing is happening in Native communities. So our challenge as parents in those communities is to make it really cool to be Indian. Powwows are really important for that. So are ceremonies and gatherings. Of course, my kids are into rebellion, too. My son just cut his hair! That's what he did.

For me, fighting deculturalizing takes many forms. When I moved back to White Earth, for instance, I could have, as an individual, secured my own land. But the fact was that 90 percent of White Earth land was held by non-Indians. And everybody was in the same boat that I was. Now, America would teach you that you should take care of yourself. But I have always felt that that's not right.

If I want to live in a community, then I have to make that community the kind of community that I want to live in. And if the structural causes of poverty in my community don't change—insecure land tenure, Bureau of Indian Affairs-controlled institutions, Tribal Councils dominated by BIA values, economic control that is outside of the community—then my kids, my children and I are not in a healthy community.

That's why I have my children in tribal school. I was the principal of that school when I came back. The Tribal Council fired me. Fired me for insubordination. I was proud of that. But I put my children in that school because I wanted them to be in the Indian community. It's a mediocre rural school at best, with some Indian infused in it, but barely enough. Our battle and our work is to transform it into a much better school that teaches a lot more Ojibwe language. Now students have twelve years of Ojibwe instruction, but at the end of their studies they can barely speak.

So we have a problem in our school system. It comes from a couple of sources. There are a lot of white teachers who would have preferred to work in a white school but they couldn't get jobs so they come to us. That's the first problem. My daughter's kindergarten and first grade teachers are excellent teachers. But a lot aren't. The other problem is that the Tribal Council does not make education a priority. So our struggle is to try to transform that school. We run an early childhood language immersion program that my four-year-old son is in. We also run evening programs for adults and children, weekend classes in language immersion, and in-school programming in two of the schools.

But we're battling the school system. We really are. My thinking, my political strategy is to transform the school system so that my children have peers in their own community. I can do that best in my own school system. I am going to have a lot less pull in a non-Indian school system off reservation where Indians are just a small percentage. I could probably try to pull a bunch of strings and get my kids into a private school someplace. But that's not going to address the problem. Then my kids will have an education that someone says is a good education. But they won't be in the community. So that's how I'm thinking.

In our community, both men and women have a pretty significant role. I would say that the berries are more the women's responsibility and the syruping is more the men's responsibility. As for corn, we planted a bunch of hominy corn last year and a man planted it—and you know, when those ears came up they were about 90 percent male! So we're going to do a test this year. He's going to plant one field and I'm going to plant the other. And we'll see what happens. I didn't even know that there were male and female ears until some Six Nations people showed me that. We are just relearning our corn knowledge. Anyway, at White Earth there's a lot of balance between men and women.

But nationally, a lot of the leadership for grassroots native environmental organizations comes from women. Native Action at North Cheyenne reservation is run by a woman, Gail Small. Then you go to Dine Care, and it's run by Laurie Goodman. Indians for Cultural Environmental Protection, which is fighting toxic sewage and sludge from San Diego, is run by Marina Ortega. Grace Thorpe fought her own tribal council when they wanted to accept nuclear waste. Grace and her daughter Dagmar are a really good example of women's leadership around these issues.

There's a lot of people who say that this era, this time, is led by women. There's a lot of recognition of that. I hear it from a lot of elders. Because women didn't have enough vested interest to get corrupted. My view is that when the tribal council system, and a lot of the jobs programs, came into the reservations, women were relegated to second-class status. And consequently they didn't get as much patronage or as much vested interest. They were marginalized and thus ended up knowing more who they were. That's why a lot of that resistance started with women.

On my reservation the Tribal Council is all male. Every once in a while you get a woman in there but it's totally male dominated. And I'll tell you, those guys hate me. On the other hand, they work with me because they know what we're doing is right and because they're afraid that I'm going to bring a lot of press or that I'm going to go and fight them. They want to take credit for what we're doing. And we let them take credit for it. It doesn't matter to me. Everyone knows that they didn't do it. But they hate me because I'm everything that scares them, because I'm educated and because I'm a woman. And because I don't agree with them.

On the other hand, I'm supported by a lot of men in our community. Our community is split between the council and everyone else. Between the haves and the have-nots. We're the have-nots. The chairman of the tribal council makes $250,000 a year. For everyone else at White Earth, the per capita income is $10,000 a year.

There are a lot of Native women out in their communities fighting tribal councils and fighting corporations. Many went to college and went back to work in their communities. And what we're finding is that our relationship with each other is really what sustains us, to know that there are women who are your peers, that there are more women of my vintage. We have a point of reference, a political and human view that are similar.

A bunch of us came together in 1985 to talk about these issues and to encourage women's participation at the local, national and international levels. We wanted to talk about organizing, and strategies that are working and challenges that we're facing—and despair and hope and all those pieces. So we hosted a conference in Yelm, Washington, that drew about 500 women. And out of that came the Indigenous Women's Network.

There was a mandate to try to form something to continue that work. So IWN is about encouraging women's political and other participation, whether it is by honoring them, or raising money to support their work, or just by being a network so that they know there's other women out there. Sometimes we found ourselves battling with women's organizations and environmental groups to say that we have a voice too, whether it's in the Native community or the broader community. That's our thinking.

And so we publish a magazine a couple of times a year. We've raised money for a Venezuelan women's health project, a diaper service in Moose Factory, Ontario. We went to Geneva to the United Nations conference. And in 1993 we did a tour with the Indigo Girls that raised $58,000 for native women's projects.

On our White Earth Reservation, Ojibwe women have joined together in a marketing collective, seeking a fair price for crafts and wild rice. On the reservation, 75 percent of the people hunt, 45 percent harvest wild rice, and about the same number make handicrafts. They produce more than they can use, and women are seeking to market the surplus themselves. The collective hopes to leave out generally unscrupulous middlemen or, at the very least, capture the "value added" of their resources themselves.

The ethical code of my own Anishinabeg culture keeps communities and individuals in line with natural law. *Minobimaatisiiwin*, which means both the "good life" and "continuous rebirth," is central to our value system. In *minobimaatisiiwin*, we honor one another, we honor women as the givers of our lives, and we honor our *Chi Anishinabeg*, our old people and ancestors who hold the knowledge. We honor our children as the continuity from generations, and we honor ourselves as a part of creation.

Implicit in *minobimaatisiiwin* is a continuous habitation of place, an intimate understanding of the relationship between humans and the ecosystem and of the need to maintain this balance. That value system has made it possible for many indigenous peoples to maintain their economic, political and religious institutions for generations in a way that would now be termed sustainable.

Throughout North America, Native women, joined with families and the men of their communities, both resist environmentally and culturally destructive projects, and engage in rebuilding efforts. We have a place. And many women are positive that the best security for themselves and their families isn't in the context of the modern industrial world but in a self-defined context of our own cultures and ways of living.

So, bringing the conversation back to parenting and politics—back home, a lot of our life is about simple things. Right now we're in maple syruping season. So my children spend a lot of time in the sugarbush. I try to keep our life-style simple. I'm most comfortable in a fairly rural life-style; that way of life reiterates my values. And, you know, I would probably have a much harder time parenting if I lived somewhere else. Because I think that parenting is about living how you believe.

SUBSISTENCE STRUGGLES

Overview

Mothers and the Politics of Feeding Hungry Children

Annelise Orleck

In the history of poor people's struggles for subsistence in the United States, mothers have always played a central role. From the American Revolution—when crowds of women seized essential goods from merchants whom they believed to be hoarding—to housewives' flour riots during the economic crises of the 1830s, immigrant milk, bread and meat strikes during the early twentieth century, and nationwide housewives' meat boycotts in 1935, 1948 and 1951, women of many different cultural backgrounds have asserted their "right" as mothers to provide affordable, decent-quality food to their families. Mother-activism on behalf of a "just price" for food and housing is a phenomenon that has transcended time and place. But there are few countries where it has occurred as frequently or over such a long period as in the United States. In the pages that follow, we offer four examinations of recent subsistence activism by mothers in the United States.

Mary Childers, a scholar of working-class women's autobiographies and currently the Affirmation Action Officer at Dartmouth College, offers an intimate view into the life of her mother—a white welfare recipient who raised her children in the Bronx during the 1960s. Childers' memoir is moving and jarring precisely because it is a personal portrait of the kind of woman who is rarely allowed human dimension. Usually, women like Sandy Childers are the subjects of impersonal analyses by scholars or journalists concerned with "the plight of the urban poor." In an unflinching reminiscence, Childers describes women who were deeply trapped by "by the contradictory relations between sexuality and motherhood, the cognitive lapses produced by living in a state of economic insecurity and physical fear, and the entombing effect of accepting the identity of 'a welfare mother.'" At the same time she sees good mothers who labored tirelessly and cheerfully for their children as building superintendents, doing plumbing and carpentry, women who "reveled in competencies for which they were not compensated—while, at the same time, policymakers and the people my neighbors called 'know-it-all know-nothings' reviled them for being lazy, ignorant baby machines."

The poor mothers Childers remembers possessed dignity and strength; they were capable of anger on behalf of themselves and their children, expressed in spontaneous outbursts like the march to the Bronx courthouse that she describes here. But they were nevertheless unable to overcome divisions of race, and the strangling effects of personal alienation, to organize any sustained kind of political action. Childers, refreshingly, does not place blame in this essay: instead she tries to understand, and to help us understand, by allowing us to see her mother as fully human and flawed like all mothers, like our own mothers.

The African-American welfare rights activists of West Las Vegas, described in historian Annelise Orleck's essay and in an interview with movement leader Ruby Duncan, shared both the strengths and the deep disillusionment of the women among whom Mary Childers was raised. In stark contrast, however, the women of West Las Vegas were able to create a lasting mothers' movement that dramatically expanded the social welfare system in the state of Nevada and that changed the lives of poor women in their own community. Ironically, the strength of their movement derived in part from their shared experience of racism—first in the Mississippi Delta towns from which most of them had emigrated and then in Las Vegas itself, where they were forced to live in a crowded, geographically isolated ghetto. Raised in a southern culture that nurtured extended kinship networks, the women in West Las Vegas did not need to make so large a leap from caring for their own children to caring for others as did other mother-activists. Belief in collective responsibility suffused their community life and formed a strong foundation for the alternative social welfare system that they built—run by poor mothers for poor women and their children. The powerful vision of community that they articulated enabled the women of West Las Vegas to attract allies across lines of race, class and gender. For people of all kinds saw in this mother-led movement an ethic of caring that promised to solve the worst problems of poor women and children, and that offered a hope of fruitful coalition-building at a time of despair among progressive activists.

Historian Xiaolan Bao, an immigrant from southern China and an activist in the student democracy movement, takes us into the new sweatshops that honeycomb New York's Chinatown. For the working-class Chinese immi-grant mothers about whom Bao writes, the harsh experiences of immigration to and sweated labor in the United States have been simultaneously degrading and empowering. For these women came from a culture where ancient Con-fucian gender-role designations still restricted the role of mothers to bearing and caring for children. A mother could exercise power only by making her sons into her liaisons with the outside world, Bao notes. A sonless woman was seen as incomplete, even failed as a mother. "Motherhood," Bao concludes, "therefore carried a very oppressive meaning for many Chinese women."

Once in the United States, where economic hardship forced women as well as men to work outside the home, Chinese mothers found themselves taking on the traditional roles both of mother-nurturer and father-provider. The in-fluence of mothers within the immigrant family increased dramatically. And, as they achieved greater power within the home, they developed a sense of entitlement and confidence in their struggles to improve the horrendous con-ditions in the shops where they worked. Becoming militant labor union activ-ists, these women smashed not only the sexist and ethnocentric stereotypes held by non-Chinese union leaders, but also the thick walls that traditional Chinese culture placed around mothers to limit and control their behavior.

All of the pieces in this section trace remarkable processes of political education among the most disfranchised and reviled sector of U.S. society, poor mothers. They examine the ways that poor mothers have been able to renegotiate their identities and take control of their lives as they organize to win concessions from "bosses" in the welfare bureaucracy, the garment shops and the unions. In the Bronx, in Las Vegas, and in Chinatown, militant poor mothers won deep respect from their children for taking a stand on behalf of their families. But there were also tensions and conflicts created in the home by these women's radicalization, resistance on the part of insecure husbands or boyfriends that sometimes took violent form—as Bao's statistics on domes-tic violence and suicide in the Chinese immigrant community starkly illus-trate. These pieces illuminate the complex links between poor mothers' rela-tionship to external authorities and to their own children and partners. They also provide an important corrective to the rhetoric of politicians and the cardboard characterizations of writers and scholars who see poor women as a distinct and alien species, somehow not quite so human as the rest of us.

A Spontaneous Welfare Rights Protest by Politically Inactive Mothers

A Daughter's Reflections

Mary M. Childers

Although no one would have hired these women as skilled laborers, and unions would not have certified them, they fixed boilers, plumbing and electrical wiring. They painted vacant apartments and hallways. They reveled in competencies for which they were not compensated—while, at the same time, policymakers and the people my neighbors called "know-it-all know-nothings" reviled them for being lazy, ignorant baby machines.

T he story I want to tell is as much about the process of memory as it is about a particular political protest. The thinking that this recollection stirs in me, a daughter recalling a deceased mother, is as much about how daughters see their mothers as participants in history as it is about a long-ago demonstration that my mother helped organize, for the details cannot be detached from the motivated distortions of filial memory.

I believe it was in the summer of 1963 that my mother shuffled all six of her children then living at home three miles to the 161st Street courthouse in the Bronx. Her two toddlers were crammed in a stroller; the two teenagers sullenly scraped their (probably) newspaper-padded shoes all the way there; and the other two children—one of them eleven-year-old me—skipped and danced with some other welfare kids from our block who were enjoying this sunny day for a protest. The second diaper bag dangling from the back of the stroller had sandwiches made from blocks of army surplus cheddar cheese that people on welfare used to get, at least in New York. (These were the pre-Food-Stamp days when women with shopping carts and kids walked miles to pick up free worm-ridden bags of rice, boxes of cheese, and much-coveted peanut butter.) By the time we got to the courthouse, there must have been one hundred children there eating cheese sandwiches and flicking white bread cheese balls at one another after rolling them in their mouths.

All those welfare mothers and their children had turned out to protest their caseworkers' refusal to let them have telephones. I cannot remember if we descended on the courthouse before or after the day when our mothers signed a petition demanding dental care that covered more than extractions. These are the only injustices I recall my neighbors joining together to protest. I wish I could remember more about why these women, who were usually—for so many good and frightening reasons—politically inert, took action on those two occasions, and, as far as I know, no other.

I wish the mothers I knew had challenged the welfare policies that forced their children to drop out of high school at sixteen and go to work to decrease the number of family members on AFDC; [Aid to Families with Dependent Children] the policies that forced seasonally employed fathers like my Dad, Hillbilly Phil, to abandon their families so that the children could eat regularly; the sex-segregated job training programs on antiquated equipment for jobs that did not exist; and the racist inequities that led to black and Puerto Rican women not getting the additional school clothing allowances that white families like mine got . . . I will stop there. Anyone who knows anything about the welfare system knows I could write an epic about the wrong-headed policies that could and should have been challenged. Anyone who knows anything about the welfare system knows how little time, energy and hope these women had for political actions, or for any action that would change their lives.

These women were ticked off and depressed a lot of the time, about so many things that political action was not usually part of their repertoire. They had a capacity to empathize with others in a way that was potentially political. But their complete distrust of politicians and bureaucracies translated into self-destructive disinterest in the possibility of participating in change. Most importantly, these women were exhausted because, contrary to popular belief, a majority of them worked outside the home in addition to receiving welfare checks. They worked off the books at subminimum wage, for either the men who owned their buildings or the men who owned the neighborhood stores that supplied household goods to all those female-headed families. These women had to work to supplement their welfare checks, which were always insufficient. They had to work off the books because if they reported the income, they would have forfeited much of their welfare allowance—and they simply couldn't support their kids on the minimum wage jobs they could get.

By knocking mothers off welfare if they made wages that approximated the welfare check, the bureaucracy determined several things. One was that these women never had a chance to improve their lives. Another was that adults on welfare communicated to their children that work was a form of cheating and being cheated. Mothers were simultaneously furtive about working and open about how little extra they could provide with their subminimum, under-the-table pay. Yet another outcome of this policy was that small businessmen had a perfectly exploitable pool of surplus female labor. Most of these factors were so much a part of the political economy and sexual politics of welfare mothers' lives that they were not even recognized as political issues.

My mother, Sandy Childers, was the unpaid superintendent of a five-story building. Instead of payment, many landlords let the women who ran their buildings keep the rent money allocated by welfare. (This meant, among other things, that they had less taxable income and so found it easier to declare financial duress to justify not adequately repairing buildings.) These women superintendents helped keep their communities alive in the days before human-scale tenements were wiped out and replaced by huge projects. In those days, all the women could look out the window and see their kids playing—and help socialize one another's children rather than fear them.

Women like my mother who were superintendents were in a unique position. Because they ran individual small buildings, they could keep track of all the goings on. They collected rent. They knew when caseworkers were visiting. Some of them judged character with such confidence that cops came to them for advice about family disputes; some landlords took their word that this or that family would make up back rent and shouldn't be served eviction notices. They mediated between families arguing with one another about noise, money owed, and squabbles among their children. When pregnant, unmarried teenagers were temporarily thrown out of their houses by their mothers, superintendents had the most up-to-date information on who had a bed to spare on a temporary basis before mother and daughter reconciled. Superintendents scrubbed floors and hauled huge aluminum cans crammed with garbage out to the street for pickup and back.

They also developed skills that they shared with one another across lines of ethnicity and race; the five women who exchanged information with my mother about their unofficial trades were black, white, Cuban and Puerto Rican. Although no one would have hired these women as skilled laborers, and unions would not have certified them, they fixed boilers, plumbing and electrical wiring. They painted vacant apartments and hallways. They reveled in competencies for which they were not compensated—while, at the same time, policymakers and the people my neighbors called "know-it-all know-nothings" reviled them for being lazy; ignorant baby machines. I don't remember these women ever translating their pleasure and confidence in their skills into demands that they be given the wages and occupational range of men. They certainly didn't encourage their daughters to train for employment. But I have cherished for many years the memory of hearing our neighbor Magda say about my mother, "Give Sandy a wrench, and she'll fix the world." Given all of this overwork, deprivation and exploitation, you may understand why these women rarely voted, and couldn't counsel their daughters about how to protect their futures with much better advice than "keep your legs together." You may also understand the political potential in finding out what galvanized them into mass action.

For on this particular day, my mother and some of her friends got it together to protest. In my memory, which may be condensing time, it was only the day before the protest that the hallways and streets were buzzing with gossip. Somebody's daughter had been stranded someplace all night and her mother had been worried to death that some creep had jumped her. And yet people knew that this daughter had done the right thing by not calling anyone in the middle of the night—even though it meant that her mother was left with a night of heart palpitations and lurid visions. Everyone knew the code: only in a dire emergency did you contact a neighbor who had a phone to relay a message to your own phoneless family. To take advantage of a neighbor's generosity and risk losing a scarce resource was definitely not allowed. The only solution was to have your own phone.

The next morning, I heard the women talking with more excitement than usual. "We gotta make that bastard let us have phones." That was the issue: most caseworkers did not allow their people to have luxury items. And telephones were labeled luxuries. That meant that your kids couldn't stay in touch, you couldn't call in sick to the job you supposedly did not have, you couldn't make a quick call to the school to ask about a kid's grade or report of a fight or of a teacher yelling or hitting. (Most positively, that also meant that people had to physically be with one another to gossip and get the only non-work exercise most got—by walking, sometimes long distances, to see friends who had moved to other neighborhoods.) But by the summer of 1963, these women wanted to be connected to the world in the same way that most people were in New York City—by telephone. These women weren't asking for bigger checks to cover the cost of a telephone; they simply didn't want to be thrown off welfare for having one. They would find a way to cut corners even more to have phones.

Ironically, though, I think it was the lack of phones that made this particular protest so successful in terms of the number of women who turned out. They organized woman to woman, door to door, saying, "No excuses. I gotta clean my floors and do something about the cockroaches, too, but the bastard is gonna be there and we gotta tell him what's what." "What about your daughter?" "What about your son?" "The weather report is good." "You can borrow so-and-so's carriage since yours is broken."

I haven't the slightest idea who that bastard was (though I am fantasizing that it was the mayor with full awareness that such fantasy can produce the feel of sharp, authentic memory). I remember the word bastard being used a lot because, although my mother and most of her friends could swear like longshoremen—in the company of anyone who wasn't wearing a clerical collar—it was rare for them as a group to let loose in front of each other's children. A lot of us kids were giggling at their language that day.

I think now that the vilification of an individual man—whoever he was— was probably more energizing for these women than any more recognizably political target. Any man could be the lightning rod for frantic rage or flamboyant hope because so many of these women had been plunged into poverty by the surprise departures of men; because the larger culture barely acknowledged the worlds of adult women without men; because men distributed jobs, apartments and love in arbitrary ways; and because men were the mythical creatures who might rescue a woman from poverty and loneliness. Lacking an analysis of a political structure and economy controlled by a select group of men, many of these women saw individual men as the holders of all power. An individual man could embody regrets, resurgent hopes and righteous anger in a way that a political structure or institution could not. And an individual man seemed manageable and approachable, at least at times. Social structures did not.

Some of the women who were drawn to the fight were not on welfare; they scraped by through other means but were also angry at the system. An Italian woman who joined the ranks supported herself and four kids by waitressing and getting money from her succession of married boyfriends. She was the woman in our building who, during the years when owning a television was a violation of welfare policy, had left her door unlocked during the day so people could hide their televisions if the caseworkers were coming. She screamed at her kids if they made fun of people on welfare the same way my mother, a white woman, screamed if she heard any of her kids say the word "nigger." This woman, unlike some of the other hoity-toity women on our block who separated themselves from the poor in the hopes that they could move from being working class to being middle class, loved to encourage women on welfare. "I don't know how you do it," she'd say. It was from her phone that my mother and another woman took turns trying to get through to newspaper offices and televisions stations to get coverage for the demonstration that was shaping up.

I have long assumed, by the way, that this protest was spontaneous, that these mothers acted on a bit of information they had—that the bastard was going to be at the 161st Street courthouse—because one of their own was not able to get a call from her daughter. But maybe the National Welfare Rights Organization (the NWRO) or some other organization was, invisibly to my unfocused eyes, behind this action. I tend to believe, however, that if any organization had been involved, my mother and her friends would not have followed so many false leads trying to figure out how you get in touch with the right office at a newspaper or TV station. Still, it is hard to reconcile the degree of organization and controlled fury I remember with the idea of this action being entirely spontaneous.

The women were loud. The children were happy. And we caused an uproar at the courthouse so malevolently depicted in *Bonfire of the Vanities* as a place surrounded by violent men rather than families still fighting cockroaches. There were reporters, but I wonder if any of them listened seriously to these women who clearly had too little money and too many kids. There were photographers. I remember people days later carefully scrutinizing a newspaper photograph to see if they or anyone they knew was in it. They delighted in the knowledge that journalists had covered the event.

It was not long before caseworkers informed their clients that they could sign up for telephone service. It turned out that there had never been an official city or state policy against telephones; individual caseworkers had been allowed discretion in determining if phones were or were not luxury items. Neither my memory nor research makes it possible for me to know if the protest just described was solely responsible for this change, but I do know that many more protests were needed to bring about more substantial changes. My mother, however, to my knowledge, never participated in another protest by welfare mothers.

By the time I was thirteen my family had a telephone, but it was years before I had anyone to call. We still ran down the street to ring bells or hoot for friends to hang out with. My mother still walked up five flights of stairs to ask her best friend if she wanted to come downstairs for tea. The phone was reserved for emergencies and special occasions. That did not include passing the word about political activity. No calls reminding neighbors that it was time to vote, or that it was time to march on the police station because they beat up on another black kid or because another little girl was raped by that candy store owner. With their kids and jobs and worries, these women still had too much to do to change the circumstances that made their poverty so intractable. Getting those telephones didn't, in the end, make much of a difference. One of my sisters who was dragged through the streets of the Bronx with me that day ended up raising kids on welfare. One of her kids is now raising kids on welfare. I reveal this particular detail about my own family because in this political climate it is important to challenge the TV-inflicted image that almost exclusively associates people of color with a cross-generational pattern of welfare dependence.

Generalizing broadly about the lives of poor women like the women on welfare I have described makes it is easy to transform them into a tableau for the historical imagination. Frozen in time, they represent what many of us yearn for: evidence of virtual collectives of poor women struggling and thriving together. This tableau also pleases because it directly displaces the image so often offered in the media: the characterization of a group called "welfare mothers" as though they all have the same psychology and belong to some separate, lazy, dangerous species.

But I want to offer an analysis that is psychological and individualistic in ways that rarely punctuate discussions of working-class political subjects. Poor women especially appear in historical narrative as an undifferentiated mass, in part because so few have written autobiographical narratives that can compete with the cachet of those white middle-class women whose stories initially shaped so much of what we know as women's history. But if we are to understand more about what makes political action in one's own self-interests more likely, we need to recognize that working-class people are not unindividuated members of "the masses" or "the people" or "the underclass." They too are capable of ambivalence and contradiction and wisdom.

In speaking of my mother, I want particularly to think about why political action on her part was so rare. I have already suggested that the material conditions of my mother's life kept her from more political activism. Those circumstances have significant explanatory power, but there are many other dimensions to the ways in which the culture of motherhood and the culture of poverty can inhibit women in need of political solutions from participating in the culture of politics. I would like to suggest that in my mother's case— which may or may not be representative—severe, strangling inhibitions were produced by the contradictory relations between sexuality and motherhood, the cognitive lapses produced by living in a state of economic insecurity and physical fear, and the entombing effect of accepting the identity of "a welfare mother". To get at those contradictions, I now want to depart from the way I have so far described this woman Sandy, my mother, whom I am trying to remember as having a separate life from my own, one deserving of a narrative very different from that produced by daughters who still imagine that they should have been the centers of their mother's lives.

As an infant, Sandy Childers was abandoned in a train station. By the time she was found, an infection in one eye left her half blind for life. Hustled from foster home to foster home, she was begrudgingly cared for and eagerly used as cleaning and child-care help by other desperate women. Raised in environments in which women were expected to be economically supported by men and psychologically nourished by Catholicism, she was unprepared for life. The training to submit to your husband and not to use birth control and the unavailability of decent work made her extremely vulnerable.

If you looked at some aspects of my mother's adult life through a magnifying glass, you might choose to see a notorious welfare queen: a beer-guzzling, man-chasing, irresponsible breeder of neglected children. She slept late rather than seeing us off to school, so some of my siblings skipped classes from an early age and, to no one's surprise, virtually stopped going altogether by high school. This woman, who should have known better and should have behaved better, blasted the television all night instead of creating conditions in which her horde of kids could study; she spent other people's tax dollars on cigarettes, hair dye and *Modern Romance* magazine rather than fruits and vegetables.

Of course, I fear having my words used to confirm damaging, politically cynical versions of what it means to be a "welfare mother"—a label that goes beyond "she who receives public assistance for herself and her children." The phrase instead conjures up a monstrously dependent and manipulative breeding creature who sends grubby, irresponsible, needy children into the world. She is the perfect misogynist image: the woman parasite who causes social problems. I've had teachers who reflected my own mother back to me as this monster, and all of my adult life I have been washed with fury at politicians and journalists who do the same.

So is it safe to say, yes, my mother did not understand personal responsibility much of the time? She was indeed dependent. It is only safe to make these concessions when it is also safe to say that many people not on welfare are also irresponsible—and that many people on welfare are not. She does deserve the excuse that she had so many fewer escapes from her circumstances than materially comfortable people. More importantly, as we are fed all these contemptuous images of women like my mother, we might choose instead to examine the particularistic, individual histories that made them so vulnerable. We might also honor their triumphs and resistances.

No one would choose to raise seven children on welfare. Life is so hard; the chances for the children were and are so restricted. But how could my mother ever let herself say clearly and remember distinctly that she did not choose this life, that early ideas of romance and motherhood as well as poverty had confused her? In her mind, I think, repudiating her circumstances vigorously would have entailed qualifying her love for her children—an act barred by prevailing ideologies of motherhood. Her preference was for dreaming. Though she verbally and physically abused most of her children as often as she expressed love, she refused to explicitly acknowledge any feeling other than love. Though her heart had been broken many times by men, she intermittently announced her belief that the right man would come along and rescue her and her children.

Like a lot of mothers, she passed her dreams on to her daughters, all six of them, feeding us such lines as, "My daughters have nothing to worry about. None of them are dogs." It rarely occurred to her to encourage a sense of agency in our lives because she had little to spare. She gazed into the faces of her daughters and watched their developing bodies with a sense that the promise she once felt about her own life must be fulfilled in theirs. That promise, however, was restricted to and shaped by the apotheosis of the female face and figure on the screen or the music stage, the popular culture forms that, along with romance magazines, particularly influenced her. Interchangeable with the image of the movie star was the image of a woman securely located in a male-supported nuclear family, the *Good Housekeeping* or *Ladies Home Journal* image. I imagine that these images were equally otherwordly and static in my mother's head. In both images, the faces of the women glowed and their eyes sparkled for some unspecified others controlled simply by a woman's body. Both lives were envisioned as essentially uneventful; they were not lives in which daily struggle and hard choices took place. What they promised my mother was a world completely removed from her daily hand-to-mouth existence.

Such dreaming makes it very hard to say, "I am a lower-class woman." The adjective "lower-class" is not experienced as a positive source of identification; it is a put-down. The ideology of U.S. democracy encourages its castoffs to avoid thinking about how class is permanently assigned to most of us. In my own family, class somehow meant being classy, and one is classy by acting like a lady. It is not ladylike to fight with landlords for heat, eat rice with vegetable oil three days in a row, and pad your shoes with newspaper. But who wants to admit to not being a lady after watching the young Katherine Hepburn and Lauren Bacall? One's identity as a woman could be shaken by realizing that being a lady is not an option, and so my mother chose a certain unreality instead. The image of being a lady was separate in her imagination from her actual behavior as a survivor and a hard worker.

Still, maybe it was because of her dreaming that my mother was a survivor. Her dreams renewed her after many hours of work. She comforted herself by holding on to confused messages about emotional and economic dependence and independence. A woman alone can make do, she told herself, but only a man could make her happy—too bad all men are such bums. You're supposed to spend your life dreaming about what you can't have while putting up with everything else and doing everything you can to survive. Because survival was such a surprise, it was hard for her to get around to thinking about how she might actually thrive. Someone else was supposed to make the truly positive happen. This ideological trajectory moves in a very different direction from the ideologies that lead to political action and self improvement.

Certainly a longing for intimacy prompted my mother to turn eagerly to even the saddest specimens of maleness on occasion. Her loneliness was matched by an economic desperateness that, I think, produced in her mind and in the minds of many women a connection between economic and sexual dependence. Just as, after my father disappeared, she compulsively turned to men for a falsified pleasure, she looked to them for economic support. She never developed any standards for genuine heterosexual companionship or mutual emotional support. She kept anticipating a boon, but all she ever got was an occasional date who paid for a baby-sitter or handed one of us kids a couple of bucks. Whatever she got had to be wheedled out of the men, most of whom did not have very much money themselves. To her they seemed rich if they had steady jobs with predictable paychecks.

The same wheedling, feminized behavior my mother practiced with dates came into play in her dealings with the welfare system. Even though several of the social workers who visited our house were women, I think my mother saw the welfare system in the figure of a male. If a check for children's clothing was smaller than expected or late in coming, she would say things like, "The Man is trying to gyp me. The Man is holding out on me." Personalized and gendered in this way, the welfare system was something she experienced as a permanent relationship she still had the chance of getting the best of. The fact that the first chairwoman of the NWRO, Johnnie Tillmon, also called the welfare system The Man may indicate that my mother was involved in that organization. Whatever the source of the phrase, on some level my mother understood that welfare was a gender issue.

The unreality that made it hard for my mother to make better choices— such as using birth control—was also highly adaptive. How else does one live day in and out with constant worry about money and safety? Sometimes my mother fed us nothing but rice three days in a row while manically insisting repeatedly, "It's better than nothing; it's better than nothing; it's better than nothing." There were periods, that in retrospect seem endless, of living in our basement apartment without lights because it just had not been possible to pay the electric bill. We kept candles going at night and feared fire. In the summer, when the cockroaches really had the run of the place, we went to sleep knowing they would crawl across our faces. My mother worried constantly about what would happen if she couldn't come up with more money, somehow, if only . . .

By the mid-1960s, money was not the only cause of my mother's severe anxiety and survival-oriented escapism. She also had to worry constantly about what was going to happen to her and her children on the increasingly dangerous streets of our part of the Bronx. Stories of rapes, robberies and beatings were part of neighborhood lore. In one year my mother was mugged five times, always by young men clearly trying to support drug habits.

If you have always lived in safety, you probably cannot fathom what it is like to live in fear, as so many families now do. My mother came to fear all alleys and dark spaces. Unexplained sounds in the night startled her awake and made her tense with alertness. This burden of alertness and fear makes one suspicious in many situations where it is inappropriate; it can ultimately affect all judgment. Worrying about money and safety ultimately strangled my mother psychologically in such a way that the possibilities of political action decreased as she got older.

But men and poverty and the ceaseless fear of violence were not the only things that scarred my mother. Many people on welfare are wounded not just by the system, but also by the ways its recipients are depicted by both critics and advocates. When you are on welfare, you know that you are a parasite, living on the taxes of reluctant people who wish you didn't exist. Having made so many bad choices, having done things that her early upbringing in a Catholic orphanage and in foster homes branded her for in her own mind, my mother recognized herself in the disparaging characterizations of welfare mothers; she looked in the mirror and saw an image that deserved public disdain. In that completely understandable act of capitulation, she further diminished the notion of herself as an active citizen. The very public discourse that could address the problems of the welfare system today tells women and children that they are the problem. This identity, when it is shamefully internalized by people already weakened by want and danger, this acceptance of one's own worthlessness, is much more responsible for the cycle of dependency than the causes so often identified by the Right.

Too early in her life, my mother lost her vigor as a worker and became, in truth, quite often the prevailing image of the lazy welfare mother. That laziness was not primarily a failure of character or of morality, nor was it caused by her dependence on the state. Unemployment and the impossibility of ever having enough are the most relevant causes of the resignation and depression that antagonists of welfare define as laziness. The loss of political agency, the loss of a belief that change is possible, results when the public identity imposed on welfare mothers is braided together with the debilitating circumstances of daily life. The solution to the crisis is not workfare; it is political and personal pride and vastly improved material circumstances. The "lazy" behavior of the small percentage of women who exhibit a cross-generational pattern of welfare dependence would be more compassionately viewed as depression in middle-class women who are not tugging on public funds in such visible ways.

Public willingness to fund AFDC is at an all-time low. Welfare mothers have become a symbol of the deterioration of the U.S. work ethic and "family" values—and a scapegoat for people who feel desperate about the prospect of working harder and harder for less return. Women like my mother, one of my sisters, and her daughter are readily available screens for other people who need to project their fears about the future of the United States and the fairness of working conditions with which most of us struggle.

And yet my mother, too, worked hard. She died young after an adulthood sapped by many pregnancies, self-destructive behavior, hard work, and grinding poverty. My mother died at the age of sixty-three, after a long struggle with cervical cancer and the substandard medical treatment poor women receive. As excessive radiation slowly burned out one organ after another before the cancer returned, she barely resembled the woman whose cynicism and grit I want to end this essay by honoring. For her dependencies were matched by resilience and resistance.

So far, I have mentioned what wore Sandy Childers down and how she submitted. But, at the same time, she frequently busted up ideas about women and created an environment in which most of her daughters could take advantage of societal changes that came too late for her. Although on her deathbed her priest tormented her with fears that she would be punished for it, my mother was openly supportive of her lesbian daughter. As a superintendent, she secured apartments for gay and lesbian households—not out of a political commitment but because it was the right thing to do. And though she would not sign petitions to fund abortions for poor women, she quietly supported several of her daughters' choices not to have children when they followed the ways of the neighborhood and got pregnant as teenagers. It is because she communicated so clearly that having children would keep you permanently poor—even as she articulated inanely positive ideologies of romance and motherhood—that only two of her six daughters had children and the rest managed to become economically independent of individual men and the state.

Sandy Childers was too distracted to follow through on much, too anxious to be a member of any political group, but she was a complicated, engaged woman. And I suspect that she would have been pleased to have her story told to flesh out the truth about this scapegoat stick figure: "The welfare mother."

"If It Wasn't for You I'd Have Shoes for My Children"

The Political Education of Las Vegas Welfare Mothers

Annelise Orleck

I said, "Which one you said is keeping us from getting shoes for our children?" And they said, "Senator Lamb" . . . I went up to him and I said: "You're the man that's keeping us from getting shoes for our children! . . ." I just felt good inside that all of this piled up stuff I didn't know was pressing on me was finally coming out. —Ruby Duncan at the Nevada Legislature, 1969

Growth has been a way of life in Las Vegas, Nevada, since it burst from the desert floor and became the nation's gambling capital in the years after World War II. Construction of the eye-catching kind—fast, big and glittering—has characterized the sprawling city. But there is one area that never seems to change much. That neighborhood is known as the Westside. It is almost exclusively poor and African-American, as it has been since it was first settled in the 1940s by migrants from the Mississippi Delta who came seeking work in the city's new hotels and casinos.

Today, the Westside looks much as it did a quarter-century ago. Trash-strewn empty lots abut bleak, cracking public housing developments. Here and there a store or restaurant dots the dusty streets, sporting hand-painted signs on window glass or stucco walls because their owners never clear enough profit to invest in neon or even plastic lettering. Though it sprawls, half-vacant right in the middle of bustling, gaudy, round-the-clock Las Vegas, a strange silence hovers over the Westside. There is too little of everything that makes a community vital—too few businesses, too few buses, too few public buildings, hardly any place for kids to play except the streets. What the neighborhood has lots of is hunger, and drugs sold on street corners, and violence of both the criminal and police-sponsored kinds.

But twenty-five years ago, a movement took root here that held the promise of turning this community around. And it began out of a very simple desire on the part of a group of poor mothers: to see that their children had proper shoes and decent clothing to start school in the fall of 1969. That summer, a group of Westside welfare mothers decided that their daughters and sons deserved better. Led by a former hotel maid and mother of seven named Ruby Duncan, the Westside mothers marched, rallied and mounted class-action suits to try and move the state welfare bureaucracy to provide better food, clothing and medical care for their children. By 1974, they had lost faith in the promises of politicians and professional welfare administrators. "We can do it and do it better," they told themselves.[1]

In that spirit, they created a nonprofit corporation called Operation Life (OL) to provide quality social services for the mothers and children of the Westside. They tore the boards off the windows and doors of an abandoned hotel on a desolate and violent corner of the Westside and declared it their official headquarters. Through 110-degree summer days and freezing desert winter nights they repaired plumbing, rewired, recarpeted, painted and brainstormed.

Their dream was to build an alternative social welfare system administered by poor mothers for other poor mothers and their children. That vision was more successful than they ever imagined that it could be. Over the next fifteen years, this group of uneducated single mothers brought the Westside its first medical clinic, library, and job-training program for women. Using welfare mothers as administrators and staff, OL created a day-care center, after-school program, teen recreation center, and summer-lunch program.

Over time they grew more sophisticated in their understanding of federal and private funding sources. By the late 1970s, the OL women had founded a community development corporation that raised millions of dollars for the construction and rehabilitation of low-income housing, for mortgage assistance and solar energy collectors. OL even built the neighborhood's first low-income senior citizen housing development—which Ruby Duncan's daughter continues to manage to this day. The history of this woman-run social service organization, its creation, its contributions, and its suffocation by local, state and federal officials is a parable of welfare rights and reforms. It is a story of what worked and what didn't in the much-maligned Great Society programs, who reaps the benefits when welfare costs increase, and what happens to communities when relief programs are gutted.[2]

The Westside mothers' movement was born under conditions that should be fairly familiar to 1990s readers. Twenty-five years before Newt Gingrich made headlines by suggesting that babies of poor single mothers be taken away and raised in orphanages, an earlier generation of ambitious politicians was boosting their political careers by blaming welfare recipients for most of the nation's problems. By the end of the 1960s, a heated debate over welfare burned brightly in Congress, daily newspapers and in the courts. Expert pronouncements on the pathology of the woman-headed household and campaign rhetoric warned the middle class of a new internal enemy—the welfare queen—who quickly came to rival the Communist bogey for her hold on the American imagination. The "irresponsible" welfare mother and her "criminal" progeny became icons of American politics.

While President Richard Nixon and governors Ronald Reagan of California and Nelson Rockefeller of New York vied with one another for the position of America's fiercest anti-welfare warrior, an unknown bureaucrat in the sparsely populated state of Nevada abruptly raised the stakes. In December 1970, without warning or hearings, Nevada welfare administrator George Miller cut half of the state's welfare recipients off the rolls. The result was immediate and dramatic. Thousands of mothers and children were left without adequate food or money for rent.

Faced with hunger and homelessness, a group of African-American single mothers from the Westside took to the streets to protest the mass cutoff. The state's precipitous action had tapped a deep well of resentment and frustration among the Las Vegas working poor. A movement was born out of the realization that, no matter how hard they worked, they would never be able to give their children even a whiff of the American Dream. For these women, like so many mothers on welfare, had long been wage workers. They had performed back-breaking labor in low-paying jobs to keep their children fed and clothed. But, due to injury, lack of medical coverage, and limited job opportunities for women and people of color, they found themselves unable to fully support their dependents without help. The women's frustration was intensified by living in the shadow of the Las Vegas Strip, where millions of dollars were literally thrown away every year. By cutting the assistance that their families received, the state forced the women to act on behalf of their hungry children.

What began as a battle to win shoes and food for their children evolved into a twenty-year struggle between poor women and government officials. Before it was over, many of the women had freed themselves from public assistance, and they had permanently changed the administration of welfare programs in the state of Nevada. But they were not hailed as heroes or held up as role models by the politicians and preachers calling for welfare reform. Instead, the combined forces of local, city, state and federal officials worked to crush the programs they had created. The successes and failures of this poor women's movement, the allies they attracted from all races and classes, and the bitter enemies they made among politicians, welfare professionals and community leaders suggest the power of their dream. But they also reveal the overwhelming assault of hostile forces arrayed against single mothers who seek to raise themselves out of poverty.

THE CREATION OF AN UNDERCLASS

As historian Jacqueline Jones has reminded us, poverty has a history and a social context. Communities of poor people do not spontaneously generate. They are created in a nexus of social, political, and economic forces that are sometimes regional, sometimes global and almost always serve the interests of others besides poor women. The emergence of an underclass in Las Vegas can be traced back half a century to the economic upheavals that followed World War II. The city's rapid growth over the next decades in many ways typified that of urban centers throughout the Southwest. For this reason and because Las Vegas has, since 1945, been the final stop for hundreds of thousands of migrants seeking work, the history of poverty there offers insights into the lives of poor families in cities and towns far removed from its neon-lit desert sprawl.[3]

Few, if any, of the women who organized against the state's welfare cuts in the late 1960s and 1970s were born in Las Vegas. Almost all of them had grown up as fieldhands, "cotton choppers" and "bean pickers" in the Delta towns of Tallulah, Louisiana, and Fordyce, Arkansas. Like most African-Americans growing up in the Delta before 1970, their schooling was fitted around their time in the fields, both because white planters demanded it, and because the subsistence level at which sharecroppers lived left them no choice. As a result, many black children never advanced beyond elementary school. And those who did make it to high school, like Ruby Duncan, "could never seem to do better than four or five months a year."[4]

Duncan might have carried on that grueling existence that prematurely aged and ultimately killed both of her parents. But the introduction of mechanized cotton pickers in the years after World War II created massive agricultural layoffs across the South. Excluded from the relief rolls by discriminatory local policies, many of the Delta's black residents began to seek opportunity elsewhere.[5]

It was just at this time that the wild success of Bugsy Siegel's Flamingo Hotel set off a fever of hotel construction that would turn Las Vegas from a small-time Western gambling town into the symbol of post-War prosperity. In little more than a decade, a neon oasis rose from the desert floor, watered by a vast infusion of organized crime money. And all those new casino hotels—the Flamingo, the Desert Inn, the Sands, the Dunes, the Stardust, the Tropicana—

needed porters, maids, laundry workers and kitchen help. Casino owners and union leaders sent agents south to recruit a cheap labor force. Word spread, triggering a migration that virtually emptied whole Delta towns and brought a black community to Las Vegas. Fewer than 200 blacks lived in Las Vegas in 1940; by 1955, there were more than 16,000 on the Westside.[6]

Like many of the women who came to work as maids in the big hotels, Ruby Duncan saw her migration to Las Vegas as the chance to raise her two young sons far from the terrors of the Mississippi Delta. Tallulah, Louisiana—where Duncan and many of the black migrants to Las Vegas came from—was known among its residents as "the lynching capital of the Delta." Duncan's childhood had been punctuated by horrified nights of hiding, as the Ku Klux Klan searched her home, looking to punish her uncle and brothers for the crime of joining the NAACP. Essie Henderson, Duncan's friend and co-organizer in Operation Life, fled a Texas cotton plantation where she watched her mother dragged for a mile from the back of a pickup truck for trying to stop an overseer from beating up her son.[7]

But these women did not leave racism behind when they fled the South, nor did they escape segregation. In Las Vegas, as in many Southern towns, railroad tracks divided white from black. Bars and hotels east of the tracks refused to serve African-American customers. Downtown landlords would not rent, nor would realtors sell, to anyone who wasn't white. And city officials reinforced racial divisions by refusing to renew licenses for downtown black businesses unless they moved to the Westside.[8]

If Las Vegas in the 1950s represented a high-rolling fantasy for white middle-class tourists, for the African-Americans who lived there it was a plantation. The high-visibility, well-paid positions—as croupiers, cashiers, barmaids and waitresses—were strictly off-limits to blacks. When migrants from the Delta applied for jobs, always at the back door if they hoped to be hired, they were put to work behind the scenes.

Still, the lure of hotel maid work was irresistible for women with children to support. To former field workers accustomed to making between fifty cents and two dollars a day, the hotel wages seemed too good to be true. Leola Harris left Tallulah for Las Vegas in 1950 because "the jobs were good here. You could get here one day and start to work the same day . . . The first day, I got a job doing maid work." "I remember my first paycheck after two weeks," says Alversa Beals, who came from Mississippi. "It was $100. I couldn't believe all that money was for me."[9]

Every women inured to heavy physical labor found the work back-breaking. Mary Wesley, who many years later worked on a sanitation truck, found that job a snap compared to what she had to do as a hotel maid. "When I came home at the end of a day on the truck I was so relaxed," she says. "I took a shower, painted the house. When I came home at the end of a day of being a maid I was so tired I just fell across the bed. I couldn't move." In 1964, after five years of working at one of Las Vegas' best hotels, Ruby Duncan had had enough. Announcing that "slavery is over," she protested the inhuman work load. She was immediately fired and forced to find kitchen work at another hotel on the Strip.[10]

Hard as they worked, the women found that they couldn't support themselves and their children on a single job. Wesley and Duncan, like many of the women of West Las Vegas, had lost their husbands to divorce, alcoholism or disease. Many of the women began working both day and night jobs. "I was working day shift as a maid in the Showboat and night shift as a cocktail waitress on the Westside," says Wesley. "And I was paying one check to the baby-sitter and the other for rent. I just couldn't do it." She finally broke down physically. While she was in the hospital, a social worker told her about welfare. Duncan, too, ended up on welfare in the late 1960s after she slipped on a pool of cooking oil and suffered a disabling injury.[11]

In 1967, welfare mothers at the Marble Manor public housing project on the Westside got wind of a new movement, the National Welfare Rights Organization. The NWRO had been founded that year by an African-American chemistry professor named George Wiley and two white social scientists—Francis Fox Piven and Richard Cloward—and it was chaired by a Watts welfare mother named Johnnie Tillmon. Two years later, in 1969, the Marble Manor women formed the Clark County Welfare Rights Organization. And a tough, sardonic woman named Rosie Seals was elected its first president.[12]

Hearing word of the National Welfare Rights Organization lit sparks that fueled a process of political education. Before NWRO existed, they didn't know that they had any rights. Ruby Duncan had to be dragged by a neighbor to her first meeting that spring. "You can't ask people for money," she told her friend. And Mary Wesley recalls being too ashamed to ever complain about the iniquities of the welfare system.

For Wesley, as for many of the Westside women, the first step toward politicization was coming to understand that welfare mothers were citizens, with the same rights and responsibilities as other citizens. "When I first heard George Wiley talk about welfare, that's what made me know not to be ashamed," Wesley recalls. "He said it was taxpayers' money. Now my father had died when I was three. He worked and his money was put into taxes and he never drew anything from it. And all of my friends and relatives who had worked had taxes taken out of their checks, whether they wanted it or not. Then I didn't feel ashamed no more."[13]

The concept of welfare *rights* transformed these women's shame into a sense of entitlement. And the more they learned about state and federal politics, the greater that sense of entitlement became, enabling Duncan, Wesley and the others to channel deep anger over years of abuse and humiliation into political action.

The next step was figuring out what action to take. "I liked what I heard," Ruby Duncan says of her first welfare rights meeting.

We could have shoes for our children if it wasn't for Sen. Lamb being the chairman of the Finance Committee in the legislature. We could have clothing for school if it wasn't for . . . all of those in Ways and Means . . . Then I looked around and I asked 'em, "What is a legislature?" I didn't know what the legislature was. That was in 1969.

Her appetite whetted by this first taste of politics, Duncan hungered for more. When the local League of Women Voters called for mothers to lobby in the state capital at Carson City, she volunteered. Armed with little more than what former Clark County Legal Services Attorney Jack Anderson calls "her fundamental sense of justice," Duncan took on the chairman of the Senate Finance Committee just moments after she arrived in Carson:

I said, "Which one you said is keeping us from getting shoes for our children?" And they said "Senator Lamb" . . . I went up to him and I said: "You're the man that's keeping us from getting shoes for our children. You!" And I just went off on him. He said: "You've got to understand!" And I said: "No, you can't tell me anything that will make me understand that." . . . I just felt good inside that all of this piled up stuff I didn't know was pressing on me was finally coming out.

This was the third step in the political education of Ruby Duncan: recognizing that she had a talent for politics, and that she enjoyed making an impact. It was a heady realization to think that "a welfare mama" could become a political player. The next week, Duncan was elected president of the Clark County Welfare Rights Organization. The men in Carson City would see a great deal more of her over the next decade.[14]

The politicization of Nevada welfare mothers was speeded up and intensified by the sudden state assault on their families. In the summer of 1969 Republican governor and casino-owner Paul Laxalt announced an audit to weed out any welfare recipient who failed to report outside income. Cutting the "undeserving" poor from the rolls would save the state money it needed to take care of the "truly deserving," said state welfare director George Miller. But this explanation was disingenuous. Nevada spent less than 2.5% of its budget on welfare and had the lowest benefits of any state outside of the Deep South. Nevada had intentionally kept welfare grants low to insure a supply of cheap labor for the hotels. As a result, most of Nevada's poor families needed both wages and welfare checks to survive—a fact that was well known to state legislators, many of whom invested heavily in the hotel industry.

Still they argued for welfare cuts, saying that there was always work for the state's poor women if they really wanted it—if not in the casino/hotels, then in the state's other major industry: prostitution. Indeed, one white welfare mother from Reno, Joanna "Cookie" Bustamonte, would later claim she had been told by state welfare workers on three separate occasions to "save the taxpayers' money" by going to work in a brothel.[15]

When Nevada announced late in 1970 that it was waging a war on "cheating" by cutting thousands from its welfare rolls, angry mothers from across the state vowed "to strike Nevada where it hurts." With assistance from the National Welfare Rights Organization (NWRO) they planned a counterattack that they knew the state could not ignore. On March 6, 1971, joined by civil rights leaders, entertainers, film stars and welfare activists from across the United States, Las Vegas welfare mothers and their children streamed onto the glittering stretch of desert highway known as The Strip. Their goal was to shut down gambling and tourism and, in the process, force the state to listen to them.[16]

The idea of targeting the casinos had come from Ruby Duncan. "I got to dreamin'," she says, about what would happen if "welfare mamas" could disrupt the gambling casinos. "This is the main vein of Nevada," Duncan told NWRO leaders. "This is *the* pocketbook." If it is shut down even for an hour, she said confidently, the state will feel the sting.[17]

The point of marching was not only to inflict economic pain on Las Vegas but also to point out how ill-suited Nevada, whose revenues depended on legal gambling and prostitution, was for its self-proclaimed role as enforcer of poor women's morality. Duncan believed that she could expose the hypocrisy of Nevada's campaign against "welfare cheaters" by casting the conflict as one between mothers trying to feed their children and a state that based its economy on feeding the human appetite for vice.

On the day of that first Strip march, Rev. Ralph Abernathy, Jane Fonda, Sammy Davis, Jr., and Irish revolutionary Bernadette Devlin ensured press attention as poor Nevada mothers and children marched and chanted their way past one extravagant resort after another. They stopped at the casino that was then the height of conspicuous consumption: Caesar's Palace. Security guards and police watched in puzzlement as the demonstrators marched through the outer courtyard—past the bronze Caesar and fountains shooting colored water—and entered the red velvet and marble casino.

Circling the crap tables, they began to clap and sing: "We are into Caesar's Palace. We Shall Not Be Moved." Guests and dealers alike ran for cover. The mothers were triumphant. "We stopped 'em," says march organizer Ruby Duncan. "Everybody was reaching for the covers and putting away the money . . . The hotel across the street, the Flamingo Hilton, had to close their doors. No hotel had ever closed its doors in Las Vegas."[18]

To make matters worse for the tourist trade, Duncan was quoted in the

New York Times, describing the struggles of families who lived on little more than $1,000 a year in the shadow of the Strip where gamblers spent $600 million annually. Newspapers and TV stations across the country ran photos of crap tables surrounded by children, who carried signs that said "Don't Gamble With Human Lives," and "Nevada Starves Children." Worried about the economic fallout from such images, the Nevada Resort Association loudly urged the Clark County Commission to ban future demonstrations on the Strip. And behind closed doors, a group of Las Vegas' unofficial enforcers, managers of the major Strip hotels, voted on whether to have Duncan killed. According to one account, only fear of riots caused them to decide against it.[19]

The mothers knew that they had hit a nerve. Elated at their first taste of success, the women vowed to disrupt gambling every week until the welfare cuts were restored. Duncan and the Clark County Welfare Rights Organization struck again one week later, at Howard Hughes' Sands Hotel. Nearly twisting the revolving doors off their hinges, the demonstrators fought guards who blocked their entrance to the casino. After briefly threatening to "burn the Sands down," the mothers decided instead to sit down on the Strip itself. Mary Wesley was working as a maid at the Sands when the melee erupted. Warned not to leave her post unless she wanted to lose her job, she turned to her supervisor in disbelief. "Lose my job?" she asked. "As a maid?" She rushed through the doors in time to join the other mothers as they formed a human chain across the strip. It was a heady moment. Wesley proudly asserts: "We slowed up traffic all the way to Los Angeles."[20]

Nearly a hundred were arrested that afternoon, but few seemed fazed. Las Vegas welfare mothers had begun, after lifetimes of subjection, to feel that they might wield some power. They also had no doubt that they were fighting on the side of justice. Ruby Duncan spoke brazenly to the judge who tried her case: "Your honor, I'm not guilty. I'm not guilty for trying to help the poor."[21]

Two weeks later, a federal judge ordered Nevada to reinstate all the families whose welfare benefits had been suspended. But the mothers' movement did not then disappear, as most observers expected it would. Unlike so many spontaneous movements that fade after immediate goals have been reached, the Las Vegas mothers had a long-range vision that was far more threatening than shutting down the Strip for a few hours: political and economic empowerment for poor mothers.

Over the next few years—aided by Legal Services attorneys, the Nevada League of Women Voters, the state Democratic party and a local Franciscan order—the women educated themselves about their rights and entitlements under county, state and federal law. That process enhanced their self-esteem and improved their daily living conditions. But it did more. It enabled them to drag Nevada—kicking and screaming—into the twentieth century, forcing it for the first time to accept federal programs aimed at insuring adequate nutrition and medical care for poor women and their children.

For more than a decade after the National Welfare Rights Organization passed out of existence in 1975, welfare mothers continued to organize politically and economically on the Westside of Las Vegas. Indeed, what begun as a protest march on March 6, 1971, evolved into one of the most enduring movements by U.S. welfare mothers to improve their lives and the lives of their children.

With the help of Legal Services and the League of Women Voters, the women of West Las Vegas created a nonprofit corporation through which they could apply for funds to help revitalize their devastated community. They called their new organization Operation Life and set up shop in an abandoned Westside landmark, the Cove Hotel. In the days before integration, black entertainers who performed on the Strip would spend the night there. Sammy Davis, Jr., and Lena Horne, among others, had frequented the Cove. Now the empty shell stood on a drug- and crime-infested corner, both an eyesore and a menace.[22]

In a flurry of activity, the Westside women convinced a local bank to give rent-free leases for the Cove and adjoining Westside properties by dropping their proposal off at the homes of the bank's board of trustees, "just to let them know we knew where they lived," says Duncan. As soon as they had won their lease, the women created a battery of programs. Soon the Cove housed the Westside's first day-care center, teen recreation program, public swimming pool, and community-run press. An abandoned building across the street was transformed into a restaurant to train community residents in food preparation and restaurant management. Mary Wesley recalls being so excited by it all that she "couldn't sleep at night thinking about what I was going to do next."

Most of this was achieved through lobbying and fund raising. But when gentle suasion did not prevail, the women turned again to direct action. The city, for example, was at first unwilling to open a library on the Westside, despite the women's contention that their children needed a quiet place to study. But when the mothers brought hundreds of children to stage "read-ins" in downtown libraries, the city found the money for a Westside branch.[23]

While they worked to expand state and local social services to their community, they recognized that the federal government possessed far greater resources. Since Nevada officials were unwilling to take advantage of federal poverty programs, Operation Life decided to apply directly to the federal government. The women's first success came in 1973, when they brought in the Early Periodic Screening and Diagnostic Testing program, a Department of Health, Education and Welfare (HEW) program to improve health care for poor children. Initially the women had hoped only to get a contract to do community outreach for the clinic. But the doctors who'd won the lucrative contract to run the clinic soon welched on their promise to grant the women outreach jobs. And to make matters worse, they opened the clinic in mob-affiliated Sunrise hospital, several bus rides away from the Westside.[24]

After one meeting with the physicians, Operation Life women realized that they knew more about the goals and requirements of the program than the doctors. And after visiting the clinic—where doctors were chronically absent and the minimal screening was done by an untrained staff—the women decided to set up their own clinic at the Cove. They found doctors who agreed to donate their time, and labs that would do the testing for a fraction of the cost Sunrise had quoted them. A private foundation, impressed by Ruby Duncan's lobbying the year before, provided funds for renovations. By the end of 1973, Operation Life had opened the first medical facility of any kind on the Westside of Las Vegas.[25]

Between 1974 and 1976, the Operation Life Health Center screened a higher percentage of eligible children than any such clinic in the country. As a result, Nevada soon led the nation in health screening for poor children, treating nearly three times more children, per capita, than the national average. When HEW held up the Operation Life Health Center as the model for other EPSDT programs, the women were validated in their slogan: "We can do it and do it better." For theirs was the only EPSDT program in the country administered by welfare women.

In 1974, the Department of Agriculture awarded Operation Life a contract to operate the first Women and Infant Child nutrition program in the state of Nevada. It was the first and only WIC program in the country to be administered by poor women themselves. They applied for and were granted CETA and VISTA funds to train and pay Westside women to help run the program. Those programs also trained and paid women to staff the Operation Life Day Care Center, in-school tutorial program, a training program for women seeking work, and a summer feeding program for children dependent on free school lunches.[26]

Four years later, the federal Office of Economic Opportunity approved Operation Life's application to become a Community Development Corporation. By 1981 it had brought millions of dollars in federal grant monies and investments into the Westside. Operation Life, which had begun land banking, was now the largest property owner in the community. It had constructed a senior citizen housing project, several units of low-income housing, and would soon begin building a modern, fully equipped community medical center.[27]

And Duncan had become a national figure. She led a delegation of Operation Life women to the 1976 and 1980 Democratic national conventions. Invited with a group of community activists to the White House shortly after

Jimmy Carter's innauguration, Duncan was appointed to the National Advisory Council on Economic Opportunity. She traveled frequently to the nation's capital in those years, to lobby the House and Senate on welfare reform. Her favorite sparring partner was Senate Ways and Means committee chairman Russell Long of Louisiana, who, a decade earlier, had referred to welfare mothers as "brood mares." By the late 1970s, Long would make a practice of catching Duncan's eye at hearings to gauge her response to welfare reform proposals. It seemed as though the Duncan model for empowering poor women in communities might influence the future of welfare policy.[28]

But even at the height of Operation Life's success, financial limitations were denying many Westside women the chance to realize their dreams of economic independence. The CETA and VISTA salaries paid to many of the women were simply not sufficient to get their families completely off welfare. And with the election of Ronald Reagan in 1980, the women of Operation Life were forced to pay a price for continued federal funding. For while the Carter administration had hailed the women as examples to those who sought to break the cycle of welfare dependency, the Reagan and then Bush administrations decided that they were not qualified to run their own programs. Instead, the organization had to hire credentialed professionals. Only Duncan and her right-hand woman, Operation Life manager Aldeen Weams, were permitted to keep their salaries.[29]

"We were dumb enough to bring those programs in," Mary Wesley says bitterly, "but then when they came we were too dumb to run them." Many of the women stayed on as volunteers. But Wesley now calls that a mistake:

If I had to do it again I wouldn't volunteer. I would insist that they train us, give us an education . . . That really hurt me when the government took the programs away . . . I don't think Ruby knew that we wouldn't be able to keep those jobs after the money came in. Because that's what we would always tell ourselves: soon we're going to be off of welfare, as soon as the money comes in . . . That's why we worked so hard, worked our heads off and our hearts off because we wanted to get off welfare.

The Reagan-Bush era reintroduced "the welfare queen" into national political discourse, and soon doors in Washington were no longer open to the likes of Ruby Duncan. Operation Life held on through the Reagan years, largely because Duncan had become effective at raising private money to supplement federal funding. But through it all, Duncan and the other women had to battle an array of powerful forces bent on seeing the women fail. Maya Miller remembers being shocked at the cruelty with which legislators mocked Duncan to her face. Casino owners lambasted Duncan as well, alternately calling her a violent militant and a false Messiah.

And then there was George Miller, the Nevada state welfare administrator who went on to become Ronald Reagan's regional administrator for Health and Human Services. Miller and state prosecutors repeatedly charged Duncan and Operation Life with fraud, forcing the organization to devote vital energy and resources to defending themselves. Prosecutors were so abusive—going so far as to call Duncan "an animal"—that after one cross-examination, Duncan collapsed and had to be carried out of court. One judge accused prosecutors of playing not to the jury but to state higher-ups, and ordered them to tone down their attacks. Duncan and Operation Life were exonerated each time. But the continual attacks took their toll.[30]

By the late 1980s, Duncan's health was deteriorating, her associates were aging, and the essential Aldeen Weams was dying of cancer. In 1989, HHS delivered a staggering blow. The order came down from Washington that Operation Life, which had just constructed a $1.5-million medical building, had to operate their clinic jointly with a more conservative local group seeking federal monies to open a health center. If Operation Life refused it would lose its HHS funding. With Duncan temporarily out of commission due to ill health, the new group took control of the joint management board. When Duncan returned and tried to fight the takeover, HHS awarded the newcomers contracts to run all the programs the women had brought to the Westside.

And with those contracts came the right to move all equipment bought with federal monies out of the Operation Life building to a new clinic down the block. It was a bitter defeat. Operation Life veteran Mary Southern recalls walking through the building after all the medical equipment was gone. The plumbing and lighting fixtures had literally been torn from the walls. "And in the trash," she says angrily, "they left a bottle of champagne. They wanted us to know they enjoyed it."[31]

Renee Diamond believes the closing of the Operation Life clinic was one manifestation of a larger Reagan and Bush policy of "taking funding out of the hands of militant community groups, particularly black organizations, and giving what little federal money there was in the eighties to more conservative groups." But she also sees it as the response of local officials who could not accept even the idea of poor, uneducated black women administering anything—much less multi-million-dollar programs. "This community, more than any I've ever seen, has a vision of people's place," she says. "And Ruby would never give in to that."[32]

The women of Operation Life are proud that many of their children have gone to college, happy that they have grown up healthy and strong because Clark County Welfare Rights won them better food than the state of Nevada wanted them to have. They are pleased that there is a beautiful new library on the Westside, and a clinic where there was none before, even if they don't get to run it. They point to their senior citizen housing complex, Ruby Duncan

Manor, and make it a point to tell visitors that, in what Duncan calls "the frustrations" following the first Rodney King verdict, no one laid a hand on any of the buildings owned by Operation Life. Renee Diamond believes that the Las Vegas welfare mothers' movement has left a legacy, too, in the "Ruby Duncan model" that she and other movement allies practice in their advocacy of poor women and children: stressing the importance of education, economic independence and political empowerment.

The Las Vegas welfare rights movement illustrates a remarkable evolution in political consciousness. In 1969, the women of the Westside didn't know that they had any rights under the law. They didn't know that there were two major political parties in the United States. They did not know what a legislature was. Seven years later they were delegates to the national Democratic Convention. And President Carter was consulting them on welfare reform because the poverty programs they had created in Las Vegas were more effective and efficient than those administered by professionals in other states.

During the 1970s when Ruby Duncan testified before numerous local, state and federal hearings, she pointed to the incredible motivation and dedication displayed by the Operation Life women. Cutting welfare programs, she insisted, does nothing to motivate poor mothers to improve themselves. "It is cruel," she argued before Congress in 1976, "to tell women who have no shoes that they need to pull themselves up by their bootstraps." Poor mothers don't enjoy welfare, she says bluntly. They hate it. The women in her community wanted nothing more than to find decently paying work with medical coverage for their children, and were willing to do most anything to ensure that their children could get the education they needed to break the cycle of poverty and dependence. What they asked from government was not handouts but funding for programs to help them help themselves.

The principle behind Operation Life was simple: no one is more expert on the problems of women and children living in poverty than poor mothers themselves. As mothers, they know best what their children need. As workers, they know which local jobs pay well enough for them to be able to support their families, and they know what training they needed to get those jobs. And as community residents they know what their neighborhoods lack in terms of housing, medical care, senior citizen and youth services. All poor women want, Duncan argued, is a real chance to pull themselves up.

But when poor women do what their critics demand of them, when they struggle to get an education, to organize, to develop programs that enhance services to their communities—as the Las Vegas women and as women's groups across the United States did in the 1970s—they are faced with fierce resistance from the same state workers, ministers and politicians who speak so fervently about welfare mothers' responsibility to become independent. The history of Operation Life offers important lessons to those who seriously hope to reform the system by which this nation provides a minimum standard of living to its poor. One is that there are deeper and more complex causes for the entrenched poverty of so many women and children in this country than eroding family values or the much vaunted "culture of poverty." Another is far simpler: that we can never hope to solve the problems of poverty in this country until we begin to listen to the solutions that poor mothers propose.

One hot afternoon on the Westside recently, Ruby Duncan watched a group of skinny, teenaged girls lope about an empty lot and sighed. "There's so much potential in those young women, I wish I could touch it. We could do so much if we still had the programs." Nobody, least of all the women of the Westside, would argue with the assertion that the current welfare system is broken. What pains and galls the veterans of Operation Life is that they pooled their talents and energies and built a genuinely workable system for delivering social services to poor families in their community, and then had to watch it torn apart piece by piece. Their story, and those of hundreds of other poor women's economic development organizations that were slowly suffocated over the past fifteen years, need to be carefully thought through before the next politician boosts his or her career by blaming the poor for the waste in the welfare system.

NOTES

1. Author's interview with Jack Anderson, September 9, 1992, Oakland, California.

2. Specific footnotes will follow, but the bulk of information on the Las Vegas mothers' movement contained in this paper comes from a series of interviews conducted in September 1992 and December 1994 with Operation Life activists Ruby Duncan, Dorothy Jean Poole, Mary Southern, Emma Stampley, Mary Wesley, Alversa Beales, Leola Harris, Roma Jean Hunt and Ruby Price; former National League of Women Voters welfare director Maya Miller; former VISTA volunteer Marty Makower; former Legal Services attorneys Jack Anderson and Mahlon Brown III; and former state Assemblywoman Renee Diamond. With the exception of Maya Miller and Mary Makower, who were interviewed in Carson City, Nevada, and Jack Anderson, who was interviewed in Oakland, California, all interviews were conducted in Las Vegas, Nevada. There were two major archival sources for this paper: the Operation Life Collection, in the possession of David Phillips, Esq., and the Maya Miller Collection, in the possession of Maya Miller.

3. Jacqueline Jones, *The Dispossessed: America's Underclasses from the Civil War to the Present* (New York: Basic Books, 1992); Eugene Moehring, *Resort City in the Sunbelt: Las Vegas, 1930–1970* (Reno: University of Nevada Press, 1989).

4. Interview with Ruby Duncan, September 7, 1992; Alexis Jetter, "Mississippi Learning," *New York Times Magazine*, February 21, 1993.

5. For the most complete analysis of the African-American migration north and west after World War II, see Jones, *The Dispossessed*; Nicholas Lemann, *The Promised Land: The Great Black Migration and How It Changed America* (New

York: Vintage Books, 1991); Richard Cloward and Frances Fox Piven, *Poor People's Movements: Why They Succeed and How They Fail* (New York: Vintage Books, 1979).

6. Moehring, *Resort City in the Sunbelt* pp. 41–106, 176–184; "The Road to Las Vegas," documentary in the collection of the University of Nevada at Las Vegas archives; interviews with Duncan, Beals, Wesley, Poole, see note 2.

7. Interview with Ruby Duncan and Essie Henderson, December 10, 1994, Las Vegas, Nevada.

8. Ed Reid and Ovid Demaris, *The Green Felt Jungle* (New York: Trident Press, 1963), pp. 161–164; Moehring, *Resort City in the Sunbelt*, pp. 178–179; Duncan interview, September 7, 1992.

9. Interview with Alversa Beals, September 5, 1992; interview with Leola Harris, September 7, 1992.

10. Interview with Mary Wesley, September 7, 1992; *Las Vegas Metropolitan*, February 12, 1988.

11. Wesley interview, see note 2; Duncan interview, 1992.

12. Interview with Rosie Seals, September 5, 1992. For information on the formation and activities of the National Welfare Rights Organization see Guida West, *The National Welfare Rights Movement: The Social Protest of Poor Women* (New York: Praeger, 1981); Susan Handley Hertz, *The Welfare Mothers' Movement: A Decade of Change for Poor Women?* (Washington, D.C.: University Press of America, 1981); Cloward and Piven, *Poor People's Movements*, pp. 264–359.

13. Wesley interview.

14. Duncan interview, 1992; interview with Jack Anderson, September 9, 1992.

15. *Nevada State Journal*, February 23, 28, 1971; *Reno Evening Gazette*, March 9, 11, 1971; *San Francisco Examiner*, March 10, 11, 1971; Teresa Traber, "The Impact of Operation Nevada," unpublished undergraduate history thesis, University of Michigan, 1980; interviews with Maya Miller and Marty Makower, September 2–3, 1992.

16. *Las Vegas Sun*, March 5, 7, 1971; *Las Vegas Review-Journal*, March 7, 14, 1971; *Washington Post*, March 7, 14, 1971; *New York Times* March 7, 21, 1971; TV news footage in "Ruby Duncan: A Moving Spirit," Franciscan Communications Productions, Los Angeles, California, 1974.

17. Duncan interview, 1992.

18. Duncan interview, 1992; *Washington Post*, March 7, 1971.

19. Interview with David Phillips, December 9, 1994; *Washington Post*, March 7, 1971; *Los Angeles Times*, March 19, 1971; *Nevada State Journal*, March 5, 6, 7, 1971; *New York Times*, March 7, 21, 23, April 3, 1971.

20. Wesley interview; *Nevada State Journal*, March 15, 1971. The national newspapers cited earlier covered the event as well.

21. Duncan interview, 1992; *Sacramento Bee*, March 14, 1971.

22. Anderson, Makower, Miller, Duncan, Stampley, Poole interviews. See also Traber, "The Impact of Operation Nevada," pp. 177–180.

23. Proposal Operation Life, "submitted to Ray Christensen, July 12, 1973, in the Operation Life collection. See also *Operation Life Community Press*, November 26, 1973; *Las Vegas Review-Journal Magazine*, January 28, 1973; *Las Vegas Review-Journal*, June 17, 28, July 2, 12, 1973.

24. Interviews with Anderson and with Duncan, 1992. Reid and Demaris describe the somewhat shady origins and financial backers of Sunrise Hospital, pp. 102–106.

25. Anderson interview; *Las Vegas Review-Journal Magazine*, May 16, 1976.

26. Traber, "The Impact of Operation Nevada," p. 181; Duncan and Anderson interviews, 1992; *Las Vegas Review-Journal*, June 30, 1974; Ruby Duncan, "Ruby Says," column in the *Las Vegas Voice*, August 6, 12, 1976; "Women After Remuneration," proposal in the Operation Life papers.

27. *Las Vegas Metropolitan*, February 12, 1988; Duncan interviews, 1992 and 1994; Miller, Anderson interviews.

28. Interview with Renee Diamond, Sept. 5, 1992; Duncan interview, 1992; Miller interview.

29. Duncan, Wesley, Anderson, Makower, Miller interviews.

30. Miller, Makower, Diamond, Duncan interviews.

31. Interview with Mary Southern, September 5, 1992.

32. Interviews with Renee Diamond, September 5, 1992, and December 9, 1994.

"I Got to Dreamin'"

An Interview with Ruby Duncan

Conducted and edited by Annelise Orleck

The story needed to be told, our story as welfare mamas. So therefore I became somebody who was very vocal and angry about society. And all of a sudden, I really began to understand.

My name is Ruby Duncan. I'm the mother of seven—I have five men and two women. I'm the grandmother of fourteen, the great-grandmother of two. I come from the backwoods of Tallulah, Louisiana. Out of the cotton patch, corn patch, and bean patch, whichever one you want to name. My parents died when I was two and a half. My mother, so they say, died from overwork. I had to go to work when I was eight years old, chopping cotton and helping my uncle plow the cotton. Didn't have the chance to put in time in school. I could never seem to do better than four or five months a year.

I was about eighteen when I left Louisiana. There was what you call a migration from the little towns of Louisiana to Las Vegas during the 1950s. Because everyone thought that you could make a good living there. At that time my aunt was working at the new Vegas hotels and they was making something like $9.50 a day. And back in Louisiana we was making like fifty cents a pound for all the cotton that you could pick.

The majority of my family had already came from Tallulah to Las Vegas. And I decided to come out too. It took me about ten years to get used to Las Vegas. At the time when we came out, we was living in an old motel that was run down. And our family all got together and fixed it up a little bit so we could live in it. Whenever the wind would blow the dust blew sand into your food. And we had to haul our water from the next town, Henderson, Nevada. This was 1952, '53, '54, '55.

Finally I got tired one day of just eating sand and not being able to take a real bath. Besides, I knew we had to move because of the factory out there. They came along one day to tell us to make sure our children would not go down into this ditch where they were building, because the water was polluted. So I began looking for a place and I moved into West Las Vegas. West Las Vegas was the only place in town black people could live in those days. It was dusty. There wasn't any paved streets at all. But the West side had its own dignity at that time. All of my children were born there except three.

I worked at a lot of the hotels on the Strip, maybe fourteen, fifteen years. The first job that I got was doing maid work for a comedian, Hank Henry, who performed at the Old Frontier. Then I was at the Flamingo. I got fired from there for refusing to work overtime for no pay. I said: "It's not slavery time any more." After that I couldn't get a maid job. I worked at the Sahara Hotel in the kitchen until I got hurt. I was holding this big pan full of vegetables. I didn't know that someone had spilled a big bucket of oil and grease and I had all this. I was coming up and nobody said "stop" or anything. Before I knew anything I had hit the floor and the wall and everything went everywhere. I had to stop working. And I had a pretty bad time for a while. I was divorced by that time. So I had to go on welfare to take care of my children. We moved in the projects. The organizing started out of my living room at 824 Weaver Drive.

I first got interested in politics through welfare rights. A girlfriend of mine by the name of Olestina Walker that I went to school with in Tallulah, she gave me a call one day when things were hard. She said, "Ruby, we have a welfare mother organizing going on and we would love for you to come." I said, "A welfare mother organizing? What on earth are you talking about?" She said, "Well, you know, we have a right to get clothing and shoes and more money for our children to go to school." I said, "You gotta be crazy. We can't be going down there and asking people for money." So she said, "Just come to the meeting." I said, "No, no, I don't think so." So she came to the house one night and she said, "Ruby, I've come to get you. You're going with me."

And I followed her and I heard all this strange language. We could have shoes for our children if it wasn't for Senator Lamb being the chairman of the finance committee in the legislature. We could have clothing if it wasn't for Senator Young and all of those in the Ways and Means at the legislature. So I looks around I asks 'em, "What is a legislature?" I didn't know what the legislature was. That was in 1969.

So they said, "A legislature is where a body of people get elected and they make laws on all of the programs including welfare. They make laws about the welfare you get. Yes. They're the reason why your children don't get adequate nutrition."

So they said, "We need a couple of ladies to go up with us to Carson City. And we can't find any because all of the mothers have to stay with their babies." And so I was promised if I would go that they would keep my children. And I did. Myself and a couple of more ladies, Essie and Earlene.

Anyway, once we got up there, they said we had to wear these signs and walk around the legislative building. I said, "Which one you said is keeping us from getting shoes for our children?" And they said, "Senator Lamb." So I said, "Well, give me his." So I had one on the back and one on the front. And we're marching around the legislative building and he ran down to the gate and he come after me because I'm the only one with the guts to put on his sign because at that time the Lambs of Nevada were powerful people.

So after that, they wanted someone to come up to the legislature and talk about welfare. You must understand that never in my life had I spoken before seven people. I said, "Me? Speak? Oh no, never." But one of the ladies from the anti-poverty, she said, "Why don't you just tell them about how the Welfare Department is treating you." So I thought, "That's easy to do."

I just began babbling about how they did not give us enough money to take care of our families who were living in the projects; that even living in the projects we did not have enough money to buy our children clothing. Oh, I just went on and on and somewhere along the line I lost what I was saying and I just talked.

Before we left the legislature that evening, we had to meet with the Ways and Means Committee because they were going to tell us the budget of different kinds of programs of the types of business throughout Nevada and how taxes pay for them and all this stuff I'd never heard in my life.

So I'm standing at this desk talking, and at the table was nothing but all white men in silk suits, silk ties, silk socks, bright and beautiful shiny loafers and shoes. And I said, "You don't have the money for welfare? You sitting here in silk suits! When we say we are the mothers and fathers of our children and we do the best we can for our children, we are telling you that you must do better with the welfare program." So Senator Young—it's twenty years ago, but I'll never forget that evening—he goes and starts laughing. And I had tears coming out of my eyes because I was totally sincere. I said, "Did you laugh at me?" He said, "Oh, no." I said, "I will never forget. I will be back. You just inspired me to come back."

The story needed to be told, our story as welfare mamas, whatever needed to be said, had to be said. So therefore I become somebody just very vocal and mad and angry about society. And all of a sudden, I really began to understand.

You see, I hated welfare. I hated it. Because I hated the social workers coming in to my home snooping and looking. It was ugly. So by then other welfare mamas such as Johnnie Tillmon from the National Welfare Rights Organization and other ladies had started talking. I went to a meeting in Washington and I began to hear so much. I heard them say, "to make them listen and pay attention you have to hit them in the pocketbook." And I'm saying to myself, I'm gonna wait and see what they mean by the pocketbook. So they began to march on different stores. They began to march on the banks. And I said to myself, Well, why not the Strip.

So I came back and when the welfare rights people came to town, I took them for a drive down the main strip. And I said, "This is the main vein in Nevada. This is *the* pocketbook!" The Strip sure seemed a good place to begin hitting them in the pocketbook.

So all the national people came in. I think we had something like 150 attorneys in here, even William Kunstler. We had Jane Fonda. We had the young lady from over in Ireland—Bernadette Devlin. We had Dr. Ralph Abernathy. We had all the leaders, international and national leaders that we wanted to work with us and to walk down the Strip.

And we had busloads of welfare mamas. They came from every crack and corner of the United States. From Canada to New York. From New York to Detroit, San Francisco, Seattle, Oregon. They came from Utah. They came from all over this country. From Mississippi, Louisiana, from every which way. We had so many great people who came in. And they were so ready and willing to work.

The march we had on the Strip was the greatest satisfaction of my life. I could look back and see long long strips of people. They were all the way backed downtown. And some guy was walking in front of me. He was about six-foot-eight and he was saying, "Go to work. Go to work." And I wanted to push this man out of my face. But I didn't. There was just so many of us and it was such a great feeling.

It gave me a feeling of self-worth to help others. Because the need was so great. Welfare rights was a great movement for us in Nevada. It taught us so much. But I never forgot where I came from. Welfare rights changed me to be more strong, to learn more about the politics of the county, the city, the state and then the nation. I found out that I could speak out and talk about the needs of the mothers and children and where we came from and why we needed to march.

That's how I learned to get into politics. Once the marches and all that movement was over, Mike O'Callahan, who was the governor at that time, he told a friend of ours, Harriet Trudell: "They need to stop marching and learn how to do politics. They need to get into the Democratic Party. They need to learn how to get out the vote. They need to learn how to work with the politicians."

So Harriet was the person who showed us how. Harriet would take me to every meeting. We were like salt and pepper. I would say, "Oh, I'm so tired." She would say, "Just drink some water or something and come on. You gotta go." We went from place to place. I began to learn. I began to listen. I would drag all the ladies to all the meetings in Las Vegas. I had an old station wagon and I would fill it with the women and say, "Let's ride around and just watch and see." And everywhere we'd see a group of cars we'd go in and sit and listen. Because we wanted to hear. And ask, "What are you doing for us outside of just sitting here talking?" And then we started to working on the preachers. And they become our friends. We started with the city, the county and then the state. We even got elected delegates to the Democratic national convention in 1976 and again in 1980. By then we had our community development corporation.

See, after the demonstrations we decided that welfare rights is really great and that we needed to stay an organization. So we named ourselves Operation Life. And from then, it was time for programs. The first was when Food Research and Action Center called me to say they needed me and two welfare mothers to sue the federal government because Senator Humphrey had carved out a piece of the U.S. Department of Agriculture budget for pregnant women and infants and children. But no one had actually gotten any of the money. That was right up my alley. So I said, "Send the papers on." And we did. And we signed them. And we sued USDA. And we won. We became the first WIC program in the United States of America. I like to say that. Because there was no program any place else then. So by us suing them and winning I began to have a lot of faith that almost everything we wanted we could get. It was a great feeling to know that these women and children were getting milk, cheese, peanut butter. All this high-protein food is very important for the body of a pregnant woman, or for a child, or for an infant.

Then we lobbied the state for Food Stamps because Nevada was the last state in the country without a Food Stamp program. The reason why the lobbying for Food Stamps was so heavy was because at that time the county was issuing us nothing but dog meat in the cans. And peanut butter with no oil in it. Powdered milk. Sugar, caro syrup and a big five-pound block of cheese. That was it. We decided, we need more. So, at that time, the legislators all used to get on a plane on Sunday afternoon to be in Carson for the legislature on Monday. Every Sunday, I got on the plane with them. And they said, Ruby where you going? I said, "I'm going up to Carson with y'all." And they said, "Yeah, what are you gonna do up there?" I said, "I'm coming to lobby y'all for some Food Stamps."

They were shouting in the plane: "Ruby's going up to lobby us, everybody!" And they were all ho ho ho. It was funny. So I got up there and started walking those halls day and night. I was just about the only black person walking around in those halls in those days. And a female at that. And a welfare mama at that. When they got up in the morning, I was there. When they went to the bar at night, I was there. I would drink right along with them. Except I was drinking orange juice. And listening.

So meanwhile all of the ladies back home were meeting and talking to people and calling the politicians and saying please vote for Food Stamps. They had a real kind of chain going on. But it just didn't look like we were going to win. And then, all of a sudden, we decided to call the grocery stores' association and tell them how much money they could make. And that was quite interesting to food businesses. Like we told 'em, "You know how the WIC program brought you in an extra quarter of a million dollars a week in this state. Think about what the Food Stamp program would bring you. So you must come up or write a letter to the Ways and Means." They had a full-time lobbyist in the state and he wrote a letter that would have made you cry. So on the last day of the session, Senator Lamb came out and he said to me, "Congratulations, you won. Ruby, you got the Food Stamp program." And that was really rewarding to me.

In 1972, our legal services attorney Jack Anderson sent us a little piece in the paper saying HEW has discretionary grants for community organizations to get community clinics. And he called me and said, "I'm going to send this down." I said, "Okay." So he sent down the little paragraph about community centers. And at that time in the National Welfare Rights Organization, community health centers was a big thing. And we felt, "Okay, it's our time." So Jack began to help us put it together. And we finally got a grant. It was the first health center anywhere on the West Side of Las Vegas.

And we didn't only do welfare rights programs. We also started talking about economic development. Because working in the community, living in the community, I could see what was needed next. For example, I knew we need a day-care program to teach low-income women how to branch out and develop their own day-care centers. And I understood we had resources to do that through state and city and federal programs. So we would bring in the state people and all the people that was professionals to show us how.

And I went to Washington. I went to talk to Senator Russell Long. And I testified in front of Senator Kennedy's committee about how welfare mothers didn't want to be on welfare. They wanted to work. But they needed child care. And they had to have decent clothes to wear to look for a job. We didn't want them to buy us a whole wardrobe. Just something decent.

I also began finding out what part of the government I should go to, to ask for money for our Operation Life programs. I must have paced those dark dungeon halls of Washington forever. Through Health and Human Services. Throughout the Commerce Building. Throughout the Labor Department. And when I went to sell a proposal I would never give them a chance to talk. I did *all* the talking. Till finally someone would scream, "You got it! You got the money."

So once we started getting money, I would keep having visions of what program we needed next. Like I would say we need to start such and such a program. For example, we started one, for job training, called Women After Remuneration: WAR. Women would be trained to go to work on the Strip. Some could do the valet parking. Some could, in a show, they could do the spotlighting. I always looked at the bigger picture of what they could do. Some of them could do construction. We could do all that. So we got people in good jobs. Good union paying jobs. And once that was over, then I could see another program that we really needed.

We had a group called Low-Income Women that helped women become businesswomen: beauticians, beauty suppliers, all kinds of little bitty kinds of business that they can do. I went from Washington, D.C., to San Francisco to the Rockefellers, to the Ford Foundation, all of them. And I would talk and talk. Our goals were to develop community cooperation and we did. We built homes, affordable homes, for the working poor, senior citizen complexes for poor senior citizens so they wouldn't have to take all of their social security money to pay for rent. We built a large medical and health center. All these ways, we tried to raise up healthy children.

I remember one day, after we was marching, I was so tired because we had got fingerprinted and we all went to jail. Three of my babies went to jail with me and we were all piled in my bed when we got home with my big German shepherd dog. And my son David says to me, "Mama," he says, "we gotta have a lawyer in the family." I said, "A lawyer? Honey, mamma don't have no money for a lawyer. We cannot afford a lawyer." He said, "Yes, mama. I know. But we need a lawyer. You get in too much trouble." So I said, "Okay, why don't you be the lawyer!" And off to school he went. He went to the University of Nevada. He got his law degree at Howard University and now he has one of the largest groups of clients that any lawyer in Nevada has.

My children—my men and women–make me so happy. But I'll be frank with you. I don't feel like I did enough. I feel like I could have done more. But maybe the timing wasn't for me to do more. And here I sit. Maybe I was a little bit ahead of my time. Maybe it would be a little easier for a woman in politics now.

The one thing I wish I could have done is I would have liked to work with a lot of young women, to train them in how they have to politic their way through to being completely independent. And therefore maybe a lot of the young women I know that are in trouble now might not be in the trouble that they're in. I worked with the older mothers that were along with me. I'm too sick now but if I get healthy again, maybe I'll try to train some young women. There are lots of young women want to do something.

Now there's all this talk about welfare reform. Well, welfare reformers should look at a program like the one we started with Operation Life. We were really doing well, running programs and running business projects. That the government came, in 1987, 1988, 1989 and 1990, and took it away from us to run it themselves, that told me the story. They didn't know what to do. But we did. Oh, the dreams that were in our minds! We started them, put them together, ran them, made them work. Then the feds, the state, the county, the city came in and took them away. But it really doesn't make me feel that bad. Other women feel sick about it. But I feel good because it makes me know that they didn't know how to do it. They had to learn from us. What I think about what happened to us and about all this welfare reform talk too, is that they don't want poor people to survive and get strong. They want as many people as they can to get nothing so they can be controlled by whatever measure they want to control us. Who started welfare in the first place? Congress did.

But I'm not giving up yet. I've got a few new ideas I'm working on. We're going to go back to education and reach out to the younger women. There's so much potential there. I think the need is even greater now than it was in our day. All I can say is: Poor, grassroots women must dream their highest dreams, and never stop.

Chinese Mothers in New York City's New Sweatshops

Xiaolan Bao

Even a baseball will bounce when it is beaten, not to mention us human beings.
—Shui Mak Ka, mother, garment worker and major organizer of the 1982 Chinese garment workers' strike in New York's Chinatown

If the meaning of language shifts with changes in context, so too does the meaning of words used to designate social roles. Motherhood, with its multifaceted nature, has different implications for women in different contexts. This essay explores how the meaning of motherhood changed for Chinese families in New York City's Chinatown as a result of the immigrant experience and Chinatown's changing economy between the 1960s and the present. It also explores how changing notions of motherhood contributed to political activism among Chinese women workers in the garment industry, culminating in the largest labor strike in Chinatown's history.

I begin with a brief account of the history of the Chinese women garment workers in New York and trace their growing importance to the economic stability of their families. By assuming a greater economic role, Chinese mothers transformed their self-perceptions, their family relations, and their consciousness as workers. Functioning for the first time both as nurturers and breadwinners, Chinese women began to receive greater respect from their children at home, while in the shops they became trade unionists, shattering the stereotypes of married Chinese women as meek and incapable of protest.

Chinese women are relative newcomers among New York's immigrants. From 1882 to 1943, the Chinese Exclusion Act barred male Chinese laborers from bringing their families to the United States. As a result, New York's

Chinatown was a long-time enclave of forced bachelors. The striking imbalance in the sex ratio of early Chinatown added to its exoticism in the eyes of Americans, who were tainted with the prejudice of the time.[1]

With the repeal of the Chinese Exclusion Act in 1943 and the passage of the War Brides Act in 1945, a small immigration of Chinese women began. The inflow of women transformed the Chinese community in New York City. Family life terminated the "sojourner" status of many male immigrants, and mitigated the problems of gambling, prostitution and opium addiction that had long plagued its bachelor society. But Chinese women did not come to the United States in large numbers until discriminatory quotes were abolished in the immigration reform acts of 1965.[2]

This large influx of Chinese immigrant women coincided with rapid growth of the garment industry in Chinatown. Within a decade, Chinese women garment workers became the largest group of organized Asian working-class women on the East Coast. Since 1974, Chinese women workers have constituted over 80 percent of the membership in International Ladies' Garment Workers' Union (ILGWU) Local 23–25, one of the largest locals in the union.[3] The growth of garment manufacturing in New York's Chinatown not only revitalized the economy of the immigrant community. With mothers entering the industry in large numbers, Chinese immigrant family culture was transformed as well, for over 70 percent of these Chinese union women are married with young children.[4]

But change in women's social status was slow. Before 1982, Chinese women workers in the garment industry were largely ignored by both their community and their unions. They were belittled by some in their community as a group of *ah sim ah mo*, the Taishan dialect for "aunties and grannies." The words have a derogatory connotation of women who know nothing but "the kitchen trivial" and gossip. At the same time they were brushed aside by the ILGWU's largely male leadership as a group of culturally bound slaves who "don't understand the meaning of [a] strike."[5]

But in 1982, much to the astonishment of their Chinese employers, their husbands, their union and the general public, 20,000 Chinese women garment workers took to the streets to press for a new union contract, galvanizing the largest labor strike in the history of New York's Chinatown. How can we understand the dynamics of the Chinese women's political activism? What were the driving forces behind their militancy? My study shows that the changing meaning of motherhood in their families and in the immigrant community played an important role in stimulating activism among women workers.[6]

This has to be understood against the context of a changing economic structure in the Chinese community of New York City. Before the late 1960s, the garment industry was not a major part of the Chinese immigrant economy. The two traditional Chinese businesses in New York city were the hand laundry and restaurant trades, which employed the majority of adult males in the community and were the major sources of income for Chinese immigrant families.[7] Although garment shops appeared in Chinatown as early as 1948, and women formed the majority of garment workers from the outset, the number of shops remained small.[8]

Given Chinese males' better job opportunities, even women who worked outside the home continued to be seen primarily as wives and mothers. This had much to do with the influence of traditional Chinese family culture, in which household chores and child care were solely women's responsibilities. Children's relations with their father tended to be formal and distant. Fathers were expected to be disciplinarians, fitting a culturally constructed image of *yan fu*, Mandarin for "stern father." Mothers, on the other hand, fulfilled the culturally constructed role of *ci mu*, or "loving mother." The public/private sphere was similarly divided up. Married women were addressed by their husbands as *nei zi*, meaning the one who took care of domestic affairs, while wives addressed their husbands as *wai zi*, the one who dealt with the outside world. Men were the only legitimate breadwinners in the family, and they reigned over their families as patriarchs.

What then was the meaning of motherhood in this context? In Confucian culture, childbearing was a woman's most important role. Mencius, a disciple of Confucius, once said that "there are three major impieties in the world, of which the most unforgivable is to be without an heir." Since family lines could only be carried on by sons, it was of paramount importance for a family to have a son. This became the prime mission of a married woman's life. And what gave this role social importance was a mother's role in the early education and training of sons.

As anthropologist Margery Wolf has noted, Chinese women could derive a degree of power from bearing and nurturing sons. However, they also bore dire consequences for not being able to do so. Motherhood thus became a metaphor both for power and the lack of it. Women could form close ties with their sons as a strategy to exert influence over the male-dominated family. This strong tie between mothers and sons, underscored by Confucian values of filial piety, would in many cases lead the son to act as a spokesman for the mother in the public world. But a sonless woman was believed to have no permanent tie with her husband's family and therefore was disposable as a wife. Women's value in the family was determined by their reproductive functions. Motherhood, in this sense, carried a very oppressive meaning for many Chinese women.[9]

Once Chinese immigrants arrived in New York, the oppressive meaning of motherhood was reinforced by the lack of economic opportunities for women. Among women who immigrated before the 1960s, the experience of "Aunt"

Chen of Brooklyn (Aunt is an honorific used to address old women) was not uncommon. In an interview done in 1986, Aunt Chen, who came to the United States to join her husband in the early 1950s, revealed that she had spent so many hours working in the family laundry business and caring for her children that she still didn't know how to get around the city without her husband or children. "I am, indeed, blind with a pair of seeing eyes," she described herself sadly.[10]

But by the late 1960s, as the economic structure of the community changed, and employment opportunities for Chinese immigrant women increased, their isolation eased. The flip side, however, was that jobs for male Chinese immigrants became endangered. The Chinese-owned hand laundry business started to die out, and the restaurant business became the only major source of adult Chinese male employment in the city. Employment in the restaurant business became increasingly competitive and unstable, and Chinese working-class families were badly in need of a second income. It was exactly at this time that the garment industry began to take off in New York's Chinatown. This timely development eased conditions for many hard-pressed Chinese families.

Women began to play an increasingly important role in Chinese working-class families, as the role of fathers faltered. Because of the irregular nature of restaurant work, with its long hours and split shifts, and because restaurant work pay varied so much, Chinese women garment workers suddenly became both the major breadwinner and primary parent in their families. They became both *nei zi*, the guardian of domestic affairs, and *wai zi*, the parent who dealt with the outside world. The role of fathers in these families became confused and uncertain. A new formation began to become common among Chinese working-class families in New York: the mother-centered family.

Did this depatriarchalizing process necessarily lead to improving women's status in the family? The impact was mixed. Like working women in most parts of the world, Chinese women garment workers were forced to shoulder an unprecedentedly heavy burden in their lives. In the shop, they were driven by the piecework system to work like a "headless fly," as one worker put it, "taking no time for lunch or to go to the toilet. Even so, during their work day, they had to think about when they would squeeze in time between work and home to shop for dinner and pick up children from school.

This work did not cease on weekends. In addition to routine weekend housekeeping, these women often took their children to Chinatown to study Chinese language and culture. Laboring day and night in the shop and for their families, they had hardly any time left to explore the horizon of life beyond these two territories. Life was particularly difficult for mothers of young children.

Another factor determining immigrant women's new status in the family was the response of husbands. Men's reaction to women's greater role in family life varied. More cooperative and interdependent relationships could be found among some recent immigrant families whose male family heads had steady work. Weijung Wang and his wife, Tang Wei, came to New York in 1981. A dim sum chef whose work day ends in the mid-afternoon, Mr. Wang picks up his daughter at school, shares housework in the evening, supervises the girl's homework and cooks dinner for the family so that his wife Tang Wei, a garment worker, can take English lessons at night. In an interview, he explained why:

To get a better job in this country we need to learn English. I tried very hard when I first came here, but I just didn't have the brain for that. Tang Wei is much better at language. In addition it is easier for women to move out of Chinatown than men. They can find a job in an American garment shop if they know a little bit of English. But how can I make dim sum in an American restaurant?[11]

However, not every husband of a woman worker shared this attitude. Many of them found it hard to adjust to their new roles both in the family and in the society. Cases of domestic violence were not uncommon among Chinese garment workers. The most extreme case of wife abuse was the case of Dong Lu Chen. Chen came to this country in 1986. His wife, Jian Wan, found work in Chinatown, but Chen had to commute to Maryland for a restaurant job. Limited by the lack of job and language skills, he vented his frustration on his wife in the form of physical violence and excessive sexual demands. Chen claimed that on September 7, 1987, Jian Wan admitted to him that she had been having an affair. That is disputed. What is not disputed is his crime: Chen beat his wife to death with a claw hammer.[12]

The tragedy of Jian Wan Chen symbolized the plight of women in a number of Chinese working-class families in New York City. Although no reliable statistics are available, my interviews with women workers suggest that wife abuse in the Chinese community is not unusual among working-class families. There is also a high rate of female suicide in immigrant families. Though the rate fell during the 1980s, in 1988 it remained twice the national average.[13]

Despite these tragic statistics, the challenge of life in their new land has also had some very positive impacts on the life of Chinese women workers. One of the greatest rewards for their hard labor, according to women I have interviewed, was the increased respect they received from their children. Many sons and daughters, now pursuing successful careers, say that their mothers made critical contributions both to their family economies and to their upbringing.

This heightened esteem of mothers strengthened relations with their children, who became the major source of emotional support for women workers in an otherwise alienating new land. This was particularly true for workers with strained marital relationships. Some women I interviewed described relations with their children as "the only ray of light" in their lives. Their children's increased respect for them dramatically improved women workers' own sense of self. It was exactly this increased self-esteem and confidence that encouraged them to begin fighting the multifarious forms of injustice that they encountered in the workplace.

The life experience of Alice Ip, now a business agent for ILGWU Local 23–25, provides a telling example. Born to a relatively impoverished family in Hong Kong, Ip had aspired to a better life since she was a child. She hastily married a young overseas Chinese from Holland when she was barely eighteen. "We married after having known each other for only six months, even before I finished my high school education," Ip recalls. "I was pregnant two months after the marriage." In 1976, she migrated to the United States.[14]

On her second day in New York, Ip found work in a Chinatown garment shop. Despite the hard work, wage-earning labor infused her life with new hope. With her limited income, she managed to sustain the family even without the support of her husband, who worked on and off, never earning a steady income. Also, says Ip, "he was a gambler and a womanizer."

Alice Ip's fortitude in overcoming the difficulties in her life won her the sympathy and respect of her children. Thus, in turn, gave her the confidence to help her fellow workers, and in October 1976 she joined Local 23–25 of the ILGWU. Though her English was limited, she was more fluent than many Chinese immigrant women. So she read union publications to her fellow workers and helped them to understand their rights as union members. She also made timely reports to the union about the misconduct of employers and pressured the union to enforce its contracts on the shop floor.

"At that time," Ip recalls, "I had a lot of trust in the union. I believed that with the backing of the union, I was powerful. I would think of going to the union even when I had problems with my own family. Once I even dreamed of talking to the president of the ILGWU about all my sufferings in life!"

Despite the enthusiasm that Ip and others expressed for the union, white male union leaders had little faith in their ability to organize. "It is part of the Chinese culture to work long hours," ILGWU president Sol Chaikin said in a television documentary in June 1982, just two months before the women's strike. "These women are able to sit at a sewing machine for eight, nine hours . . . It's hard to make them understand the provision for overtime pay."[15]

Jay Mazur, another ILGWU leader, believed that cultural differences, rather than the language barrier, were the real problem. Echoing Mazar's sentiments, Ben Fee—a Chinese business agent of the local—stated: "China is not an industrial society . . . The immigrants don't understand the meaning of [a] strike. They are hard-working people who grab as much as they can so as to make a dollar more. Any benefits that come their way are considered gravy."[16]

In describing Chinese workers as culturally bound, passive and willing slaves with no understanding of labor militancy, white union leaders seem to have missed an irony. These same traits were once attributed to the last wave of militant garment workers: their own mothers.

Indeed, it wasn't easy being a union activist and a mother. But the conflicts forced women to talk honestly to their children about the political work they considered so essential. Alice Ip, who was hired as an ILGWU organizer in 1982, recalls:

At first there were certainly some conflicts. My children did not want me to work in the union. They hoped that I could spend more time with them. It was very difficult especially when they were young. I tried my best to explain to them the significance of my work, helping them to understand me. My mother-in-law didn't want me to work in the union either, because she thought I would become too good for her son!

Balancing work and childcare was exhausting for the Chinese women workers. After sending her children off to school and kindergarten, Ip would go to work at the garment shop early in the morning and work until 3 P.M. Then she'd pick up her children at school, and with few other options, took them back to work with her, where they would stay until the shop closed at 7 or 8 P.M. Ip recalls: "Since most of the shops had a wide hallway outside, I would lay a mattress in the hallway in the summer and let my children take a nap or play there. In winter, however, I could not do so. Then I would take them home and let the older one take care of the younger ones."

Child care was an overwhelming problem for the Chinese women workers. In 1977, while more than 10,000 slots in day care centers were needed in Chinatown, only 500 were available.[17] Many women were forced to take their children to work. But taking children to the shops was both illegal and dangerous. Not only was the dusty air in the shops harmful to the children's health, but other hazards could literally be fatal.[18] Frightened by terrible conditions in the shops, some workers chose to leave their children home alone, which was equally dangerous. One child fell out of the window at home while her mother was toiling for her future at a Chinatown garment shop on the eve of Mother's Day.

Not surprisingly, then, the women's most sustained struggle prior to the 1982 strike was a battle for union day-care centers. Beginning in 1977, groups of women workers started writing to the union to open a day-care center in an abandoned public school building. In 1981, to convince their union, the women spent their lunch hours carrying the petition up and down the narrow stairs of the small shops in Chinatown to gather signatures from the workers.

After they had amassed 2,500 signatures, they held a formal conference with the union officials. Due to the lack of child care, many of them came to the union office carrying babies on their backs or holding children by the hand, clear evidence of the seriousness of the problem. Surrounded by children, secretary-manager Jay Mazur nonetheless insisted that child care was not a union concern. He turned down the petition. But he was clearly rattled. At one point Mazur got so angry that he banged his fist on a table, startling a sleeping child from his sweet dream in his mother's arms. The baby started wailing.[19]

The women day-care activists refused to give up. They began to organize meetings among workers in the shops. The work was extremely difficult. Most did not have any organizing experience. The majority were mothers of young children and could not attend meetings most days of the week. At the meetings, the sound of children crying was omnipresent. And still the day-care activists persisted. Their efforts finally paid off in 1984 when the ILGWU opened the Garment Industry Day Care Center of Chinatown, paid for by the workers, the manufacturers, the union and the city. Although the center cared for only seventy prekindergarten children of union members, it represented a great achievement. The Chinese women workers had, for the first time, pressured and cajoled established institutions to respond to their needs.[20]

Just as importantly, the women's battle for the center laid the groundwork for the 1982 strike. Although the day-care center didn't open until 1984, the women's long crusade fostered a group of rank-and-file labor activists who constituted an important part of the workers' leadership for the 1982 strike.

In the summer of 1982, a group of Chinese shop owners set out to break the union. Appealing to the women workers' ethnic solidarity, these Chinese employers refused to renew the union contract. "The bosses' friends and relatives are all workers," one contractor said on a radio broadcast. "How could they exploit their own family?"[21]

Trapped in the middle were the workers. They were torn by two very limited options: to ally either with the distant and indifferent union or with the familiar but exploitative employers. However, the women knew very well which side they should stand on. Ip recalls, "When the Chinese bosses showed no signs of backing away from their position, I said to the bosses that no matter whether you care about our position or not, we would make you care! What impressed me most was the response of the workers. They tried all means to help out: organizing phone banks, delivering flyers, talking to each other, and spreading the news among themselves."

Reacting vigorously to every move of the contractors and the union, the women talked in the shops, on the phone, in the streets, on the trains and at home. Indignant at the bosses' outrageous position, many workers wrote articles to the Chinese newspapers, condemning what the bosses were doing, and they asked their English-speaking sons and daughters or fellow workers to call the union for a strike.

On June 24 and July 15, 1982, New York's Chinatown witnessed two historic events. To show their determination to press for agreements on the union's contract, 10,000 to 20,000 women garment workers walked out and staged pro-union rallies in Chinatown's Columbus Park. Never before had so many people, much less women, turned out over a labor issue in Chinatown. Quoting from a Mao Zedong poem as she addressed the crowd on July 15, strike organizer Shui Mak Ka said that the Chinatown contractors' attempt to break the union was just like "a grasshopper trying to stop a car in its tracks." The contractors are daydreaming in broad daylight, she told the assembled women. Again quoting Mao Zedong, Ka exclaimed: The contractors are "acting like a blind bat trying to knock down a tree." Her speech evoked great response from the women workers.[22]

The women led a spectacular march after the rally. A Chinese dragon escorting the union banners danced forward. Following it were the children, playing drums and cymbals, and the women. Their furious outcry shook the old world of the Chinese community. The workers set up picket lines and struck the shops after the march. The Chinese contractors were so frightened by the women's militant action that one contractor after another emerged into the street to sign the interim contract. The strike lasted only half a day before the manufacturers settled.

By 1 P.M. there was only one shop left that had not signed the agreement. Twenty excited women workers, impatient with the thrill of imminent victory, ran up the stairs of the last shop holding out, only to find that the owner had disappeared. "Could we call this our final victory?" Mrs. Ka asked. "Of course, no!" the workers passionately responded. "We must dig the man out of his hole!" On the advice of two old workers, the strikers searched out their boss in his favorite restaurant, enjoying *dim sum*. He could not but consent to sign. By that afternoon, all the shops in Chinatown were once again under union contract.

Over the past decade, the women have continued to organize, always with an eye toward improving life for their children as well. In response to their demands, the union established the Immigration Project to ease citizenship problems for members, and it created a scholarship program for the children of the workers. In 1985, to increase their political influence, the Chinese women labor activists formed a Chinese chapter of the Coalition of Labor Union Women (CLUW) They have taken an active part in combating anti-Asian violence in the city, and have kept morale high among workers by organizing cooking and singing groups. They have also extended their help to Chinese women garment workers in other U.S. cities.

Looking back, Alice Ip sees a reciprocal relationship between union involvement and greater closeness with her children. "The most rewarding thing was my children's increased respect for me," she says. "I gained tremendous condolence from what they have said." The changing meaning of motherhood for Chinese women workers endowed them with increased self-esteem and confidence.

Without understanding this, we cannot fully understand the militancy displayed by Chinese women workers in the 1982 strike, or their deepening sense of power and achievement ever since. "I don't believe that one's life is predestined and unchangeable," says Ip. "I believe in my own effort. I believe that if you don't try hard and help yourself, even the heavens can do nothing to help you."

NOTES

1. In 1910, the gender ratio of the Chinese population in New York State was twenty-five males to one female. Even in 1940, it remained six to one (*U.S. Census of Population 1910–1940*). For the prejudiced accounts of New York City's Chinese early bachelor society, see Stuart Creighton Miller, *The Unwelcome Immigrant: The American Image of the Chinese, 1785–1882* (Berkeley: University of California Press, 1969), chapter 8, passim, particularly pp. 185–86. The best accounts that cover the change in U.S. immigration laws concerning Chinese and other Asian immigration over the past century are Harry H. L. Kitano and Roger Daniels, *Asian Americans: Emerging Minorities* (New Jersey: Prentice Hall, 1995), pp. 12–20, and Sucheng Chan, *Asian Americans: An Interpretive History* (Boston Twayne Publishers, 1991), passim.

2. The number of Chinese women immigrants increased from an average of 2,600 annually between 1960 and 1965 to an average of 13,500 between 1966 and 1979. (Immigration and Naturalization Services, *Annual Reports 1960–1979*).

3. On the Move: A Report Made During the Years from 1971 to 1974 and Plans for the Future," a 1974 special issue of the *Local 23–25 News* and *Justice* 56, no. 15 (August 1974).

4. Min Zhon, *Chinatown: The Socioeconomic Potential of an Urban Enclave* (Philadelphia: Temple University Press, 1992), p. 173.

5. A Chinese business agent of ILGWU local 23–25 quoted in *New York Times*, August 5, 1972, p. 16.

6. Xiaolan Bao, *Holding Up More Than Half the Sky: A History of Women Garment Workers in New York's Chinatown, 1948–1991* (Urbana: University of Illinois Press, forthcoming.)

7. Bernard Wong, *Chinatown: Economic Adaptation and Ethnic Identity of the Chinese* (New York: Holt, Rinehart and Winston, 1982), p. 37.

8. Guo Zhengzhi, *The Vicissitude of a Chinatown: The History of New York's Chinatown* (Hong Kong: Buoyi Press, 1985), pp. 88–89.

9. For a detailed discussion of the mother/son relationship and the mother-centered uterine family in traditional Chinese culture, see Margery Wolf, *Chinese Families in Rural Taiwan* (Stanford: Stanford University Press, 1975), passim, and Kay Ann Johnson, *Women, Family and Peasant Revolution in China* (Chicago: University of Chicago Press, 1983), pp. 10, 18–20.

10. Author's interview with Aunt Chen, April 7, 1986. Brooklyn, New York. Conducted in the Taishan dialect.

11. Author's interview with Tang Wei, March 19, 1989, Brooklyn, New York.

12. Alexis Jetter, "Fear Is Legacy of Wife Killing in Chinatown: Battered Asians Shocked by Husband's Probation," *New York Newsday*, November 26, 1989.

13. *New York Times* February 20, 1988; *China Daily News*, November 17, 1981.

14. This and other information in this paper about Alice Ip is based on the author's interview with her December 12, 1994, New York City.

15. Sol Chaikin, quoted in the PBS documentary, "Trouble on Fashion Avenue," cited in *Women's Wear Daily*, June 17, 1982.

16. *New York Times*, August 5, 1972, p. 16.

17. *Chicago Daily News*, September 21, 1977; *Migration World* 14, no. 1/2: 46–49; and interview with Katie Quan, April 27, 1989.

18. During the winter of 1979, a girl fell to her death as she left her mother's shop, which was in an old building with a broken elevator. *China Daily News*, February 22, 1979.

19. *Central Daily News*, November 16, 1981.

20. *New York Times*, March 30 and April 1, 1988.

21. *Central Daily News*, June 18, 1982.

22. Author's interviews with Shui Mak Ka, March 1, 9, 17, 1989, New York City. For descriptions of the strike, see also author's interviews with Alice Ip and Leung Se Moi, March 23, 1989, New York City, in Bao, *Holding Up More Than Half the Sky*.

MOTHERS' RESISTANCE AGAINST THE STATE

Overview

Mothers and the State

Diana Taylor

This section examines how motherhood has functioned as a political resource, deployed strategically for and against the state. From Israel to the Gaza Strip, from Argentina to Kenya to New York City, mothers have participated in political battles of all kinds. Some mothers, like those who fought in the Aba women's war, used their maternal bodies as weapons against their oppressors. They stripped, challenging the soldiers to "shoot your mothers" (Kaplan). Others, such as the Argentine Mothers of the Plaza de Mayo, made a show of their aged, defenseless bodies. They too stalemated the military dictatorship. How could the armed forces, who were supposedly defending family and Christian values, kill unarmed women? In some of these essays, women struggle for political visibility in a society that has appropriated, and even militarized, motherhood (Sharoni, Hammami, Bardenstein, Taylor). "National" motherhood often pits a woman's duty to her country against her personal obligations to her children. Other mothers recall how their political activism affected their children, who often did not understand that their mothers would seemingly abandon them to pursue some higher good (Partnoy, Paley). Caught between the political and the personal, these women pay a heavy emotional cost. The women represented here link their role as mothers to their role as activists—exploring how their responsibility toward their own children either fueled or complicated their activism. The various essays reflect the painful tensions or contradictions in their competing roles.

Three of the essays in this section focus on the political uses of motherhood in the context of the Israeli-Palestinian conflict. Interestingly, Israeli scholar Simona Sharoni and Palestinian scholar-activist Rema Hammami describe an analogous situation on opposite sides of the political divide. In both societies, women have attempted to empower themselves by using the very role that has traditionally delimited their political participation—motherhood. The institutionalization and militarization of motherhood, accentuated by the seemingly unending conflict, has long been a major obstacle for Israeli and Palestinian women's search for equality. As the war claimed more and more children, women's reproductive function was transformed into a form of state service. "Heroine mothers," Sharoni writes of Israeli women, had ten or more children. Hammami describes how Palestinian mothers have come to embody the national ideal of steadfastness and rootedness to the land, or *sumud*. Yet, in both contexts, active women were simultaneously needed for the war effort and severely attacked by their own governments. Israeli conservatives and Palestinian fundamentalists began to crack down on activist women. Sharoni and Hammami trace various women's and mother's movements dedicated to empowering women as *women*, rather than as *mothers*, as they work for peace. Carol Bardenstein, a scholar who studies both Palestinian and Israeli women's movements, illustrates how Palestinian women have resisted the nationalist appropriation of motherhood within the context of the ongoing political struggle.

The following two pieces focus on Argentina's Dirty War (1976–1983), analyzing the role of mothers, and the military appropriation of motherhood by the ruling junta. The Mothers of the Plaza de Mayo, as the Latin Americanist scholar Diana Taylor documents, took to the main square of Buenos Aires to demand information about their missing children. Their public demonstration of sorrow, outrage and determination became a model for women's resistance movements throughout Latin America. The Mothers worked within a double bind—"good" mothers were supposed to stay home, keep out of politics, and look after their children. But in a situation in which their children were being abducted, tortured and "disappeared," they couldn't be good (i.e., submissive) mothers and fulfill their maternal obligations. Their activism started as a direct response to military provocation, but continued to establish a stable human rights movement. The Mothers' demonstration elucidates how those groups that most belabor the essentialist, natural and immutable qualities associated with mothers are often the very ones that make most effective political use of the icons and roles traditionally assigned to them.

Alicia Partnoy, an Argentine writer and human rights activist, was one of the 30,000 "disappeared" in Argentina's Dirty War. She was one of only 1,500 to "reappear." She explains how she, and a whole generation of committed university students and activists, opposed the dictatorship's anti-democratic political and economic practices. The students published and distributed leaflets protesting the junta's quasi-fascist methods and ideology. In her collection of short stories, *The Little School: Tales of Disappearance and Survival in Argentina*, she describes her experience in an Argentine concentration camp. In the portrait included here, she relates her painful choice to stop breastfeeding her young daughter, knowing that at any moment she might be abducted and killed. The military, she tells us, not only routinely tortured women, it tortured them through their motherhood. Pregnant women were allowed to live until they gave birth. The jailers would then steal their babies and give them to a military family. Many of the mothers were then drugged, taken aboard a plane, and thrown naked and alive into the Rio de la Plata far below.

Short story writer, poet and activist Grace Paley picks up Partnoy's theme of impossible choices in a very different context. In "Six Days: Some Rememberings," she recalls her six-day jail sentence for sitting down in front of a military parade in protest of the Vietnam War. Her body served as an eloquent signal of maternal protest, but it also led to conflict with her family: "I received a note from home," she writes, "telling me that since I'd chosen to spend the first week of July in jail, my son would probably not go to summer camp because I had neglected to raise the money I'd promised. I read this note and burst into tears [. . .] It was true: Thinking about other people's grown boys I had betrayed my little son."

Temma Kaplan, a professor of history and women's studies, describes the Nigerian women involved in the Aba war, who also used their maternal bodies to confront the State. Like the Mothers of the Plaza de Mayo, they used the patriarchal institution of motherhood for their own political aims. They used their bodies to "shame" their men into behaving appropriately, and to protest political measures that they feared would hurt their children. Kaplan explores how Western fears of maternal sexuality worked to opposite effect in Nigeria—empowering the women who used their sexuality to their own ends.

There is, clearly, a political strength that comes from claiming "mother" politics—even in societies that have usurped "motherhood" to control women and their relationship to children. And yet the mother–child relationship puts women in a vulnerable social situation. So why do U.S. politicians, and male power brokers from military dictatorships (such as Argentina's), feel so threatened by it? Why does masculinist ideology try so hard to control procreative capabilities? Why is everyone so nervous about maternal sexuality? How can that nervousness be turned into a vehicle for activism? The women activists represented here refuse to give in to the masculinist ideology that objectifies and controls the maternal body. They work against the diminishment of their social roles as women, mothers and social actors.

Motherhood and the Politics of Women's Resistance

Israeli Women Organizing for Peace

Simona Sharoni

In the past two decades, the discourse of motherhood has become central to women's organizing for peace in Israel. This phenomenon, however, is not unique to the Israeli case; symbols and images associated with motherhood such as those of life giving and care giving have informed the struggles of women peace activists around the world at least since the turn of the century. At the same time, to understand the centrality of the discourse of motherhood within the Israeli women's peace movement, it is essential not only to trace its origin, but also to critically examine the social and political context of women's anti-war resistance in Israel. This article examines the use of motherhood as a primary discourse of struggle during the Israeli invasion of Lebanon (1982–1985) and during the Palestinian uprising, known as the *intifada*, which began in December 1987. The principal argument is that given the limited space for women's political dissent in Israel, the appropriation of symbols and images associated with motherhood by women peace activists is not simply as a natural choice. Rather, it reflects a strategic decision designed to mobilize broad support for peace without appearing threatening and being relegated to the margins of Israeli-Jewish collectivity.

An exploration of the space available for women's organizing for peace in Israel must begin with a critical examination of popular representations of Israeli women. Two popular images have shaped the way women in Israel are viewed. One is the tough, powerful and exceedingly unfeminine Golda Meier, the former Israeli prime minister. The other is the sexy, exotic woman soldier, in military fatigues, with a machine gun slung over her shoulder, ready to fight for her country. These images have fueled a myth about gender equality and women's political participation in Israel that, unfortunately, has helped reinforce the marginalization of women within Israeli society and politics.[1]

The image of the liberated and sexy woman soldier became popular after the 1967 war, nurtured both in Israel and abroad to garnish Israel's victory. On the one hand, the public display of Israeli women soldiers was intended to emphasize that Israel was fighting for its very existence and therefore women had to contribute to the national effort. On the other hand, women's participation in the military was also presented as proof of the modern and democratic character of Israel. This image of the allegedly liberated, modern Israeli woman soldier was then contrasted with images of veiled, powerless Arab women in order to depict the neighboring Arab countries as undemocratic and culturally backward, thus demonstrating Israel's role as an outpost of the West.[2]

The other image associated with Israeli women—that of former prime minister Golda Meir—is also related to the politics of the Arab-Israeli conflict in that it was used mainly abroad to mobilize support for Israel. The powerful woman prime minister came to stand as a symbol for a supposedly progressive society fighting for its survival. Despite her coarse personality and tough rhetoric, the very fact that she was a woman rather than a retired general made Israel appear more vulnerable and thus generated more sympathy abroad. In particular, it helped obscure Israel's militaristic ethos, with its aggressive posturing and tendency toward territorial expansion. Even more damning to the progressive connotations of Meir's leadership for women was that she was no champion of women's rights and was especially unsympathetic to the feminist movement in Israel, which first crystallized during her time in office.

Rather than accurately reflecting women's roles and positions in Israeli society, popular images such as those of Golda Meir and of Israeli women soldiers reflect the role of the Arab-Israeli conflict in generating idealized notions of womanhood. These idealized notions have complicated Israeli feminists' struggles for gender equality. Given this context, it may be easier to understand why and how the discourse of motherhood and the powerful images it inspired became so central to Israeli women's struggles for peace in the Middle East.

FEMINISM AND THE POLITICS OF MOTHERHOOD

There have been different perspectives and strategies of struggles that have marked women's organizing for peace since the turn of the century. Adrienne

Harris and Ynestra King have explored some of the changes and transformations in women's perspectives that occurred over time.[3] They point out that at the beginning of the twentieth century, women's peace organizing involved mainly middle-class women inspired by traditional and idealized visions of womanhood and femininity:

As mothers, as preservers of life, as "angels of consolation," they spoke and acted in the name of peace. It was a brilliant strategy. Consigned to the relative powerlessness of the private sphere, women moved into public political life while maintaining the protective cover of their traditional role. Caretakers and spiritual centers in the domestic sphere, they thought they could take public power only by becoming housekeepers and moral mothers to the nation . . . Protest was conducted in a ladylike manner. Women took pains to present themselves as decorous and respectable. The appeal to peace was often made in the name of the children.[4]

Over the years changes occurred in the demographics of women's participation in anti-war struggles as well as in the strategies of struggle and the major arguments which characterized them. It seems, however, that motherhood remained a powerful symbol of women's resistance. Throughout the years, women's peace initiatives around the world have combined radical feminism with anti-war perspectives and militance with creativity. For example, at Greenham Common and the Women's Pentagon Action, women activists combined civil disobedience with guerrilla street theater to dramatize the threat posed by wars and by expanding nuclear arsenals.[5]

Symbols and images associated with motherhood, life and care played a significant role in the messages put forth by women peace activists. Sara Ruddick, for example, calls attention to "[w]omen who put pillowcases, toys, and other artifacts of 'attachment' against the barbed wire fences of missile bases."[6] For Ruddick, these symbols "are 'words' of a developing language which is spoken by women in public in order to resist violations of care in care's name."[7] In many cases, the use of symbols associated with motherhood, life and care were used in conjunction with the philosophy of nonviolent resistance. Thus, a central underlying assumption of feminist struggles for peace and social justice, especially in Europe and North America, has been that women's struggles for peace ought to be grounded in a commitment both to the value of life preservation in the name of motherhood and to nonviolent philosophies.

But the self-understandings, images and symbols that women around the world have utilized to articulate their positions on war, peace and conflict resolution are not simply reflections of women's identities and gendered consciousness. Rather, they may reflect deliberate political strategies designed to mobilize broad public support for a particular cause. For example, in order to mobilize massive opposition against a war, many women may decide to cover their radical feminist anti-war critiques and instead use the language and symbolism of motherhood and the "rationality of care" to express concern for "our troops." Therefore, the central role of symbols and metaphors associated with motherhood should not be treated as natural but rather problematized.

This is not to deny that there are many women peace activists who honestly believe that mothers are inherently more peaceful than men because of their ability to give life, nurture and care. It is to recognize that there are also women who treat these ideas quite skeptically, but nevertheless find the images of motherhood politically useful in many cases. These women may decide to use the symbols of motherhood and the "rationality of care" subversively to challenge what Carol Cohn termed "the technostrategic language of war," which ignores the human costs and social dimensions of militarization and glorifies war and fighting.[8] Overall, the language, images and symbols that have informed women's struggles for peace are indicative of the state of gender relations and the available space for women to voice dissent in a particular context, at a particular historical moment. To see that, one must look at particular struggles through feminist lenses and situate the emergence of motherhood as a central discourse of women's struggles for peace in historical context.

MOTHERHOOD AND THE HISTORY OF WOMEN'S STRUGGLES IN ISRAEL

The origins of Jewish women's political organizing date back to the turn of the century, which was marked by a gradual immigration of Jews to settle in Palestine. The founding of the Women's Workers' Movement in 1911 represents the first example of Jewish women's political organizing in Palestine. Established within the Labor Zionist movement, it grew out of the disappointment of a small group of women with the limited roles assigned to them in the emerging society. These women had come to Palestine to participate more fully in social life than they had been permitted to do in the middle-class circles of their Jewish communities in Eastern Europe. They did not expect, nor had they prepared themselves, to struggle for equal rights. As Dafna Izraeli stresses, "they thought equality would be an accompanying feature of their move to the new homeland."[9] Many of these expectations had their origins in the nationalist-socialist ideology prevalent in the Zionist movement at the time. The struggle for gender equality during this period involved a conflict between two competing projects: one designed to put women's self-transformation on the agenda of the Labor Zionist movement, and the other to turn the Women's Workers' Movement into a social service organization. The conflict came to a partial resolution in 1930 when the movement became more social service oriented and changed its name to the Organization of

Working Mothers in an attempt to resolve the tensions between women's work outside the home and their roles as wives and mothers.[10]

This transformation gave legitimacy to a gendered division of labor and power. As a result, occupational training took on the task of preparing girls and women for socially accepted feminine roles such as hairdressers, dressmakers, nursemaids and nursery teachers and left political decisions, trade union activities and economic policy in the hands of the male establishment. A number of interrelated factors led to this dramatic transformation in both the vision and the strategies of the Jewish women's movement in Palestine: (1) the exaltation of aggressive masculinity by both men and women; (2) the organization of production according to traditional definitions of gender roles; and (3) the centrality of mothering to women's identity and its conceptualization as a woman's responsibility.[11]

The difficult conditions in Palestine at the time served to increase the importance of qualities considered masculine; physical strength became one of the first criteria for the distribution of social prestige and power within the community. Because physical strength was seen as a key to productivity, and given that the *kvutza* was fighting for recognition of its economic viability, women were defined from the beginning as being less productive than men.[12] In their struggle for gender equality, women emulated the masculine model and sought "to make the functions, qualities and goals of men their own, without demanding a similar change on the part of men, without demanding that they 'feminize.'"[13]

Organization of production according to principles of productivity and profitability helped solidify the development of two spheres of economic activity along distinct gender lines. Consequently, it became impossible for women to win the prestige enjoyed by men as full-time farmers—the true pioneer ideal, a central fixation of Jewish collective identity in Palestine. Within this broader context, which valued masculinity and profitability and directly linked the two, motherhood could only undermine the status of women. Fogiel-Bijaoui describes how "when the first children were born the care of the newborn was immediately entrusted to the mother. And even though demands were made here and there that fathers participate in the care of children, such a solution was never seriously considered . . . It seemed totally dysfunctional and illogical within the realm of agriculture to exchange a man, a 'productive worker,' for a woman, a 'less productive worker.'"[14] The institutionalization of motherhood became a major impediment to women's struggles for equality during the prestate period and helped reinforce a gendered division of labor and power within the Jewish community in Palestine.

With the establishment of the state of Israel in 1948 and with the escalation of the Arab-Israeli conflict, the exaltation of masculinity was reinforced. This time, however, the pretext for privileging masculinity was not profitability like it was during the prestate period, but rather national survival and national identity. The belief that Israel was a nation under siege provided the basis for maintaining national unity in the face of external enemies, and men were assigned the primary role of safeguarding the existence of the state. This shift in the individual and collective identity of Israeli–Jewish men had direct consequences for women's lives and struggles at the time. Natalie Rein summarizes this period as one where "the hopes and aspirations of Israeli women toward equality and egalitarianism faded. The country turned its back on humanism and pursued a policy for nationalism, militarism and Zionism."[15] From 1948 onward, women had no space to assert themselves outside the confines of their role as male supporters or to protest the erosion in their status. In order to be part of the Jewish state they had to constantly support and express gratitude for their male "liberators" and "protectors," thus adopting the gendered division of labor and power.

This was the climate in which a particular ideal of motherhood became institutionalized as the major venue through which Israeli–Jewish women could contribute to the national project. In the early 1950s, Israel's first prime minister, David Ben-Gurion, turned the issue of women's fertility into a national priority, arguing that "increasing the Jewish birthrate is a vital need for the existence of Israel, and [that] a Jewish woman who does not bring at least four children into the world is defrauding the Jewish mission."[16] "If the Jewish birthrate is not increased," Ben-Gurion recounted in his projections at the time, "it is doubtful that the Jewish state will survive."[17] In other words, while Israeli men defended Israel on the battlefield, women were asked to secure Israel's survival on the homefront.

Ben-Gurion took this analogy further by comparing "any Jewish woman who, as far as it depends on her, does not bring into the world at least four healthy children" to "a soldier who evades military service."[18] Based on these convictions, Ben-Gurion initiated a special state fund designed to pass out symbolic money rewards to "heroine mothers"—women who had 10 children or more.[19] The analogy between women's "special" role as reproductive units and the military service of men has defined the Israeli national project, with its gendered assumptions and practices to this day.

With the militarization of motherhood and the additional national glory attached to the production of sons—as future soldiers—and given their limited access to decision-making levels of social and political institutions, women had few options other than the socially accepted roles of wives and mothers. They did not mobilize to protest their collective social and political predicament, nor did they take explicit political positions *as women*, especially not on questions of war, peace and security. This nonmobilization can be attributed both to the absence of an organizational framework and to the broad political and social consensus taken by many as a sign of unity, essential to the survival of the nation.

The most dramatic changes affecting Israeli women's lives and struggles prior to 1977 were related to the escalation of the Arab-Israeli conflict, mostly through warfare and preparations for war. The 1977 elections and their aftermath introduced changes of a different sort, although they were still connected to the politics of war and peace in the region. Among those changes were the victory of the right-wing Likud party in the 1977 elections after 29 years of Labor-led governments in Israel, the founding of an extraparliamentary pressure group called Peace Now, and the signing of the Camp David Accords between Israel and Egypt.

Despite the changes in the political arena and the emergence of a distinct peace movement, the roles of Israeli women remained constrained by the unchallenged assumption that their primary contribution to the nation was via their roles as mothers. In the 1980s, three decades after Ben-Gurion declared motherhood and childbearing a national priority, this theme was once again invoked to fit the political agenda of the time. The newly formed Efrat Committee for the Encouragement of Higher Birth Rates linked the public debate on abortion at the time to the widely disseminated worry among Israelis that Israel's survival depended on its victory over Palestinians in what they saw as a demographic war. Utilizing the rhetoric of religious anti-abortion groups, and the memory of the Holocaust, the Efrat Committee called upon Jewish women to fulfill their national duty by bearing more children to replace the Jewish children killed by the Nazis during the Holocaust. In addition Haim Sadan, then advisor to the minister of health, proposed to force every Jewish woman considering an abortion to watch a slide show that included, along with grotesque slides of dead fetuses in rubbish bins, pictures of dead Jewish children in the Nazi concentration camps.[20] This proposal was narrowly defeated, but its message was clear: abortion was an act of national treason while bearing more children turned Israeli–Jewish mothers into national heroines.

Attempts to promote the virtues of heroine mothers have been prevalent in many national movements because, along with praising women's participation in the national struggle, they reinforce a certain understanding of femininity and womanhood grounded in women's reproductive role and nurturing capabilities. In the Palestinian context, for example, the tendency to depict women as "mothers of the nation," which gained particular importance during the first three years of the *intifada*, embodied both the steadfastness and cultural continuity associated with Palestinian national liberation and the warmth, care and compassion associated with womanhood. As Nahla Abdo points out, "the construction of motherhood equals nationhood within the

Palestinian context emerged as an expression of Palestinian lived reality. Expulsion from the homeland and refugeeism in foreign territories provided the impetus for the mother–nation relationship."[21]

Despite significant differences in context, women in both the Palestinian and Israeli cases were encouraged to participate in nationalist projects but were publicly praised only when they participated as women. In other words, to fulfill their national duty women had to accept primary responsibility for reproduction and cultural transmission of their respective communities. The "mothers of the nation" have nonetheless often been relegated to the margins of their collectivities. Despite this, the intensity of the Israeli-Palestinian conflict and its centrality in people's everyday lives have naturalized the tendency to overlook differences within one's imagined community, particularly the narrow roles allotted to women, and tamed, until recently, possible resistance on the part of women.

The Israeli women's movement, which emerged in the 1970s, focused on issues such as women's reproductive freedom, equal opportunity and legal rights. These issues echoed in many ways the concerns of women's movements in North America and in Europe. In other words, the chief concerns of the feminist movement in Israel at that time were not grounded in the unique social and political context within which it emerged. For the most part, Israeli feminists have avoided taking explicit positions on the Arab-Israeli conflict; there was a fear among feminists that a further discussion of national and international politics would divert attention from women's issues and result in a further fragmentation of the already fragile movement. With the Israeli invasion of Lebanon in 1982, however, the women's movement could no longer ignore the broader political picture.

MOTHERHOOD, FEMINISM AND POLITICAL PROTEST:
THE ISRAELI INVASION OF LEBANON AND ITS AFTERMATH

The 1982 Israeli invasion of Lebanon gave rise to the first example of Israeli women organizing explicitly against war. It also marked a turning point for the Israeli peace movement as a whole, sparking the emergence of a distinctive peace movement in Israel.[22] Peace Now—founded in 1978 by a group of Israeli reserve officers and soldiers who were not convinced that the government was doing enough to bring about peace with Egypt—situated itself at the center of the emerging Israeli peace movement through its superior resources and its ability to define peace as an issue of national security. Some Israeli women, on the other hand, searched for different peace frameworks and new strategies of resistance and activism against the war.[23]

Two major women's protest groups emerged during that period: Women

Against the Invasion of Lebanon and Parents Against Silence. Both groups opposed the Israeli invasion of Lebanon and demanded an immediate withdrawal of Israeli forces from Lebanon. The groups differed, however, not only in their origins and in the positions they articulated against the war, but also in the different strategies they used to achieve goals—particularly in the ways they linked (or did not link) their gender identity with their political positions.

The establishment of Parents Against Silence a year after the invasion was triggered by a letter to the editor published in the Israeli daily *Ha'aretz*. Shoshana Shmueli, a teacher and a mother of two, wrote the letter with a message that appealed to mothers' and fathers' sense of responsibility for their children fighting the war. She urged those with similar sentiments and concerns "to cease to be silent, to protest against those who bear the responsibility for this cursed war . . . and not to relinquish the struggle until our sons come home."[24] A week after the publication of the letter, Shmueli convened the first meeting of Parents Against Silence.

The group was comprised of between forty and fifty women (and a few men who gave support primarily behind the scenes). The organization maintained a high level of activity for two years. Its scope included holding demonstrations and protest rallies, publishing proclamations, issuing press releases, distributing stickers and explanatory material at supermarkets, beaches and demonstrations, and collecting signatures on petitions. Major protest rallies were held near the prime minister's office in Jerusalem, in one of Tel-Aviv's main squares, and near the ministry of defense in Tel-Aviv.[25]

The members of Parents Against Silence, which the media and the Israeli public called Mothers Against Silence, publicly disassociated themselves from feminism and tried to project an image that would not be threatening to most Israelis. They insisted that they were simply mothers (and fathers) who were worried about their sons in combat.[26] Women Against the Invasion of Lebanon, on the other hand, was made up of women who had been active in the Israeli feminist movement and articulated their opposition to the war in the form of a feminist anti-militarist position. They stressed the connections between their oppression as women and other forms of oppression and domination suffered by Palestinians as a result of Israeli military occupation both in Lebanon and in the West Bank and Gaza Strip.

Israeli society and its mainstream media were sympathetic to Parents Against Silence, but did not tolerate the feminist anti-war and anti-occupation positions articulated by Women Against the Invasion of Lebanon. Gadi Wolfsfeld points out that "unlike the feminist group, Parents Against Silence were pictured as mainstream Israel: mothers worrying about their sons in combat. To oppose the group politically was equivalent to insulting motherhood and the army at the same time."[27] The hostile public reaction toward Women Against the Invasion of Lebanon, however, revealed that Israeli society was not able to address the oppression of Palestinians in the Occupied Territories nor the subordination of Israeli women, and especially not the links between the two.

Parents Against Silence dispersed soon after the Israeli army pulled out of most of Lebanon in 1985. The active women in the group did not join feminist groups or other political organizations. Women Against the Invasion of Lebanon, on the other hand, changed its name to Women Against the Occupation (WAO) and expanded its anti-war focus to include solidarity campaigns with Palestinian women in the West Bank and Gaza Strip.[28]

In sum, the Israeli invasion of Lebanon in June 1982 triggered for the first time massive anti-war protests in Israel and galvanized a peace movement. Yet women had little room to challenge as women, let alone as feminists, the dominant rhetoric of national security, which prescribed the ideological notion of an Israeli woman who backs her sons and on occasion, only in the name of care and protection, may question government policies. Feminism was viewed as an extreme movement that posed a threat to the stability of Israeli society, particularly in times of crisis. This crisis atmosphere helped generate public hostility toward Women Against the Invasion of Lebanon, in contrast to the empathetic attitude toward Parents Against Silence.

The women who founded Parents Against Silence stressed time and again that they were not feminists but rather mothers concerned with their sons on the battlefield. Such a position might have been a strategic decision designed to mobilize broad support for their cause without having to confront the dominant political discourse in Israel, but this does not appear likely in this particular case. What remains significant, however, is the centrality of the discourse of motherhood for women's peace activism in Israel and its broader legitimacy within Israeli society.

Despite the insistence of Parents Against Silence that their group included both mothers and fathers, the media and the public consistently called the group Mothers Against Silence. This indicates that the "task" of care, in Israel as in other places, is associated primarily with the experience of mothering and, as such, seriously limits social and political movements seeking a radical transformation of the prevailing political and social order including gender relations. Only with the outbreak of the *intifada* has feminism gained some prominence among women peace activists in Israel.

THE SEARCH FOR ALTERNATIVE FEMINIST DISCOURSES OF PEACE:
THE INTIFADA AS A TURNING POINT

The outbreak of the *intifada* was a watershed for the political involvement of women in Israel. Exclusively female (and largely feminist) peace groups burst on the scene, initiating activities that had two major goals: to mobilize public opinion in Israel and abroad against the occupation, and to build bridges of solidarity with Palestinian women in the West Bank and Gaza Strip. Groups such as Women in Black, the Women's Organizations for Women Political Prisoners (WOFPP), Israeli Women Against the Occupation (SHANI), the Women and Peace Coalition, and Israeli Women's Peace Net (RESHET) provided new frameworks for the political mobilization and activism of women in Israel. These newly founded women's peace groups initiated numerous demonstrations, letter campaigns, local and international peace conferences and solidarity visits to the West Bank and Gaza Strip.[29]

The emergence of a multitude of women's peace groups provided many Israeli women with new opportunities to step out of their prevailing roles as mothers and keepers of the homefront and to take positions on the most crucial matter in Israeli politics: the Israeli-Palestinian conflict. In this context, Israeli women have gradually come to realize that the broad array of concern and problems previously defined as "women's issues" cannot be treated anymore in isolation without reference to broader structures of militarization, inequality, and oppression reinforced by the Occupation.

The first reactions by women in Israel to the *intifada* were spontaneous, involving primarily those who had been previously active in either the Israeli left or the feminist movement or both. Acting within existing frameworks and channels, these women explored various ideas and strategies to educate the Israeli public about the *intifada*. In January 1988, a few weeks after the outbreak of the *intifada*, a group of women in West Jerusalem, members of a mixed-gender group, *Dai L'Kibbush* (Hebrew for "End the Occupation"), held a silent vigil under a banner bearing those words. This is how Women in Black in Jerusalem began. Hagar Rovlev, one of the seven women who organized the first vigil, insists that its origins were largely experimental and that its success was highly contingent.[30] Nevertheless, the overwhelmingly supportive response by women to the idea led to its weekly institutionalization. In January 1988, women in Jerusalem, and soon thereafter throughout the country, began holding silent vigils on Friday afternoons. The women dressed in black to symbolize the tragedy of both Israeli and Palestinian peoples and held signs in Arabic, English, and Hebrew, which called for an end to the Israeli occupation of the West Bank and Gaza Strip.

The *intifada* represented a significant turning point in the development of feminist discourses on peace and security. Rachel Ostrowitz, a prominent figure in feminist circles as well as in the Israeli women's peace movement, points out that the Palestinian uprising represented a new stage in the history of the feminist movement in Israel in that it triggered attempts to explore and articulate linkages between feminist praxis and the Israeli-Palestinian conflict. According to Ostrowitz:

For years we tried to avoid dealing with the Israeli-Palestinian conflict in our feminist activities. When subjects such as the occupation, the Arab-Israeli conflict or our attitudes toward Arabs came up, the tendency was not to link those topics with our struggles as feminists . . . This was partially since we tried to attract many women, regardless of their political views, to the women's movement. Given the ongoing backlash against feminism in Israel, we felt that it was not appropriate to confront the public with the most delicate topic for the majority of Israelis: the political situation.[31]

Only with the outbreak of the *intifada* did Jewish women begin to make the connections between feminism and the politics of the Israeli-Palestinian conflict more explicit. These newly articulated connections have formed the basis for the emergence of what can be called "local feminist discourses."[32]

What stands out about local feminist discourses is that they are not grounded in any one particular theory, nor have they been directly informed by conflict resolution scholarship on the Israeli-Palestinian conflict or by existing feminist frameworks on the relationship between women and peace. They represent a search for a context-specific feminist standpoint, for a theory of struggle "from below." Local feminist discourses are dynamic and transformative in that they have emerged from and are grounded in particular experiences of struggle. These experiences of struggle have given rise to perspectives and interpretive frameworks that inform women's actions and seek to relate feminist politics to the struggles to end the occupation and to end social injustice in Israel.

Local feminist discourses reflect attempts made by women peace activists in Israel to situate their struggles for gender equality within the particular socioeconomic and political context in Israel and in relation to the Israeli-Palestinian conflict and Middle East politics.

These discourses broaden conventional understandings of "women's issues" by making explicit several sets of connections which should be of concern to Israeli feminists: (1) between different systems of domination and structured inequalities along lines of gender, class, race, ethnicity or sexuality; (2) between practices of violence used by Israeli soldiers against Palestinians in the Occupied Territories and the increase in violence against women in Israel; and (3) between struggles of Palestinians in the Occupied Territories and of women in Israel for liberation and self-determination.

Hannah Safran, a founding member of Women in Black in Haifa, has described some of the conditions in which these local feminist discourses emerged:

In Israel, there is not much theoretical debate on feminism as a social and political theory. The same is true about theoretical debates around the relationship of women and peace. We don't have access to the emerging literature on these issues so it is almost like we try to invent the wheel every time we are confronted with a new question. But, in fact, there were women before us, in different parts of the world that engaged in protests against wars and articulated feminist frameworks for peace and conflict resolution. This information about women's struggles for peace in other parts of the world could be very enriching and I think it is crucial for our ongoing struggles.[33]

As a result, most of the connections articulated by women peace activists are informed by their own particular experiences as women and as Israeli citizens who oppose the Israeli occupation of the West Bank and Gaza Strip. Furthermore, there are many women who now identify themselves as feminists but who were not active in the Israeli women's movement before they joined the women's peace movement. The emergence of an indigenous women's peace movement in Israel seems to have provided a context, at least for some women, to make sense of their everyday lives as women in relation to the Israeli-Palestinian conflict. The process of articulating connections such as between women and nonviolence or between militarism and sexism enables women to reevaluate what they once saw as their *personal* experiences with a *political* understanding. It is these reevaluations and new political understandings that have inspired the search for local feminist discourses in Israel.

What is particularly significant about the emergence of local feminist discourses in Israel is that they represent attempts to move beyond the conventional and often uncritical use of motherhood as the primary discourse to articulate the relationship between women and peace. While it is true that many women in the Israeli women's peace movement, as in other conflict-torn regions around the world, have utilized this discourse to articulate visions for peace and conflict resolution, the relationship between women, motherhood and peace is not as natural nor as politically significant as it is made to seem.

In many cases women who wish to voice political dissent have no other "choice" but to reify the institution of motherhood, which reduces feminism to simply recognizing biological gender differences between men and women. This reduction of feminist politics is no doubt related to the limited space available in the political arena for women's voices and perspectives that explicitly challenge the hegemonic discourse of militarized masculinity and to the lack of alternative discourses of struggle that address the relationship between women and peace.

Feminist peace activist Hannah Safran expressed her uneasiness with the overwhelming use of motherhood as a primary discourse of dissent in the Israeli women's peace movement:

Is our primary role as a women's peace movement to stress that we are mothers and based on the idealization of motherhood argue that we refuse to keep sending our sons to fight? Maybe it is time for us to also stress other identities. To point out that we are not just mothers, that some of us are not mothers (either by choice or not), that we are lesbians and heterosexual, Ashkenazi and Sephardic, young and old, wealthy and poor, and that all these diverse identities constitute legitimate locations from which we can voice opposition to war and conquest.[34]

Safran emphasized the need to listen to the multiplicity of voices within the women's peace movement and to search for alternative discourses of struggle that will be able to capture and celebrate these differences. The emergence of local feminist discourses is encouraging precisely because it has inspired compelling alternatives and enabled the articulation of new perspectives on the Israeli-Palestinian conflict.

CONCLUSION

More than two years after the signing of the Declaration of Principles between the Palestinian Liberation Organization (PLO) and the Israeli government, the women's peace movement in Israel is facing one of its most serious crises. Women in Black vigils have gradually disappeared from the scene, and other women's peace groups have decreased their volume of activism or folded altogether. Many of the founding members of various women's peace groups in Israel have been engaged for the past year in attempts to examine the causes of the present crisis and the ways to overcome it.

There is no doubt that the crisis in the women's peace movement has been prompted, among other things, by the change in government from Likud to Labor and by the exclusive public attention to official diplomacy, which resulted in the narrowing of political discussions to statements for or against the Madrid Peace Process, for or against the Gaza and Jericho First Plan, and the Declaration of Principles signed by Yitzhak Shamir and Yasser Arafat. As a result, grassroots initiatives in general and women's political organizing toward a just and lasting resolution of the Israeli-Palestinian conflict have been marginalized and rendered insignificant.

Another possible explanation for the crisis involves the history of the Israeli women's movement, which, like the histories of resistance movements around the world, has been riven by attempts to overlook differences in political ideology and direction in order to reach a broad consensus designed to mobilize large segments of Israeli society. This search for a consensus in the women's peace movement has often suppressed differences—between women who joined Women in Black as mothers of sons who serve in the Occupied Territories and women who were strongly in favor of Israeli soldiers' refusal to serve in the West Bank and Gaza Strip, and between women who joined the vigil because of the sexist nature of the Israeli peace movement and radical feminists whose participation in the vigil is grounded in a principled position against any type of oppression. Other suppressed differences concern women's positions on feminism and Zionism and their perspectives on the long-term solution to the Israeli-Palestinian conflict.[35]

In addition to marginalizing differences within the movement, women peace activists have been reluctant to publicly address the connections between gender and the politics of the Israeli-Palestinian conflict, which are inherent in the structural underpinning and legitimization of the relationship between militarism and sexism and between violence against women in Israel and the violence and oppression of Palestinians in the Occupied Territories. Given the present political situation, the ability of women peace activists not only to overcome the present crisis but also to emerge as a politically significant force in Israel requires the courage to acknowledge and address these differences and uncomfortable connections.

In conclusion, the present crisis facing the Israeli women's movement cannot be overcome by time or by a new catchy slogan around which most women peace activists will unite because it is not only a crisis of direction and political strategy. Rather, it is first and foremost an identity crisis. As such, it calls for a critical rethinking of not only strategies of struggle, but also the very basis of women's organizing around questions of peace and security. One positive outcome that may result from this critical rethinking is a move beyond a focus on motherhood as the only legitimate discourse of women's struggles for peace and a strengthening of local feminist discourses.

The spontaneous large-scale political mobilization of women in Israel during the first years of the *intifada* confirms that Israeli women are ready and determined to struggle for a distinct voice and place within the peace movement and in the broader political arena in Israel. It would be a grave mistake, therefore, to interpret the inability of the women's peace movement to confront the unexpected political developments of the past two years as a sign of failure or burnout. Such an interpretation, which is common among women activists themselves, is indicative of the reactive nature of peace activism in Israel; the common view is that it is the task of grassroots activists to immediately respond to events unfolding in the official political arena. This limited understanding of resistance has narrowed the parameters of possible responses by the women's peace movement in Israel.

The present crisis presents women peace activists in Israel with a unique opportunity to rethink the dominant understandings of resistance and activism and to explore new venues to address the connections between gender and the Israeli-Palestinian conflict that have affected their lives in powerful ways. Such an analysis, however, should not begin with the question of women's support of or opposition to war or peace, nor should it be limited to motherhood as a primary discourse of struggle. Rather, it should focus on the implications of particular political developments in the Middle East for women's lives and struggles on both sides of the Israeli-Palestinian divide.

NOTES

1. For a more detailed discussion, see Simona Sharoni, *Gender and the Israeli-Palestinian Conflict: The Politics of Women's Resistance* (Syracuse: Syracuse University Press, 1995), pp. 90–91.

2. Ibid., pp. 90–91.

3. Adrienne Harris and Ynestra King, eds., *Rocking the Ship of State: Toward a Feminist Peace Politics* (Boulder, Colo.: Westview Press, 1989).

4. Ibid., p. 1.

5. For more on Greenham Common, see, for example, Gwyn Kirk, "Our Greenham Common: Not Just a Place, But a Movement," in *Rocking the Ship of State,* pp. 263–280, and Jill Liddington, *The Road to Greenham Common: Feminism and Anti-Militarism in Britain Since 1820* (Syracuse: Syracuse University Press, 1991). For more on the Women's Pentagon Action, see Harriet Hyman Alonso, *Peace as a Women's Issue: A History of the U.S. Movement for World Peace and Women's Rights* (Syracuse: Syracuse University Press, 1993).

6. Sara Ruddick, "The Rationality of Care," in *Women, Militarism, and War: Essays in History, Politics, and Social Theory,* ed. Jean Bethke Elshtain and Sheila Tobias (Totowa, N.J.: Rowman & Littlefield, 1990), p. 239.

7. Ibid., p. 239.

8. Carol Cohn, "Sex and Death in the Rational World of Defense Intellectuals," *Signs: Journal of Women in Culture and Society* 12, no. 4 (summer 1987):690–691.

9. Dafna Izraeli, "The Women's Workers' Movement: First Wave Feminism in Pre-State Israel," in *Pioneers and Homemakers: Jewish Women in Pre-State Israel,* ed. Deborah Bernstein (Albany, N.Y.: State University of New York Press, 1992), p. 184.

10. Ibid., pp. 204–206.

11. Fogiel-Bijaoui, "From Revolution to Motherhood: The Case of Women in the Kibbutz, 1910–1948," in Bernstein, ed., *Pioneers and Homemakers,* p. 215.

12. The *kvutza* was a small collective settlement in which all were equally to share the work. The *kvutza* laid the ideological and structural foundations for the development of the *kibbutz* in the 1920s. While the *kvutza* often restricted its membership to 20 or 30, the *kibbutz* was a larger social unit with 100 members or more.

13. Fogiel-Bijaoui, "From Revolution to Motherhood," p. 215.

14. Ibid., p. 216.

15. Natalie Rein, *Daughters of Rachel: Women in Israel* (New York: Penguin, 1980), p. 65.

16. Quoted in Lesley Hazleton, *Israeli Women: The Reality Behind the Myths* (New York: Simon and Schuster, 1977), p. 63.

17. David Ben-Gurion, *Israel: A Personal History* (New York: Funk & Wagnalls, 1971), p. 8.

18. Ibid., p. 78.

19. See Nira Yuval-Davis, "The Jewish Collectivity," in *Women in the Middle*

East, ed. The Khamsin Collective (London and Atlantic Highlands, N.J.: Zed Books, 1987).

20. Yuval-Davis, "The Jewish Collectivity," pp. 82–84.

21. Nahla Abdo, "Women of the Intifada: Gender, Class and National Liberation," *Race & Class* 32, no. 4 (1991):25.

22. See Mordechi Bar-On, *Peace Now: The Portrait of a Movement* (Tel-Aviv: Hkibbutz Hameuchad, 1985) (Hebrew); Reuven Kaminer, "The Protest Movement in Israel," in *Intifada: The Palestinian Uprising Against Israeli Occupation*, eds. Zachary Lockman and Joel Beinin (Boston: South End Press & MERIP, 1989), pp. 231–245; and Gadi Wolfsfeld, *The Politics of Provocation: Participation and Protest in Israel* (Albany: State University of New York Press, 1988).

23. See Nurit Gillath, *The Thundering Silence: Parents Against Silence* (unpublished Master's thesis, University of Haifa, Haifa, Israel, 1987; Hebrew), and Gillath, "Women Against War: Parents Against Silence," in *Calling the Equality Bluff: Women in Israel*, ed. Barbara Swirsky and Marilyn P. Safir (New York: Pergamon Press, 1991), pp. 142–146.

24. Quoted in Gillath, *The Thundering Silence*, pp. 142–143.

25. Ibid., pp. 142–143.

26. Ibid., pp. 142–143.

27. Wolfsfeld, *The Politics of Provocation*, p. 130.

28. Ghada Talhami, "Women Under Occupation: The Great Transformation," in *Images and Realities: Palestinian Women Under Occupation*, ed. Suha Sabbagh and Ghada Talhami (Washington, D.C.: Institute of Arab Women's Studies, 1990), pp. 15–27.

29. For detailed overviews of women's peace activism since the Intifada, see Naomi Chazan, "Israeli Women and Peace Activism," in *Calling the Equality Bluff*, pp. 152–164; Yvonne Deutsch, "Israeli Women: From Protest to a Culture of Peace," in *Walking the Red Line: Israelis in Search of Justice for Palestine*, ed. Deena Hurwitz (Philadelphia, Pa.: New Society Publishers, 1991); and Simona Sharoni, "Conflict Resolution through Feminist Lenses: Theorizing the Israeli-Palestinian Conflict from the Perspectives of Women Peace Activists in Israel" (Ph.D. diss., George Mason University, 1993).

30. Sharoni, "Conflict Resolution Through Feminist Lenses," p. 182.

31. Interview with the author, May 1990, Tel-Aviv, Israel.

32. Sharoni, "Conflict Resolution Through Feminist Lenses," pp. 223–230.

33. Interview with the author, May 1990, Haifa, Israel.

34. Ibid.

35. See, for example, Tikva Honig-Parnass, "Feminism and Peace Struggle in Israel," *News From Within*, 10/11 (Oct-Nov 1992), pp. 2–5; and Erella Shadmi, "Women, Palestinians, Zionism: A Personal View," *News From Within* 10/11 (October–November 1992): pp. 6–13.

Palestinian Motherhood and Political Activism on the West Bank and Gaza Strip

Rema Hammami

Motherhood is the way in which Palestinian women gain authority within their communities. It gives women the ability to assert their right to resources, and it is the most socially acceptable way for women to be political activists. The Palestinian women's movement and the nationalist movement have at different times tried to use the identity of motherhood as a way to mobilize women politically. But this is where a women's movement that identifies itself as a women's movement has a problem.

When people think about Middle Eastern women they think immediately of Islam, and assume that Islam defines and determines much of what goes on in women's lives. But the peasant background of Palestinian society is in many ways much more important than Islamic ideology in determining the boundaries of women's lives and their socially ordained goals and values.

Until this century, Palestine's Mediterranean, peasant-based society, its social and economic logic, was organized around the village system and peasant production. The family was the basic economic unit of production. Local politics was also organized around family alliances, and political power was based on creating a large enough linkage of family alliances across villages. Basically this meant that the family and children were pivotal. And despite the massive dislocations that have taken place through dispossession, domestic transformation and proletarianization, family ideology is still incredibly important—even among refugees for whom the land-based logic of this ideology ceases to exist.

As a result, the basic logic of life, not just for Palestinian women but for Palestinian men, is marriage. Marriage is the goal in life for the whole society. And the goal of marriage is children. A recent survey of women over twenty years old who live in the Occupied Territories showed that more than 90 percent were married and almost 80 percent had a child within the second year of marriage. In a very bland, empirical way, the results show how life is defined, and how women are primarily defined by their family identity. Men have the ability to have socially acceptable dual identities, whereas women are primarily defined as mothers, and their goal is to become mothers. It is the primary way in which most Palestinian women socially identify themselves.

It is also the way in which the society identifies them. In most Middle Eastern and Arab societies, both parents take on the name of their oldest son at birth. So parents with an oldest son called Hamad would be referred to as Umm Hamad and Abu Hamad (the mother and father of Hamad, respectively) as a sign of respect. Among women of the younger generation this is looked upon as very old fashioned; we want to be treated as our individual selves. But it shows how incredibly important parenthood is to the older generations.

Motherhood is the way in which Palestinian women gain authority within their communities. It gives women the ability to assert their right to resources, and it is the most socially acceptable way for women to be political activists. The Palestinian women's movement and the nationalist movement have at different times tried to use the identity of motherhood as a way to mobilize women politically. But this is where a women's movement that identifies itself as a women's movement has a problem.

There is an inherent contradiction between the conceptualization of women as feminists, as individuals working for women's rights, and the mother-identified woman for whom everybody else's needs come first. Motherhood in our context—in the Palestinian context—is not based on female individualism: she's acting as a mother, not as a woman. And therefore she doesn't threaten the gender social boundaries of this society. She is actually acting within them.

This inherent contradiction is vividly illustrated by the images of women in the national media. In the Palestinian context, where you don't have a national technical media—radio or television—poster art has been very important since the 1950s in representing the national movement to people in everyday life. Palestinian nationalist artists—most Palestinian artists are nationalist artists—have been very pivotal in this movement. It is very interesting to look at the transformation in images of women in nationalist poster art since the 1950s, because the mother is something that keeps coming back again and again.

In the early 1950s some of the first nationalist art was done by Ismail Shamut, a man from the Gaza Strip. The topic of his paintings, which were then turned into very popular posters, was the *Hijra* or the experience of going into exile. The paintings always depicted a peasant woman in peasant dress carrying her child and fleeing. There's a very famous one of a mother working and in the corner you can see an old man sitting there, bent, completely overwhelmed. That represented a reality. In the period when most of the population became refugees, men went into shock. Women, mothers specifically, didn't have the luxury to go into shock. Mothers had to keep everything going. They were the real motors of the community that helped the community survive and keep going. That typification of the peasant woman as the guardian, as savior, was predominant throughout the 1950s.

In the mid-1960s, socialist realism entered Palestinian art. This was the period of Arab nationalism, socialism, revolutionary movements. Socialist realism fit the mood of the day. And the typification of women in this socialist realist style, although attempting to represent militancy, was actually very reactionary. Mothers didn't figure in it at all. What you had were young women. Some were supposed to represent young militant women. But they were represented much more as the young virgin, as though the nation were a young virgin that had been occupied and taken. They have taken our women, they have despoiled them—that type of thing. Some of these posters are very lurid. As Carol Bardenstein's essay in this volume illustrates, much of the nationalist poetry from that period had the same typification of women, of Palestine, as the virgin, the bride; it was about longing and desire.

In the 1970s, poster art and its depiction of women continued to mirror Palestinian nationalist ideology and political strategy. During this period, there was a shift away from a strategy of underground military resistance against the occupation. Instead, the notion of *sumud*—steadfastness—emerged, and became the main ideology for Palestinians inside the West Bank and Gaza Strip. The occupation was trying to dispossess people of their land, to move the population out either through direct means of deportation or through creating economic hardship so that people would emigrate. The *sumud* strategy dictated that, in the absence of armed struggle, Palestinians should resist the Israeli occupation by remaining steadfast, by staying rooted in the land. The mother was the absolutely perfect representation of *sumud* ideology. This was also the period of the heritage movement—folklore and heritage. And all this work depicted very round, pregnant peasant women, who were the real icons of *sumud*.

By the time of the *intifada*, the imagery of women had changed to reflect a new dualism in Palestinian women's activism: those who participated in the *intifada* primarily through their motherhood, and those who engaged as political individuals, as combatants. In the *intifada*, the nation was the child. And the rebellion was embodied in the militance of children. The nation was the young child going into the streets, throwing rocks at soldiers. That was the nation being born. So the child really took center stage. And that drama was captured, as never before, in photographs. Photography was the mass visual art of the *intifada*. It was very accessible to the society, and a lot of it was made into posters. The photographs showed two different images of women. One was the young activist woman demonstrating in the streets. The other was of the mother, confronting the soldier, wrestling with the soldier over her son. And that was a very, very powerful visual image.

The same dualism was captured in the text of the Palestinian Declaration of Independence, issued in 1989. When the Declaration addresses the rights of the Palestinian people, it includes women. It says they contributed to the creation of the nation and should be granted equal rights. In the epilogue, however, there's a poetic text that romanticizes mothers as being "the guardians of our collective past, the keepers of the flame of the nation," and "the wellsprings of our future."

This double image was rooted in the reality of Palestinian women's participation in the national struggle. From the beginning of the occupation of Gaza and the West Bank that followed the Six Day War of 1967, a number of women were involved in the armed resistance. They fell into two categories. There were young women fighters who set a major precedent in the West Bank and Gaza by forcing a very radical redefinition of what women could do. The other women in the armed resistance were mothers of male combatants. They were, in a certain sense, above ground: they made food for the fighters, they passed messages, they sometimes transported arms. When the resistance was finally crushed in the Gaza Strip in 1973, many of these women were either imprisoned or deported.

Following a prisoner exchange in the early 1980s, a number of the women fighters were released and returned as heroes to their communities. The nationalist movement valorized them as female role models. But for the women themselves, reintegration into the community was very difficult. Most never married. In the United States, this may not seem to be such a terrible thing. But in the West Bank and Gaza, it is a very, very difficult situation for a woman from the class background that most of these women fighters came from. The mothers, on the other hand, emerged as very socially acceptable symbols of women's political struggle: mother-activists. They are empowered in their communities to this day, where many are authoritative figures who command great respect.

Such divergent treatment—of women combatants and of mothers—has its roots not only in nationalist art but in the history of Palestinian women's organizing prior to the 1970s. In the Palestinian women's movement, the role of motherhood has conflicted and sometimes integrated with various women's organizing strategies. And changes in women's activism have mirrored changes in the larger Palestinian resistance movement.

Prior to the 1970s, much of women's activism took place within charitable societies that were service- and relief-oriented. They were staffed by middle- and upper-class women, many of them very elitist. These organizations were not interested in a wider transformation of gender roles in Palestinian society. One was literally called the Society for the Preservation of the Family. It was founded just prior to the occupation of 1967. Its members believed that the family was the backbone of society—the core of society—and that to help society continue, women need help preserving their families. The organization helped traditional women market their embroidery products and find sources of income for traditional women's work: knitting, sewing and cooking. It also taught economics and motherhood skills.

The director of the organization is a powerful figure who, despite being the nominal head of the local general union of Palestinian Women, is often at loggerheads with the women's movement when it comes to issues of women's equality. Umm Khalil is what she calls herself—she's the mother of Khalil. She used to give annual prizes to women who had large numbers of children. Umm Khalil and other women from the charitable societies valorized the role of the mother, although they themselves didn't always act out this role very well. They promoted motherhood as the singular contribution of women to the national struggle. Their position was that there wasn't any other way for women to contribute to the national struggle besides being a good mother and a mother of many children. (Ironically, Umm Khalil was the only person to challenge Yasser Arafat for president in the January 1996 Palestinian legislative council elections. She received a respectable total of 22,000 votes.)

In the 1970s, after armed resistance gave way to *sumud* and militants moved from underground cell activity to mass mobilization, a new generation of women organizers emerged. If you have read at all about Palestinian women in West Bank and Gaza Strip, mostly what you hear about are the women's committees. The goal of women's committees, as they were originally conceived, was to mobilize women for the national movement.

A few decisive factors helped the women's committees to mobilize young women in the mid- to late 1970s. This was a time when more and more women were entering the workforce, decreasing their isolation and increasing their chances for politicization. But perhaps the most important development was the opening of the universities, through subsidies, to a larger population of people who would never have had the chance to go to the university before. Many women from rural backgrounds, from refugee camp backgrounds, enrolled for the first time. Here they came into contact with activities of the nationalist movement.

What's interesting is that the leaders and activists of the women's committees were some of the first Palestinian women to politicize their individual female identities. In other words, they organized women as women, not as wives or mothers. These women were educated: some in fact had university jobs. But when they mobilized beyond the university and the school, and reached out to women in refugee camps and villages, they often mobilized using the motherhood model. In trying to organize women in traditional contexts, motherhood was a major way to forge links. Thus, much of the work of the women's committees involved basic bread-and-butter issues.

Take day care, for instance. Up until 1992 there were more than 240 day-care centers in the Gaza Strip alone. The day-care centers that the women's committees established in the refugee camps served not just working mothers but mothers of many children. This way the mothers could put their children in the day-care centers and have a rest or a chance to do other things. This was an incredibly important service, and brought a wide swath of women into contact with the women's committees. It was also a very positive way of representing the women's committees not just to mothers but to the wider society.

The women's committees stress political education, ideology and organizing for their activists. They also do political mobilization of mothers on specific issues. For instance, if there is a hunger strike of prisoners, the women's committee will organize a sit-in by prisoners' mothers at the Red Cross office. These sit-ins at the Red Cross offices are a very regular occurrence—sometimes lasting for weeks. Mothers and sisters of prisoners from many social backgrounds—from the countryside as well as from refugee camps—are brought in by women's committees and tend to make up the backbone of the demonstrators.

The women's committees also work with mothers of martyrs. In the *intifada*, the mothers of martyrs were brought to public events to be acknowledged for their role in the national struggle. International Women's Days in the West Bank and Gaza throughout the late 1980s and early 1990s were events of this kind. At one such Women's Day celebration in the early 1990s, a group of approximately seventy mothers of martyrs from the Gaza Strip was the event's main focus. One by one, each woman climbed onstage and announced herself, saying: "I am the mother of the martyr Hammad al-Dweik." And then the people would clap and praise her. This is a very difficult phenomenon for people in the United States to comprehend. In the United States, death is considered a private matter. However, in the context of struggle in Palestine, collective recognition and sharing of one's child's death is extremely important both emotionally and politically. It is critical for the political work of the women's committees and nationalist organizations that these mothers' losses be recognized as contributions to the nation.

These women's committees have scored some real achievements, not the least of which are their efforts to stretch and transform definitions of how Palestinian women can be politically active. By the time of the *intifada*, the women's committees had attracted a large membership of young and married women who'd gotten involved not just through the universities and the schools but also through organizing the villages and refugee camps. Working with mothers was very positive. Not only did it recognize the mothers' political activity, but it made political arenas more accessible to them. It also made the women's committees and their activists less threatening to the larger society, because throughout this whole period the women's committees never challenged the traditional role of motherhood. They tended to valorize it as a way that many women have contributed to the nation.

But the vulnerability of the strategy became very clear during the repression and breakdown of the *intifada* after its first two years. The beginning of the *intifada* was marked by spontaneous, mass mobilization rather than organized protest. And in that very first period of mass spontaneity, traditional identities were suspended. Women weren't going down to the streets as mothers, women weren't going down as workers. Really, literally, everybody took to the streets as Palestinians. The women's committees were initially able to absorb the large numbers of young women coming into the streets, and they gave their spontaneous activism order, resources and logic.

Simultaneously, older mothers were able to keep women's activism going for quite a while. Mother-activism tended to stay as it was—very informal and unplanned, spontaneous. In direct confrontation with soldiers, mother-activism was in many ways more successful than women's activism. Soldiers were in shock when these old traditional mothers in peasant dresses physically grabbed them and struggled with them. This challenged all of their racism and sexism against Palestinian society. Young women, on the other hand, were much less successful in direct confrontation. Young women were seen as just political activists. It became very clear, at least in the beginning stages of the *intifada*, that older women were much less likely to be beaten, and were much more successful in getting a person away from a soldier and out of harm's way than were young women—who were sometimes dragged away and arrested themselves. An underlying issue was the potential threat to young women's sexual integrity that physical confrontation with soldiers entailed. That wasn't an issue with mother-activists, who were older and, in the public mind, desexed. But for younger women this was a very major problem.

After the first few years of the *intifada* there was a terrible backlash. You had the backlash of the occupation authorities. You also had a backlash of fundamentalists, much more so in the Gaza Strip than in the West Bank. The occupational authorities very strategically went after women activists, not only the leadership but also young women activists from villages and refugee camps. That completely terrified families. And, in an increasingly conservative context, the Israeli crackdown on women activists was a very difficult thing for the women's movement to deal with. For Palestinian Islamic fundamentalists were directly attacking women activists at the same time. The very idea of women acting as individuals was very threatening to fundamentalist ideology. Mother-activists, on the other hand, were not attacked by the Israelis or by the fundamentalists. The Israelis saw them as politically unorganized. To the fundamentalists, motherhood activism was the only acceptable way for women to be active.

This is a time of real reassessment for the women's movement in Palestine. The types of discussions taking place today are about the need to look beyond the mother role when presenting positive images of women's activism to the larger society. The women's committees didn't try to redefine in a deep way how women could be activists in this society. There has been a growing recognition that motherhood needs to be seen not only in the mythic and romantic ways it has been represented, but also in terms of the practical burdens and constraints it puts on women. Simultaneously, women activists have recently recognized the need to create legitimacy for women's political activism as individuals outside the accepted parameters of family or motherhood roles.

Some of this redefinition has begun through activist women addressing their own issues as mothers. Like women in national movements anywhere in the world, they once tried to hide their motherhood. They didn't want to make it an issue, because having to deal with mother issues might make them seem not as strong, or not as able within their political movements. But in recent years at women's conferences women activists have been openly calling for a re-division of labor within the home. Day care is seen as only a partial answer. The question is: Why is it acceptable that a politically active or working father leaves the care of his children and the home in the hands of an equally active or working mother?

Clearly, we need a redefinition of roles with our spouses. Palestinian mothers are no longer willing to remain the mythic mothers of the nation and icon of *sumud* while the real burdens of motherhood are left unrecognized. Moreover, the historic tradeoff of being an activist Superwoman—whose motherhood is incidental—is just as untenable. Female individualism and motherhood do not have to be diametrically opposed. The status of one need not be at the cost of the other in terms of material and social supports, nor in terms of the social and political roles women are allowed to assume in society. For Palestinian women, struggling against this dualism remains one of their greatest challenges.

Raped Brides and Steadfast Mothers

Appropriations of Palestinian Motherhood

Carol Bardenstein

Do the women in the tents give birth to entire armies?
—Muzaffar al-Nawaab, from the poem "Bridge of Old Delights"
on *samizdat* casette[1]

This line of poetry succinctly articulates one of the most charged and potent, if perhaps also one of the most "literal," ways in which Palestinian mothers and motherhood have been mobilized and enlisted in the service of the Palestinian resistance and struggle for survival. While the construction of childbearing as a woman's most valued contribution to the national struggle figures prominently in Palestinian political and literary discourse, other phases and aspects of motherhood have been appropriated as well: subverted motherhood, "mothers-in-the-making," mothers as providers, and bereft mothers defined by the loss or "sacrifice" of their children to the struggle.[2]

In this essay I would like to sketch some of the particular ways in which Palestinian motherhood has been articulated, by mothers and others, as a mode of resistance, as well as other ways it has figured in discourses of Palestinian nationalism. I pay particular attention to the ways that traditional articulations of motherhood have been adapted and modified within the context of crisis and national struggle.

UNNATURAL UNIONS AND SUBVERTED MOTHERHOOD

Portrayals of the "homeland as woman" abound in the modern Arabic literary tradition as in so many others, replete with (sons) yearning for the homeland, longing to unite or reunite with it, and to defend its honor against invaders.[3] These portrayals may be viewed as more recent manifestations of a long tradition in Arabic literature of idealized unions with a feminized Other, longed for and realized, as in Sufi and profane love poetry. Those that have emerged within the contemporary Palestinian context are most pointedly shaped by the specific experience of occupation and resistance.

A recurring version of the "idealized union" in representations of Palestinian experience is the union between the land and its people, with Palestine often cast in the role of the would-be bride of the hoped-for marriage. If matters were running their predictable and natural course, such a union would take place in a normal fashion, representing a "natural" stage of life. In the Palestinian context, however, the phase of marriage, and the natural progression from it to consummation, conception, and birth (and thereby to natural continuity in history), is violently disrupted from the time of the traumatic primal scene of Palestinian dissociation from the land in 1948, commonly referred to as the *nakba*, or catastrophe.

One of the most widely known and circulated representations of this scenario of unnatural disruption is found in a poem entitled "Night Strings"[4] by the renowned underground poet Muzaffar al-Nawaab. Composed between 1970 and 1975, this two-hour-long poem has circulated widely in *samizdat* cassette form throughout the Arab world, where nearly all of this poet's work in published form is banned. During the Palestinian uprising of the late 1980s, this poem was actively revived, listened to and recited by Palestinians in the Occupied Territories of the West Bank and the Gaza Strip, where locally printed editions of a transcription of the cassette appeared in circulation as well. The poem recounts and laments some of the vicissitudes of the Arab world's recent history, including scathing words aimed at leaders (and, to a lesser extent, peoples) of the Arab world who did nothing to prevent the *nakba* from happening. In this segment, Palestine (referred to as "Jerusalem") is portrayed as a bride on her wedding night. Cast in a twisted, grotesque version of the "idealized marriage" turned nightmare, she is forced by the invading enemy into an unnatural union and violently raped.

The image of Palestine as the virgin bride raped on her wedding night has great potency as a graphic and disturbing image with a powerful effect on the reading and listening audience. The image also conspicuously reinscribes traditional configurations of power drawn along gender lines, as a variation of the theme of the "master rescue narrative." Men (here specifically Arab men and, most pointedly, Arab rulers), as the "real" subjects and actors in history, are being called upon to enact the traditional rescue narrative of the helpless woman, and are being harshly rebuked and insulted for not having done so at the crucial moment. The shocking image of the raped bride is used here to arouse feelings of guilt, horror, and a sense of duty and responsibility in "real" male subjects:

Jerusalem is the bride of your Arabness!!
So why did you usher all the fornicators of the night into her room,
And stand eavesdropping from behind the door
    to the screams of her torn virginity
You drew your daggers, and swelled with pride
And you yelled at her to keep quiet, for honor's sake
How honorable of you!!
Sons of bitches, can a woman being raped keep quiet?
You sons of bitches! I'm not ashamed to tell you what you really are!
A pigstye is cleaner than the cleanest of you.
Even a tombstone would be moved,
But you?! Not a single fiber in you flinches!
I scream at you: where is your decency?!!⁵

In the continuation of this image, however, Palestine—the raped, passive bride—takes action, and she does so specifically in her capacity as a mother-in-the-making: she physically and forcibly reverses the unnatural pregnancy resulting from the rape by vomiting it out of her, and onto the onlookers who delivered her to her fate:

Jerusalem is the bride of your Arabness! . . . .
What cuckolds you are! . . . .
Go ahead and leave her all bloodied in the sun,
    without a midwife to tend to her
She'll tear at her braids, and she'll vomit the pregnancy out onto you
She'll vomit the pregnancy all over your glory
She'll vomit the pregnancy over the sound of your broadcasts
She'll vomit the pregnancy onto you house by house, and she'll poke her
    fingers into your eyes, saying: It's *you* who are my rapists!

The bride Palestine has disrupted the sequence of consummation, pregnancy and motherhood by aborting her own motherhood. This would appear to be the "right thing," if possibly the *only* thing, for Palestine to do, given the nature of the impregnation and the resulting "mongrel" pregnancy, and given, as portrayed in the poem, the fact that none of her "men-folk"[6] proved able or willing to prevent the dreaded impregnation from taking place. In this instance, motherhood is mobilized in the context of a masculinist discourse. The threat of Palestine refusing motherhood and choosing to remain barren—and the challenge to regain control over who is to do the impregnating—are used to shame and goad men into active resistance. The poem continues:

> Be sterile, oh land of Palestine,
> For this is a frightening pregnancy!
> Be barren, oh mother of martyrs, from this time on,
> For this pregnancy by the enemies is ugly, deformed and frightening.
> This land will be fertilized by none but the Arabic language.

Michel Khleifi's 1987 film *Wedding in Galilee*[7] presents a somewhat different version of the disruption and abnormality of the marital union, in the unnatural context of a village under Israeli domination. In this film, a wedding is scheduled to take place, but the Israeli authorities have imposed a curfew on the village, rendering any kind of public gathering, including a wedding, unlawful. Under these circumstances, in which attempts to conduct everyday life and to engage in normal phases of the community's life cycle are thwarted or rendered illegal, the bridegroom's father strikes a deal with the Israeli authorities—one that is viewed as a humiliating capitulation by many of the villagers, particularly the younger generation who are the bridegroom's peers.

In order to receive permission from the Israeli authorities for the wedding to take place, the father has agreed to their conditions: an entourage from the Israeli military will be "invited" as guests to attend the wedding. Their unnatural and imposed insertion of themselves into Palestinian life, at the wedding as well as in the overall political context, affects every aspect of the wedding's festivities, and perhaps most pointedly seems to have the effect of rendering the bridegroom impotent on his wedding night, incapable of the insertion that all the wedding guests are anxiously awaiting evidence of—the blood-stained cloth of consummation. An additional unnatural insertion replaces the one anticipated: in a rather graphic scene, the melancholic Palestinian bride undertakes the act of insertion herself, tearing her hymen with her own fingers to provide the necessary drops of blood, thereby covering up her groom's impotence. With normal life disrupted, idealized Palestinian unions become joyless and humiliating rituals, and actual consummation and motherhood are put at bay and ultimately prove impossible.

BEARING CHILDREN AS RESISTANCE: MOTHERHOOD REVOLUTIONIZED

If in the examples cited so far the threat of motherhood unrealized has been articulated in powerful and disturbing ways, in other contexts, motherhood *realized* has been presented as a powerful weapon, and as one of the most substantial ways for women to participate in the Palestinian resistance. Independent of the conflict with Israel, and preceding it, bearing children (and more specifically, bearing sons) tended to be valorized in traditional Palestinian society. It granted a certain degree of social legitimization and status to women. If, for example, offspring translated into vital and valued "manpower" in a traditional agricultural economy, then the logic of "strength in numbers" takes on a related but redefined significance in the context of Palestinian resistance and struggle for survival. Julie Peteet has cited numerous examples of Palestinian women articulating their contribution to the national struggle in terms of their reproductive capacity, and has shown how this "credentialization" has been recognized and lauded within their communities in a variety of ways.[8]

The eminently traditional act of bearing children, when appropriated into the discourse of Palestinian resistance, is redefined and "radicalized" as an act of furnishing weapons and providing soldiers for the "war effort." This reconfiguration of Palestinian motherhood finds expression in a wide variety of literary and cultural representations. A chilling example of this is found in another poem by Muzaffar al-Nawaab that has circulated widely in cassette form. The poem is entitled "The Bridge of Old Delights,"[9] but is more commonly referred to as "Tel al-Zaatar," because of a well-known section of the poem treating the siege and subsequent massacre of Palestinians in the Tel al-Zaatar refugee camp in Lebanon in 1976. Focusing on women and children, graphic scenes of horror are recounted: a starving pregnant woman eating the vomit of her feverish child; charred and dismembered body parts—a woman's breast, a child's hands; a young boy trying to cover the exposed thighs of his murdered grandmother. In the face of these incomprehensible horrors, and at a loss to explain what could have possibly led anyone to do this to innocent women and children, the narrator indignantly asks, "Do the women in the tents give birth to entire armies?" The implied question is: Could the enemy possibly feel that the women in the camps deserve to be starved and killed because they believe these women are guilty of giving birth to an army of soldiers for the resistance?

While the manner in which this question is raised has the effect of implying an answer in the negative, that is, that the women in the tents do not give birth to soldiers, a latter segment of the poem would appear to affirm that this is in fact assumed to be the case:

They've torn out a womb in which a *fedayee*[10] is created
   during the night,
. . . Have you heard, you accursed Arabs
The hatred has reached the wombs
Have you heard, you accursed Arabs, that Palestine is being torn
   from the womb.

Ghassan Kanafani's portrayal of an idealized and quintessentially steadfast Palestinian mother, *Umm Saad*, is a "classic" within the corpus of Palestinian literature of resistance.[11] The title of the book is the name of its protagonist, Umm Saad, which in Arabic means "the mother of Saad." It is a common practice within Arab societies for a mother or a father to be called by the name "the mother" (*Umm*) or "the father" (*Abu*) of their first son to the extent that their original first name falls into virtual disuse. However, this named identification of a mother as the "producer" of that son is highlighted and elevated within the discourse of Palestinian resistance. In Kanafani's portrayal, the character Umm Saad articulates her motherhood, her ability to bear children, and the specific accomplishment of having given birth to Saad and his brother, who have joined the resistance, as a central component of her identity and as one of her primary contributions to the Palestinian resistance. When Umm Saad tells the narrator that Saad has left the camp to join the resistance with other *fedayeen*, he asks her if she is sad or angry about it. "No," she responds, "like I told my neighbor this morning, I only wish I had ten more like him to offer."[12]

Umm Saad's husband is proud that their two sons are fighting in the resistance, and in expressing his pride, he gives all the credit to Umm Saad for having produced the sons. On a day that guns are brought into the camp, the two proud parents watch their younger son from the balcony as he shows other young men what to do in combat. Another admiring onlooker, an old man, comments to Abu Saad that if their generation had been like this, they could have prevented the *nakba* from happening. Admiring the sight of the young men handling guns, Abu Saad replies, "This woman gives birth to children who then become *fedayeen*; she provides the children for Palestine!"[13] In tacit acknowledgment of the impotence of his generation of men, Abu Saad takes none of the credit for having produced these potent sons, and insinuates that women of his generation have more of a connection to the vitality of the new generation of young men through having given birth to them.

MOTHERS WHO PROVIDE

Several other aspects of traditionally defined motherhood, besides childbearing, have been substantially altered and redefined within the context of the Palestinian resistance. The traditional role of mother as provider of nourishment, shelter and protection for her children has been significantly expanded in scope and politicized as Palestinian mothers have come to consider themselves, and to be considered by others, as actors in the resistance.

The "providing" and nurturing energies of Palestinian mothers have traditionally been confined, as for so many mothers, to the home, focused on the smaller community of the immediate nuclear and extended family. In the context of the nationalist struggle, the scope of "community"—considered the rightful and deserving recipient of those "mothering" energies—has greatly expanded. The particulars of this process have varied in different periods and among different Palestinian communities, but the massive grassroots mobilization of women during the *intifada*, or uprising, in the Occupied Territories in the late 1980s pointedly illustrates this phenomenon.

Palestinian women in the Occupied Territories have participated in public political life under the rubric of a nationalist agenda largely defined by men since the turn of the century, working in socially acceptable and largely traditional "women's" venues such as charitable societies, fund-raising efforts, sometimes participating in demonstrations, and so on, with a preponderance of urban women from social and economic elites engaged in such activities. In the context of the *intifada*, the scope of these activities expanded extensively, with the proliferation of women's centers and committees outside of these already established in major urban centers, spreading to towns, villages and rural areas, with an increase in the sheer number of women participating in such activities, and involving a substantially broader socioeconomic spectrum of women.[14]

Women's centers and committees throughout the Occupied Territories became actively engaged in a variety of educational undertakings. With the closing of major universities and secondary and even primary schools for long periods of time during the *intifada*—some for as long as four years—the women's centers helped create alternative educational channels, including "home education kits" that enabled students to continue their education independently, or with the help of parents or teachers. Some women's centers developed literacy programs geared primarily toward middle-aged and older women who either had not completed or had never had any formal education. In the face of the tremendous number of casualties inflicted in confrontations with the Israeli military, programs were established that trained women in basic first aid techniques, in which they learned to treat injuries resulting from tear gas, beatings, and bullets.

During the *intifada*, a substantial number of women's centers instituted day care for children, freeing mothers to pursue a variety of activities outside of the home. Some women's centers established programs for providing "precooked" meals for the families of women engaged in work and other activities outside of the home as well. A wide variety of other food production projects has been undertaken by the centers as well, as another of the many nonviolent modes of resistance characteristic of the *intifada*. Most often these have been very small-scale centers or "factories" for the production of goods using local seasonal produce, such as juice, jam, or pickled foods.[15] The idea behind these food production projects has been twofold: to provide cheap food goods for the needs of the immediate community, and to contribute, even on a modest scale, to the development of a more self-sufficient economic infrastructure designed to decrease dependence on Israeli products and the Israeli economy.

Vocational cooperatives and training programs have been a salient feature of many women's centers, training women in skills such as sewing clothing and making sweaters on simple machines, providing the training and access to equipment and materials for nominal subsidized fees or free of charge. These cooperatives are designed to enable women to provide for their family's clothing needs more affordably, and, it is hoped, to earn an income from their newly acquired skills and to contribute to the development of an independent economic infrastructure as well. Vocational cooperatives at women's centers that teach women traditional Palestinian decorative embroidery serve these same goals, with the additional objective of reviving and disseminating traditional folk arts among Palestinians. Women's centers have developed and supported workshops in which women learn to produce other kinds of crafts and artwork as well, such as copper enamel decorative pieces, paintings, wall-hangings, and leatherwork, most of which articulates nationalistic sentiments and depictions of national struggle.[16]

With the exception of this last type of craft workshop, virtually all of these modes of women's grassroots participation in the resistance can be viewed as extensions of the traditional and sanctioned "mothering" roles of nurturing—providing nourishment, clothing and protection—and transmitting culture and education.[17] But due to heightened solidarity among Palestinians during the uprising, some of these conventional energies have been mobilized and redefined as modes of political resistance, channeled away from the home to a more broadly defined family or community—although not without difficulty.

To depict these women's activities as extensions of traditional "mothering" roles is not to detract from the fact that these extensions constituted a substantial transformation and significant development. For many women, particularly those not from elite social and economic backgrounds, it was quite a struggle to convince their husbands and families to allow them to channel some of their energies away from the home. One woman I spoke with at length told me it had taken her a full year of persistent "lobbying" to convince her family to allow her to enroll in a six-month course at the local women's center (just a few blocks away from her home) to learn to sew clothing on sewing machines provided by the cooperative.[18]

These nurturing and care-giving aspects of motherhood and their expansion or transformation within the context of Palestinian national resistance are also found in a variety of literary and visual representations. In Kanafani's *Umm Saad*, when Umm Saad first learns that her son has joined the armed resistance with the *fedayeen*, her first concern is whether he is being fed properly at the "front." Even though the narrator assures her that Saad is fed adequately, she comments, "I wish he were nearby, then I could take him my home-made food every day!" In an interesting expression of the displacement of strictly family-based nurturing for the sake of nurturing the national struggle, Umm Saad continues, "You know, children are slavery! If I didn't have these two infants at home, I would go and join him [Saad]. I would go and live with him there. Tents? Some tents are different than others![19] I would go and live with them, and cook their food for them. I would serve them myself, but children are slavery."[20] Umm Saad shifts smoothly and deftly in mid-utterance from "him" to "them," from Saad as son and freedom fighter, to his fellow freedom fighters (or all freedom fighters) as sons whom she yearns to feed. Coupled with her expressed irritation at having to provide for her non-*fedayee* children at home, this desire to nurture the guerrilla fighters illustrates the shifting boundaries of motherhood and "motherly" energies in the context of struggle and resistance.

The narrator tells Umm Saad that there is no need for her to visit Saad at the front, and that she should leave him to manage for himself, since "once a man has joined the *fedayeen* he no longer needs the care of his mother."[21] Upon further examination, however, the implication appears to be that a collective mother–son relationship subsumes or takes the place of the individual or particular mother–son relationship. Umm Saad tells the narrator that Saad came home for a short period after being wounded on a mission, and that when he was leaving again, she asked him why he didn't kiss her after such a long time of their not having seen each other. Saad answered that he had, in fact, seen her while he was away. He then proceeded to tell her about a time when he and his companions were on a mission, and had to wait in hiding without access to food or water for over a week. Just as they were getting desperate, a woman who looked just like Umm Saad appeared, and Saad, certain that it was indeed his mother, called out to her, "Mama, mama we want food." When they met, she too called him "my son," embraced him and wept as if he were her son, and brought food to Saad and his companions for the next five days, saving their lives. After Umm Saad has finished relating this story to the narrator, she turns to leave, and after she has taken a few steps, the narrator (who is not her son) relates "and suddenly I heard myself call 'Mama!.' And she stopped."[22] It is implicit in this appropriation of Palestinian motherhood in Kanafani's novel that in the context of national struggle, all mothers become the mothers of all sons. In spite of their displacement as "individual" mothers, particular mothers such as Umm Saad are to take comfort in the fact that the "collective" mother is taking care of her children, and that she has a meaning-ful role in taking care of a "collective" son.

Representations of this collective maternal figure appear in many of the nationalistic crafts produced at women's centers in the Occupied Territories, such as copper enamel pieces, embroidered wall-hangings, calendars and paint-ings. While one may find portrayals of women in roles clearly exceeding an exclusively "motherly" rubric,[23] the more prevalent images of women are those that reinscribe traditional roles of providing and bearing children. A classic "providing" image, found on embroidered calendars as well as copper enamel pieces, is that of a conspicuously maternal-looking woman providing a young fighter with ammunition. The mother is portrayed as taking stones from a pile that she has presumably collected, and is handing them to a young man who is throwing them either with his bare hands or with a sling-shot. Although this image most commonly occurs with one woman providing the ammunition for one young man, the discourse of an "every-mother" providing for an "every-son" is strongly reinforced. The articulation of a col-lective mother–son relationship within discourses of Palestinian resistance plays a pivotal role in absorbing and providing solace for the inevitable next phase of this national struggle, namely, the loss and death of sons, and the figure of the bereft mother.

BEREFT MOTHERS

Once someone has joined the armed resistance, and become a *fedayee*, that person's life is presumed to have been "sacrificed," preceding and distinct from actual physical death. The word *fedayee*[24] means one who is willing to sacrifice, or one who has ransomed or sacrificed his own life for the sake of a higher cause; in contemporary usage, the cause has generally been one's coun-try or national struggle. As in religious analogues to this phenomenon, once a child's life has been ransomed or dedicated to the higher cause,[25] the mother no longer has a traditional motherly "claim" to the life of her child. In *Umm Saad*, Saad's mother has had to learn to adapt her motherly claim to Saad, and her impulse to protect him from harm, in the context of the armed struggle. Umm Saad asks the narrator if she should go to Saad's chief at the front and tell him to be sure to take care of him and protect him, and then asks if the narrator himself might do so for her. The narrator explains to Umm Saad that it makes no sense to ask anyone to keep a *fedayee* out of danger, since the defining function and most desirable task for a *fedayee* is to be sent to the front to fight, where he will most certainly be exposed to danger.[26]

The "willing sacrifice" of one's son to the cause has been conspicuously articulated as a substantial contribution by women to the Palestinian resistance, and its importance is valorized further if that son dies in battle, upon which the mother becomes *umm al-shahid*, or "the mother of the martyr." As Julie Peteet has discussed in considerable detail, the contribution of mothers of martyrs has been institutionally and ritually recognized in a wide variety of contexts and occasions, at funerals and on a number of religious and national holidays.[27] The particular ways in which this is manifest in communal contexts strongly reinforces the sense that both the loss and the "mother-son" relationship are collective. This seems to facilitate the wrenching transformation of a parent's indescribable and incomprehensible grief at the loss of a child, into a meaningful contribution that has its place in the broader context of the national struggle for survival.

One of the qualities that would enable a bereft parent or mother to transform such painful experiences in this manner is a ubiquitous one that runs through a great deal of Palestinian political and literary discourse of resistance, namely, the quality of *sumud*, or "steadfastness" in the face of adversity, the ability to withstand, to hold out against, to outlive or survive even the most difficult circumstances and experiences.[28] Although this feature is by no means attributed exclusively to women or mothers, it is manifest in its own specific and particular ways in articulations of "motherly" Palestinian resistance. The thread of steadfastness runs through the portrayal of the bride who proves resiliant even though her respective wedding night has turned into a catastrophe, the bride who is capable of physically reversing a pregnancy resulting from rape, and the bride who takes her own virginity when her bridegroom proves incapable of doing so. Mothers are seen as remaining steadfast in the traditional roles of providing, nurturing, and protecting, even when circumstances require that they substantially adapt these roles, and expand the scope of the "family" considered the rightful recipients of their "mothering" energies. Mothers are portrayed as steadfast and resilient in continuing to bear children, even though the national struggle requires the sacrifice and loss of the children they produce.

These and other representations of Palestinian motherhood have figured as a salient and vital part of the literary and political discourse of Palestinian nationalism and resistance, at times in ways that reinscribe the most traditional aspects of motherhood, and at others in ways that seem to challenge the boundaries of such conventional roles. With the field constantly changing and expanding to include threads of Islamist and other discourses, the long-term social and political ramifications of the varying appropriations of Palestinian motherhood are still unclear and remain to be seen.

NOTES

1. This is one of a number of poems by this Iraqi-born poet, who has lived in exile from Iraq for over thirty years. With his poetry banned throughout much of the Arab world, his works have been pushed underground, and they enjoy an astonishingly wide circulation on *samizdat* cassette tapes of live performances by him, and in informal publications. He is notorious for his open criticism and harpooning of Arab leaders.

2. Most of the following discussion will treat appropriations of mothers as "mothers of sons" as opposed to mothers of daughters or of children in general, since it is portrayals of mothers of sons that are most commonly and persistently articulated.

3. Such as the well-known line of Iraqi poet Abd al-Wahhab al-Bayaati, "I want a woman, a homeland . . . ," among countless other examples.

4. *"Watariyat Layliya."*

5. It is important to note that al-Nawaab's dramatically emotive and confrontational style of performance of his poetry augments the intensity of its effect on listeners.

6. The reference here is not to Palestinian men, who are implicitly subsumed within the construct of a feminized and dominated Palestine, but rather men and male leaders from the rest of the Arab world.

7. *Urs bil-Jalil.*

8. With particular reference to Palestinian women in refugee camps in Lebanon, see Julie Peteet, "Authenticity and Gender: The Presentation of Culture," in *Arab Women: Old Boundaries, New Frontiers*, ed. Judith Tucker (Bloomington: Indiana University Press, 1993); Julie Peteet; *Gender in Crisis: Women and the Palestinian Resistance Movement* (New York: Columbia University Press, 1991).

9. *"Jisr al-Mabahij al-Qadima,"* composed and performed shortly after 1976.

10. Guerrilla fighter.

11. Ghassan Kanafani, *Umm Saad* (Beirut: Mu àssasat al-Abhath al-Àrabiyya, 1969).

12. *Umm Saad*, p. 27.

13. Kanafani, *Umm Saad*, p. 70.

14. For a detailed account of the various networks of women's centers, with discussion of party or faction affiliation, class composition, and more extensive description of activities, see, for example, Souad Dajani, "Palestinian Women Under Israeli Occupation: Implications for Development," in Tucker, ed., *Arab Women: Old Boundaries, New Frontiers*. See also Phillipa Strum *The Women Are Marching: The Second Sex and the Palestinian Revolution* (New York: Lawrence Hill Books, 1992).

15. While in several of the older, more established urban women's centers these food production enterprises are quite large and extensive, many of these "facto-

ries" in towns, villages and refugee camps are far more modest in scale, sometimes confined to one small room.

16. The preceding brief sketch of women's activities during the *intifada* is by no means exhaustive, but is meant to summarize the most common, salient and sustained of women's modes of participation facilitated through the networks of women's centers. It is based on my visits to such centers, the most recent of these being in the summer of 1992, as well as extensive conversations with women involved in various capacities at these centers.

17. Palestinian women have participated in the *intifada* as well as in other periods and contexts of national resistance in a variety of ways that are not extensions of "mothering" roles, but that is not the focus of this article.

18. To what extent these expanded venues for women will be sustained beyond the context of focused national struggle remains to be seen.

19. Allusion here is made to the tents of the refugee camps and the tents of the guerrilla encampments, implying that the tents of the *fedayeen* are different from, and preferable to, the tents of the refugee camps. The implication is that it would be "preferable" to be providing food for her child in the guerrilla tent than to those at the "home" tent, although she is ultimately compelled by the duty of the "home" tent.

20. Kanafani, *Umm Saad*, p. 28. Representations of women's role in the national resistances struggles as providers of food to soldiers or guerrilla fighters are, of course, found in other literatures as well. In Assia Djebar's *Fantasia: An Algerian Cavalcade* (London: Quartet Books, 1985), which describes Algerian peasant women's participation in the resistance against the French, providing food to freedom fighters figures prominently.

21. Kanafani, *Umm Saad*, p. 28.

22. Kanafani, *Umm Saad*, pp. 37–42.

23. It is common to find artistic portrayals of women carrying a baby in one arm and a gun in another. Most of the traditional depictions of fighters are male: among baskets full of small copper enamel pins of individual *milaththamin*— young male fighters with a black and white *kaffieh* headgear wrapped around their heads concealing all but their eyes. But one can find a very small number of these in which the fighters are clearly female, with eyes conspicuously outlined with eye kohl.

24. In standardized transcription, *fidaai*, but I have used the form more familiar to English readers throughout the present essay.

25. In certain Biblical narratives, for example, in return for a miraculous and often prayed-for birth, a child is promised and "sacrificed" to the service of God.

26. See Peteet, "Authenticity and Gender," pp. 54–58.

27. See Peteet, "Authenticity and Gender," pp. 54–58.

28. Raja Shehadeh's *Samed: The Diary of a West Bank Palestinian* (New York: Adama Books, 1984) is one of a number of works that pointedly explore the different layers and manifestations of *sumud*, here within the specific context of life in the Occupied Territories.

Making a Spectacle

The Mothers of the Plaza de Mayo

Diana Taylor

A rm in arm, wearing their white head scarves, the Mothers of the Plaza de Mayo slowly walk around the Plaza de Mayo, Argentina's central square. Some carry huge placards with the smiling faces of their missing children. Others hang small photographs around their necks. Turning their bodies into walking billboards, they carry banners demanding *"Aparición con vida"* — that their children be brought "back alive." On any given Thursday afternoon at 3:30, hundreds of women meet in the square to demand justice for the human rights violations committed by the brutal military dictatorship that abducted, tortured, and permanently "disappeared" 30,000 Argentineans between 1976 and 1983, a period that came to be known as the "Dirty War." The plaza, facing the presidential palace, lies in the heart of Buenos Aires' financial and economic district. Businessmen and politicians hurry to and fro, sometimes crossing the street to distance themselves from the Mothers. The women continue to talk and comfort each other as they walk, stopping every so often to gather around the microphone and loudspeakers from which they and their leader, Hebe de Bonafini, broadcast their accusations to the country's president. *Where are our children? We want them back alive! Why did their torturers and murders get away with murder? When will justice be done?* Until these issues are resolved, the women claim, the Dirty War will not be over. Nor will their demonstrations.

The spectacle of elderly women in white scarves carrying placards with the huge faces of their missing children has become an icon of women's resistance movements, especially in Latin America where their group has become the model for dozens of similar grassroots, human rights organizations. This essay focuses on how the Mothers of the Plaza de Mayo staged their opposition to the three consecutive military juntas that controlled Argentina between 1976 and 1983. While much has been written on the Mother's movement, few people have looked at how their spectacle fit into or contested the military junta's spectacle of national identity and cohesion. As the political Fathers of the nation persecuted and killed its opposition in the name of Christian, western and family values, the Mothers made visible the violence and hypocrisy that underwrote the junta's "process of national reorganization."

In its first pronouncement immediately following the coup (literally, *blow*), published on the front page of a major centrist daily paper, *La Nación*, on March 24, 1976, the junta declared itself the "supreme organ of the Nation" ready to "fill the void of power" embodied by Perón's widow, María Estela Martínez de Perón ("Isabelita"), Argentina's constitutional president. With a show of muscle, the junta undertook its exercise in national body building, determined to transform the "infirm," inert, Argentine masses into an authentic, implicitly masculine, "national being." The military heralded its accession to power as the "dawning of a fecund epoch," although the generative process was not, as it recognized, strictly speaking "natural." "Isabelita's" government was sick; its "productive apparatus" was exhausted; "natural" solutions were no longer sufficient to insure a full "recuperation." As Argentina's military leaders made clear in their first blueprint to their "process of national reorganization," opposition would be fought in interior and private spaces. If need be, the Motherland would be turned upside down and inside out, but both "open and hidden subversion would be eradicated."

The military represented itself as a disciplined masculine body, aggressively visible, all surface, identifiable by its uniforms, ubiquitous, on parade for all the world to see. The display of the military leaders in church or with the Catholic archbishops aligned military and sacred power. Staging order was perceived as a way of making order happen. The junta's display both reenacted and constituted the new social order: all male, Catholic and strictly hierarchical. The unholy trinity—Army, Navy and Air Force—were depicted as one entity, set apart as in religious iconography, the embodiment of national aspirations of grandeur. They spoke as one central, unified subject; their "we" supposedly included everyone. Visually, the spectacle affirmed the centrality of the junta and emphasized the importance of hierarchy and rank by distancing the great leaders from their undifferentiated followers. As opposed to the highlighted images of the junta leaders in isolation, their subordinates were presented in linear formations of seemingly identical bodies in military attire. The military body was represented as alert, always ready for action, always under control. But it also presented itself, conspicuously and perhaps even consciously, as a threateningly sexualized phallic body/machine. Soldiers would drive up and down the streets of Buenos Aires flashing their machine guns out of the car windows. Passers-by might at any moment be confronted by a weapon thrust in their faces.

From its opening address, the junta made explicit that the maternal image of the Patria or Motherland justified the civil violence. The military claimed it had to save "her," for "she" was being "raped," "penetrated" and "infiltrated" by her enemies.[1] But "she" was also the site of the conflict, as the Dirty War was carried out in the interstices of the Patria, in her very entrails. General Jorge Videla, President of the junta, declared that the Patria was "bleeding to death. When it most urgently needs her children, more and more of them are submerged in her blood."[2] But it is interesting to note that *Patria*, which comes from *padre* or father, does not mean "fatherland" in Spanish. Rather, the word Patria signals the image of motherland as envisioned by patriarchy. Thus, the word itself alerts us to the dangerously slippery positioning of the "feminine" in this discourse. There is no woman behind the maternal image invoked by the military. The term *Patria* merely projects the masculinist version of maternity—patriarchy in drag. In the name of the Patria, this non-existent yet "pure" feminine image, the military justified its attack on its own population. However, depicting the physical site of violence as feminine had devastating repercussions on the lives of real-life women. The very notion of the feminine was split in two—into the "good" woman and the "bad" woman. On the one hand, the junta honored the symbolic image of pure motherhood associated with the Patria, the "good" woman, and made clear to women that their role was also to be "pure," that is, nonpolitical, mothers confined to the private sphere. On the other hand, active women were "bad" women, associated with deviance and subversion. Women who were not content to stay home were often targeted as enemies of the State. "Subversives," the military stressed, were not only those who bore arms against the government—any and all "ideological" opposition constituted a crime. The crimes ranged from progressive Catholicism to Protestantism and Judaism, from alcoholism and prostitution to divorce and homosexuality, from human rights to women's rights and pacifism. Furthermore, anyone associated with or sympathetic to this expanding and amorphous group of "subversives" might well become the next victim.

During the Dirty War—so called because it was a terrorist civil conflict rather than a conventional war with two armed sides that abide by the international rules of war—there were mothers who were willing to go along with the junta's version of "good" women. They supported the military's mission and encouraged it to exercise even more control over the public good. In 1977, the League of Mothers of Families, sounding much like the Christian Right in

the United States today, urged their rulers to ensure that "education strengthened traditional and Christian values" and asked that "the media be truly
instruments of culture, diffusing good examples and healthy entertainment."[3]
The media, under military direction, not surprisingly carried interviews and
reports on "good" women, those who were happiest in the home, looking after
their children, those whose gravest concern was buying groceries at reasonable prices. Mothers were warned that their children were in grave danger
because the *guerrillas* were just waiting to lure their children into subversion.
("Today, education is free, at least classes are. But what happens when he
leaves school? What alternatives does a boy have? He vegetates, emigrates, or
grabs a machine gun. Is this the country we want for our children?")[4] Soon,
however, even traditional roles for women were called into question. Notions
of a woman's domestic sphere, conceived as a nonpolitical space, "disappeared" as women were accused of not properly controlling their children.
The radio, television, and magazines bombarded women with the question,
"Señora, do you know where your children are?" The junta demanded that
women put State interests over familial bonds. The nocturnal raids on homes,
the abduction of family members, the practice of raping and torturing loved
ones in front of each other revealed the armed forces' uneasiness with the
family as a separate space and organizational unit. As the junta had warned, all
the interior and formerly "private" spaces were turned inside out.

The resistant female was represented as embodying opposition. The military accused her of using motherhood as a shield to cover her subversive
activities. One article, "The Guerrilleras: The Bloody Story of Women in
Terrorism," published in the pro-military magazine *Somos*, states the following:

Little by little we have got the Argentineans to understand that the word "war"
reflects a reality. Now we have to get them to understand that war is not peculiar
to men. In the guerrilla, the woman is *as* or *more* important than the man. She
serves as ideologue, she serves as a combatant, she infiltrates all spaces (even the
most innocent, the most frivolous, the most banal), she seduces, lies, deforms, gets
information, indoctrinates, "keeps a lookout," and she defends herself by attacking the most permeable facets of human sensibility: the respect for pregnancy,
maternity and natural feminine fragility.[5]

Guerrilleras, or female guerrillas, the article states, are "unhappy, lonely
adolescents" who are initially led astray by a man, but then want to "be" like
a man, and finally want to overtake men altogether (p. 13). The *guerrillera* is
promiscuous ("*mujer de muchos hombres*," p. 14), and she uses her sexuality
as a weapon of war: "She will try to get pregnant because she knows that she
will be handled more gently. She will hold her son in front of her like a shield"
(p. 14). She will falsely charge that she has been raped, "creating thus a conflict
between her interrogator and his boss" (p. 14). The journalist quotes a high-

ranking military official who claims, "As far as I'm concerned, women are worse than men" (p. 15). However, the article goes on to gloat that once in a while, women become live bait in the military's attempt to catch their male partners.

The gendering of the enemy on a metaphoric level played itself out on the physical bodies of those detained during the junta's seven years in power. In the concentration camp known as Olimpo (Olympus), the distinction between "good" women and "bad" women was made brutally evident as military soldiers tortured female prisoners in front of the image of the Virgin Mary.[6] The negative image of the "public" or active woman provoked and enabled the systematic assault on the reproductive organs of all females held in captivity. Women were reduced to their sexual "parts." Testimonies by survivors repeatedly allude to guns shot into vaginas and wombs, to pounded breasts and buttocks. Abducted women, who made up a third of the 30,000 victims, were raped as a matter of course. Pregnant women, who made up 3 percent of the disappeared, were often abducted, raped and tortured simply because they were pregnant.[7] If and when they gave birth, they were beaten, humiliated, and often killed. After the fall of the dictatorship and the famous "Trial of the Generals" (1985), during which the leaders of the three juntas were put on trial for crimes against humanity, one of the survivors, the physicist Adriana Calvo de Laborde, recounted her ordeal. She was seven and a half months pregnant when she was abducted. She was beaten and tortured. When she was due to deliver, she was shoved, blindfolded and handcuffed, into the backseat of a police car. "Lucrecia," one of the very few women known to have tortured during the Dirty War, sat in the back with her. In spite of Calvo de Laborde's screams that her child was being born, the guards did not stop the car, nor did Lucretia do anything to help her. The baby, a girl, was born and fell onto the floor. Finally Calvo de Laborde was taken to another concentration camp where a physician looked her over while the baby was abandoned on a table and the guards looked on. "With one shove, he took out the placenta and threw it on the floor as he insulted me. . . . They made me get up, they brought me two buckets of water and made me scrub the floor and wash the stretcher. They made me clean everything. I had to this in front of the guards, who were all laughing."[8] She was naked—a spectacle for their amusement and deprecation. Finally, the men allowed her to wash her dress and put it on. She was then permitted to pick up and care for her daughter.

Children born in prison were usually killed or given away to military families.[9] The military also tried to destroy mothers in captivity, not only by torturing pregnant women, and stealing the children born to mothers who were disappeared, but also by threatening to kill the children of all disappeared women and by allowing women prisoners in jail no physical contact with their children (a privilege enjoyed by male prisoners). As Alicia Partnoy—one of the few "disappeared" who "reappeared"—states, the military "attacked us as mothers, in our motherhood."[10] Thus the armed forces enshrined the glory of "motherhood" in the image of the Patria even as they targeted mothers and familial bonds as a way of breaking down the social fabric.

In the midst of this brutal political climate, when most members of the opposition were either in exile, in hiding, in concentration camps or in jails, the Mothers went to the Plaza de Mayo, the most public space in Argentina, to protest that the military was "disappearing" their children. The Mothers attempted to manipulate the maternal image that was already rigorously controlled by the State. They claimed that it was precisely their maternal responsibilities as "good" mothers that took them to the plaza in search of their children.

For those unfamiliar with the Mothers' movement, here is a brief overview. In 1977, fourteen women first took to the plaza to collectively demand information concerning the whereabouts of their missing children. They had met in government offices, prisons and courts looking for any sign of their sons and daughters. Little by little, the women came to identify as a group, and called themselves simply the "Mothers of the Plaza de Mayo." They started wearing white head kerchiefs to recognize each other and to be recognized by onlookers. The Mothers realized that only by being visible could they be politically effective. Only by being visible could they stay alive in a society in which all opposition was annihilated by the military. The role of "mother" offered the women a certain security in the initial phase of their movement. The junta, which legitimated its mission with the rhetoric of Christian and family values, could hardly gun down defenseless mothers in public. So it tried dismissing the Mothers as "crazy old women" or *locas* and threatened the women individually in their homes and on their way to and from the plaza. But even after the Mothers were threatened, they returned to the plaza every Thursday afternoon to walk counterclockwise around the obelisk in front of the presidential Casa Rosada.

Gradually, the number of women grew. They belonged to different social classes, though the majority were working class. They represented different religious groups and came from different parts of Argentina. In July there were 150 *Madres*. Public response to their activities was mixed. Most Argentines tried to ignore them, crossing the street to distance themselves as much as possible from the women. Some passers-by insulted them. Others whispered support and solidarity. On October 5, 1977, the Mothers placed an ad in *La Prensa* demanding the "truth" about 237 disappeared persons, accompanied by pictures of the victims and the signatures and identity card numbers of the women in the movement. They got no reply. Ten days later, hundreds of women delivered a petition with 24,000 signatures demanding an investigation into the disappearances. The police tried to disperse them—spraying tear gas at the women, shooting bullets into the air and detaining over 300 of them for questioning. Foreign correspondents, the only ones to cover the event, were also arrested.

News of the Mothers and their anti-junta activities soon spread internationally. The battle for visibility commanded more and more spectators. Largely due to the public recognition and financial support from human rights groups from the Netherlands, Sweden, France and Italy, the Mothers were able to survive politically and financially. Amnesty International sent a mission to Argentina in 1976 to report on the disappeared. In 1977, President Carter sent Patricia Derian, U.S. Assistant Secretary of State, to investigate the accusations of human rights abuses. She estimated that 3,000 people had been executed and 5,000 disappeared.[11] The United States cut military aid to Argentina and canceled $270 million in loans. The junta realized that they could not dismiss the Mothers as "madwomen"; they had to get rid of them. So in December 1977, the junta infiltrated the Mothers' organization and kidnapped and disappeared 12 women, including their leader, Azucena de Vicenti, and two French nuns who were working with the Mothers' movement. But in spite of the danger, the Mothers returned to the plaza. During 1978, the military intensified its harassment and detentions. In 1979, it became impossible for the Mothers to enter the plaza, which was cordoned off by heavily armed police. The women would stand around the plaza and raid it—dashing across the square before the police could stop them, only to remind the world and themselves that this was still their space.

In 1979, the Organization of American States (OAS) sent the Inter-American Human Rights Commission to Argentina. The Mothers brought women from all over the country to testify before the commission in Buenos Aires. As many as 3000 people lined up at a time to meet with the commission. The junta, unable to block the investigation, launched its own counterattack, inscribing slogans on people, and mimicking the visual strategies the Mothers used. They made up posters and used people's bodies as walking billboards marked with a pun on human rights: "*Somos derechos y humanos*" ("We are right and human"). That same year, practically banished from the plaza, the Mothers formed the Association of the Madres de Plaza de Mayo. In January 1980, the Mothers returned to the plaza, ready to face death before relinquishing it again.

The Mother's performance of motherhood tried to bridge the schism between the "good" woman and the "bad" woman belabored by the military. The women consciously modeled themselves on the Virgin Mary, the ultimate mother who transcends the public/private bind by carrying her privacy with her even in public. Thus, Christian and Jewish women alike initially played the Mater Dolorosa and exploited a system of representations and stereotypes that had so effectively limited most forms of female visibility and expression: "At first they marched as if in ritual procession: faces serious, eyes turned upward in supplication, heads covered . . . peaceful, rapt, pleading" (Alejandro Diago, *Hebe Bonafini: Memoria y Esperanza* [Buenos Aires: Ediciones Dialéctia, 1988], p. 29). The virginal role allowed the women to perform traditionally acceptable "feminine" qualities—self-sacrifice, suffering, irrationality. Even as they took one of the most daring steps imaginable in their particular political arena, they affirmed their passivity and powerlessness. Yet even that virginal role—sanctified by Argentine society though it was—did not protect the women for long. The women's public exposure resulted in their being ostracized from the church. They had gone beyond the representational constraints of the role: pain was permissible, perhaps, but not anger. Silence, maybe, but not protest. As one of the church leaders, Monsignor Quarracino, commented, "I can't imagine the Virgin Mary yelling, protesting and planting the seeds of hate when her son, our Lord, was torn from her hands."[12]

Over the years, the Mothers' notion of motherhood had gradually became political rather than biological. They came to consider themselves the mothers of all the disappeared, not just their own offspring. Their spectacles became larger and increasingly dramatic. They organized massive manifestations and marches, some of them involving up to 200,000 people: the March of Resistance in 1981, and again the following year; in 1982 the March for Life and the March for Democracy; in 1983, at the end of the last military junta, they plastered Buenos Aires with the names and silhouettes of the disappeared. However, even with the return of a democratic government, their demands for information about the fate of the children and justice for their tormentors had not been addressed. In spite of the Trial of the Generals, only a handful of the military leaders had been sentenced to prison terms. All those who had served as torturers and on the paramilitary "task forces" that abducted, tortured and killed thousands of people were still free. In 1986, when it became clear that Raúl Alfonsín's elected government would do nothing meaningful to punish those responsible for the atrocities, the Mothers staged the March for Human Rights as a procession of masks.

The Mothers spoiled the junta's parade by responding to the military spectacle with a spectacle that inverted the focus. What had been invisible before— from domestic women to "subversives"—was now visible for the world to see. Through their bodies, they wanted to show the absence/presence of all those who had disappeared without a trace, without leaving a body. Clearly, the confrontation between the Mothers and the military centered on the physical and symbolic location of the missing body—object of exchange in this battle of images. While the military attempted to make their victims invisible and anonymous by burying them in unmarked graves, dumping their bodies into the sea or cutting them up and burning them in ovens, the Mothers insisted that the disappeared had names and faces. They were people; people did not simply disappear; their bodies, dead or alive, were somewhere; someone had done something to them. Instead of the military's ahistorical forgetting, the Mothers inscribed the time and dates of the disappearances. Instead of dismembering, remembering. The Mothers challenged the generals' claim to history by writing themselves and the "disappeared" into the narrative, literally as well as figuratively. Their bodies, inscribed with names, dates and faces were "written into the message," to borrow a phrase from Ross Chambers.[13] Opposed to the image projected by the junta of a lone, heroic male leaving family and community behind, the Mothers emphasized community and family ties. Instead of the military's performance of hierarchy, represented by means of rigid, straight rows, the Mothers' circular movements around the plaza, characterized by their informal talk and pace, bespoke values based on egalitarianism and communication. While the soldiers' uniforms, paraphernalia and body language emphasized the performative aspects of gender, the Mothers too were highly conscious of the importance of their gender role, specifically their maternal role, and played it accordingly. The Mothers also had their "uniforms," though these may not have been immediately identifiable as such. They presented themselves as elderly, physically weak and sexually nonactive women. Yet they resisted even the most brutal treatment. When the military tried to force the women from the plaza, they marked their presence indelibly by painting white kerchiefs around the circle where they usually walked. Instead of the empty streets and public spaces mandated by the military curfew, the Mothers orchestrated the return of the repressed. Buenos Aires was once again filled with people: spectacular bodies, ghostly, looming figures who refused to stay invisible. The public spaces overflowed with demonstrators as the terrorized population gradually followed the Mothers' example and took to the streets.

However, redefining motherhood was a painful process for the Mothers. Individually, many of the women admitted that they had lost hope of finding their children alive: "We know we're not going to find our children by going to the square, but it's an obligation we have to all the *desaparecidos*" (Fisher, *Mothers of the Disappeared*, p. 153). The tension between the biological death of their children and the living political issue of disappearance and criminal politics placed them in a conflicted situation. Were they now simply the mothers of dead children? If so, should they claim the dead bodies offered up by forensic specialists, accept compensation for their loss, and get on with their lives? Or did they need to hold onto the image of the "disappeared" in order to bring the military to justice and continue their political movement? Could the Mothers, now a political organization, survive the death of their children? By 1986, the dilemma had split the group in two.[14] The division continues to shape the political movement. The group that now calls itself the

Madres de la Plaza de Mayo, headed by Hebe de Bonafini (as opposed to the "Linea Fundadora" or the "Founding Group" of the fourteen original members, headed by Renee Epelbaum) felt committed to keeping the *"desaparecidos"* alive. They continue to demand *"Aparición con vida"* ("Back alive") for all the disappeared. They refuse to give up the struggle until justice has been served. The Linea Fundadora, though accepting that their children are dead, continues to work to bring the perpetrators to justice. However, the women felt that many of the working-class members of the organization needed the economic compensation offered by the government in order to keep up their struggle. Members of both groups travel, lecture abroad and document their history. Both groups—made up mainly of women in their sixties and seventies—continue to march around the Plaza de Mayo.

Commentators find it hard to agree on the short- and long-term effects of the Mothers' activism. During the Dirty War, the Mothers provided the families of the disappeared a model of resistance to atrocity as well as a network of communication and support. The Mothers would find out information about a detained or disappeared person and transmit it nationally. The women raised money to allow families around the country to travel to ask about their missing children or to visit a political prisoner. The Mothers' organization contributed money to raise the children of the disappeared who had been left behind with relatives or friends. In the long term, however, some commentators stress that the Mothers changed little in Argentina. There were fewer women voted into positions of power after the Dirty War than before. Some say that the Mothers' grassroots movement lacked any lasting organizational structure. The women undoubtedly called international attention to civil rights violations taking place in Argentina. But that, in itself, did not topple the dictatorship. The downfall of the military came with its invasion of the Islas Malvinas, the British-owned Falkland Islands that lie off the coast of Argentina. Plagued by a crashing economy and an increasingly irate population, the military decided to bolster their popular support by taking back the islands. The armed forces miscalculated Britain's resolve to keep the islands—for one thing, the islands have substantial oil deposits, and for another, Margaret Thatcher herself needed a boost in popular opinion. The humiliating defeat of the Argentine military, which was also held responsible for the deaths of hundreds of very young conscripts who had not been trained or prepared for war, brought down the last of the three juntas.

Moreover, though the Mothers's spectacle was a powerful manifestation of personal courage and moral resistance to oppression, it did little to stop international aid to the armed forces. Though Carter took the atrocity seriously and cut aid to Argentina, the United States under Reagan increased its support of the armed forces and their "war" on subversion.

So how are we to assess and understand the Mothers' movement? Commentators interested in the Mothers' and other women's political groups in and outside Latin America have pointed out the many contradictions posed by their movement—it attacked the legitimacy of the military but left a restrictive patriarchal system basically unchallenged. The Mothers won significant political power, but they claim not to want that power, at least not for themselves but only for their children. The women's shared struggle for missing children bridged class and religious barriers in Argentina, but the Mothers have not politicized those issues. They recognize that "women are doubly oppressed, especially in Catholic-Hispanic countries" (Fisher, *Mothers of the Disappeared*, p. 155), and they have formed alliances with women's coalitions in Nicaragua, El Salvador, Uruguay, Colombia, Chile and other Latin American countries. But they are not feminists, if by feminism one refers to the politicization of the women's subordinate status. Hebe de Bonafini states the following: "I don't think the Mothers are feminists, but we point a way forward for the liberation of women. We support the struggle of women against this *machista* world and sometimes this means that we have to fight against men. But we also have to work together with men to change this society. We aren't feminists because I think feminism, when its taken too far, is the same as *machismo*."[15] The Mothers left the confines of their homes, physically and politically, but they have not altered the politics of the home—for example, the gendered division of labor. After coming home from their demonstrations most of them still cooked and did housework for their remaining family, even in those cases in which the husbands were at home full time. The Mothers took to the streets in order to protect their children and families; nonetheless, their political activity estranged many of them from the surviving members of their families who were not prepared to accept the women's new roles: "They say if you stop going to the square, you're one of us again. My family now are the Mothers of the Plaza de Mayo," says one Mother (Fisher, *Mothers of the Disappeared*, p. 156). Having left home, they have established a new *casa* (or "home") for their new family. There, they continue their unpaid labor, their political activity. There, too, they nurture the young people who come to talk to them: "We cook for them, we worry about their problems, we look out for them much as we did for our children" (Diago, *Hebe Bonafini*, p. 187).

How do we explain these contradictions? Some of them can be understood, I believe, by distinguishing between the Mothers' performance of motherhood and the essentialist notions of motherhood sometimes attributed to them and that, in all fairness, the Mothers themselves often accentuate. Although much has been written about the Mothers' strategy of politicizing motherhood, little has been said about the fact that motherhood—as a role—had already been socialized and politicized in their patriarchal society. What we see, then, are conflicting performances of motherhood, one supporting the military's version of social order, one defying it.[16] Once the Mothers decided to march, their self-representation was as theatrical as the military's. The Mothers' movement did not begin when the individual mothers became acquainted in their search for their children. It originated when the women consciously decided to protest and agitate *as* mothers. That *as* marks the conceptual distance between the essentialist notion of motherhood attributed to the Mothers and the self-conscious manipulation of the maternal role that makes the movement the powerful and intensely dramatic spectacle that it has been. The women, most of whom had no political background or experience, realized that they were a part of a national spectacle and decided to actively play the role that had traditionally been assigned to them—the "good" women who look after their children. Yet, they shifted the site of their enactment from the private sphere—where it could be constructed as essentialist—to the public—where it became a bid for political recognition and a direct challenge to the junta. The Mothers' decision to make their presence visible in the plaza, stage center so to speak, was a brilliant and courageous move. While the plaza had often been used as a political stage throughout Argentina's history, no one had used it as the Mothers did, much less during a state of siege in which public space was heavily policed. They perceived and literally acted out the difference between motherhood as an individual identity (which for many of them it was) and motherhood as a collective, political performance that would allow women to protest in the face of a criminal dictatorship. The role of mother was attractive, not because it was "natural," but because it was viable and practical. It offered the women a certain legitimacy and authority in a society that values mothers almost to the exclusion of all other women. It offered them visibility in a representational system that rendered most women invisible. For once, they manipulated the images that had previously controlled them.

Looking beyond the maternal role, however, and looking at the individual women who walked away from the plaza, I see a group of women who redefined the meaning of "mothers," "family" and "home" in a patriarchal society. Mothers, flesh and blood women, are now more free to act and take to the streets. They can be bold, independent, political and outraged even as they take on the role of the submissive, domestic creature. Their new "home" is a negotiated space; their new "family" is founded on political rather than biological ties. What has been accepted as the Mothers' traditionalism in fact has more to do with the negotiated alliances advocated by feminists. The women may choose to adhere to their old ways, recreate a "family," and cook for the younger members of the group, but that is now a choice they exercise. Their political activism, explicitly designed to empower the new "Man," in fact made new people out of the Mothers, people with options. As Hebe says, "For me cooking for twenty is the same as cooking for one, and we like to eat together because this is also a part of our struggle and our militancy. I want to continue being the person I've always been. Sometimes I'm criticized for wearing a housecoat and slippers in public but I'm not going to change. Of course my life is different" (Fisher, *Mothers of the Disappeared*, p. 158). The performance of motherhood has created a distance between "I" and the "person I've always been." It is as if the women's conscious performance of motherhood—limited though it was—freed them from the socially restrictive role of motherhood that had previously kept them in their place. The performance offered that disruptive space, that moment of transition between the "I" who was a mother and the "I" who chooses to perform motherhood.

The performative aspect of their movement, though seldom commented upon, was a politically vital and personally liberating aspect of the Mothers' activism in several ways. For one, the demonstrations offered the women a way of coping with their grief and channeling it into life-affirming action. Rather than trivialize or eclipse their loss, the performative nature of their demonstrations gave the women a way of dealing with it. Much as in the case of mourning rites, aesthetic distancing is an enabling response to pain, not its negation. For another, the ritualistic and "restored" nature of their demonstrations succeeded in drawing much-needed public attention to their cause, both nationally and internationally. This put them in contact with human rights organizations worldwide and provided them with financial and moral support as well as the much-needed legitimacy to offset the junta's claims that the women were only raving "madwomen." Moreover, the "restored" nature of their public action in itself was a way of restoring the disappeared into the public sphere, of making visible their absence. And, by bringing motherhood out of the domestic closet, the Mothers revealed the predicament facing women in Argentina and the world over. Traditionally, mothers have been idealized as existing somehow beyond or above the political arena. Confined to the home, they have been made responsible for their children. But what happens to the mothers who, by virtue of that same responsibility to their children, must go looking for them outside the home and confront the powers that be? Do they cease to be mothers? Or must onlookers renounce notions of mothers as apolitical? Their transgression of traditional roles made evident how restrictive and oppressive those roles had been. Thus their performance of mothers as activists challenged traditional maternal roles and called attention to the fact that motherhood was a social, not just biological, construct.

The Mothers' performance, like all performances, challenged the onlooker. Would the national and international spectators applaud their actions, or look away? Join their movement or cross the street to avoid them? One letter to the editor of *La Nación* asked the authorities to put an end "to the sad spectacle that we must endure week after week" (June 1, 1981, p. 6). But there were spectators who were able to respond as reliable audiences/witnesses, either because they saw the event from a safe distance or because they felt they had nothing more to lose. They helped introduce different perspectives and disrupt the show the military was staging about itself. The fact that the Madres could not do *everything*—that is, seriously challenge patriarchal authority—does not mean that they did *nothing* to ruin their parade. The Mothers' efficacy and survival relied on capturing the attention of spectators—Argentines who might dare to reinterpret the junta's version of events, as well as the foreign spectators who might feel compelled to bring pressure to bear on their governments.

The Mothers had the courage to show the world what was happening in Argentina. They still continue their walk around the Plaza at 3:30 on Thursday afternoons. They vow to do so until the government officially explains what happened to their missing children and brings their murderers to justice. There has been no closure. The drama of disappearance is not over.

NOTES

1. President Videla of the junta in his first address to the nation on March 25, 1976, claimed that the "subversives" were "raping" the society (*La Nación*, p. 14), and other military spokespeople warned against "Marxist penetration" and "ideological infiltration" (*La Nación*, Aug. 5, 1976, p. 1).

2. In Oscar Troncoso, *El Proceso de Reorganizaíon Nacional*, vol. 1 (Buenos Aires: Centro Editor de America Latin, 1984), p. 59.

3. Andres Avellanada, *Censura, Autoritarismo y Cultura: Argentina 1960–1983*, vol. 2 (Buenos Aires: Biblioteca Politica Argentina, 1986), p. 148.

4. From the weekly news magazine *Gente*, May 6, 1976, pp. 12–13.

5. Carlos Penguin, "Las Guerrilleras: La cruenta historia de la mujer en el terrorismo,"*Somos* (Oct. 12, 1976):10–17.

6. Ximena Bunster-Burotto, "Surviving Beyond Fear: Women and Torture in Latin America," in June Nash and Helen Safa, *Women and Change in Latin America* (Boston: Bergin & Garvey Publishers, Inc., 1986), p. 299.

7. See Horacio Verbitsky's *Rodolfo Walsh y la prensa clandestina 1976–1978* (Buenos Aires: Ediciones de la Vrraca, 1985), pp. 87–88.

8. Adriana Calvo de Laborde's testimony in *El Libro del Juicio: Testimonies* (Buenos Aires: Editorial Testigo, 1985), pp. 38–39.

9. General Ramón J. Camps explained the rationale for disappearing babies: "It wasn't people that disappeared, but subversives. Personally I never killed a child; what I did was to hand over some of them to charitable organizations so that they could be given new parents. Subversive parents educate their children for subversion. This has to be stopped" (quoted in Jo Fisher, *Mothers of the Disappeared* (Boston: South End Press, 1989), p. 102). Verbitsky cites several instances in which children were killed by the military. In one case, witnesses heard one of the members of the armed forces who was taking away a ten-year-old boy, "We'd better kill you now, so you don't grow up." The boy was never seen again (Verbitsky, *Rodolfo Walsh*, p. 62).

10. Redefining Motherhood Conference, Hanover, N.H., May 1993.

11. Figures quoted in John Simpson and Jana Bennett, *The Disappeared: Voices from a Secret War* (London: Robson Books, 1985), p. 279.

12. Quoted by Laura Rossi, "¿Cómo pensar a las Madres de Plaza de Mayo?," p. 149 in *Nuevo Texto Critico*, no. 4 (11), ed. Pratt and Morello Frosch (Stanford: Standford University Press, 1989).

13. Ross Chambers, "No Montagues Without Capulets: Some Thoughts on Cultural Identity," Public Lecture, School of Criticism and Theory, Darthmouth College, Summer 1992. My discussion later on "identity politics" and "cultural politics" is based in part on his observations.

14. I disagree with Ann Snitow's assessment in "A Gender Diary" (in *Rocking the Ship of State: Toward a Feminist Peace Politics*, ed. Adrienne Harris and Ynestra King (Boulder: Westview Press, 1989), that the Madres split "along the feminist divide." Both groups, as I see it, have an ambivalent relationship to feminism. According to the Madres de la Plaza faction, tensions started in the group after Alfonsín came to office at the end of 1983. The Linea Fundadora, they maintain, wanted to negotiate with Alfonsín and take a more pacifist line. There was also an election in the movement in January 1986, which intensified the suspicion and resentment among the women and provoked the final rupture.

15. In Jo Fisher, *Mothers of the Disappeared*, p. 158.

16. There was a pro-military league of mothers, who called themselves *La Liga de Madres de Familia*, that organized to ask the junta for a more forceful implementation of "family values": "Of our leaders we ask for legislation to protect and defend the family, the pillar of society: an ordinance in favor of education that secures traditional and Christian values, and the necessary means so that the media can be a true instrument of culture, broadcasting good example and healthy diversion" (Avellaneda, *Censura, Autoritarismo y Cultura: Argentina 1960–1983*, p. 148.)

Alicia Partnoy

A Portrait

Diana Taylor

When I got involved in politics after the military coup, I thought: "I'm doing this for my child, because I don't want her to grow up in this society." But at the same time, I, like other activist mothers, was torn. We are willing to put our lives on the line, but we don't want our children putting their lives on the line. And when we get into activism, we're putting their lives on the line. And we're depriving them—for the sake of their future and the future of all society—of the *present* in which we should be building a relationship with them.

Alicia Partnoy was abducted from her home in the middle of a hot, sunny afternoon in January 1977. In the months that followed the military coup of March 1976, thousands of Argentines, especially young people in their late teens and twenties, had been "disappeared," tortured in clandestine concentration camps, and killed. As uniformed military men dragged Alicia out, blindfolded, in broad daylight, her daughter, then a year and a half old, was left behind crying in the empty house. It would be months before Alicia, one of the few "disappeared" to miraculously "reappear," would know what became of her daughter. "The moment of detention," she says, "goes through my mind like a movie." This is one of the reasons that she describes the incident in the third person in her collection of autobiographical short stories, *The Little School: Tales of Disappearance & Survival in Argentina*: (Pittsburgh: Cleis Press, 1986): "She realized who was at the door and ran toward the backyard. She lost the first slipper in the corridor, before reaching the place where Ruth, her little girl, was standing. She lost the second slipper while leaping over the brick wall. By then the shouts and kicks at the door were brutal. Ruth burst into tears in the doorway" (pp. 25–26).

What had Alicia done to be targeted by the military? She was politically active in the university, one of the many students who believed in justice and in a democratic system. "My generation, people between sixteen and twenty-five, had grown up under military dictatorships. I entered the university in 1973, and we were all very excited about the possibility of change. At the university, we were trying to rewrite the curriculum, change the syllabi. We were tired of being taught things that were alien to our culture. I got involved in the Peronist movement, a movement which is so complex that, at times, it's even hard for me to understand it, but suffice it to say here that it has a left, center and right wing to it. A lot of the trade-unionists and professors involved in it were on the left, and we were working for social change." With the military coup of 1976, the possibility of change seemed remote. In her introduction to *The Little School*, Partnoy writes that after the coup, "[a]ttending school became hazardous. I had to pass between two soldiers who were sitting with machine guns at the entrance of the building. A highly ranked officer would request my I.D., check it against a list of "wanted" activists and search my belongings. I did not know when my name would appear on that list. I stopped going to classes" (Introduction to *The Little School*, p. 13).

Partnoy began handing out leaflets and painting slogans on walls. She recalls:

I made the decision to get involved—at this point we were still talking about options. But it was because of my daughter that I got involved, for her future. I remember my mother asking me, "but what about your child?" We all knew we could get arrested and disappeared. And I'd tell my mother, "It's because of my child that I am doing this." My daughter gave me strength. I was willing to risk everything for her. But that was because I wasn't alone; there was a whole movement. We were all eighteen and nineteen, we had kids and we were in college. I didn't want my child to grow up in a repressive society; I wanted a better world for her. I decided to stop breast-feeding her when she was about eight or nine months old, not because it was time but because I was afraid that I would be disappeared or arrested. I didn't want them to take me away without having gone through this process with her.

Alicia was taken to the "Little School," an old building near the headquarters of the army in her home town of Bahía Blanca which had been used for military training. She recalls:

They took me there blindfolded, and I remained blindfolded the whole time I was there. We couldn't talk to each other. We were constantly beaten and sexually harassed. We tried to beat the system. For example, I would try talking only once during a shift. When the guard was replaced, I'd try again. I, personally, was never tortured with electricity. I was lucky because the doctor wasn't there when I was brought to the Little School. So the torturers did not use electricity on us women. They were afraid that we might die on them, before our time. But I did hear them torturing my husband. They applied an electric cattle prod, 220 watts, to the most sensitive parts of his body. But it didn't occur to me that it was him—all that night I thought it was some animal screaming. My mind was protecting me.

"Sometimes people ask me if women are tortured worse than men. And I say, 'it's not even ethical to ask that question. Torture is torture is torture is torture.' But the military does tailor torture to women. They attack women sexually in torture sessions, but they also attack women through their motherhood. They tortured me psychologically by saying that they were going to kill my daughter." Alicia Partnoy did not know until months later that her neighbors had taken her daughter to live with her parents. "By severing the link between the mother and the child, they attack women in their most vulnerable spot. They destroy both the women and their children, and that's done very consciously. They destroy the women through their motherhood. In this concentration camp, there was a pregnant woman with me, Graciela Romero. They tortured her with electricity; on her way to the Little School, they applied electric shocks to her abdomen. They did that to pregnant women." When the children were born, many of them were given to military families who brought them up as their own. More than a decade after the fall of the dictatorship, the Grandmothers of the Plaza de Mayo continue to search for the four hundred disappeared children who were either born in concentration camps or kidnapped with their parents.

In April 1977, when she was in the Little School, the Mothers of the Plaza de Mayo started to march in front of the government buildings. The Mothers' demonstration reassured the disappeared who were still alive that people still cared. "It was very important to me—they brought me back to life, which is why I always say that the Mothers gave birth to me. In most cases, they did not recover their own children. After five months in the concentration camp, I miraculously reappeared and was sent to a jail for political prisoners."

The Mothers' movement also focused international attention on the situation in Argentina. Amnesty International, the Organization of American States and other human rights groups were beginning to get involved. The Argentine government chose to materialize some prisoners to show that, contrary to international accusations, it did keep political prisoners and treated them humanely. In jail, prisoners received better food and medical attention. The Red Cross was allowed to inspect the premises. The women's jail, Partnoy states, came to be known as the *vidriera* or showcase, designed to keep public attention away from the disappeared in the concentration camps. "We were there to be shown to the world."

While Partnoy's reemergence as a recognized political prisoner was a stra-tegical move on the part of the government, the disappeared who were killed also functioned as political pawns. As Partnoy puts it, "we were hostages, and the military used us according to their needs. They kept records, which of course they have either hidden or destroyed, in which they recorded very informed decisions of why they were keeping some of us alive, why they were killing most of us, and the ways they were doing it." Usually, it was the destruction of the "disappeared" rather than their well-being, that legitimated those in authority: "They took my friend Zulma and her boyfriend out of the concentration camp. They put them in a house, put them to sleep with an injection, then they shot them and scattered political flyers around them. They staged a fake confrontation in which soldiers inside the house shot at soldiers outside the house. Then they'd call the press. This was a common practice. After Argentina's return to democracy in 1983, the body of Zulma was shown to her mother. An autopsy was performed and it was clear that she had been killed at close range. There had been no confrontation with the army whatsoever. Most of the people in the concentration camp were never seen again." The fate of the prisoners in the concentration camps was closely tied to what was happening in Argentina at large. The "need" for more military force resulted in more fake confrontations with so-called armed terrorists. But when human rights organizations increased their pressure on the government it would deny charges of human rights violations by upgrading the "disap-peared" to political prisoners.

Alicia Partnoy, however, was one of the fortunate ones transferred to a jail for political prisoners, where she was kept for two and a half years without being charged with any wrongdoing. "Once we were in jail, in this women's prison in Buenos Aires, I was able to see my daughter through a thick glass. We had to speak through a microphone. We women prisoners were not allowed to touch our kids, though the male prisoners could—they had no glass, no mi-crophones. The guards could beat the men but they attacked us in other ways. The military tailored its way of destroying us. Women were not allowed to send short stories, poems, or drawings to our kids. That was our way of com-municating with them. But they always came back censored; the censors said they were escape plots."

The military's strategy, as Alicia Partnoy makes clear, was to attack three generations simultaneously—the target generation, their parents, and their children. Parents lived in fear of doing too much or too little for their disap-peared children. Were they putting their children at greater risk by demanding to know their whereabouts? Or were the ceaseless inquiries the only way to get them back? The military spread rumors that many of the political activists had fled abroad, thus tormenting parents with the hope that their offspring were still alive somewhere. Some members of the military concocted financial schemes to fleece the families of the disappeared by selling false information regarding the missing people. It continued to be painful, Partnoy notes, for parents like her own whose children had, in fact, reappeared: "It was very painful for my mother, first that I was disappeared and later that I was in prison. But it was hard too because she had to go through the painful routine of jail visitations with her granddaughter. When my daughter made an effort to touch me through the glass the female guard would come and make her sit down in the chair. How do you communicate with a two-year-old?"

The consequences of this treatment cannot be measured on the generation that followed, Partnoy says. "My daughter at least was lucky to get us back. I am in touch with kids whose parents did not reappear." Some of the children of the disappeared, anxious to come to terms with their traumatic histories, have formed support networks to help each other survive intact. Other children of the disappeared who were brought up by military families resist separating from the only families they have ever known, even when they suspect that their adoptive parents were somehow implicated in the death of their biological parents.

But the repression also affected the younger generation who was not directly touched by the conflict. Not everyone who lived under the dictatorship has reacted to Argentina's recent history of atrocity in the same way. There were those who believed the version of events that the military told them— that a group of communist "subversives" was trying to end Western civilization as Argentines knew it. After all, these young people grew up, for a while at least, deprived of information. There was censorship, books were burned, professors who could have educated them were in fear of their lives, out of work, in exile, or had already been disappeared. Others resisted whatever evidence they did see. They did not want to know more. They did not want to "get involved." They focused on material things, on their individual well-being. "But there was a part of the population that wanted to know more," says Partnoy, and that is what gives her a little hope.

In thinking back on her experience in relation to the Redefining Motherhood Conference, Partnoy concluded that women had been targeted specifically through their motherhood, through the severance of the mother–child bond. She tells about the experience of women political prisoners in jail, as described in a book of short stories, *Pasos bajo el agua* (Steps Under Water), by Alicia Kozameh, a political prisoner who wrote about the maternal cell block. Mothers with newborns were allowed to keep their children with them for three months before the babies were given over to their families. (This was not the case for the "disappeared" children who were born in the Argentine concentration camps and who were given for adoption to friends and families of the military.) "Kozameh has a shocking story about how women would take turns staying up the whole night on duty because they were afraid that the guards would come and take away their kids," Partnoy told the audience. "The strategy of unpredictability was another way of attacking women *in* their motherhood."

However, Partnoy also sees reclaiming motherhood as a way of resisting the dehumanization and mutilation that women have suffered at the hands of the military. "One of the things that women have to do when they're in the hands of the military is not *redefine* but *reclaim* their motherhood." As an example, she turns to the Chilean poet, Valeria Varas, who wrote *Cantando me defiendo* (Singing I Defend Myself). Varas now lives in Costa Rica. "When she was taken in Chile, the military used rats to torture her. They placed them on her breasts. This book of poetry very poignantly tells about her torture. She had a child after her release. And in the process of writing about her child and breast-feeding her child, she recovered her body that was mutilated by torture. Her tortured breasts came back to life." And then Partnoy laughs as she adds that Valeria Varas has also gone on to criticize Nestlé: "we can't avoid the politicizing our bodies and our lives. Varas starts this crusade for breast-feeding—so you see how coherent a person can be."

The Mothers of the Plaza de Mayo, Partnoy believes, have also been saved by their motherhood. When the military tried to devalue them as "madwomen" and "mothers of subversives," the women clung to their children and made their connection to the disappeared visible.

Sometimes, even the best-intentioned people, even the solidarity movement at times, has made the mistake of separating the women from their children. By making the mothers seem innocent and separating them from their children, the implication is that the children are not innocent. This justifies the nature of the repression. When we say "innocent," that seems to suggest innocent of not having been involved in politics. Even when society accepts the mothers, they will reject the children for whom they were fighting.

Now when I look back and realize how much we have invested, in terms of our lives and the lives of our kids, I become frustrated and desperate. We are at point zero. Sure, we have a democracy now, but it's a democracy without justice. The people responsible for the disappearances and killings are walking the streets. The generals who ordered the disappearances and tortures went to trial in 1985, and some of them were sent to jail for a few years. But that's all that happened. For the kids to come, there is no assurance that something like this will not happen again. There is no hope to pass on to the next generation.

I have spoken about my oldest daughter. She felt left out at times when I was so active and traveling and denouncing. And of course, she felt destroyed when we were disappeared, and had to live without us during the three years that I spent in jail. Now I'm writing a play (with Judith Weiss) called *Paper House* about my experience with my daughter. I've been working on it for the past five years. It's taken me a long time to come to terms with this. One of the reasons it's so difficult for me to handle this is that I've had another daughter, Eva Victoria. She is now the age that my eldest daughter was when I was disappeared. So I'm recovering that period now. But my eldest daughter of course hasn't been able to recover her childhood. She left me when my second daughter was born. She went to live with her father, my ex-husband, in Seattle. She could hardly bear to see her sister growing up with her parents, in her country. Every time she looked at Eva she could see the innocence that she had lost and she was reminded of everything that she never had. So the consequences of political repression on our children will mark their entire lives.

It has been very difficult for me to write. But in thinking about this conference and about motherhood, I came up with the last correction for this play. Here is an excerpt from that play:

ROSA (Voice Off): Dear daughter: Last week you didn't get my letter because I was sending a poem that the guards didn't like . . . I wrote it for you and I think it's pretty. Although there are some words in there that you may not understand, I'm sure that when you grow up you will like it too.

Listen:
My throat befriends the wind
To reach you, tender heart, fresh eyes.
Listen:
Hold a seashell to your ear,
Bring your ear close to this infamous earphone . . .
Listen:
The reason
Is so simple and so pure,
As a drop of water
Or a seed
That fits in the palm of your hand.
The reason is simple:
I just couldn't stop fighting for the happiness
of those we call sisters and brothers."
(*Paper House*, Scene 26)

But I want to end on a happy note. On Mother's Day, I got the best present from my eldest daughter. She spoke out against street violence in a demonstration in Seattle. And as she prepared her speech, she said to me: "Mom, you have to understand. It's not a racial problem, it's a class problem!" And I pretended I didn't understand so I could hear her explain how it was a class problem [laughs]. So, they come around, they come back to us.

Six Days

Some Rememberings[1]

Grace Paley

I was in jail. I had been sentenced to six days in the Women's House of
Detention, a fourteen-story prison right in the middle of Greenwich Village, my own neighborhood. This happened during the American War in
Vietnam. I have forgotten which important year of the famous '60s. The civil
disobedience for which I was paying a small penalty probably consisted of
sitting down to impede or slow some military parade.

I was surprised at the sentence. Others had been given two days or dismissed. I think the judge was particularly angry with me. After all, I was not a
kid. He thought I was old enough to know better, a forty-five-year-old woman,
a mother and teacher. I ought to be too busy to waste time on causes I couldn't
possibly understand.

I was herded with about twenty other women, about 90 percent black and
Puerto Rican, into the bull pen, an odd name for a women's holding facility.
There, through someone else's lawyer, I received a note from home, telling me
that since I'd chosen to spend the first week of July in jail, my son would
probably not go to summer camp because I had neglected to raise the money
I'd promised. I read this note and burst into tears, real running down the cheek
tears. It was true: Thinking about other people's grown boys I had betrayed my
little son. The summer, starting that day, July 1, stood up before me day after
day, steaming the city streets, the after-work crowded city pool.

I guess I attracted some attention. You—you white girl you—you never been arrested before? A black woman about a head taller than I put her arm on my shoulder.—It ain't so bad. What's your time sugar? I gotta do three years. You huh?

Six days.

Six days? What the fuck for?

I explained, sniffling, embarrassed.

You got six days for sitting down front of a horse? Cop on the horse? Horse step on you? Jesus in hell, cops gettin crazier and stupider and meaner. Maybe we get you out.

No, no, I said. I wasn't crying because of that. I didn't want her to think I was scared. I wasn't. She paid no attention. Shoving a couple of women aside.—Don't stand in front of me, bitch. Move over. What you looking at? She took hold of the bars of our cage, commenced to hang on them, shook them mightily, screaming—Hear me now, you mother fuckers, you grotty pigs, get this housewife out of here! She returned to comfort me.—Six days in this low-down hole for sitting front of a horse!

Before we were distributed among our cells, we were dressed in a kind of nurse's aide scrub uniform, blue or green, a little too large or a little too small. We had had to submit to a physical in which all our hiding places were investigated for drugs. These examinations were not too difficult, mostly because a young woman named Andrea Dworkin had fought them, refused a grosser, more painful examination some months earlier. She had been arrested, protesting the war in front of the U.S. mission to the UN. I had been there too, but I don't think I was arrested that day. She was mocked for that determined struggle at the Women's House, as she has been for other braveries, but according to the women I questioned, certain humiliating—perhaps sadistic—customs had ended, for that period at least.

My cellmate was a beautiful young woman, twenty-three years old, a prostitute who'd never been arrested before. She was nervous, but she had been given the name of an important long-termer. She explained it in a businesslike way that she *was* beautiful, and would need protection. She'd be OK once she found that woman. In the two days we spent together, she tried *not* to talk to the other women on our cell block. She said they were mostly street whores and addicts. She would never be on the street. Her man wouldn't allow it anyway.

I slept well for some reason, probably the hard mattress. I don't seem to mind where I am. Also I must tell you, I could look out the window at the end of our corridor and see my children or their friends, on their way to music lessons or Greenwich House pottery. Looking slantwise I could see right into Sutter's Bakery, then on the corner of 10th Street. These were my neighbors at coffee and cake.

Sometimes the cell block was open, but not our twelve cells. Other times the reverse. Visitors came by: they were prisoners, detainees not yet sentenced. They seemed to have a strolling freedom, though several, unsentenced, unable to make bail, had been there for months. One woman peering into the cells stopped when she saw me. Grace! Hi! I knew her from the neighborhood, maybe the park, couldn't really remember her name.

What are you in for? I asked.

Oh nothing—well a stupid drug bust. I don't even use—oh well forget it. I've been here six weeks. They keep putting the trial off. Are you OK?

Then I complained. I had planned not to complain about anything while living among people who'd be here in these clanging cells a long time; it didn't seem right. But I said, I don't have anything to read and they took away my pen and I don't have paper.

Oh you'll get all that eventually—she said. Keep asking.

Well they have all my hair pins. I'm a mess.

No no she said—you're OK. You look nice.

(A couple of years later, the war continuing, I was arrested in Washington. My hair was still quite long. I wore it in a kind of bun on top of my head. My hair pins gone, my hair straggled wildly every which way. Muriel Rukeyser, arrested that day along with about thirty other women, made the same generous sisterly remark. No no Grace; love you with your hair down, you really ought to always wear it this way.)

The very next morning, my friend brought me *The Collected Stories of William Carlos Williams*. These OK?

God! OK—Yes!

My trial is coming up tomorrow, she said. I think I'm getting off with time already done. Over done. See you around?

That afternoon, my cellmate came for her things—I'm moving to the fourth floor. Working in the kitchen. Couldn't be better.—We were sitting outside our cells, she wanted me to know something. She'd already told me, but said it again.—I still can't believe it. This creep, this guy, this cop, he waits he just waits till he's fucked and fine, pulls his pants up, pays me, and arrests me. It's not legal. It's not. My man's so mad, he like to kill *me*, but he's not that kind of—he's not a criminal type, *my* man. She never said the word pimp. Maybe no one did. Maybe that was our word.

I had made friends with some of the women in the cells across the aisle. How can I say "made friends." I just sat and spoke when spoken to, I was at school. I answered questions—simple ones. Why I would do such a fool thing on purpose? How old were my children? My man any good? Then, you live around the corner? That was a good idea, Evelyn said, to have a prison in your own neighborhood, so you could keep in touch, yelling out the window. As in fact we were able to do right here and now, calling and being called from Sixth Avenue, by mothers, children, boyfriends.

About the children: One woman took me aside. Her daughter was brilliant, she was in Hunter High School, had taken a test. No she hardly ever saw her, but she wasn't a whore—it was the drugs. Her daughter was ashamed, the grandmother, the father's mother made the child ashamed. When she got out in six months it would be different. This made Evelyn and Rita, right across from my cell, laugh. Different, I swear. Different. Laughing. But she *could* make it, I said. Then they really laughed. Their first laugh was a bare giggle compared to these convulsive roars. Change her ways? That dumb bitch? Ha!!

Another woman, Helen, the only other white woman on the cell block, wanted to talk to me. She wanted me to know that she was not only white, but Jewish. She came from Brighton Beach. Her father, he should rest in peace, thank God, was dead. Her arms were covered with puncture marks almost like sleeve patterns. But she needed to talk to me, because I was Jewish (I'd been asked by Rita and Evelyn—was I Irish? No, Jewish. Oh, they answered). She walked me to the barred window at the end of the corridor, the window that looked down on W. 10th Street. She said—How come you so friends with those black whores? You don't hardly talk to me. I said I liked them, but I like her too. She said, if you knew them for true, you wouldn't like them. They nothing but street whores. You know, once I was friends with them. We done a lot of things together, I knew them fifteen years Evy and Rita maybe twenty, I been in the streets with them, side by side, Amsterdam, Lenox, West Harlem; in bad weather we covered each other. Then one day along come Malcolm X and they don't know me no more, they ain't talking to me. You too white, I ain't all that white. Twenty years. They ain't talking.

My friend Myrt called one day, that is called from the street, called—Grace, Grace.—I heard and ran to the window. A policeman, the regular beat cop was addressing her. She looked up, then walked away before I could yell my answer. Later on she told me that he'd said—I don't think Grace would appreciate you calling her name out like that.

What a mistake! For years, going to the park with my children, or simply walking down Sixth Avenue on a summer night past the Women's House, we would often have to thread our way through whole families calling up—bellowing, screaming to the third, seventh, tenth floor, to figures, shadows behind bars and screened windows—How you feeling? Here's Glena. She got big. Mami mami you like my dress? We gettin you out baby. New lawyer come by.

And the replies, among which I was privileged to live for a few days—shouted down.—You lookin beautiful. What he say? Fuck you James. I got a chance? Bye bye. Come next week.

Then the guards, the heavy clanking of cell doors. Keys. Night.

I still had no pen or paper despite the great history of prison literature. I was suffering a kind of frustration, a sickness in the way claustrophobia is a sickness—this paper-and-penlessness was a terrible pain in the area of my heart, a nausea. I was surprised.

In the evening, at lights out (a little like the army or on good days a strict, unpleasant camp), women called softly from their cells. Rita hey Rita sing that song—Come on sister sing. A few more importunings and then Rita in the cell diagonal to mine would begin with a ballad. A song about two women and a man. It was familiar to everyone but me. The two women were prison sweethearts. The man was her outside lover. One woman, the singer, was being paroled. The ballad told her sorrow about having been parted from him when she was sentenced, now she would leave her loved woman after three years. There were about twenty stanzas of joy and grief.

Well, I was so angry not to have pen and paper to get some of it down that I lost it all—all but the sorrowful plot. Of course she had this long song in her head and in the next few nights she sang and chanted others, sometimes with a small chorus.

Which is how I finally understood that I didn't lack pen and paper but my own memorizing mind. It had been given away with a hundred poems, called rote learning, old-fashioned, backward, an enemy of creative thinking, a great human gift, disowned.

Now there's a garden where the Women's House of Detention once stood. A green place, safely fenced in, with protected daffodils and tulips; roses bloom in it too, sometimes into November.

The big women's warehouse and its barred blind windows have been removed from Greenwich Village's affluent throat. I was sorry when it happened; the bricks came roaring down, great trucks carried them away.

I have always agreed with Rita and Evelyn that if there are prisons, they ought to be in the neighborhood, near a subway—not way out in distant suburbs, where families have to take cars, buses, ferries, trains, and the population that considers itself innocent forgets, denies, chooses to never know that there is a whole huge country of the bad and the unlucky and the self-hurters, a country with a population greater than that of many nations in our world.

NOTES

1. This story first appeared in the *Alaska Quarterly Review* (Anchorage: University of Alaska, 1994).

Naked Mothers and Maternal Sexuality

Some Reactions to the Aba Women's War

Temma Kaplan

Not every society idealizes prepubescent girls and denigrates fuller bodies re-shaped by childbirth. In certain cultures, mothers' bodies occupy a special place of honor, one associated with fertility and power. But in our society, where we as feminists have worked so hard to separate reproduction and sexuality . . . we take our stands as feminists, not as mothers . . . It makes many of us as femi-nists more fearful and less able to consider the relationship between fertility and power that women in Aba took for granted. What guided these mothers to ex-press scorn—using their own bodies as distorting mirrors, and reflecting an im-age of authority designed to humiliate those in power—was a different sense of legitimacy than feminism provides.

Skimpily attired in a diaphanous scarf over a gold-lamé bikini, an accom-plished visual artist in her fifties performed a near-striptease to a rap song she had written celebrating her loss of fifty pounds. Among the racially mixed audience at an art gallery, the artist of color's adult daughter stared at her feet and twisted her hands as she watched her mother's perfor-mance. If, as one of my friends says, the role of parents is to embarrass their children, the artist was certainly a good mother. But why were the daughter and I so uncomfortable?

Remembering how my mother often went around half-naked and tried to tell me more about sex than I wanted to know, I certainly could empathize with the daughter—and feel ashamed about my lack of solidarity with the mother. Wasn't fat a feminist issue, and hadn't the artist's health required her weight loss? Accustomed to great subjectivity in her work, why shouldn't she craft her own body and present it in any way she chose? But there was a further problem. The mother still did not conform to current American cultural ideals of thin, muscular women. Were the daughter and I offended by the mother's public display, or did we think she wasn't skinny enough to carry it off?

The artist-mother, having fought against men controlling her fertility, her sexuality, and her availability, no matter what she wore or where she was, should have been able to show her own body anywhere she wished without ceding power to her daughter (or to me) to determine her behavior. I wondered at the time whether the daughter and I were just prudes who, despite years of demonstrating in outlandish ways for political causes, wanted to deny the mother the same right. Wasn't the artist the only one who should determine the meaning of her motherhood and sexuality, enjoying, even flaunting, her own body as she wished?

Though very much a product of North American culture, where we as feminists have created a space for nonreproductive sexuality, I nevertheless work with women inside and outside the United States for whom their role as a mother provides a fundamental part of their political and personal identity. I've also studied many cases of women, who, in the name of motherhood, pit their own semiclothed or naked bodies against authorities, and, in the process, enrage and humiliate police and soldiers, making them appear brutal and ridiculous for daring to attack mothers. Though I applaud such women, I myself don't like seeing anyone's mother in the flesh; even being in the audience made me feel nervous.

This issue arose again a few years later at a feminist conference, when I spoke about the Aba Women's War of 1929, a movement in Eastern Nigeria where local mothers resisted the imposition of taxes that would have reduced their ability to provide for their families. Focusing on what the British called the Aba Riots—and what local people referred to as the Women's War of December 1929—I began with a quote by a near-contemporary British woman who had spoken with women who had participated in the uprising: "[S]ome ten thousand women, scantily clothed, girdled with green leaves, carrying sticks [approached Aba]. Singing angry songs against the chiefs and court messengers, the women proceeded to attack and loot the European trading stores and Barclay's Bank, and to break into the prison and release the prisoners."[1]

Whatever else we might know about the administrator who reported on these events, or the testimony given by the women who participated in the inquiries following the uprising, it is clear that the Igbo–Ibibio women of Eastern Nigeria knew what they were doing while not dressing or acting as the missionaries would have liked. According to Nina Emma Mba, one of the movement's leading historians, "the women were very conscious of the special role of women, the importance of women to society, and the assertion of their rights as women vis-à-vis the men. They consistently drew attention to their sexual identity through their dress, body gestures, and songs."[2]

With vines on their heads and waists, banging their cooking implements, ten to fifteen thousand women from two provinces converged on the towns of Utu Etim Ekpo, Opobo, and Aba. The women attacked the warrant chiefs, male villagers—some of whom held traditional authority—whom the British had appointed to rule over the villages. The women stole the hats that symbolized the men's high office, and rubbed their naked bottoms over the faces and bodies of court officers. As the women flexed their own muscles, they also humiliated the British. Once in Aba, the enraged women attacked the British merchants they held responsible for the declining price of palm products—the women's main cash crop—and the high costs of imported goods like soap and kerosene. But twenty Igbo policemen, understanding the meaning of the demonstration, were able to restore the peace, despite the overwhelming number of women.

The situation was considerably more violent when four to five thousand women faced British troops faced at the Utu Etim Ekpo bridge. The women, realizing that their kitchen knives, pestles, and sticks were no match for the armed soldiers, used the only weapons they had: bawdiness and sexual ridicule. They lifted their skirts and challenged the soldiers to "shoot your mothers." Following the order of a white officer, the white soldiers complied. Eighteen women died in the confrontation and nineteen were wounded. The following day at Opobo, another sixty-three women were gunned down, of whom thirty-two died.[3]

In the two government inquiries following the uprising, women survivors expressed bewilderment that soldiers would shoot women. I too find it shocking, and yet wonder why killing women is worse than killing men. In fact, for over a decade I have been trying to explain a paradox: Authorities are often confused about how to treat militant mothers who accept the gender prescriptions of motherhood in their culture and historical period, but also presume the right to protect their communities—a conviction I call "female consciousness."[4] At first glance, women with female consciousness seem "traditional," since they uphold the views their societies have of proper gender behavior. In periods of stress, however, when the women's families and communities are threatened, such women will sometimes take matters into their own hands and act in ways that outsiders might consider far from traditional. Confronted with such mothers, police and soldiers from their own racial or ethnic groups sometimes support the women acting in their capacity as mothers, and mutiny rather than attack them.

Since I'm constantly pondering what goes on when crowds of women use their own bodies to show scorn for authorities, I looked forward to a general discussion at the conference where I talked about the Aba women. Among feminists, I thought, we might have an open dialogue about the ways women sometimes have to be seen in order to be heard—and the lengths of exhibitionism to which some women must go to get their messages across. Puzzled about why women sometimes violate taboos in their own societies in order to shame or ridicule those in power, I wondered why real women's bawdiness gets so little attention. Since feminist literary theory has revealed a great deal about transgressive behavior, performance and masquerades, I was disappointed that in the question-and-answer period that followed my presentation the issue of the Aba women's dress, raucous behavior and the possible meanings of their actions never came up.

When Wangari Maathai, founder of the Green Belt movement in Kenya and an internationally acclaimed grassroots leader, talked to the same audience about women in Kenya, she called attention to the 1992 activities of mothers of political prisoners, who "when the authority challenged them with beatings and tear gas, . . . used an old tradition to ward off the attackers. [S]ome of them stripped naked and shocked the oppressors and the onlookers alike. Women decided to use their bodies to fight injustices against their children."[5] In the lively discussion following Maathai's presentation, the feminist audience never asked her to situate the mothers' strategy of using their own nakedness in the context of Kenyan history and culture. Neither I nor anyone else asked whether the relationships among sexuality, reproduction and desire gave women's naked bodies a different meaning in Kenya than in the United States.

Had the performance artist's daughter or the distracted feminist audience been the only examples I'd recently encountered of troubled silences about the nakedness of mature women, I'd have chalked these reactions up to individual idiosyncracies. But, six months later, in my graduate feminist theory course, I met the same nervousness and shame—this time from some of my own graduate students, whom I think are among the most sophisticated feminists I know.

My students were offended by three readings I assigned by anthropologists: one dealing with women's participation in Mau Mau rebellion in Kenya; one on the use of menstrual blood by women in New Guinea to negotiate with recalcitrant husbands; and one on peace activists at England's Greenham Common.[6] The students were particularly hard on the women of Greenham.

"Don't they realize," one student earnestly beseeched me, "that by going naked and by rubbing ashes on themselves, they antagonized a lot of people?"

"Well, yes," I responded. "That was the idea."

Another volunteered that the women were demeaning themselves by undressing before their enemies. Now these same students read and enjoyed Judith Butler's work on "performativity," attended a lecture by Jane Gallop entitled "The Teacher's Breast," and listened to Eve Kosofsky Sedgwick's discussion of the excitement of shame, with interest and understanding.[7] These students debate questions about whether all spectatorship is necessarily sadistic and whether the gaze is necessarily male. They view themselves as open, curious and liberated from petty qualms. They are tutored in theory but are skeptical about Freud, especially the influence of psychoanalysis on feminist film criticism; they are wary about the gender insensitivity many of them find in Foucault.

So, how come they seem so squeamish when mature women, many of them mothers, use their bodies to achieve political goals? One person in the class, a performance artist and member of Riot Girrrls, a feminist punk contingent, immediately understood the power of being outrageous, especially as a means of expressing rage, frustration, and inability to make oneself heard in any other way. But the women with whom she is familiar proclaim their freedom as women and artists, not as mothers. And, like performance artists Karen Finley and Holly Hughes, they are generally young. Maybe that's where the difficulty lies.

Not every society idealizes prepubescent girls and denigrates fuller bodies reshaped by childbirth. In certain cultures, mothers' bodies occupy a special place of honor, one associated with fertility and power. But in our society, where we as feminists have worked so hard to separate reproduction and sexuality and to demonstrate our right to look like anything we want, we take our stand as feminists, not as mothers. One of my friends, a grandmother, says that whenever she hears about disputes between mothers and daughters, she identifies with the daughters. We seem to feel a great deal of uneasiness when considering ourselves, and our bodies, as maternal. And older female bodies, particularly those of mothers, cause the most uneasiness.

This anxiety, which permeates white, black, Latino and Asian cultures in the United States to different degrees, is rooted in our efforts to view desire and sexuality as separate from reproduction. It makes many of us as feminists more fearful and less able to consider the relationship between fertility and power that women in Aba took for granted. What guided these mothers to express scorn, using their own bodies as distorting mirrors, reflecting an image of authority designed to humiliate those in power, was a different sense of legitimacy than feminism provides. To understand the process, it's worth considering in more detail what happened during the Aba Women's War.

Although extremely variable from one culture to another, rural West Africa in the early 20th century generally maintained what political scientist Kamene Okonjo has called "the dual-sex political system."[8] According to those patterns, married women, who produced the subsistence crops necessary to maintain the family, also had associations, governed by rituals and systems of law, that managed women's affairs and maintained their power. Some of these associations were devoted to shaping cultural views about reproduction and fertility.

In Igbo–Ibibio culture, where masculinity and femininity were not considered to be the inverse of one another, women could challenge patriarchal authority by insisting on their own fertility and control of reproduction, linking motherhood and sexuality. The ceremonies following the birth of a new baby were usually bawdy free-for-alls of language and gesture, as the women simulated intercourse, pregnancy, and birth, while doing their famous Crotch Dance. In the *Ohie N'Ole?* dance, "women of all ages, miming intercourse and pregnancy and childbirth, standing wide-legged, rocking on their heels, throwing their hands into the air and slapping their crotches in unison . . . jointly answered the lead singer's question: Where do they all come from?"[9]

Igbo-Ibibio women also maintained political institutions over which the men had no control. Once the village women's association, consisting of married women who had become mothers, reached a decision, its rules were binding. Those women who chose to ignore it faced humiliation, including ostracism, destruction of goods, and even physical injury.[10] Since the council of women acted as a popular court, adjudicating disputes among women, between wives and husbands, or between all the village men and women, these councils wielded great social power locally.

While men's institutions dominated those of women, when the two groups came into conflict, the women could initiate direct action. In a manner of speaking, they engaged in a system of gendered politics. But the British, who had developed the single-sex system to perfection, were not aware of the African women's customs, and were certainly not supportive of the association of wives of the village and the women's secret societies. These organizations empowered women not only to supervise puberty rituals but also to officiate over women's rights in the village.

Although the British were well acquainted with protests—they'd even engaged with their own fierce suffragettes before the First World War—the British authorities in Nigeria had never encountered adversaries quite like the militantly bawdy Nigerian women.[11] Men's ridicule of women and their bodily functions frequently helps build male solidarity, and British soldiers undoubtedly acted lewdly in their barracks and men's clubs.[12] But bawdy women seem to have confused them.

Bawdiness does not, in fact, seem to be symmetrical in any culture. The act of displaying their bodies may have a different meaning for women than for the men who ogle, caricature, or ridicule them. And once again, the female body in question is presumably young and unmarried. But when mothers, generally clothed among the Igbo–Ibibio as among the British, violate taboos, disrobe, and perform nakedly, they seem to call male authority into question. Displaying mothers' bodies—not just women's bodies—may challenge authority itself, but just how? The example of Aba demonstrates one way.

Agalaba Uzo, which the British shortened to Aba, the capital city of a territory covering two provinces and containing two million people, went up in flames for about a week in December 1929, in what local people called *ogu umunwanye* (women's war). One of the major anti-imperialist struggles in Africa before the advent of Mau Mau, the uprising resulted in the death of more than fifty-five women. The relative absence of local men in the insurrection led the British to believe that the men had surreptitiously instigated the rebellion and then stepped back, letting the women do the fighting. The British simply could not believe that men had not played a role, for the British were ignorant of the sex–gender systems that prevailed in West Africa.

Married women had a systematic way of shaming men who violated acceptable behavior, according to feminist researcher Judith Van Allen. Although the practice had become merely a memory by the 1929 uprising, the women resurrected it when their grievances had reached a limit.[13] The Igbo–Ibibio, who were polygamous, had carefully regulated patterns, enforced by married women, to make sure men did their share to support all their wives and children. If a man did not provide the yams necessary for ceremonial occasions, or if he allowed his cows to eat the coco yams from a woman's field, or if he abused or ridiculed his wives or any other women, the married women of the hamlet, linked in loose associations, would visit his hut. They would explain the rules to him and ask him to mend his ways. If he failed to comply, they would order his wives not to cook for him or sleep with him, and they would ridicule him in lewd songs. If he continued to disobey the women, they would deface or even burn down his hut or sit on his face while naked. This entire process was called "sitting on a man" or "making war on a man."

By sexually humiliating the perpetrator of domestic violence, for example, married women could impose sanctions on batterers in their communities. When an Igbo or Ibibio woman was badly beaten, the other women at the market might pass twigs as a sign of collective grievance. They would accompany her to confront her husband in his compound. T. Obinkaram Echewa's novel, *I Saw the Sky Catch Fire*, provides an account of one such incident. The women recited a bawdy song:

> Ozurumba, Ozurumba, you like to beat your wife!
> You will beat all of us tonight,
> Until your arms fall off!
> Ozurumba, Ozurumba, you have the biggest prick in town
> You will fuck all of us tonight,
> Until your prick falls off![14]

More than forty women surrounded a man who had beaten his pregnant wife, stripped his loin cloth from him, killed his goat, threw him to the ground, lifted their own garments, and then nakedly sat on every portion of his body. Later in the novel, the wife-beater reflects upon the humiliation he has suffered. He thinks that a "disgrace beyond repetition had been visited upon him, the ignominy and shame of a lifetime. Their smelly and sweaty bottoms on his face, their rank wetness and the prickly hair of their things in his mouth and eyes! Unspeakable abomination. He would rather have fallen into a latrine. How could he ever show his face in public again!"[15] Although this is a fictional depiction, it reflects a widespread practice.

If the British had realized that the women of different compounds had such effective means of expressing their wrath against men who violated their rights, could contact one another across two provinces, and could do so on relatively short notice, they might have organized their efforts to tax the women differently. Instead, authorities decreed a census of women, children, and livestock. Women were alarmed, for a similar census had preceded taxation of men two years before. Word went out along the market routes of women who traded in small items. Women's societies comprised of mothers and elders spread the rumor about taxes to their colleagues in the next compound. The women were already outraged at the all-male British warrant chiefs, who had been using their power to sexually harass women and take their crops.[16] And so word—and fury—about their newest outrage spread quickly.

The first woman who faced the census taker, a local school teacher, had recently lost her daughter-in-law. She seems to have associated her daughter-in-law's death with the census-taking, as her remark makes clear. "Are you still counting? . . . Last year my son's wife who was pregnant died. What am I to count? I have been mourning the death of that woman."[17] Not wanting to have her livestock tallied, the women of Oloko passed palm leaves and twigs, spreading the news to other female neighbors as they attempted to "sit on" the teacher, Emeruwa, and the chief who had sent him.[18]

Taxation raised economic issues for mothers and their families, but that was not the only problem. Under any circumstances, the women would have resented being asked to pay taxes. But the 1920s had been a period of drought, when the palm trees produced fewer palm nuts and a lower grade and quantity of palm oil, the women's main cash crop. With declining production, the women had less money to feed their families. Even the cassava and yams they produced for their own consumption suffered because of the drought.

Beyond the economic issues was a crisis in authority that threatened fertility. In a duel-sex system, women not only have special responsibilities. They have special privileges. One of the women who gave testimony to the court of inquiry following the uprising asked, "What have we women done to warrant our being taxed? We women are like trees which bear fruit. You should tell us the reason why women who bear seeds should be counted."[19] The link between women and fruit trees was both metaphoric and symbolic. The women passed palm leaves from one village to another; they also wore them on their heads and around their waists. In some places, passing the leaves and branches meant peace; in other places, war; sometimes they were signs of mourning. Elsewhere, women appeared with sticks around which were wrapped young palms. Fern leaves apparently formed crowns upon their heads. Although the Europeans were baffled by the foliage, the Africans knew the leaves "meant war."[20]

A few days after the first women were counted in Owerri in November 1929, a delegation of about fifty women from the Bende Division, incorporating Oloko and villages to the south and west, went to the regional capital at Port Harcourt to secure promises from the warrant officers that the women would not be taxed.[21] Despite assurances that the census did not foretell taxes, the women's rage spread across the provinces of Owerri and Calabar. Some demonstrated at Ukam on December 2, and another group of women marched on the Native Court at Owerrinta, demanding to be heard. By December 16, the women, who were initially concerned only about their own taxation, now began questioning why the men should submit to taxes. Grievances about prices, market regulations, the corruption of court messengers, and the failure of the warrant chief system all surfaced. The women's war spread to many towns and villages across the southeastern provinces. The women who participated in the great march to Aba called themselves *Oha nd'inyom*, which historian Nina Emma Mba translates as "a gathering of women." She adds that during the course of the uprising the women overcame ethnic differences among Igbo, Ibibio, Annang, and Ogoni women by identifying themselves only as *oha nd'inyom*.[22]

Two provinces went up in flames as women demanded reforms. By December 9, 1929, one thousand women were thronging the roads leading to the court in Owerri. Singing their song, "We are dying, our hearts are not good, for death is standing before us," the mothers marched on the courts.[23] They stole the court records, the hats of the warrant chiefs, and they marched on the residences of the court who enforced the warrant chiefs' orders. The women mowed down everyone in their path, including the court messengers. They undressed them and "sat on" them, and then took possession of the courthouse, drove the chiefs away, and freed the prisoners in the jail.[24] The women who had converged on Owerri were pushed back on December 16, and fresh contingents of women from Oguta were dissuaded from supporting the Owerri women by the movement of a platoon of troops and by assurances from British officials in Lagos that the women would not be taxed.[25]

In the aftermath of the insurrection, the British banned all women's societies. As in the case of the men, the British attempted to structure and monopolize all forms of authority. The mothers as individuals still had recourse to the native courts, but collective demonstrations, including dressing in traditional garb, singing bawdy songs and banging implements, was forbidden. After the uprising, such public behavior presented too great a threat to the British authority, which increasingly monopolized spectacles as well as force.

Spectacles such as the ones the Igbo–Ibibio women carried out had a broad political purpose rooted in a culture that authorized mothers to defend their collective fertility and their livelihoods—but not their own individual independence. By local standards, the Igbo–Ibibio women would have been bad mothers had they simply accepted the census and the taxation they believed would follow. Women who went off on their own, however, attempting to escape the collectivity to act as individuals, also suffered the wrath of the women's community. Echewa portrays one such woman, whose mother and mother-in-law stage a raucous spectacle outside her dwelling in the city, where she had gone, leaving her children behind.[26]

Returning to the question of Northern feminists' difficulties in granting mothers power to use their bodies bawdily, I have to confront the issue of Anglo-American prudery. Despite nearly thirty years of second-wave feminism, many of us are wary about mothers acting provocatively. In trying to provide space for all women's choices, we as feminists have attempted to honor both motherhood and nonreproductive sexuality. But recent discussions of bawdiness have sometimes revealed worries and concomitant rigidities among us. On one hand, there is Madonna, who toys with the Madonna/whore polarity so fascinating to Northern cultures. Then there are the performance artists who, like the mother I described at the beginning of this essay, act out and against cultural stereotypes. One can also refer to Demi Moore's pregnant, nude body on the cover of *Vanity Fair*, and the scandal it caused, in part, because pregnant women's bodies are considered the antithesis of female beauty in our society. Exhibitionism finds its limits when it confronts the presumed asexuality of mothers. In one of the few feminist studies of the sexuality of mothers, psychologist Susan (Contratto) Weisskopf argues that "maternal sexuality is a topic that makes virtually everyone anxious" and attributes this discomfort to "the embarrassment, guilt, disgust, and anger that accompany tabooed behaviors and feelings."[27]

The boundaries that theoretically separate women's bodies engaged in sexual intercourse, in childbirth and nursing, in aggressive acts, and on display are frequently blurred in the Northern mind. Look at sexual insults. My friend Ann Farnsworth-Alvear remembers "Your mother wears combat boots" (now highly acceptable) as one of the greatest insults you could make in grade school, implying that your mother cross-dressed, and was not fully a woman. "Motherfucker" reflects badly not just on you, but on your mother. Among my Mexican-American friends, *"puta madre,"* calling mothers prostitutes, tops the list of insults. While in Spain, *"me cago en la leche de tu madre"* ("I shit in your mother's milk") can end in a brawl. Like so much else in maternal imagery, these slurs don't have much to do with sexual women at all. Rather, they are part of an elaborate policing system governing the imagery of motherhood and enforcing patriarchal authority.

In the United States, where fewer than 25 percent of all women breast-fed their children in the 1970s, discomfort with the multiple uses of women's bodies—as avenues of our own sexual pleasure, as means by which to nurture, as weapons to express our disdain for authority (and sometimes as all three)—has caused many mothers to be ashamed of their own bodies and of themselves as sexual beings.[28] Another reason sexualized maternity presents such problems to Anglo-American women is that, despite broad concerns with reproduction, ranging from the needs of children born to women on welfare to in vitro fertilization to abortion rights, many Northern feminists have rejected the connection between fertility, sexuality, and desire.

The contrast with the plight of the Aba women could not be clearer. Those responsible for maintaining fertility among the Igbo–Ibibio were the associations of mothers. They expressed their fertility by wearing and showing ferns and palm leaves—and little else—and by observing certain patterns of behavior. Fertility, viewed as a matter of community survival, remained one of women's preoccupations.

Bawdiness against errant men maintained the continuity of this gender-structured community. Such men, once humiliated, lost face with other men. By violating community practices in their treatment of women, batterers and scoundrels unmanned themselves—or rather were emasculated by the women. "Sitting on a man" redressed the gender imbalance an unmanly man created by violating the rules.

The British and their allies among the warrant chiefs, who should have known better, also threatened community survival. Taxing women challenged the maintenance of the entire community, especially in light of the growing depression of the late 1920s. But economic crises appeared to women not only as loss of goods, but as a threat to their fertility.

Did the Igbo–Ibibio women convey the wrong message by disrobing, wearing little more than palm leaves, "sitting on" court messengers, and antagonizing the troops by their bawdiness? What did the performance artist's striptease mean? Was the daughter merely embarrassed that the mother, whatever her health needs, seemed to be conforming to Madison Avenue's dictates about thin women? Or that she wasn't thin enough? In contrast to what my students might say—and the anxiety the daughter and I might feel about the mother's appearance—nakedness has many meanings. When displayed by the Aba women, naked mothers' bodies may have shown women's collective power over their own sexuality and fertility; the women baring their bodies weren't victims, but adversaries of authority. The British paid women the backhanded compliment of treating them as subversives. Unlike some contemporary feminists, who sometimes view bawdy women as naive, the British feared their antagonism and shot them down.

Why then do Northern feminists like the daughter, my students, the college audience of feminists, and I have so much trouble dealing with nude mothers' bodies in the past and the present, here and elsewhere? Nakedness is common in art, and nude self-portraits are routine among feminist artists. But right now, when violence is ever-present and Northern women feel especially vulnerable physically, nakedness seems to present a special threat. For those concerned with the effects of pornography and victimhood, mothers displaying their bodies offer problems of interpretation with which we still have trouble. Moreover, at a time when Northern feminists are divided about the meaning of visual representation in pornography, and anthropologists are self-consciously examining their own position in relation to people from diverse cultures, interpreting what women of color were doing in Kenya or Nigeria raises more problems than most feminists from industrialized countries want to deal with. Despite all this, running away, invalidating our own perceptions because we may be foreign to the culture in question, and refusing to look at the mother's naked body solve nothing. Maybe it's time to read the palms and confront our anxieties about the power inherent in maternal sexuality.[29]

NOTES

1. Sylvia Leith-Ross, *African Women: A Study of the Ibo of Nigeria* (London: Routledge & Kegan Paul, 1939; reprinted New York: A.M. Sedition, 1978), p. 26; for the complete records of the British hearings following the war, see *Report of the Commission of Inquiry appointed to Inquire into the Disturbances in the Calabar and Owerri Provinces, December 1929*; the *Memorandum as to the Origin and Causes of Recent Disturbances in the Owerri and Calabar Provinces*; and the *Proceedings Before the Commission of Inquiry into Disturbances in the Calabar and Owerri Provinces*, available in *The Igbo "Women's War" of 1929; Documents Relating to the Aba Riots in Eastern Nigeria*, D.C. Dorward, ed. (East Ardsley, Wakefield, Yorkshire, England: Microform Limited, 1983; New York: Distributed by Clearwater Publishing Co., 1983).

2. Nina Emma Mba, *Nigerian Women Mobilized: Women's Political Activity in Southern Nigeria 1900–1965*, Institute of International Studies Research Series No. 48 (Berkeley: University of California, 1982), p. 90.

3. Dorward, ed., *The Igbo "Women's War" of 1929*, p. 157; T. Obinkaram Echewa, *I Saw the Sky Catch Fire* (New York: Putman, 1980) combines the two incidents and says that 100 women were shot, pp. 208–209, 214–215.

4. I have developed these ideas about female consciousness in three published articles and my forthcoming book: "Female Consciousness and Collective Action: The Case of Barcelona, 1910–1918," *Signs: Journal of Women in Culture and*

Society, 7, no. 3 (spring 1982):545–566, reprinted in *Feminist Theory, A Critique of Ideology*, ed. Nannerl O. Keahane, Michelle Z. Rosaldo, and Barbara Gelpi (Chicago: University of Chicago Press, 1982, 1990); "Women's Communal Strikes in the Crisis of 1917–22" (in Russia, Italy, Spain, and Veracruz, Mexico), in *Becoming Visible: Women in European History*, 2nd ed., ed. Renate Bridenthal, Claudia Koonz, and Susan Mosher Stuard (Boston: Houghton Mifflin, 1987), pp. 429–449; "Community and Resistance in Women's Political Cultures in Chile and South Africa," *Dialectical Anthropology* 15 (1990):259–267; and *Crazy for Democracy: Women in Grassroots Movements* (New York and London: Routledge, 1996).

5. Wangari Maathai, Keynote Address, "Women and the Earth," Redefining Motherhood Conference, Hanover, N.H., May 15, 1993.

6. Tabitha Kanogo, "Kikuyu women and the politics of protest: Mau Mau," Jessica Mayer, "Women and the Pacification of Men in New Guinea," and Lynne Jones, "Perceptions of 'Peace Women' at Greenham Common 1981–5," in *Images of Women in Peace & War Cross-Cultural & Historical Perspectives*, ed. Sharon MacDonald, Pat Holden and Shirley Ardener (Madison: University of Wisconsin Press, 1988), pp. 78–99, 148–165, 179–204.

7. Judith Butler, *Gender Trouble: Feminism and the Subversion of Identity* (New York and London: Routledge, 1989); Jane Gallop, "The Teacher's Breast," lecture delivered on September 23, 1993, at the Humanities Institute of Stony Brook; Eve Kosofsky Sedgwick, "Queen Performativity: Warhol's Shyness, Warhol's Childness," lecture delivered on October 14, 1993, at the Humanities Institute of Stony Brook.

8. Kamene Okonjo, "The Dual-Sex Political System in Operation: Igbo Women and Community Politics in Midwestern Nigeria," in *Women in Africa*, ed. Nancy J. Hafkin and Edna G. Bay (Stanford, Calif.: Stanford University Press, 1976), pp. 45–58, cited in Mary H. Moran, "Collective Action and the 'Representation' of African Women: A Liberian Case Study," *Feminist Studies* 15, no. 3 (Fall 1989): 443–460.

9. Echewa, *I Saw the Sky Catch Fire*, p. 14.

10. Mba, *Nigerian Women Mobilized*, p. 28.

11. To be fair, the author of the *Report of the Commission of Inquiry*, published in 1930, did, in fact, appreciate the similarities between the British and Nigerian women, saying that "In some measure the movement [in Nigeria] may be likened to that for women's suffrage in England where militant feminism committed breaches of the law with a view to drawing the widest possible attention to what they believed to be the inherent justice of their cause" (Dorward, ed., *The Igbo "Women's War" of 1929*, p. 20).

12. Mikhail Bakhtin, *Rabelais and His World*, trans. by Helene Iswolsky (Cambridge, Mass.: MIT Press, 1968). Among the most useful of the numerous commentaries of this work is the work of Peter Stallybrass and Allon White, *The Politics and Poetics of Transgression* (Ithaca, N.Y.: Cornell University Press, 1986).

13. Judith Van Allen, " 'Sitting on a Man,' Colonialism and Lost Political Institutions of Igbo Women," *Canadian Journal of African Studies* 6, no. 2 (1972): p. 165–181; "Aba Riots or Igbo Women's War: Ideology, Stratification, and the Invisibility of Women," in Hafkin and Bay, eds., *Women in Africa*, pp. 59–85.

14. Echewa, *I Saw the Sky Catch Fire*, p. 145.

15. Echewa, *I Saw the Sky Catch Fire*, pp. 145–146, 151–152.

16. A. E. Afigbo, *The Warrant Chiefs: Indirect Rule in Southeastern Nigeria 1891–1929* (London: Longman Group, 1972).

17. Quoted in Mba, *Nigerian Women Mobilized*, p. 77.

18. Johnson Elewhemba Nnaia Nwaguru, *Aba and British Rule: The Evolution and Administrative Developments of the Old Aba Division of Igboland 1896–1960* (Enugu, Nigeria: Santana Press and Publishing Co., 1973), p. 101; Mba, *Nigerian Women Mobilized*, p. 77. In the fictionalized account presented in Echewa's *I Saw the Sky Catch Fire*, the elder of the compound tried to prevent the women from marching on the chief's house, but without success. They claimed the men were taking no action, and therefore it was up to the women to take command (p. 163).

19. The comparison between women and fruit trees seems obvious to historian A. E. Afigbo, who claims that the analogy "lies at the root of certain indigenous social and ethical philosophy. First, just as one cannot, in the interest of human beings, joke with the survival of fruit-bearing, one could not play with the fate of women." A. E. Afigbo, "Revolution and reaction in Eastern Nigeria 1900–1929," *Journal of the Historical Society of Nigeria* (Ibadan), 3, no. 3, (1966: 539–557; p. 553 ff. quoted in Mba, *Nigerian Women Mobilized*, p. 76. For attitudes about sexuality and fertility in other West African countries, see Shirley Ardener, "Sexual Insult and Female Militancy," in *Perceiving Women*, ed. Shirley Ardener (London: Malaby Press, 1975), pp. 127–157.

20. Margery Perham, *Native Administration in Nigeria* (London and New York: Oxford University Press, 1937, 1962), pp. 207, 209, 209–210, 212.

21. Susan M. Martin, *Palm Oil and Protest: An Economic History of the Nga Region, Southeastern Nigeria, 1800–1980* (New York and Cambridge: Cambridge University Press, 1988), p. 113.

22. Mba, *Nigerian Women Mobilized*, p. 91.

23. From the Aba Commission of Inquiry, cited in Nwaguru, *Aba and British Rule*, p. 102.

24. Echewa, *I Saw the Sky Catch Fire*, p. 174; Nwaguru, *British Administration*, p. 102.

25. Mba, *Nigerian Women Mobilized*, p. 94.

26. Echewa, *I Saw the Sky Catch Fire*, pp. 44–72.

27. Susan (Contratto) Weisskopf, "Review Essay: Maternal Sexuality and Asexual Motherhood," *SIGNS* 5, no. 4 (Spring 1980): pp. 766–782; p. 767. Thanks to Marianne Hirsch for recommending this article.

28. The figure on nursing comes from Weisskopf, "Review Essay: Maternal Sexuality and Asexual Motherhood," p. 778.

29. I am grateful to Ann Farnsworth-Alvear, Marianne Hirsch, Alexis Jetter, Robert Moeller, Annelise Orleck, Bennett Sims, and Diana Taylor for their useful comments.

NATIONALIST MOTHERHOOD

Overview

Good Motherhood as Patriotism: Mothers on the Right

Annelise Orleck

The rise of conservative movements and political parties around the world during the 1980s and 1990s has been accompanied by a surge of right-wing women's activism. In western democracies, like the United States and Italy, conservative and religious fundamentalist women have built on the gains made by feminists during the 1970s to open up a place for women as candidates, lobbyists and strategists for right-wing political parties and organizations. In the countries of Eastern Europe, including Poland and republics of the former Soviet Union, where Communist dictatorships have only recently given way to democratic regimes, resurgent nationalist sentiment has dovetailed with calls for a return to traditional gender roles. In all of these shifting constellations, the politics of motherhood has occupied a central position.

Blaming "bad mothers" for a descent into chaos, and asserting the important role to be played by "good mothers" in restoring order has been key to the organizing successes of right-wing movements in the 1980s and 1990s. The much-reviled "bad mothers" are the same in many parts of the world: they are women "tainted" by feminism, women who insist on the right to use birth control, the right to safe and legal abortion, the right to child care so that they can continue working. In the United States, "bad motherhood" is also conflated with race, class and sexuality: poor mothers of color and lesbian mothers have become the repository for social anxiety about changing gender roles and family dynamics. As such they have served as very effective organizing tools for the right. In Eastern Europe ethnicity has played an equally powerful part in nationalist gender-ideology as "good motherhood" becomes freighted with the responsibility for maintaining ethnic purity. This section examines the role that mothers and motherhood have played in right-wing and racist movements in the United States, Eastern Europe and Italy. Much of the research and analysis is groundbreaking, as there has been little study of the integral ties between motherhood and right-wing politics.

In the section's opening essay, historian Claudia Koonz—author of *Mothers in the Fatherland: Women in Nazi Germany*—offers a theoretical framework for analyzing recent right-wing activism by women. Koonz argues that there is a linkage between misogyny, xenophobia and maternal concern that has energized many, if not most, "backlash conservative" movements during the 1990s. Koonz differentiates backlash conservatism from conventional conservatism in this way: conventional conservatives seek to retain the status quo, while backlash conservatives long to return to a way of life, real or imagined, that has been replaced by a more flexible and open value system. Nostalgia for good old-fashioned mothers suffuses backlash rhetoric; after all, if the kids are acting out, it must be the fault of failed mothering or "bad" mothers.

Koonz argues that backlash conservatism, fueled largely by fear, has been particularly potent when economic downturns follow partially successful drives to expand women's rights and social welfare entitlements. That scenario paved the way for radical right-wing movements from the United States to Italy to Eastern Europe during this decade: in each of these cases self-identified "good mothers" promise relief from the social disorder created by "selfish feminist mothers" and mobilize to ward off the threat of race or ethnic mixing. Focusing particularly on post-Cold War Eastern Europe, Koonz provides powerful evidence of the murderous potential of women who defend "maternal concerns" that underwrite the oppression of other women.

Following Koonz are two closer examinations of racist motherhood in the United States. Sociologist Kathleen Blee—author of *Women of the Klan*—traces the history of mothers in race-hate movements in the United States. Blee challenges our assumptions that either maternal sentiment or feminism need necessarily be opposed to bigotry, patriarchy and misogyny. Her research has led her to the inescapable conclusion that "women, and mothers, have played significant roles in almost every race-hate movement in the 20th century United States." Blee focuses here on two—the Ku Klux Klan of the 1920s and the neo-Nazi movement of the past fifteen years—in which mothers and motherhood have been foregrounded and manipulated. Essential to racist motherhood in Blee's formulation is an inability, or perhaps an unwillingness, to make the full transition from caring for one's own children to caring for all children. The women Blee writes about stop somewhere in between, identifying only with other children who are *like their own*. For these children, racist mothers are willing to fight.

Still, not all racist mothers are alike. Blee finds two different kinds of mothers within race-hate movements: one that fits Koonz's backlash conservative model, calling on mothers to reclaim a primary responsibility for child rearing and to step back from public activism; and another that identifies as racist-feminist, seeing motherhood as a means to greater influence within white power movements. Despite their differences, these mothers are united in the sense that they see no disjuncture between claims of maternal concern and calls to violent race-war. As in her book on Indiana Klanswomen, Blee argues that mothers in race-hate movements are seeking a sense of community and a social network in which to immerse themselves. Within these worlds, violent racism is the norm and "good motherhood" is defined by one's commitment to white supremacy and violent opposition to "race mixing." It is that banality of evil that Blee finds most disturbing and most dangerous.

Journalist Kathy Dobie—who has interviewed and profiled a range of "bad girls" from high school outcasts to prostitutes—here chronicles the life and times of a group of teenage skinhead mothers in Portland, Oregon. These are self-proclaimed racist-feminists who at first seek to prove their importance to the movement by being as violent as the boys. With time, however, they come to believe that their greatest contribution to empowering the white race will be as mothers, raising up the next generation of pure Aryan racists, acting as anchors for a separatist white community life of the future. Seeking to understand rather than to judge these young women, Dobie listens as they explain their alienation from the suburban cultures in which they were raised, and as they position themselves as the counterparts of black nationalists.

Dobie admits to being drawn at first to these young women's brazenness, their willingness to be outlaws, their rejection of middle-class values. Then it becomes clear to her that the sense of alienation that has propelled these young women and men into the racist skinhead movement has nurtured a twisted backlash dream—of white wedding dresses, and white picket fences and whites-only communities. As tormented as any teenagers by the fear of not fitting in, these young people have created a community-vision in which everyone is like them and their children. Anyone different from themselves has been made to disappear, and with them any of the troubling questions of identity that life in a multicultural society gives rise to. The romance of bad girls disappears in a bland longing for a kind of conflict-free community life that differs little from the suburban dreams of their parents—except that they explicitly express the fears and hatreds that underlay the white flight of thirty years ago. We are back to the banality of evil. We must understand it if we hope to offer alternative visions.

The final essay in this section, by historian Annelise Orleck, examines a much more moderate conservative mothers' organization—Federcasalinghe, the Italian Federation of Housewives. This group was founded in 1982—as the Italian feminist movement was losing steam—to campaign for state-funded salaries for women who stay at home to raise children and to care for elderly parents. Though Federcasalinghe eschews the violence and scapegoating that characterize the other movements described in this section, it is joined to them by its assertions that social harmony is sustained by women who stay at home to perform the gender-specific tasks of nurturing and care-taking. The group's primary allegiances are to the mainstream right—the Catholic Church, and discredited former prime ministers Giulio Andreotti and Silvio Berlusconi—but it has not shied away from making shifting coalitions with feminists, left-wing parties, and "pro-family" elements in the neo-Fascist party.

The longevity and seeming indestructibility of Federcasalinghe illustrates an important dimension of maternalist politics: that it need be neither right, nor left, neither inclusive nor racist. It can be profoundly slippery in an ideological sense, subject to manipulation by opportunists. The willingness of groups like the Housewives' Federation to claim the mantle of motherhood, even as they resist being pigeonholed politically, gives them great clout at a time when the old ideological verities are being called into question. They hold forth the possibility of an independent maternalist politics, but they also highlight the dangers of maternalism unmoored from any broader ideological context.

Motherhood and Politics on the Far Right

Claudia Koonz

When uncertainty reigns . . . in an unstable political setting, or in a nation fraught with ethnic strife, masses of women may well resent feminists' emphasis on equality and individual rights and, instead, work for solidarity and community . . . Fed by a dream of close families, secure homes, ethnic uniformity, and a transcendent set of ideals, women's special abilities and qualities inspire nostalgia for an imagined bygone era of simplicity. When economic downturn looms and ethnic strife threatens, difference trumps equality.

Most of the essays in this volume examine the ways that women have mobilized for political action around concerns tied to family and community. These women's initiatives rooted in mothers' demands have succeeded because of their own dynamism, and also because the institutions against which they protested valorized the motherly ideals invoked by the protesters. Yet as we praise maternal thinking and admire the female consciousness that inspires women to unite in defense of their rights, other discordant images from television newscasts crowd in on our vision. Serbian women throw themselves in the path of U.N. armored vehicles delivering life-saving food to Bosnian women and children; popular Italian women politicians deliver blistering invectives against feminism; and in the United States, the women chanting "pro-life" slogans celebrate men who murder physicians who perform abortions. These women seem not to belong in the same moral universe as Patsy Oliver, Dollie Burwell, Ruby Duncan, and the women of the Plaza de Mayo.

While the women activists we admire struggle for equal rights, anti-feminist women leaders fight for their feminine identity, which they locate in their maternal concerns. Although the major focus of this collection is on women organizing for progressive reforms, I inquire into the sinister potential of women who defend "maternal" interests that underwrite women's oppression; not coincidently, these women also support misogynist male leaders and murderous hatred of ethnic "outsiders." In this essay I investigate the explosive connection between xenophobia, misogyny and maternal concerns as evidenced in the post–Cold War world.

For as long as citizens have mobilized for political action, women's relative conservatism has been noticed and accounted for. Many observers, from Jules Michelet and Caesare Lombroso to Otto Weininger and Helene Deutsch, have blamed female character traits—emotionalism, narcissism, and fragility, among them—for women's passivity. More recently, feminists have pointed to the ways that masochism allows the weak to adapt to their hopeless lives by glorifying constraints as challenges or even advantages, thereby giving victims a feeling of control within their limited world.[1] For at least a century, despairing feminists and socialists also have assailed women's devotion to male-dominated religious hierarchies as a major cause of women's political quiescence. More recently, scholars have attributed women's acquiescence to male domination to women's emphasis on community cohesion and their fear of creating disunity by asking for equity.[2]

Virginia Woolf trenchantly settled on one word to explain women's passivity. "Fear," she wrote in *Three Guineas*, "is a powerful reason; those who are economically dependent have strong reasons for fear."[3] This includes not only the fear of men in women's immediate surroundings, to which Woolf referred, but fear of violence from men outside the community, fear of economic insecurity, and fear of social disintegration. Centering our investigation on fear leads us away from rhetoric about "essential" feminine traits and toward an examination of the circumstances that evoke fear. By asking "when" and "how" rather than "why" women participate in repressive regimes, we may better understand the processes that transform fear into panic.

Fundamental to an understanding of women in racist, misogynist movements is the distinction between fear and panic, which underscores the difference between two types of conservatives. Since the 1930s observers have named this split in many ways. Theodor Adorno, writing about interwar Germany, wrote of conservatives and "pseudo-conservatives."[4] Seymour Martin Lipset and Earl Raab separated "backlash politics" from its conservative antecedents.[5] "Reactionary" often has been appended to "conservative" to denote a particularly virulent radical strain of traditional opposition to change. More recently, scholars have stressed the comprehensive and radical utopianism lacking among conservatives and ubiquitous among followers of the radical right. It seems that in order for conservatives to "go on the warpath," they must feel empowered by an all-encompassing vision. "Traditionalism becomes fundamentalism," Malise Ruthven has written, "when its normal critique of society is transformed by religious intellectuals into a 'systematic whole' within the frame of a salvation history which both legitimizes the critique and endows it with emotive force."[6] Rebecca Klatch, in studying conservative American women, neatly separates the "social" from the "laissez-faire conservatives."[7]

For the purpose of this essay, I distinguish between "conventional conservatives" and "backlash conservatives," without implying that the distinction between them is sharp. The former defend the status quo; the latter aim to restore a world that has already been lost. In contrast to the relatively staid conservatives, backlash leaders demonstrate an extraordinary talent for mobilizing grassroots activism with calls for a social order marked by ethnic solidarity, "natural" gender roles, and an absolutist value system. Conventional conservatives, by contrast, are more elitist, secular, and libertarian. In the post–Cold War world, both varieties of conservatives crusade for purity in a phobic, symbolic universe. In the early 1990s, the rapid proliferation of backlash movements to the point where they have largely eclipsed conventional conservative parties replays, in frightening ways, the Weimar scenario—the rise of radical right parties in the aftermath of a time of social as well as political freedom.

The "Weimar Paradigm"—which I am deriving from an analysis of Germany in the 1920s—has haunted all subsequent democracies because it reveals fault lines that may well be systemic in any representative government but that become starkly visible during times of crisis. The paradigm develops in two stages. When progressive reforms, especially in regard to women's equality and welfare entitlements, seem to have achieved some measure of success, conservatives mobilize against further change and in defense of traditional hierarchies. As long as the economy is healthy and politics stable, they achieve only limited success. If, however, in the midst of generally progressive change, economic downtown or political instability threatens business as usual, backlash parties mobilize previously apathetic or complacent citizens. One hallmark of such movements in Western Europe and the United States is a high degree of women's activism. In this essay, I examine women's activism and gender ideology on the far right, first within the context of the original German prototype, and then within post–Cold War backlash movements in the United States, Italy and nations of the former Soviet bloc.

THE WEIMAR PROTOTYPE

In the wake of a serious defeat and an unpopular peace treaty, progressive reform changed the face of German politics and society during the 1920s. In 1919, German women became the first female citizens in any major nation, except Canada, to vote; Weimar parliaments included between 7 and 10 percent women; cultural liberation brought sexual freedom to young, urban women; female film stars smoked cigarettes and seduced matinee idols; and new opportunities for women in education and employment created a highly visible category of employed women. While progressives lobbied to further extend social justice, conservatives during the 1920s warned of racial degeneration, cultural collapse and the demise of morality. Voters who shared these anxieties during the 1920s regularly shunned the fledgling Nazi Party and voted for the Catholic Center or one of the two conservative parties. Women voters exhibited a slight preference for conservative over leftist parties and, to a far greater extent than men, avoided the Nazis.

However, the cataclysmic economic depression following the collapse of international markets in late 1929 changed all that. The financial and political impact in Germany was immediate. With over 30 percent unemployment and a political system paralyzed by six major parties that could not form a coalition, voters shifted their support away from the moderate parties of the middle to the extremes: the communists and Nazis. Although the situation appeared hopeless, voter turnout remained well above 80 percent in the six major national elections between 1930 and 1932. The larger the percentage of women voters, the higher the vote for Nazi candidates. As the Nazi Party leapt from the ninth largest party (with 2.6 percent of the vote) in 1928 to the largest party (with 37 percent of the vote) in July 1932, women joined the electoral "bandwagon" at a faster rate than men. Although a complete statistical record is not available, it appears that no "gender gap" divided women from men voters.[8] At the time, reporters noted the presence of many women in the Nazi following, but they attributed this behavior to stereotypically passive "feminine" behavior. When Hitler became chancellor in 1933, one typical report noted,

A new Women's Movement is starting in the new Reich, and it is going in a direction exactly opposite to that of all other women's movements as we have known them. For it is moving away from financial independence, away from business and the professions, back-to-the-home, to the nursery, to the kitchen. It is right in line, of course, with the drive for more wedding rings and more Peterchens and Emmies.[9]

Like many at the time, this observer explained women's behavior in terms of the seemingly irresistible attraction of Hitler's call for "more masculine men and more feminine women." Yet in the 1980s a few scholars looked beyond Nazi dogma as propagated by male leaders and investigated Nazi women themselves. They found a surprising number of self-conscious, dedicated women Nazis who stood their ground against misogynist Nazi men. Some historians even used the terms like "Nazi feminism" because they were so impressed with Nazi women's aggressive leadership style and independence.[10] When we look only at male leaders' speeches, the Nazi movement appears misogynist in the extreme. But when we look at women true believers, we discover women who acted in public ways that remind us of feminists.

Rather than expand "feminism" to include Nazis, however, I consider Nazi women leaders as "backlash conservatives," akin to women in fundamentalist neo-fascist and Christian Right organizations today. What do they have in common? Women on the far right express anger at the "system," hatred of "godless" materialists, resentment against ethnic "others," and a longing for a stable and gender-distinct social order. Against the backdrop of traditionalist nostalgia, backlash conservatives develop formidable organizing skills and considerable sophistication when it comes to modern media. Frequently, their male leaders underestimate their women followers' abilities, thereby inadvertently providing them with a certain freedom from oversight, which in turn accords to ambitious women a remarkable degree of independence. Women in the Nazi movement provide the first case study in this essay's look at activist women who organize in distinctively modern ways against feminism.

After the onset of the Great Depression, thousands of women with no prior record of political activism became regional and local leaders in the Nazi movement. Although they deplored the very sight of women officials in government office and exalted the role of the traditional housewife/mother, these women Nazis behaved in stridently "inappropriate" ways: heckling speakers, marching through the streets attired in distinctively Nazi dress, smuggling illegal weapons and leaflets and traveling alone through the countryside to win new converts. Other women, following a more "feminine" calling, enhanced a sense of community among Nazis by organizing soup kitchens, sewing centers, used clothing exchanges, and SA (Stormtroopers) welfare centers. Together with Hitler's charisma and his deputies' organizing skills, women Nazis created a tightly integrated and fanatical subculture. While the men spoke of the "Nazi Party," female Nazis spoke instead of "our Freedom Movement," by which they meant an organic spiritual community. For all their hatred of crass modernity, they followed Josef Goebbels' lead in brilliantly deploying the most up-to-date communications network, including recordings, mailing lists, newsletters, and slide shows. While conventional conservatives and Nazis shared many of the same attitudes toward the "woman question," women Nazis displayed great originality, daring and energy to recruit new followers. Conservatives preserved tradition, while Nazis modernized it.

The very presence of women as political activists (not candidates) enhanced the Nazis' dynamic image, and the demand for powerful state protection of mothers also contributed to the élan of modernity. Odd as it may seem today, the Nazis' promotion of racial science, a popular cause among many progressives at the time, set them apart from conventional conservatives. Finally, for

234 : *Claudia Koonz*

Nazi women, anti-Semitism carried a special meaning because women's "biological" second-class vis-à-vis Nazi men was offset by their radical arrogance toward Jews, Slavs and other "inferiors." Without the gloss of propriety that characterized conservative parties, the Nazi Party openly demanded the expulsion of women from politics and the elimination of Jewish influence in public life. In the biologized social world, gender separation harmonized with racial segregation.

POST–COLD WAR BACKLASH

Starting in 1945, political scientists pronounced all forms of wartime fascism dead. As late as 1990, one scholar noted, "the war . . . bankrupted Nazism and Fascism as viable ideologies . . . the extreme right could only stand by, powerless, as moderates were drawn irresistibly towards the centre."[11] Salazar's Portugal and Franco's Spain disappeared once their leaders died. Until the late 1980s, few believed that xenophobic, anti-democratic parties could attract more than a tiny following. By the early 1990s, that assumption had collapsed. A second, older, axiom about political life also has disintegrated: Max Weber predicted at the opening of the twentieth century that modernization and secular values progressed apace. But during World War II, Eric Fromm had already expressed doubts when he wrote about the widespread fear of freedom that drove citizens in modern nations toward authoritarianism.

In the 1990s, it appears that modernity, far from eclipsing spiritual faith, actually creates a *habitus* in which powerful backlash movements flourish. The call for ethnic purity and conservative cultural values inspired Vlaams Blok's ultranationalists in Belgium; Franz Schönhuber's Republikaner, the neo-Nazi National Democratic Party and Gerhard Frey's German People's Union in Germany; Jorg Haider's neo-fascist Freedom Party in Austria; the neo-fascists in Italy; and Jean-Marie Le Pen's Front National in France. Although the Christian right in the United States is not conventionally labeled "neo-fascist" and continues to be courted by the Republican Party, its doctrines fall squarely within the spectrum of what Europeans call "neo-fascism." In all of these movements, the rationalist language of equality fell before an onslaught of emotional rhetoric appealing to immutable ethnic and gendered identities.

The Nazi Party, for so long seen as an aberration, seems increasingly like the prototype for post–Cold War reactionary movements, although only in Japan has a mainstream politician made the error of openly acknowledging this fact. In both backlash and conventional conservative parties, women play central roles—albeit in dramatically contrasting ways. Reactionary movements everywhere promote the expulsion of women from political and economic power and cast feminists as the enemy. In western democratic settings, women often figure prominently in backlash political parties. But in Central and Eastern Europe, women virtually never appear as public figures in newly formed political institutions or in conservative protest movements.

RIGHT-WING RESURGENCE IN TWO POST–COLD WAR DEMOCRACIES

In Western Europe and the United States, after an era of reform and economic growth, progressive social change fell short of its supporters' ideals and fulfilled its critics' worst predictions. Women appeared on both sides of this debate. Traditionalist women became alarmed by their own declining status and financial insecurity and fearful of threats to their community supposedly posed by sexual promiscuity, drugs, violent crime, and corruption. Politically, these fears coalesced into hostility against democratic institutions, welfare, "big government," sexual "deviants" and atheism.[12] Where once anticommunism forged powerful bonds among right-wing zealots, the vacuum left by Soviet disintegration was filled by a symbolic universe populated with homosexuals, promiscuous welfare mothers, and emigrants—biologicalized enemies reminiscent of the Jews, sexual disease, and cultural degeneracy excoriated by Nazi ideologues. Although it seemed paradoxical at first, since the 1970s women in the United States have begun to appear as "backlash movers, shakers, and thinkers," in Susan Faludi's language. These women did not meekly reside in their homes awaiting change from the male-dominated political or economic system, but vigorously entered public life to oppose feminism and other liberal beliefs. While rhetorically exalting motherhood and family, they broke out of the "feminine" stereotype they endorsed. Describing these New Right women, Faludi shrewdly observes: "By divorcing their personal liberation from their public stands on sexual politics, they could privately take advantage of feminism while publicly deploring its influence. They could indeed 'have it all'—by working to prevent all other women from having that same opportunity."[13] Like backlash conservatives in democracies elsewhere, they reap ample benefits from the tolerant political system they plan to destroy. Italy and the United States provide two case studies in this phenomenon.

Backlash conservatives have demonstrated an extraordinary affinity for the most technologically sophisticated forms of communication. Most dramatically, the elections of June 1994 in Italy were won by a media mogul who dominated television so totally that rival candidates had to buy air time from his network. In the United States, backlash activists pioneered in the use of direct mail, electronic mail, videocassette, toll-free numbers, televangelism and radio talk shows. Popular music genres, from rock to rap, have been perfectly imitated by skinhead, neo-fascist, and Christian groups. Like the interwar Fascist and Nazi parties, backlash leaders brilliantly harness advanced technology.

Central to these values are ethnicity, which analysts commonly recognize, and gender, which is rarely noticed.[14] On the most obvious level, belief in "biological" difference between the sexes reinforces a racialized social vision. Equally important, the preservation of gentle virtues among women in the community complements masculinist values that vindicate ruthless attacks against "outsiders." Thus, the full range of ethical choices can be captured and compartmentalized according to gender. The presence of "virtue" blunts the impact of brutality. In the United States, although all major figures in Christian Right organizations are men, women comprise the majority of the faithful. And women proudly declare their special mission. Christian author and lecturer Connie Marshner promised that "It is women who will transmit civilization and humanity to the 21st century. Make no mistake . . . This involves nothing less than a change of heart by a whole generation. To save our society, we must change our hearts . . . If our hearts are changed, our politics will change and our public policies will change."[15] While powerful male preachers and politicians thunder their message of hatred in an increasingly aggressive media world, the presence of actual females combined with maternalist rhetoric provides a human face for an incitement to social war. In Italy, when women candidates swore to clean up corruption that had sullied the male-dominated political machine, voters believed them. Precisely because they had not previously participated in politics, they could claim to remain untouched by its temptations. Feminist scholars, like Rebecca Klatch and Kathleen Blee, have documented women's role as the lieutenants and sergeants in reactionary political movements.[16]

At first glance the role of women within the political structures of the far right in Italy and the United States could not be more different. While Italian women figure prominently in government offices, fewer backlash women hold office in the U.S. Senate or House. But in the United States, to a greater extent than in Italy, several influential women have achieved considerable status as media personalities, authors, lobbyists, and public speakers. Feminine idealism shines out over the greed of televangelists and self-serving Christian Coalition leaders. In Italy and the United States, backlash women make motherhood a central political concern. As Annelise Orleck notes, Italians look to the state for the financial support that would enable any mother to decide to remain at home without working. By contrast, rightist women in the United States deplore welfare benefits, especially to black unwed mothers. If mothers need additional services, they suggest, churches and other nongovernmental organizations ought to provide it. Yet, as in Italy, scores of women have taken up careers outside their homes in backlash movements. Sometimes backlash women in the United States appear with their spouses, as in the case of Dan and Nancy Mitchell, who host a popular talk show on the new National Empowerment Television, a conservative, 24-hour-a-day cable network that reaches 11 million homes. "Bryant and Katie are replaced by "Mitchells in the Morning," a perky couple—Dan and Nancy—who drink coffee and shake their heads over the liberal outrages in the morning papers. Trendy backlash women like Nancy use mainstream communication networks to deploy their "down-home" values.[17] They enter public life, in Connie Marshner's phrase, as "new traditional women" who offer a unique commitment to community, family and selflessness. Their Italian counterparts, by contrast, proudly call themselves the "new men" and boast of their public power. Irene Pivetti, Speaker of the Italian House, refers to herself as a "cittadino cattolico" using the masculine form for "Catholic Citizen."[18]

While in the United States male backlash leaders castigate the corruption of entrenched interests inside the Beltway, their female counterparts caricature and demean feminists. Beverly LaHaye, for example, laments the disoriented and confused "restless woman" who becomes easy prey for feminists who harp on "my rights" and "my goals," "my body" above communal values. LaHaye charges that among feminists, "the 'freedom' to fornicate outside of marriage and to murder their unborn children is looked upon as a great stride forward in the status of women."[19] Blaming feminism for social chaos and moral confusion, LaHaye calls for tough countermeasures to restore an ordered and stratified world. This may mean that women, even white middle-class women like herself, would lose access to the upper echelons of the hierarchy, but the exchange of opportunity for security would make the trade-off worthwhile. When backlash males advocate ruthless competition (armed or economic) to achieve their goals, the vision of domesticated women at the heart of communal and family life helps to rationalize their merciless tactics. "Soft" feminine qualities become increasingly valuable as the public sphere disintegrates and the material conditions of daily life grow harsher.

RIGHT-WING RESURGENCE IN THE FORMER SOVIET BLOC

The crisis in the former Soviet bloc is far more devastating than disenchantment and frustration in the West. One might expect to find women in the forefront of anger at Communist rule since, as in Italy, women's lack of experience in a discredited system might provide women with a source of popularity. Then, too, when dissident organizations like Solidarity were forced to operate clandestinely, women formed the backbone of their survival strategies. In the last months of Soviet rule, women figured prominently in reformist associations like the New Forum and the Round Table in the former E.

Germany. But by 1990, women had vanished. Raging xenophobia, endemic misogyny, unemployment, and rampant lawlessness had rendered political stability fragile at best. Two case studies, Russia and the former Yugoslavia, highlight trends that span post–Cold War Central and Eastern Europe.

While we read of women who follow the newly powerful religious leaders and rally to crusade against ethnic "outsiders," we do not read about any women of influence within these movements. For centuries, soldiers have died for "Mother Russia," and today, Serbians pay reverent homage to their "motherland." This mythic adoration, far from promoting actual women to responsible positions, vindicates the drive to exclude them from civic space. Charismatic, virile leaders, from Vladimir Zhirinovsky to Franco Tudjman, glorify women who devote their lives to domestic concerns. They extol feminine virtues as part of their call for "purified" ethnic unity against the evil "outsiders," especially Jews and Muslims. Indeed, the family and ethnic community form the two ideological pillars of the entire post-Communist political spectrum. During *perestroika*, male politicians throughout the Soviet bloc openly campaigned against women's emancipation. The liberal Russian press persisted in defending traditionalist family values with slogans like "The civil duty of women is to be women." Mikhail Gorbachev told his comrades that in order for women to fulfill their "natural destiny, . . . we should help our women spend more time at home."

As the quality of life has deteriorated for most people, women who do not conform to the new stereotype have become convenient scapegoats for government failures. In Croatia, the Nationalists, who won the election of 1992, blame their subsequent failure to fulfill their promises on "women, pornography, and abortion."[20] In Russia, Nadezhda Azhgikhina reports, the "Western feminist" has become a threatening figure because she is the very antithesis of the self-sacrificing wife. This aggressive lesbian comes to Russia to corrupt innocent Russian women.[21]

Television and the print media denounce women as being "overemancipated" and "masculinized" even as they print pornographic photos of nudes in the centerfolds of daily newspapers. Under communism, they maintain, women had too many rights, and they call for a return of "strong" families.[22] In Russia, nationalists redeployed a favorite trope of Nazi propaganda in a popular draft Law on the Protection of the Family that defined the family as the "cell" of all society. The legislation proposed that only the family, under the male head of household, would be able to own property or decide on procreation. A beleaguered Russian feminist told American reporter Katrina vanden Heuvel, "you come to the conclusion that the only thing a woman will be able to do in life is to fulfill the state-approved role of motherhood, since other opportunities for self-realization are denied her."[23] Although the anti-abortion legislation has been most dramatic in Poland, opposition to abortion is a staple of backlash conservatism throughout Eastern Europe.[24] Significantly, the rationale rests on the need for a larger, stronger ethnic population, not on the putative sin of "fetus murder." To Polish women, Solidarity's reactionary stance on women's role does not come as a surprise, for they recall the early 1980s when Lech Walesa supported only reforms that fostered women's traditional roles: three-month maternity leave and improved day care.[25]

Throughout Eastern and Central Europe, feminists are caricatured in much the same terms as among the Christian Right organizations in the United States and the conservative and neo-fascist parties in Italy. As in the West, the anti-feminist initiative does not come only from men. But in the East, virtually no women appear as leaders in the campaign. Rather than being media personalities or legislators, they are writers who mainly address women readers. Russian feminist Nadezhda Azhgikhina cites a woman journalist who described leaving an international women's forum feeling dispirited: "In torment after a conversation with an unattractive, nasty and aggressive American feminist, she returns to the railroad station, where two drunken Russian men approach her and grasp her hands. This finally restores her sense of herself as a female; smiling at the men, she reflects with relief that Russian feminism will never make any headway."[26]

Irene Dölling, a feminist from the former E. Germany, pithily highlighted the shift in gender ideology for women that came with unification:

If one were to [compare] two issues of the women's magazine *Für Dich*, one from 1989 and one from 1990, . . . One set, mostly poor quality black-and-white prints, could be summarized as stating, "Women work like men and owe their allegiance to a greater unity as integral parts of a collective 'We'." The other pictures, in seductively brilliant color, [say] I am a very feminine woman who relates to the world primarily through my excellent taste for beauty and harmony.[27]

Dölling explains the popularity of the new image as the result of women's justified need for improvement in material living conditions, a longing for western "life-style," and contempt for everything communist. Azhgikhina, too, points out that a general hatred for all cultural values associated with communism produced the feeling that "all that was forbidden yesterday must be good." Part of what was forbidden was any public discussion or display of sexuality and interest in sentimental topics. A hunger for forbidden pleasures may account for the proliferation of women's magazines like *Sudarushka* ("Little Madam") and *Provornista* ("Nimble Woman") that feature sex, horoscopes, advice columns, religion, pop psychology and beauty. Azhgikhina laments, "It is the women journalists . . . who are most active in developing . . . the new images . . . No one made them do this. On the contrary, not only do almost all of the men's publications publish soft-core porn, many women's magazines do also . . . "[28] Like the desire for consumer goods, the dream of a sexualized social world was one product of a feeling of deprivation. To expect women (or anyone else) to resist the allure of emotional and material gratification would be unrealistic. As in the West, the experience of consumer society, breadwinner husbands, and capitalist free markets may in the long term produce rebellious women.

However, the politics of women's issues in the mid-1990s are bound to reverberate differently in the East than in the West because, despite communist propaganda about "stateswomen" and stalwart women comrades, actual women in Soviet block nations never experienced genuine integration into positions of power and prestige. Constitutional guarantees of equal rights for women came from "the top down" and not in response to women's mobilization. Equally important, propaganda about "emancipated" Soviet bloc women only disguised women's endemic inferior status. Impressive gains in women's education did not translate into access to power. The popular cultural image of women's equality under communism was a media creation: a stalwart worker/mother, the mirror opposite of the women in the televised "ideal" families in the United States, from "Dallas" to "Melrose Place."

On the other hand, the end of communism affected women differently than it affected men. It sharply reduced career options for women, reduced childcare and health facilities and produced higher levels of unemployment than for men. Even readers of popular women's magazines may feel nostalgia for some of the old values that offered important social welfare benefits and placed collective well-being over individual advancement.[29] The term "conservative" in formerly communist countries has a double valence, for in addition to suggesting ethnic, religious, and conservative political values, it may also connote a nostalgic longing for the safety of the old "hard-line" communist regime. The old order may not have allowed women to advance up the status hierarchy, but it did provide fundamental material security for mothers.

The post-communist era, by contrast, casts women as the dependents of their individual husbands, caretakers of their children, and members of the ethnic community. In wartime this identity is deepened. The ideology of polarized gender roles and irrevocably divided ethnic communities on occasion allows women access to public view. Given the binary Eve/Mary symbols so popular in the media, it is not surprising that women's actual roles in wartime have been polarized. In the dominant ethnic discourse, women appear as the staunch defenders of their menfolk in uniform, and also as the utterly passive victims of "enemy" men. But their identity as mothers may also empower them to protest against war. Using the former Yugoslavia and Russia as case studies, I briefly survey these trends.

Although women in theory remain tied to their homes, they may on occasion depart from the stereotypical image and enter the combat zones. Perhaps best known were the women who blocked U.N. convoys bringing food and medicine to Bosnian women in Sarajevo.[30] It goes without saying, however, that women are not encouraged to participate in "masculine" combat. The one woman Serbian nationalist who has made headlines is a Canadian woman (of Irish descent) who "converted" to the cause and created a veritable scandal when she arrived in Belgrade and asked to join the front-line troops.[31] But in genocidal war, "enemy" civilians become targets for military violence. Although many identify the war in the former Yugoslavia as uniquely "postmodern" in this respect, slaughter of helpless populations as a war aim is a venerable tradition, from the Crusades to Vietnam.[32]

Alongside lavish praise for the maternal virtues of "their" women comes contempt for "enemy" women. This vilification and victimization of women is the logical corollary of the axiom that "pure" women belong to their husbands and their ethnic community. This juxtaposition is most dramatic in the former Yugoslavia, where soldiers, while exterminating their enemies, also systematically raped "enemy" women. Estimates of the number of rape victims ran as high as thirty thousand in early 1993, when Dame Anne Warburton directed the European Community fact-finding mission.[33] The team reported also on the existence of between fifteen and seventeen "rape camps" where women prisoners were forced to endure daily, multiple rapes. In October 1993, a U.N. panel concluded that "rape was a weapon of Serbs."[34]

While rape (and slave brothels) have accompanied previous wars, the military organization of rape appears unusual, and perhaps unique, in the former Yugoslavia. At first this seems paradoxical: Why rape a woman who belongs to a group of people targeted for extermination? Two considerations render this decision "logical." Serbian and Croatian soldiers imagine their own genes to be sufficiently powerful to override female genes. They told their victims (whom they typically released from camps after it became too late to secure a legal abortion) that they had sent a traitor baby into the "enemy" community—the biological equivalent of the Trojan Horse. Systematic rape debases the ethnic "enemy" by polluting his "biological" descent. In addition, it wounds not only the women victims but the "enemy" men, to whom the women in theory belong. Professor Asim Kurjak, a Muslim physician, explained:

You see, if you want to destroy the dignity of a Muslim man, rape his wife or daughter, and he will—very often—not be able to cope with the shame. . . . This is organized, in order to achieve a kind of genocide. First of all they (Serbs) know what rape means in traditional Muslim culture. Secondly, they know that repeated rape will destroy the reproductive desires and abilities of Muslim women.[35]

Rape of the enemy's property wounds his masculine pride and, like land mines designed to maim and not kill, it inflicts lasting damage on the living.

Starting with powerful media wars against the "other" in Serbia and Croatia, the actual war has deepened national and gender identity and flattened distinctions among "alien" outsiders. Gender polarity within the "insider" ethnic community contributes to a "natural" sense of order and simultaneously divides the moral universe into ruthless men fighting against an external threat and gentle women who preserve the values worth dying for. This double binary construct—by which women identify with both a gendered and an ethnic identity—functions most obviously during ethnic wars. But on some occasions, even in the most severe crises, a few women (not necessarily acting as feminists) break ranks with their ethnic community and call for peace in the name of motherly concerns.

From the first months of the wars in the former Yugoslavia, women demonstrated publicly against the war, carrying signs, "Soldiers do not shoot women." A few courageous women in Croatia and Serbia have protested against aggression on all sides since April 1991, and the media briefly covered their "women in black" protests. But even in the absence of media attention in Croatia and Serbia, anti-war women's groups such as the Center for Antiwar Action in Belgrade and the Center for Women War Victims in Zagreb persisted in their activities. Far greater freedom of the press in Russia meant that when Russian mothers opposed the invasion of Chechnya, their actions captured world-wide media attention, particularly during the battle for Grozny in early 1995. In late January, dozens of Russian mothers traveled to the front demanding the return of their sons. In a widely publicized exchange, Chechen authorities released thirty-four Russian soldiers and received forty-three Chechen POWs.[36] Shrewdly, Chechen leaders negotiated only with Russian women and not with Yeltsin's representatives. Alla Dudayev, widow of Chechen leader Jokhar Dudayev, continued this tradition of gendered negotiating strategies in April 1996 when she offered to direct "a purely humanitarian peacemaking mission as a Russian woman who was married to a Chechen man."[37]

CONCLUSIONS

As we celebrate women activists who work for a more humane social, ecological and economic environment, other women crusaders in the public sphere give us pause to reflect on "female consciousness" and "maternal thinking." All too often "feminine" concerns seem uncomfortably close to what politicians in the United States have termed "family values," whose reach extends from a "strong" family with a man at the helm to a "pure" nation free of ethnic outsiders. With Virginia Woolf's warning about the political consequences of fear framing our interpretations, we stop short of essentializing any "typically" feminine traits. When uncertainty reigns, for example in an unstable political setting or in a nation fraught with ethnic strife, masses of women may well resent feminists' emphasis on equality and individual rights and, instead, work for solidarity and community. The call for hierarchy and sacrifice fends off dread of disintegration from within or conquest from without. Fed by a dream of close families, secure homes, ethnic uniformity, and a transcendent set of ideals, women's special abilities and qualities inspire nostalgia for an imagined bygone era of simplicity. When economic downturn looms and ethnic strife threatens, difference trumps equality.

In these unstable settings, women may or may not assume roles of public leadership. Post–Cold War developments, informed by historical experience from Weimar Germany, suggest that, where prior feminist reforms accustomed citizens to the presence of women in public spaces, backlash politicians will admit women into their ranks and even, within certain parameters, share the spotlight with them. Where, by contrast, citizens have little experience with either democracy or women's participation in visible public roles, women citizens may well support backlash causes, but no women emerge as leaders. In the post–Cold War world, ethnicity and gender shape the contours of the mythic community that provides emotional ballast in hard times. Gender distinctions constitute the "us" by which insiders define the "other." Perceiving themselves surrounded by catastrophe beyond their control, women and men in endangered communities stifle the call for individual rights and cry instead for collective liberty.

As members of a bio-political community, women can take pride in their special capacities for motherhood, grassroots morale building, nourishment, and care for the weak. Fear, as Virginia Woolf warned, blunts aspirations for women's equality and makes a very different social vision attractive. Crises frequently polarize gender roles that extol womanhood within a community and simultaneously violate women defined as outsiders. In the post–Cold War United States and Europe, the New Right has deployed polarized gender assumptions to mobilize pervasive anxieties to underwrite assaults by the powerful against the weak, whether they be mothers receiving welfare in Chicago or unarmed women in Bosnia.

NOTES

1. Tania Modleski, *Loving with a Vengeance* (New York: Methuen, 1982), pp. 38, 45. Victoria DeGrazia elaborated on this point in *How Fascism Ruled Women* (Berkeley: University of California Press), p. 254; cf. Leonore E. A. Walker, "Inadequacies of the Masochistic Personality Disorder Diagnosis for Women," *Journal of Personality Disorders* 1 & 2 (summer 1987):178.

2. Elaine Foster, "Women and the Inverted Pyramid of the Black Churches in Britain," in *Refusing Holy Orders: Women and Fundamentalism in Britain*, ed. Gita Sahgal and Nira Yuval-Davis (London: Virago Press, 1993). Also see Martin Durham, "Women and the National Front," in *Neo-Fascism in Europe*, ed. Luciano Cheles, Ronnie Ferguson and Michalina Vaughn (New York, London: Longman, 1991), pp. 278–280.

3. Virginia Woolf, *Three Guineas* (New York: Harcourt, Brace and World, 1938), p. 120.

4. Theodor W. Adorno and Max Horkheimer, *The Authoritarian Personality* (New York: Harper and Brothers, 1950). Adorno is one of the very few observers to comment on women as distinctive participants in conservative causes.

5. Seymour Martin Lipset and Earl Raab, *The Politics of Unreason: Right-Wing Extremism in America, 1790–1970* (New York: Harper & Row, 1970).

6. Malise Ruthven, "Was Weber Wrong?," *London Review of Books*, August 18, 1994.

7. Rebecca E. Klatch, *Women of the New Right* (Philadelphia: Temple University Press, 1987), pp. 4–15.

8. I take a differential of seven percent as the baseline for a gender gap. On the breakdown by sex, cf. Helen Boak, "'Our Last Hope': Women's Votes for Hitler," *German Studies Review* XII, no. 2. (May 1989):289–310.

9. Dr. William Seaver Woods, "Germany Faces a Baby Famine," *Pictorial Review* Sept. (1993):67.

10. Liliane Crips, "'Nationale-Feministische' Utopien," *Feministische Studien* 8, no. 1 (1990):128–136; and Leila Rupp, "Mothers of the Volk: The Image of Women in Nazi Ideology," *Signs* 3 (1977):362–379.

11. Roberto Chiarini, "The 'Movimento Sociale Italiano': A Historical Profile," in *Neo-Fascism in Europe*, ed. Luciano Cheles, Ronnie Ferguson, and Michalina Vaughn (New York, London: Longman, 1991), p. 20.

12. Nancy T. Ammerman, "North American Protestant Fundamentalism," in *Fundamentalisms Observed*, ed. Martin E. Marty and R. Scott Appleby (Chicago and London: University of Chicago Press, 1993), pp. 2–4.

13. Susan Faludi, *Backlash: The Undeclared War Against American Women* (New York: Doubleday Anchor, 1991), pp. 221, 256.

14. Martin E. Marty, Nancy T. Ammerman, Mortimer Ostow, and George M. Marsden. Comparative studies also overlook the ways in which women and gender function in religious activism. Gilles Kepel, "The Revenge of God: The Resurgence of Islam, Christianity and Judaism in the Modern World," *Polity*, December 16, 1990. Martin Riesebrodt, *Pious Passion: The Emergence of Modern Fundamentalism in the United States and Iran* (Berkeley: University of California Press, 1993).

15. Connaught C. Marshner, *The New Traditional Woman* (Washington, D.C.: Free Congress Research & Education Foundation, 1982), p. 3.

16. Margaret Lamberts Bendroth, *Fundamentalism and Gender, 1875 to the Present* (New Haven, CT: Yale University Press, 1994) and Gita Sahgal and Nira Yuval-Davis, ed., *Refusing Holy Orders: Women and Fundamentalism in Britain* (London: Virago Press, 1993); cf. the review of the literature on women in Islam by Bruce Lawrence, "Muslim Women and Islamic Fundamentalism," *AMEWS Newsletter, Association for Middle East Women's Studies* VII (1991):1–2, 1–5.

17. Jon Meacham, "Surfing on Newt's Network," *Newsweek*, January 30,1995, p. 36.

18. Trisha Thomas, "Women Ride Right-Wing Wave," *San Francisco Chronicle*, June 18, 1994, final edition.

19. Beverly LaHaye, *The Restless Woman* (Grand Rapids, Mich.: Zondervan, 1984), pp. 129–130.

20. Renata Salecl, "Nationalism, Anti-Semitism, and Anti-Feminism in Eastern Europe," *New German Critique* 57 (fall 1992):58–59.

21. Nadezhda Azhgikhina, "Back to the Kitchen," *Women's Review of Books* XII, 8 (May 1995):14.

22. Barbara Einhorn, *Cinderella Goes to Market: Citizenship, Gender and Women's Movements in East Central Europe* (London: Verso, 1993), pp. 156–157.

23. Katrina vanden Heuvel, "Anti-Feminist Russia, Sexploitation Meets Mandatory Motherhood," *Washington Post*, Feburary 21, 1993. Over half of all Russian families with three or more children live in poverty, and high divorce rates mean that 700,000 fathers of children under one year old leave their wives. One in five women is the sole wage earner in her family,.

24. Wanda Nowicka, "Two Steps Back: Poland's New Abortion Law," *Journal of Women's History* 5, no. 3 (winter 1994):153–156. In November 1992, a law passed the extraordinary Parliamentary Commission that outlawed contraceptives and allowed abortion only when the mother's life was in danger. An outpouring of opposition was responsible for a milder version actually passing the parliament.

25. Renata Siemienska, "Women in the Period of Systemic Changes in Poland," *Journal of Women's History* 5, no. 3 (winter 1994):72–76.

26. Azhgikhina, "Back to the Kitchen," p. 14.

27. Irene Dölling, " 'But the Pictures Stay the Same . . .' The Image of Women in the Journal *Für Dich* Before and After the 'Turning Point' " in Nanette Funk and Magda Mueller, eds., *Gender Politics and Post-Communism: Reflections from Eastern Europe and the Former Soviet Union* (New York: Routledge, 1993), p. 168.

28. Azhgikhina, "Back to the Kitchen," p. 13.

29. Vicki L. Helsi and Arthur H. Miller, "Gender and Institutional Support in Lithuania, Ukraine and Russia," *Europe-Asia Studies* 45, no. 3 (1993):505–532.

30. "20 or More Die as Serbs Pound Gorazde, Women and Children Force UN soldiers to Halt Outside Enclave," *Daily Telegraph*, April 22, 1994. Sue Masterman, "The Bosnian Serbs Threw Their Ultimate Weapon into the Arena Again Today—Women and Children," *Evening Standard*, March 1, 1994.

31. Marcia de Almeida, "Zeal of the Convert: A Canadian Chetnik," *Internews*, July 16, 1993. The 43-year-old Jewell Chandler Adan arrived in Serbia in June 1993 ready to fight. Renaming herself "Svetlana Jewell Tomic," she requested transfer to the front lines, which her commanding officers did not grant.

32. Raphaël Lemkin papers, Duke University Archives. Roger Cohen, "In Sarajevo, Victims of a 'Postmodern' War," *New York Times*, May 21, 1995. What may distinguish genocide in the 1990s is the vastly expanded number of bystanders created by video technology.

33. Linda Grant, "Rape Babies: What Do We Know?," *The Independent*, London, January 10, 1993. The BBC carried the first report of mass rapes on September 25, 1992. Judy Darnell, a registered nurse from Marlton, N.J., who worked in

Bosnia, had already reported the policy of rape in Croatia six months earlier. Judy Mann, "Report from the Front," *Washington Post*, January 15, 1993. Roy Gutman, *Witness to Genocide* (New York: Macmillan, 1993).

34. Paul Lewis, "Rape Was Weapon of Serbs," *New York Times*, October 20, 1993. The panel concluded that the overwhelming majority of victims were Muslim women and most of the rapists were Serbs, although it found violations on all sides. The panel also reduced the estimates of rapes established by the EC Commission investigation from upward of 30,000 to about 20,000.

35. "Are Serbian Forces Sowing the Seeds of Genocide?," *South China Morning Post*, February 14, 1993.

36. "Prisoners of War Exchanged in Dagestan," *Interfax*, Moscow, January 26, 1995; BBC broadcast, January 28, 1995.

37. "Chechen Deputy Premier Willing to Include Dudayev's Widow in Talks," British Broadcasting Corporation's World Service, April 29, 1996.

Mothers in Race-Hate Movements

Kathleen Blee

When the wife joins and the children participate, you know that the family is going to stay with the Klan. —1920s Ku Klux Klan field agent

In 1924, three mothers posed proudly for photographs as they pledged their newborn babies to a crusade for white and Christian supremacy at a meeting of the Women of the Ku Klux Klan. Almost seventy years later, in 1992, eighteen young women gathered on an outdoor stage—babies and rifles in their arms—to be photographed giving the Nazi salute at the First Annual Aryan Festival, in rural Pennsylvania. One of them spoke for the group, announcing that white Aryan women were now ready to do battle with ZOG (the Zionist Occupation Government) and its white-traitor supporters and that neither the threat of imprisonment nor death could deter them from this mission.[1]

The notion of women—especially mothers—as active agents in racial hate movements is both frightening and confusing. It is frightening because it suggests that maternal practices and goals can become deeply entangled with reactionary, bigoted, patriarchal and misogynist interests. It is confusing because women—in their roles as mothers—do not appear to benefit from the traditional goals of hate-based politics such as heightened nationalism, a return to earlier forms of family or community, or the preservation of existing economic arrangements. Ideas about motherhood have motivated resistance to capitalism, colonialism and imperialism—as several articles in this book document—but also have been wielded in the pursuit of nationalism, racial supremacy, class privilege and other forms of social inequality and political domination.

Women, and mothers, have played significant roles in almost every major race-hate movement in the twentieth century United States. And in at least two major waves of organized racist activity—the massive 1920s Ku Klux Klan (KKK) and modern neo-Nazi and Klan groups—mothers and the idea of "motherhood" appear in particularly prominent and complex ways. By examining these two mass racist movements, it is possible to begin to understand the contradictory ways in which a politicized motherhood may be pulled in reactionary or bigoted directions.

In the 1920s, hundreds of thousands of women joined the Women of the Ku Klux Klan, enlisting their children in "Ku Klux Kiddies," Junior Ku Klux Klans and other auxiliaries. With a total enrollment of several million men, women and children, the combined Klan groups of the 1920s mounted a powerful campaign of religious and racial bigotry, directing their message of hatred toward Catholics, Jews, African-Americans, labor radicals and others. Although women had been excluded from the first Klan, which was formed in the post–Civil War Reconstruction era, this second Klan movement welcomed white native-born Protestant women, conscious that they could deliver votes and bring substantial sums of money into the organization. The Klan appealed to mothers especially, characterizing them as the foundation of the family and the nation and suggesting that it was white Protestant women's maternal duty to ensure the racial and religious privileges of their children.[2]

Today's organized racism also counts significant numbers of women and children in its ranks. The movement ranges from neo-Nazis and white-power skinheads to the modern Ku Klux Klan and is known collectively as the "Fifth Era." One branch of the Fifth Era, the neo-Nazi or Aryan movement, is an assortment of about one hundred groups in 31 states plus an estimated four thousand other white-power skinheads and skingirls. The most prominent neo-Nazi group is the White Aryan Resistance (WAR) and its female affiliate, Aryan Women's League (AWL)—intensely racist and anti-Semitic organizations that claim to take the side of white working people against both race mixing and capitalist exploitation. These groups have been charged with stockpiling weapons in preparation for an all-out "race war" and have been named in several cases of vicious assaults and murders of minorities.[3]

A second branch of modern organized racism is Christian Identity (CI), a quasi-theological movement that believes that Anglo-Saxons are the lost tribe of Israel and that Jews, African-Americans and other people of color are inferiors sent to earth as a scourge of God. Although CI includes both male and female members, it is intensely patriarchal, with an ideology that is equal parts anti-Semitic, anti-Catholic, racist and paramilitary survivalist.[4]

Finally, the Fifth Era includes the Ku Klux Klan, which today is not an

organization per se but a name under which operate perhaps a dozen competing racist organizations organized into at least seventy-five factions. These
Klans have approximately ten thousand committed followers and five or ten
times as many sympathizers. In recent years, they have been highly visible in
recruitment efforts throughout the South and Midwest and have been accused
in a number of violent, even lethal attacks on African-Americans, immigrants, gays and lesbians and others. Women are highly visible and vocal
activists in several Klan organizations. They compose an estimated 25 percent
of the Klan's total current membership, although leadership positions continue to be largely held by men.[5]

Despite the differences in these groups, there are distinct commonalities in
how racist movements use motherhood to promote racial hatred and in the
results of using motherhood as a basis for white supremacist identities and
politics.[6] Women in these various racist groups use similar language to construct their maternal identities. They cite motives for activism that are closely
linked. And, there are strong common themes expressed by the racist political
cultures to which these women are drawn.

MATERNAL IDENTITIES

The history of race-hate politics in this country and elsewhere makes it clear
that there is no simple relationship between motherhood and politics. In
many cases, becoming a mother causes women to see more clearly the negative impact of nuclear proliferation, capitalist exploitation or social injustice
on themselves and their families. Thus, mothers have been active participants—as mothers—in numerous progressive social movements. But if
motherhood has broadened the political horizons of some women, in other
cases it has promoted a very narrow and exclusive identity for women as
guardians of their racial, social class, or national identities and futures.

Motherhood can generate racist and reactionary political attitudes and
actions for several reasons. First, the idea of motherhood is often central to
how political movements create racial identities. Racist movements have
been particularly interested in recruiting mothers because of their concern
with racial destiny, racial reproduction, racial purity, and socialization into
a racial identity—issues in which mothers have historically been central.
These groups encourage mothers to promote racial awareness and a sense of
racial superiority in their children.

In the 1920s, the Women's Klan was active in the promotion of white racial
identity across generations. It sponsored a "Tri-K-Klub" for teenaged daughters meant to teach young girls the responsibilities they would face as "future
mothers of the race" and a "Cradle Roll" through which younger children,

even infants, were enlisted in the Klan's crusade. Moreover, Klan women promoted racial identity in propaganda that heralded the achievements of white Protestant Americans and warned that interracial marriage would pollute the purity—and thus destroy the future—of the white race.[7]

Today, all groups within the neo-Nazi movement stress both Aryan childbearing and the creation of a racial, and racist, identity for whites. In the newsletter of neo-Nazi women, *White Sisters*, motherhood is portrayed as key to an Aryan-supremacist future since "one Aryan baby born in a small town is worth much more than a dozen Klan rallies."[8] The Aryan Women's League sponsors a baby-clothes exchange and a baby fund to subsidize Aryan child rearing, noting that "procreating our Race is the only way in which we survive" and insisting that every Aryan couple should strive to have three or four children.[9]

Issues of racial identity and white heritage likewise appear in nearly every publication of the modern neo-Nazi Klan movement. Christian Identity groups, in particular, place great emphasis on promoting a sense of racial distinctiveness and superiority among whites, condemning as "whoredom" all forms of cultural exchange, integration, interracial marriage and humanism. In her column, "For Women Only," Cheri Peters, wife of CI leader Peter J. Peters, recalls how her grandmother "stressed the importance of *white* skin . . . and had a difficult time understanding why white girls desired to look like Mexicans [in other words, why they wanted suntans] . . . In today's society my grandmother would be what is called a 'racist.' If only we had more 'racist' grandmothers today."[10]

Similarly, a recorded message on AWL's telephone "hate line" tells Aryan women that whites "have been programmed to feel guilty for everything—slavery, the so-called Holocaust and such"—but warns that race mixing "is one guilt that the white race has not been charged with and they should be (since) the more race-mixing that continues, the better off the Jews have of controlling the United States."[11] The AWL also has established a penpal exchange for children, Aryan-only schools and a "personals" column for young adults—efforts to prevent race mixing by ensuring that the next generation can locate white supremacist friends and marriage partners.[12]

Such broad-based appeals to race pride, however, have drawn far fewer women into racist organizations than campaigns aimed to strike at mother's fears about their children's physical safety. "Good" motherhood can provoke reactionary politics when, as for many in the twentieth century United States, it is defined fairly narrowly, as protecting and providing for one's own children, rather than as having a responsibility toward all children. Thus, although mothering can sensitize women to common experiences, promoting empathy and cooperation, the experience of being a mother also can generate fear and competition, even animosity and antagonism toward others. The

1920s Women's Klan sought to bolster its call for white Protestant supremacy by spreading rumors that African-American men were kidnapping young girls for white slavery dens and that Catholic priests routinely molested Protestant girls; mothers were urged to join the Klan to protect and defend the honor of their daughters.[13] In the 1970s, a group known as Restore Our Alienated Rights (ROAR) enlisted white working-class Boston mothers in a campaign against school desegregation in similar ways. Organizers fueled mothers' worries that their children's safety would be endangered and the quality of their education would decline if African-American children were bused to formerly all-white neighborhood schools.[14]

Propaganda issued by neo-Nazi groups today is even more explicit in playing up this danger issue. In recorded phone messages, leaflets, posters, books and newsletters, they portray all African-American men as potential rapists and victimizers of young white women.[15] Pamphlets circulated by the Aryan Women's League encourage Aryan mothers to join those who are "fighting for white survival," citing "a non-White crime wave which makes our cities unsafe for our families" and "the brain-washing, by the schools and the media, of White youth with racial self-hatred and genocidal race-mixing propaganda."[16] To underscore its warning that white children are in danger of becoming an "endangered species," Aryan-power groups in California have distributed random photos of white children, captioned "We will never forget, never forgive! We will forever be vigilant in our endeavor for our children's future. A White future!"[17]

Although glorification of the traditional social role of mothers as nurturers and protectors has often been used by supremacist groups to encourage women to participate in racial politics, appeals to white women's rights have also been used as a recruitment strategy. The 1920s Women of the Ku Klux Klan presents a particularly clear case. At the same time as the Women's Klan mounted an appeal to white Protestant women in their roles as mothers and guardians of racial destiny, it addressed women as workers and as newly enfranchised citizens, calling for passage of the Equal Rights Amendment, an end to sexual harassment, and increased legal rights for women.[18]

Moreover, even this Klan's view of motherhood was complex. Not unlike progressive and reformist groups of the early twentieth century, the Women's Klan proclaimed the potential power of a politicized motherhood. The inherently moral natures of white mothers, it argued, would contribute to elevating public morality and ending political corruption. In sharp contradiction to the glorification and extolling of homelife by the male Klan, 1920s Klanwomen spoke of motherhood, as they did housework, primarily as work—the labor of maintaining a house, a family and a nation. Some Klanswomen went so far as to campaign for the eight-hour day for mothers, suggesting that motherhood and housework deserved both social recognition and social regulation.[19] Surprisingly, they were supported in this by some male Klan members. Although many men in the 1920s Klan regarded the proper role for women with children as in the home, not in the workplace or political arena, others had a broader view of the role of mothers. As one Grand Dragon declared in 1923, "no longer will man say that in the hand of woman rests the necessity of rocking the cradle only. She has within her hand the power to rule the world."[20]

Women in today's Klan, in contrast, seem to accept a greater degree of gender inequality. Women are recruited into the Klan primarily to promote the Klan's agenda of nurturing white supremacism in the next generation and tend to support the Klan's opposition to feminism, affirmative action and abortion, all of which they regard as promoted by Jewish interests. Klanswomen separate themselves from the more militant "white power/women power" stance of some racist skingirls such as those of the SS Action Group, which support equality of the sexes.[21] But they also depart from the model of complete female submissiveness and male authority found in Christian Identity, whose female leadership proclaims that "we cannot and will not be happy in a man's world because our Creator did not make us to find our fulfillment there" and that encourages Aryan women "to fulfill their ancient roles as wives and mothers, that there may be proper male leadership in the nation."[22]

These seeming contradictions and differences in organized racist groups reflect how modern racism functions, in the phrase of historian George Mosse, as a "scavenger ideology"—a system of beliefs capable of annexing other, and different, belief systems.[23] In this sense, neither maternalism nor ideas of gender equality are always antithetical to racist beliefs. Throughout recent history there have been numerous strategies by which maternal identities have become politicized and absorbed into white supremacist politics.

MOTIVES FOR ACTIVISM

What motivates any individual's participation in politics, however, may not match very well the goals of movement leaders. Although motherhood has served as a powerful symbol for recruiting women into organized racism, there is not always a clear connection between the symbols that movements have used to recruit members and the actual reasons why people join. This is particularly true in the case of the recruitment of mothers in racist movements, since the idea of motherhood is used to symbolize many distinct political issues. For example, some mothers join racist groups because of deep-seated racist beliefs that have nothing to do with motherhood, but then insist that organized racism is necessary to protect their children's future. Conversely, other mothers join racist groups out of concern for their children's education, safety or opportunities—concerns that have little necessary connection to race—but, once involved in racist politics, becomes convinced that these are indeed racial issues.

This potential disjuncture between movement goals and member motivations illustrates the complex role of maternalist appeals in political organizing. Many racial extremists seem to package their fears and aspirations as mothers in racial terms to which they have only the most casual connections. In the 1920s, many women joined the KKK to preserve and extend their rights as white Protestant mothers, rights they feared would be eroded by immigrant, African-American or non-Protestant voters. A similar process fuels participation in modern racist movements. In the late 1980s, for example, one woman recalled that she joined the Klan because she got "fed up" that she couldn't get her children educated properly, adding only as an afterthought that their poor education must have resulted from the presence of Hispanic kids in their classrooms.[24] Another Klan woman cited the problem of "latch-key children," arguing that "the children of the world now are lost. Mother is having to work now and support them, and they have to sit on the doorstep a couple of hours before their mother ever gets home."[25]

Swelling the ranks of organized racism, therefore, are not only women—and mothers—who are motivated by racism, elitism or bigotry, but also those worried about the impact of crime on themselves and their families, the quality of their children's schools or the escalating rate of family dissolution, concerns that can not be easily described as either reactionary or progressive. One of the keys to the success of organized racism in recruiting women, and mothers, has been its ability to formulate a political agenda that appears to take account of these widely disparate maternalist concerns.

RACIST POLITICAL CULTURE

Regardless of their motives for participation, the incorporation of mothers as active members has made it possible for many racial supremacist groups to exist over time and across generations. Racist groups with significant numbers of mothers have generally taken root more deeply and have lasted longer than predominantly male racist groups. There are several reasons why this is true.

Many racist political organizations have encouraged the recruitment of mothers (and wives) in order to solidify political commitments through family ties. Throughout the twentieth century, the Ku Klux Klan has emphasized the joint enrollment of whole families. As a 1920s Klan field agent noted while defending his efforts to recruit women and children, "when the wife joins and the children participate, you know that the family is going to stay with the

Klan." In the 1980s a Georgia Klan woman made a similar point, commenting that "once you get into the Klan, it becomes your whole family, all your socializing, all your parties."[26] Modern neo-Nazi and some Klan groups recently have further increased their efforts to enlist women and adolescents in the belief that members will be more loyal and dedicated to organizations in which their entire family participates.

As race-hate groups enlist mothers and children, they tend to become less marginalized and more integrated into the communities in which they exist. Racist groups that are age restrictive (like white-power skinheads who primarily recruit among teenagers and young adults) or gender restrictive (like some paramilitary Klan groups) generally have little legitimacy or influence outside of a core of committed followers. In contrast, at least some segments of organized racism have recruited more broadly and have a greater scope of influence. In the 1920s, for example, Klan mothers brought an agenda of bigotry and intolerance into the marrow of the white Protestant communities in which the Klan was strong—spreading the Klan's poison in schools, neighborhoods and family networks. Mothers in this Klan organized a political culture of racism, with family picnics, spelling bees, dances, Klan fairs and other social activities through which the Klan's message was spread, and the zeal of its members intensified.

Today's organized racist movement is far smaller and more marginal than the 1920s Klan, but it too has shown the potential for increased influence. Former Klan and Nazi leader David Duke garnered strong and broad-based electoral support in his bids for public office in Louisiana. Hundreds of neo-Nazi families, responding to the call for a "Great Northwestern Trek" to settle an Aryan homeland in the Pacific Northwest, have established homesteads in the states of Washington, Idaho and Oregon. And "white-power" student organizations have been established on college campuses throughout the country.

Racist political cultures such as these contribute to the seeming "normalization" of racial hatred, creating a sense that racism and bigotry are acceptable, unremarkable aspects of white Protestant culture. In the 1920s, Klan mothers were central in organizing Klan-based rites of passage. Klan ceremonies marked birth and death, illness and marriage. Klan weddings bound couples together in love and Klan duty. Babies were christened amidst Klan rituals. Klan members visited the sick and served as pallbearers at the funerals of departed Klan brothers and sisters.[27]

In race-hate groups today, there is a similar attempt to project an image of normality. In this sense, what is more threatening in modern organized racism is less the groups of middle-aged Klan men who continue to parade, usually far outnumbered by anti-Klan demonstrators, but the advertisements for toddler car seats and Aryan cookbooks that appear in white-power newsletters and on Aryan electronic bulletin boards. A writer for the *Los Angeles Times* summarized her reaction to a gathering of four hundred neo-Nazis as "so benign. Everyone was so common, so average, so mannerly and nice: 'Our son, Rob, is doing so well in college,' and talk like that. There was a lot of physical holding of kids, a lot of good parenting." She recounts how a young neo-Nazi mother jotted down a recipe for gingerbread on the back of a flyer bearing a swastika and calling for "white power" and "death to race-mixing."[28]

It is this ordinariness of racism—the banality of evil, in Hannah Arendt's terms—that is found also in Aryan weddings, where white lace dresses and black tuxedos come embroidered with swastikas and rest on steel-toed boots, or white-power skinhead dances where young teens learn racial hate as easily as they learn new dance steps.[29] Such efforts to normalize racism rest largely on the absorption of ordinary social roles (like motherhood), the manipulation of ordinary events (like rites of passage) and the use of ordinary networks (like those of family and neighborhood) to build a culture of racial supremacy and racial hatred. In this, motherhood is a potentially powerful strategy and vehicle for organizing of hate groups.

It is impossible to predict how successful contemporary organized racism is likely to be, or how many women and mothers will be attracted to the politics of racial hatred. Unlike in the 1920s when the Klan captured the allegiance of a very large proportion of the white Protestant population, modern race-hate groups remain relatively small and politically marginal. The recent electoral efforts of David Duke,[30] the ability of white-power skinheads to recruit young followers across the United States and the alarming growth of organized racism and anti-Semitism across Europe and in the former Soviet Union, however, should caution against a simplistic assessment that organized racism will necessarily decline over time. To effectively counter the growth of organized racism, we need to examine seriously the many complex ways in which those from majority populations come to identify their interests with the politics of hatred and bigotry and develop progressive agendas to address the concerns that otherwise might lead people into the politics of racial hatred.

NOTES

1. Kathleen M. Blee, *Women of the Klan: Racism and Gender in the 1920s* (Berkeley: University of California Press, 1991), photograph no. 11; "White Women Practice Unity," *Aryan Action Line* 2 (winter 1992):1.

2. Blee, *Women of the Klan*, pp. 12–16, 23–33, and 157–162.

3. Southern Poverty Law Center, *Intelligence Report*, September 1993.

4. James Ridgeway, *Blood in the Face: The Ku Klux Klan, Aryan Nations, Nazi Skinheads and the Rise of a New White Culture* (New York: Thunder's Mouth Press, 1990).

5. Ridgeway, *Blood in the Face*, pp. 79–105.

6. See also Claudia Koonz, *Mothers in the Fatherland* (New York: St. Martin's

Press, 1987), and Vron Ware, *Beyond the Pale: White Women, Racism and History* (London: Verso Press, 1992).

7. *Ritual of the Tri-K Klub* (Tri-K Klub of the Women of the Ku Klux Klan, 1925).

8. *White Sisters*, a publication of the Aryan Women's League, no. 2 (winter 1991).

9. "The Baby Book Is Back," Aryan Women's League brochure, March 26, 1992; "Make More Babies, Prepare to Survive," *White Sisters*, winter 1991.

10. "Whoredom in America" and "For Women Only," *Scriptures for America* 1 (1991):1, 3–6.

11. Aryan Women's League hate line, June 11, 1990, California.

12. See Aryan Women's League, *White Sisters*, issues from 1990 to 1992.

13. See, for example, Justin D. Fulton, *Why Priests Should Wed* (L. J. King, publisher, 1911).

14. Ronald P. Formisano, *Boston Against Busing: Race, Class, and Ethnicity in the 1960s and 1970s* (Chapel Hill: University of North Carolina Press, 1991).

15. Hannah Arendt, *Eichmann in Jerusalem: A Report on the Banality of Evil* (New York, 1963); White Aryan Resistance, telephone "hate line" messages, 1991–1992.

16. "A Challenge to White People," published and distributed by the Aryan Women's League in San Francisco, 1989.

17. *White Sisters* 1 (spring 1990).

18. Alma White, *Woman's Chains* (Zarepath, N.J.: Pillar of Fire Press, 1943).

19. Grand Dragon, "A Tribute and a Challenge to American Women," in *Papers Read at the First Annual Meeting of the Knights of the Ku Klux Klan*, 1923.

20. See *Christian Century*, May 21, 1925, pp. 177–178; *Fiery Cross*, July 6, 1923, p. 23; *Imperial Night-Hawk*, September 3, 1924, p. 6.

21. Kathy Dobie, "Long Day's Journey into White," *Village Voice*, April 28, 1992, pp. 23–32; Aryan Action Line, *Communication #4* (fall 1992):2. Local skingirl groups are covered in "The Monitor," the newsletter of the Center for Democratic Renewal, Atlanta, Ga.

22. "The Masculinized Female," *Scriptures Holy Bible Newsletter*, March 1987; "For Women Only," *Scriptures for America* 8 (1988).

23. George L. Mosse, *Nationalism and Sexuality* (Madison: University of Wisconsin Press, 1985).

24. Interview of an anonymous informant in Texas, c. 1992, in the files of the Anti-Defamation League of B'nai B'rith.

25. *Greensboro Daily News*, September 12, 1982.

26. Blee, *Women of the Klan*, pp. 157–165; miscellaneous letters and internal documents of the Ku Klux Klan, no date, files in the possession of the author.

27. Blee, *Women of the Klan*, pp. 163–164.

28. "Neo-Nazi Believers—'So Average . . . It Was Surreal,'" *Los Angeles Times*, November 25, 1987.

29. Aryan Research Fellowship Newsletter, "Report from Youth Conference," June–August 1990, pp. 8–12.

30. Douglas Rose, ed., *The Emergence of David Duke and the Politics of Race* (Chapel Hill: University of North Carolina Press, 1992).

Skingirl Mothers

From Thelma and Louise to Ozzie and Harriet

Kathy Dobie

Carolyn and Kirsten were new mothers; Laurel was hugely pregnant. They'd grown their hair back to protect their children. "It's a lot easier to protect a child if you can't be singled out," Carolyn said. "Babies are more important than your hair." More important, I'm told, because these babies were the future of the white race.

I met my first skinhead girl in a San Francisco bar—a big blonde with a baseball cap jerked backward on her head, wearing a flight jacket and red braces, her blue eyes lined in black, looking like the girl who'd crashed the boys' clubhouse. Liz was a white-power skinhead, a recruiter for the American Front, a self-described "white supremacist feminist"—and the most self-assured twenty-two-year-old I've ever met. Her voice was slightly clotted; almost a murmur. It made everything Liz said, even the most outrageous comment, sound offhand.

Liz and I decided to take a road trip through the Northwest. She would introduce me to other skinhead girls. She packed her tapes of white power music and her "survival pack"—two weeks worth of Navy-issued food rations, canned water, and first aid supplies—just in case. We cut across the Bay Bridge at sunset, Liz murmuring beside me that the feds were certainly already alerted to her travel plans.

She had dubbed our road trip "Thelma and Louise." And that's what it felt like driving through the mountains at night, boot-stomping music shaking the dashboard, Liz telling me she could step out of the car right here—snow, black rock, sheer drops—and disappear. She was fearless; she was a rich man's daughter. She had blasted through girlhood and come out the other side.

In San Francisco, Liz introduced me to some skinhead men and a wannabe skingirl—a girl who was as racist as the rest of them but never quite made the grade. In Portland, Oregon, we met with five skingirls, all members of the American Front. Then we went up to the Aryan Nations compound in Hayden Lake, Idaho, to meet with the people that some skins consider "their elders" and some deride as "white trash." The skins are mostly middle-class kids; better educated and more sophisticated than a lot of the older white racists. They're proud that they've fought black gangs, gone to school with Mexican-American kids, worked under Chinese or Jewish bosses—in other words, that they aren't ignorant, trash-talking hillbillies who think if they ever come across a Jewish man, they'll know him by the hook in his nose.

For the most part, their racist elders retreat from the world—into the dream of a whites-only territory, into the Aryan Nations compound guarded by German shepherds, into increasingly paranoid visions of persecution. But the skinheads throw themselves against the world; they agitate, disturb. In San Francisco, the skinhead boys would run through a black housing project, shouting "White Power" in what Liz described as an initiation rite. A skinhead girl wore her swastika earring to work ("a little, dangly one"), knowing that Jewish customers come in every day and they would yell at her. They take part in anti-abortion demonstrations, carrying signs "White Women Awake! Abortion Equals Genocide of the White Race!"—much to the consternation of the pro-lifers. With their shaved heads and white-power tattoos, the skins are highly visible racists. They demand a relationship.

The skins reserve their bitterest hate, their most caustic criticism for other whites. "Most whites have 'victim' printed on their forehead," the skins sneer. They hate liberal whites, politically correct whites, whites who came of age in the sixties and consider themselves "progressive" or color blind. "Caucasian casualties," the skins call them.

Most of their parents fit this profile, of course, but then so do many others— their teachers, the media, their middle-class peers. One skingirl says, "Whites are supposed to feel guilty for every war that ever happened. White liberals go out of their way to blame whites for everything . . . to prove they're not racist. Most true racialist blacks hate white liberals more than anyone else. 'Here, Mr. Negro, take my home.' They're big butt-lickers and no one likes a butt-licker."

When Liz called herself a "white supremacist feminist," she simply meant that she was concerned with women's place in the movement—hers was definitely in the driver's seat. She wanted them to be politicized, active—not merely girlfriends of skinheads. She used "feminist" the way the young always use the word—in the broad, rebellious spirit of "can do" . . . just what the boys can. But most of all, I think Liz called herself a "white supremacist feminist" to shock liberal whites, to get under the feminists' skin. She knew it was too easy for whites to stand back aghast, to cluck their tongues, to dismiss the skinheads as ridiculous or dangerously alien; too easy to deny any connection to them. Liz insisted on intimacy. You just had to deal with Liz. She had about a hundred ways of challenging your comfort with yourself and your feelings of superiority to her. We took our road trip two years ago. I can still see her fists pounding out tunes on the steering wheel.

Liz was introduced to the white power movement when she was thirteen and attending boarding school in Colorado. In town, she befriended two brothers, the sons of Klan members. She found their life-style and beliefs exciting—"I saw it as an adventure as opposed to the Volvo-driven, suburban family lifestyle." She became a skinhead at fifteen. She got her "fringe" (the girls shave the middle of their heads and leave the hair long on the sides) and got "jumped in" to the movement—beat up by the other skinhead girls, as was the custom at the time. Now, only boys get jumped in, and only some of them at that. By the time I met her, Liz had been photographed so many times by various law enforcement agencies that she and the other skins joked that the cops would trade their photos like baseball cards.

"They consider the right wing so much more dangerous than the left," she said. "There was a demonstration here in San Francisco outside the recruiting office. The communists and fags were dragging out the office furniture. If those were right-wing demonstrators, anti-abortionists or Ku Klux Klan, the whole National Guard would be out. But I don't think the government takes the left seriously. They don't have to—they're always tripping themselves up. They're a bunch of wishy-washy granola munchers."

Like most skinheads, Liz thought she was punished for her beliefs, not for anything illegal she'd done. The skins are always referring to Orwell's *1984*; they say that they live among thought police. "Why is it okay to be proud that you're black but it's racist to be proud you're white?" they ask.

Liz listened to NWA[1] — "they're our counterpart." While visiting her mother, she read Dickens and her mom was taken aback. "She thinks I only read Mein Kampf," Liz said, too amused and too in control to be sarcastic. I've heard skinheads describe their politics as a "psychological mind game" they play with society. Liz, especially, enjoyed confounding expectations.

When she was in art school, Liz did a performance piece where she lay naked on the floor in a cold room for eight hours . . . to see if she could. She'd taken survivalist training. She'd learned how to control her dreams for the express purpose of saving the dream-Liz from any disaster. I don't know what Liz was afraid of—it didn't seem to be any ordinary fear—maybe not being in control of the world and all the little creatures swarming on it. I do know that none of the skinhead girls were willing to live quietly with fear, to let some nameless anxiety hang over them. Shaving their heads, looking tough and ugly as sin, coming out as white power skinheads seemed to help them face something awful, and diminish it.

Laurel, who was sixteen when we met, grew up in a black neighborhood in Portland, attended Martin Luther King, Jr., grammar school and went to a mostly black high school. The white kids there were divided into two groups, she said. Some were scared of the black kids and hid in their books; others "found black life really interesting and decided to go for that . . . probably just to upset their parents." She felt sympathy for the first group of kids, and wished they'd come over to her side "instead of just cowering away."

The day Laurel shaved her head, she seemed to have found a rock-hard identity and to have walked straight into the violence she felt shimmered everywhere. "I felt really confident, ready for anything. I felt above everybody. That's the feeling you have the whole time you have a fringe. It's weird. It's kind of a step out—you're saying that you're ready to fight for what you believe in. Now there's no turning back." She shaved her head in the summertime, shortly after her fourteenth birthday. Her first day back at school was the hardest, she said. "People let me know exactly how they felt, how they were going to kill me before the year was up." All they ever did, actually, was taunt her. "You look like a guy," they laughed. They chanted: "Skinhead-Kinhead-Pinhead."

Laurel's friend Kirsten grew up with her mother and brother in a mostly Mexican neighborhood outside Sacramento, went to a high school that was half white, half Mexican, and got into the punk scene. Kirsten met her first skinheads at the mall. She felt comfortable. "What was your attraction to them?" I asked her. She said, "Because of my school—there were so many Mexicans and the way I felt about it—with the skinheads, it was cool to talk about it. You didn't have to keep it to yourself. You could make jokes. Having other people around who felt the same way I did and who didn't hide it."

They didn't want to feel timid in any way—not just physically timid, afraid of violence, but mentally timid. If racist thoughts snuck through their heads, they weren't going to hide them or worry over them. No, they'd trumpet them loud. They wanted to be in the place where nothing—out in the world or inside their heads—would make them cringe.

When I met Jesse, the wannabe skin, she was nineteen. She'd dated some skinhead men and called herself a skinhead but the boys called her an "oi toy." Since you can't elect yourself a skin, you have to be accepted by the family, Jesse was nothing more than a garden-variety racist at a loss in the big city. "I've met some really decent men who were really able to respect a decent white woman. The problem is so many white men are liberal today." She sat at her kitchen table in a pink t-shirt and silver jewelry, coughing and smoking.

Jesse's rap was all about men, about the long line of racist, patriotic, union men she came from in Kentucky and Missouri. "Growing up, I was around a lot of older men. They're total racists—for America, for the family. They totally influenced me. Every man in my family did hard labor jobs—construction, welding—the kind of work that made this country great."

Her image of the past—when America was great—was of great big Men and sweaty biceps and drills biting rock and "being out there in the sun working hard to feed your family." It was daddy worship—erotic and childlike, and very wishful. It was a fantasy about strong men, men who are competent and secure enough to protect their families, about sweet, deep job satisfaction. And then there was the reality. Here's how Jesse described her father, a bitter, beaten man: "He's a total racist. He hates it here. He's here because of the money. He works for the city of Oakland and he's always coming home saying: 'Those goddamn niggers can't pick up their own trash. Filthy mongrels.'"

Jesse was pregnant by a skinhead man. He wanted nothing to do with her. Compared to the skingirls, Jesse was an old story—just another girl wearing men's contempt like she'd been born to it. She'd been used and abandoned by men and the skinheads don't like victims.

One night in San Francisco, I went out drinking with Liz and two skinhead men at a bar near their apartment. We sat with a punk rocker, his half-Indian girlfriend (Liz hissed "half-breed" in my ear), and a white girl. The two skinhead men, Gordon and Kiwi, played darts with "Indian Joe"—it's what Gordon called one of the "compromises" made by city skins. On her flight jacket, Liz wore an Iron Cross and a button that read: "Register Homosexuals Not Handguns." The white girl said, "Liz, I've always admired you . . . I mean I've watched you for a while and I think you've got a lot of guts." Liz looked at the girl without warmth. "Why?" Liz asked. The girl shifted in her seat uncomfortably—"Well—I like what you stand for." Liz asked, "What do I stand for?" The girl pushed back her seat. "Well . . . I j-just like admire you. You say what you think." Liz's irritation began to show, "What do I think?" The girl huffed, "Well, if you don't know, I'm not gonna tell you!" Liz yelled, "You brought it up! You like what I stand for—well, what do I stand for?" The boys interrupted then, their eyes gleaming, one of them merrily handing out beer. Liz was completely disgusted. She wanted to leave.

The way Liz saw it—this was another wimpy white girl, a closet racist who would coddle up to her in a dark bar, but never risk anything to stand by her. I saw something else—the girl was no secret racist. What she admired was Liz's flamboyance, her guts, the way Liz stood out in that grunge-hippy-multiculti bar scene, the way she didn't give a fuck what people thought about her, her ease with violence, even a kind of integrity that showed itself to me the minute she didn't let that girl falsely flatter her. Liz wouldn't tuck in her rough, ugly edges for anything—not to escape condemnation, not even in order to get love and admiration. She had a terrible freedom about her, Liz did. And I was no less stagestruck than that girl in the bar.

I'm not saying this as a confession of how I overlooked the skins' racism because some of them were so charismatic. I always saw their racism—it was the obvious thing for a reporter to be focused on when focusing on racist skinheads. What I'm saying is that for a time, I saw them as bad girls, as outlaws (racist bad girls, racist outlaws), and so I missed the essential thrust of their movement. Or as one skinhead boy put it, "the idea behind this whole fucking thing." I focused on their differences—from the scared white kids in school, from all the pretty, careful girls who aim to please, from those poisonous white adults who learn to hide their racism, even from themselves. I saw them in opposition to a Great Big Other and I couldn't have been further off the mark. As it turned out, my outlaws were dreaming of white weddings and family hearth.

OZZIE AND HARRIET

I first met Kirsten and Laurel in Portland, along with three other skingirls, and I'll never forget the sight—five skinhead girls with short fluffy hair, light makeup, pastel sweaters. Looking like the girls who volunteer to decorate the gym for the prom. Where were the bald heads, the ass-stomping uniforms?

Carolyn and Kirsten were new mothers; Laurel was hugely pregnant. They'd grown their hair back to protect their children. "It's a lot easier to protect a child if you can't be singled out," Carolyn said. "Babies are more important than your hair." More important, I'm told, because these babies were the future of the white race.

Carolyn, Kirsten and Laurel considered themselves "old skinheads." Carolyn had just turned twenty-one, but Kirsten and Laurel were only sixteen. Laurel was the last to grow out her fringe. She was tiny with almost pixie-ish features, but there was a boldness to her gaze, a hard challenge that removed all impressions of cute. "Sixteen years old is not the time to be grown-up," she said, her hands folded on top of her pregnant belly. "We just had so much fun. It was such a blast. I never used to worry about getting hurt. Kirsten and I used to go into a fight and never back off."

We met in Carolyn's apartment, which was also the headquarters of the American Front. Carolyn's red-haired daughter, named after the Viking goddess Freya, crawled around the floor. Carolyn said that when she went to the hospital to have her baby delivered, the doctor said uh-oh—"Are there going to be a lot of skinheads coming in?" About thirty of them came, since the birth of a baby is a big deal to the skins. After Carolyn got out of the hospital, the state sent a social worker to the home—"They thought we'd be goosestepping on the baby," Carolyn cackled. Kirsten, milky-skinned and brown-eyed, held her baby girl in her lap.

Sometimes the girls sounded like any group of teenagers talking about other girls—"that douchebag," "that abortion queen." Talking about the unfaithfulness of guys, but in this case, of white racist guys—"Oh yeah, the guys hate them, they're 'half-breeds,' until they spread their legs."

The girls jealously guarded their turf—on the watch for "sluts" who just want to sleep with skinhead men, and for rich girls who are just slumming—hanging with the skins, soaking up all that maschismo but ready for a quick escape, daddy's Gold Card tucked away. "It's the feline in us," Laurel laughed.

"But I think if the guys were as critical as we are, they'd keep a lot of trash out of the movement," Kirsten said, meaning the guys who join with "the gang mentality," ready only to party and fight. The girls fought girls; mostly girls from SHARP (Skinheads Against Racial Prejudice). "I think the funniest part for us is that most girls don't know how to fight. And we had no hair," Laurel said. Of course, sometimes the guys got mad—"because we beat up their dates."

The girl they called "the abortion queen" was ostracized after they learned about the abortion, and heard she was having "race-mixed" parties. "My first instinct was I'm going to beat her ass," Carolyn said. "Her ass is mine. I'll rip her hair out and stuff it into her nose." But since Carolyn had become a mother, she decided to stay out of trouble. Instead, she and her husband, Bob, left a series of messages about the abortion and the parties on the girl's parents' answering machine. "I rocked her world," Carolyn told me. "She's nothing. She's completely ousted from any white community. You don't claim to have racial pride and kill your offspring." Right about then, it occurred to Kirsten that they're always fighting other white girls.

When Liz was in Portland, she formed the Valkyries, the women's auxiliary of the American Front. She tried to hold classes in self-defense, food canning and first aid (for the coming race war), but the local skingirls laughed off her idea. Self-defense classes were fine in theory, though the girls already know how to fight, but food canning?

Instead, they wrote and distributed racist literature, planned rallies and kept in contact with those skinheads in prison. A member of the Portland gang task force told me, "I can remember four years ago, the women were really subservient. They used to run behind the men like Chinese coolies." He believed that there came a time when the girls must've realized that they were the babymakers—he imagined them all slapping their foreheads as the thought occurred—and, therefore, central to any white race movement.

I like the image, but I think he's got it backward. Of course, they've used motherhood to give themselves more power in the movement—I mean we're talking about girls who have known the good feeling of putting on a pair of Doc Martens and stomping the world down. But mostly, they work it the other way around—the girls use the movement and its racial politics to strengthen the role of mother (and wife and girlfriend). Their strongest desire is not for power; it's for connection.

The girls say that skinhead men *stay*. They won't desert their pregnant girlfriends, or their wives and kids. I doubt the absolute truth of this, but the skins do have an ideology that supports family—and it's most fervently articulated by the girls. A true skinhead man will work hard to support his family because he sees himself as protecting and preserving his race, the girls say. Liz, the unabashed mythmaker, told me, "Women are more protected and revered in the movement than in society as a whole. They see us as something that's sacred, almost mystical."

The skingirls want men who stick around, but they also want to have something bigger than themselves to live for. Babies are more important than your hair, they say, more important than any youthful (and selfish) pleasure.

They're furious at white adults for fucking up the family. Carolyn's mother was a "hippie" and Carolyn believes that most of her mother's generation was into the scene for the music and drugs, not the politics. "The hippies messed everything up," she said. "With all the drugs, have sex with anyone in the world. We're sick of seeing stuff on TV about how great that generation was. Every big hippie is now a CEO of a big corporation. Wait a minute—what happened to 'get back to nature,' to 'love everybody.' They kind of drummed all of that garbage in everybody's mind, opened a big can of worms and then went off to lunch."

Carolyn's real father died of a drug overdose when she was two months old—"And that's why I never got into drugs." Her mother and stepfather divorced when she was two. By the time Carolyn graduated from high school she and her mom had lived in Illinois (twice), Wisconsin, California (twice), and Michigan.

When Carolyn and Bob got married *before* having a baby, her mother was "like wow!"—really impressed. "I definitely know what divorce can do and I'm not putting my children through it. Bob and I have said that the only way we're getting out of this marriage is if one of us dies."

One time her mom told her: "I can't believe what I'm seeing on TV these days. All these hate crimes. All this white against black, black against white. Everybody's so hateful! What ever happened to all that love-your-neighbor we were talking about in the sixties?" Carolyn told her: "Ma, you loved the drugs back then. You didn't love your Negro neighbor."

When I met her, Kirsten was still a skinhead but her boyfriend, Kelly, wasn't anymore. He'd grown out his hair and kept his white power tatoos covered. "He really wants the nuclear family bit. He works hard," Kirsten said. "He's gonna be twenty-four. Being a skinhead at twenty-four . . ." She laughed. "You're not gonna be that Aryan warrior forever. You sit back like the older people."

"Little skinheads grow up to be big racists," Liz said. "Skinhead has a youthful, fun, spunky quality to it. I won't be doing that when I'm forty. I've served my time on the political front. It's time to retire and live with a group of white power families." Somehow I find it hard to believe in Liz's retirement— Liz who joked that when she took over the world, she was going to change "dictator" to "dictatress" in all the dictionaries. But many of the skins seemed to be looking for that next step.

Kirsten and her boyfriend were planning to marry—a regular church wedding that both their families could come to. ("I don't want to wear Doc Martens with my wedding dress!") She wouldn't be a skinhead much longer, either. There was her daughter to think about now. "No one wants their kids to grow up like that. I want her aware but I don't want her to be a skinhead."

Even pregnant Jesse was taken in by another skinhead man. Steve sounded proud when he told me that he'd raised her kid like his own. But listen to this: His role model was his Filipino boss. "He still believes in the family structure," Steve said with undisguised admiration. Most whites, on the other hand, are "DINKS—double income, no kids. They'd rather have Mercedes payments."

Their enemies have such shining qualities. If they could devour them— that is, destroy them and become them, too—I think they would. Liz described the "tragedy of being a skinhead woman" this way: "You know how Negro women say: 'All our men are in jail'? Well, all these white supremacist men are in jail, too." Our men. The skingirls like the way that sounds.

They complain that the black community is tighter, more aggressive about its survival than whites are. "If the race war happens now, we'd lose," one girl told me. "Blacks are so close together. They'd be real easy to set off and they'd all stick together but whites wouldn't. Most are confused. We'd fail miserably. We'd probably go after our own people, too."

They want the schools to teach white pride. They want a white history month. Because of their race, they're just American kids; not African-American or Asian-American or Mexican-American. Yet it makes them feel rootless, all alone, without a flag to defend. They want an ethnic community, too—but what is it? What can it be for a white American kid? They've come up with "Aryan" and complain to me, "You can't find out about Viking history!" Viking?

Their racism is infused with jealousy and admiration—for the Jews who won't forget the Holocaust, for the angry black rappers sending their message out to the brothers, for the Filipino immigrant who has a huge family and works back-breaking hours to provide for them; for anyone, that is, who has a "we" in their lives.

MR. ROGERS' NEIGHBORHOOD, OR "THE IDEA BEHIND THIS WHOLE FUCKING THING"

The great adventure ends here. Thelma and Louise sitting by the hearth. Thelma and Louise living on a street where everybody knows their name. The girls say they want to leave the city, live on farms in the wilderness, have lots of children and horses, and helpful neighbors. "I'd like to have a whole town where everybody gets along. Like the old days," Carolyn says. "A place where you know everybody else. You don't have to lock your door. If you need help, everybody will come over and help you build a barn." Hillary, another skin-girl, says her kids will walk through the woods safely, they'll play kick-the-can in the street long after dark—"you know, like it used to be."

For teenagers, they seem strikingly, absurdly nostalgic, but what they're imagining is an escape from suburban, white, middle-class loneliness, or what-ever personal loneliness they suffered always being the new kid in town or one of the few white kids in school or the daughters of self-absorbed parents.

They're trying to repair what they think were the damages of the sixties, trying to find family and a "we" in the color of their skin. They've pumped themselves up with the politics of supremacy and given to ordinary life—babies, marriage, job—a heroic mythology. They say: We're propagating and preserving the white race; we're recovering lost white working-class values. They've made the strongest sales pitch they can for the sanctity of marriage and family. But they don't stop there.

Jesse does, which is the real reason why she would never be a skin. Jesse was just looking for that one decent white man who could really respect a decent white woman. Her dream was really not the skinhead dream at all.

The skins dream of community, not merely of true love or the nuclear family. They want group loyalties, a group identity. Look at their white skin, bristled and tattooed—they want you to see flags waving, hear a battlecry, tribal chants. Perhaps you look at that white skin and instead see divorced parents (fluent in the newest self-help lingo), DINKS babying their Mercedes and an old woman sitting alone hour after hour, her hands worrying her house-dress. That's the skinhead nightmare—that being white means being selfish, sterile and all alone.

Liz told me once, "To see us just as a street gang, makes us seem less dangerous." When she first said it, I didn't understand because nothing seemed more dangerous to me than a bat to the head. But now, I know what she means. Boys with bats can be locked up, and for a very long time. Girls who like to kick ass spend most of their time kicking each other's. But young racists who have a plan, a dream of the future that is both a critique of the alienation and materialism of our culture and a solution to it, are a different matter altogether. They have staying power and drawing power.

When the skins made a mission out of raising a family, a holy crusade, they transcended the nihilism of their fight-and-fuck lifestyle—the multiplying hatreds, the drunken violence. They have something to live for now, something to love. Liz wanted me to see that the skins were much more dangerous than a street gang, and I do. But I can't help thinking that it's our loneliness that has become dangerous and now threatens us.

NOTES

1. "Niggas with Attitude"—a black rap group that became infamous for a song called "Fuck the Police."

Housewives and Motherist Politics in the New Italy

Annelise Orleck

Men in the Christian Democratic leadership convinced Italian women that the vote was like the marriage vow: You give it only once and then you're stuck for life.
—Federica Rossi Gasparrini, president of Federcasalinghe, the Italian Federation of Housewives

ITALY'S OFFICIAL MAMA'S BOYS

On a hot June day in 1994, more than a thousand well-coiffed Italian housewives from every province in the country gathered at a movie theater in Rome to discuss the problems facing wives and mothers in the 1990s. Plastered over movie posters in the theater lobby were banners celebrating "the birth of the new Italian woman . . . and soon of the new European woman: caught for so long between family and society, finally free to choose." By mid-morning the theater was packed with tailored, perfumed delegates to the Sixth National Convention of Federcasalinghe—the Italian Housewives' Federation. Jumping to their feet, the women cheered a speech by their leader, a savvy blonde middle-aged rabble-rouser named Federica Rossi Gasparrini. Campaigning for a seat in the European Parliament as "the candidate of your dreams," Gasparrini urged mothers to elect one of their own. "Politicians are mobsters," she boomed. "No more will we give a blank check to politicians who want our votes for their own gain.[1]

Without skipping a beat, and without a trace of irony, Gasparrini urged the crowd to welcome as one of their own then-prime minister Silvio Berlusconi, still glowing from his resounding victory in the national elections just two months earlier. Berlusconi smiled broadly as he accepted tribute from the traditional Italian mothers who had done so much to ensure his election. It was a remarkable political moment. Assuring Italian housewives of his empathy and respect, the slick media tycoon, who controls all of Italy's private television stations, its largest real-estate and department store empire and even its most successful soccer team, declared proudly, "I too have been a housewife! I too have done the shopping and dusted the furniture!" His words were greeted with a frenzied enthusiasm. A thousand middle-aged mothers shouted out their pet name for him as if they were teenaged girls greeting a matinee idol. "La Luce," they screamed, pounding their feet. It literally means "The Light" but it is also the name that young girls were taught to call Mussolini.[2]

It is an election year ritual in many countries for politicians to claim the mantle of the working man, but in 1994 Berlusconi turned that tradition on its head: he declared himself one with the common woman, the average wife and mother. The ardent romance between Berlusconi and Italian mothers moved critics to speak contemptuously of him as the political choice of "failed hairdressers," and of his supporters as innocents who voted for him only because he was the man who brought American soap operas to Italian television. But Berlusconi, who won 55% of the women's vote in the March 1994 election, preferred another nickname: "Italy's official mama's boy."[3]

One might wonder why the man who was then Italy's most powerful politician would campaign so hard for the allegiance of a group that has been generally considered politically powerless. One answer is that the fragile right-wing coalition that had brought his government to power was growing more fractious by the day. He needed a mark of purity that would distance him from Tangentopoli—Kickback City—the massive corruption scandal that had convulsed Italian Politics since the early 1990s. As anti-corruption investigators moved closer to his business empire, Berlusconi became increasingly anxious to present himself as untouchable. And so he sought and won a very public stamp of approval from a group that all Italians acknowledge as experts in the business of cleaning up: mothers.

But Berlusconi was not the first male politician to come courting at the back door of Federcasalinghe. The housewives' federation has been gaining influence and visibility since the early 1980s by self-consciously manipulating its members' "good motherhood" as a symbol of political trustworthiness. Its leaders have confronted Italians beleaguered by an endless stream of revelations about venality and corruption among their leaders with the promise that everything is under control: mother has arrived to straighten out the mess. A true cleanup of Italian government, Gasparrini insists, requires the involvement of mothers who will "bring to politics not the values of power-seeking but the values of service to others." Such talk is balm to the spirit of a nation weary of political machinations.[4]

The only problem is that, despite these soothing, gender-essentialist statements, the leaders of the Housewives' Federation have proven themselves as skilled at wheeling and dealing as any of the recently fallen male political icons. Since 1982 they have developed a complicated political platform that draws on several competing strains in modern Italian politics: Mussolini's pro-natalist social welfare policies, post-World War II papal pronouncements on the family, 1970s feminist wages-for-housework campaigns, and Berlusconi's version of 1980s free-market optimism. This amalgam reflects the fluidity of Italian political allegiances—but it also raises some troubling questions about motherist movements in general. Without clear ideological moorings on either the right or the left, are mother-activists willing to forge alliances with any political group that promises to honor mothers and motherhood? And at what cost?

The longevity and buoyancy of the Italian Housewives' Federation, in an era when virtually every well-known figure in Italian politics has lost credibility, illustrates the potential influence of a movement focused on empowering traditional mothers. What politician would dare to argue with a group of nicely attired women loudly proclaiming that devoted mothers are the cornerstone of a harmonious society? The simplicity of the federation's appeal is its greatest strength and its glaring weakness. Any close examination of the history of Federcasalinghe evokes the twin spectres of opportunism and backlash politics. Many worry that the federation has put "good motherhood" up for sale to the highest bidder, most recently Silvio Berlusconi. Seasoned feminist activists like American expatriate and long-time parliamentary deputy Carol Beebe Tarantelli question whether the experience of child rearing can be translated into a concrete political program—and suggest that the nebulousness of maternalist arguments may explain why the federation's press has far outstripped its legislative successes. Finally, they fear that a politics that glorifies women who stay at home to care for children somehow denigrates women who choose to work outside the home.

Some feminist politicians warn that Federcasalinghe's maternalist rhetoric threatens to erode the legislative gains that Italian women have made as individual citizens, totally separate from their motherhood. Their fears seemed to be borne out by the 1994 election, when ultraconservative women allied with Berlusconi won key posts in Parliament and the Cabinet and promised to pass legislation to shore up the traditional family. Still, Federcasalinghe cannot be easily categorized as conservative or retrograde on women's issues. The federation has created economic, political and social institutions that diminish the isolation of individual housewives while making mothers as a group into a formidable political bloc. And if the ideological slipperiness of federation leaders is suspicious, it is also part of what makes their group so intriguing. Even seasoned political insiders like Tarantelli, who are highly suspicious of Gasparrini, cannot easily write the group off. With all of its quick-change artistry, Federcasalinghe might well be just a sham, a money-making, publicity-generating machine for its leaders. But it could also be what its leaders claim: a genuinely autonomous traditional women's movement. And if that is the case, Federcasalinghe, which boasts disciplined local organizations from Milan to Palermo, is a political development worthy of note.

FLEXING MOTHER'S MUSCLE IN A WORLD OF POLITICAL PATRIARCHS

Federcasalinghe was founded in 1982 by Federica Rossi Gasparrini, a wife and mother who had never held political office. She was, however, a long-time supporter and admirer of the chief power broker of the Christian Democratic party, former prime minister Giulio Andreotti. Gasparrini told friends that she was determined to use the lessons she learned from Andreotti, her country's master of political gamesmanship, to benefit Italian mothers and children. "Political power permeates all facets of Italian life," Gasparrini said in a 1994 interview. "After years of dedicated campaigning I realized that we would never get adequate representation unless we too became political. I believe that Italian women have to enter directly into administration and politics if we want a different country. If we do not, we will always be instruments in the hands of others."[5]

It is difficult to separate the politics of the Italian housewives' movement from the personal aspirations of Gasparrini herself. She is a highly skilled and ambitious politician who likes to be on the winning side. Although she and her movement were closely tied for nearly a decade to the Christian Democratic Party (DC), which had ruled Italy since the Second World War, she pulled Federcasalinghe off a sinking Christian Democratic ship four years before the DC literally disappeared in the 1994 elections. She flirted briefly with Christian Democratic reformers who promised to further the DC's mainstream conservative agenda in a corruption-free atmosphere. Then, charging that men could not be trusted, she called for the creation of a women's political party that would offer—because women are innately so—a selfless alternative to corrupt men. But before the Pink Party, as she named it, could get off the ground, Gasparrini was lured into an alliance with Berlusconi's Forza Italia ("Let's Go Italy") party, which staked its claim to political legitimacy on the tycoon's entrepreneurial accomplishments. Breathless in her adulation of Berlusconi in his ascendancy, Gasparrini barely blinked when he toppled from power at the end of 1994. Within months, she was announcing the formation of a national union for housewives that would be free of the taint of electoral politics entirely. Amidst the wreckage of virtually all of the political parties that have governed Italy since Mussolini's day, Gasparrini has ferried her housewives' movement so smoothly from one alliance to another that the Italian press has dubbed her "Federica the Navigator."[6]

Despite the many Italian political observers who would write her off as little more than a political opportunist, all evidence seems to suggest that Gasparrini is not lying when she boasts that Federcasalinghe has galvanized 800,000 housewives into "an army in battle for laws favorable to us." Local and national leaders of the housewives' federation have promised to use those footsoldiers to marshall the economic and electoral might of Italy's more than 12 million housewives behind candidates who support their demand for full recognition of the unpaid labor of mothers in the home. Federcasalinghe leaders warn politicians to ignore them at their own risk.[7]

In 1990, the Italian housewives' movement declared its independence from the DC, claiming widespread disgust at years of unfulfilled promises. "We are sprinkling ashes on our heads for having had faith in certain men and certain parties," Gasparrini told reporters. "The DC will not see our votes again . . . Men in the Christian Democratic leadership convinced Italian women that the vote was like the marriage vow. You give it only once, and then you're stuck for life." Now that they were politically organized, she said, Italian housewives no longer needed to be dependent on men. They could and would demand "absolute independence."[8]

The surest way to achieve that political autonomy was to maximize housewives' economic clout. Toward that end, the federation mounted some extremely creative initiatives in the early 1990s. Shortly after leaving the DC, Federcasalinghe introduced the Cartadonna, a housewives' credit card. Any federation member was guaranteed a card. Husbands were not to be consulted, nor their financial records checked. And card fees included something absolutely unique in the world of credit-card sales gimmicks: divorce insurance. Cardholders were guaranteed free legal advice in case of divorce, and protected against financial calamities resulting from divorce.[9]

Next, to combat the isolation of women who work as caregivers in the home, Federcasalinghe assembled a group of drug, insurance, telecommunications and computer software companies to offer coordinated services to those who cared for sick children, husbands and parents. Finally, in 1993, the federation suggested an alternative to housewives' savings accounts: corporate investment. Entering a bid to buy SME, the massive food production conglomerate that is Italy's equivalent to Beatrice Foods, Gasparrini explained that food production was the logical business of housewives to control. "It's very simple," she told reporters who wondered why housewives would want to take on the worry of governing a major corporation. "Rather than having their savings in a little book, housewives entrust them to our financiers who can bring them dividends. Their investment will offer two practical results: discounts on their acquisition of food products, and also their own income."[10]

Some laud Gasparrini for making housewives players in the free-for-all scuffle for economic power that followed Berlusconi's promise to privatize Italy's government-owned corporations. Others are not so sure. Without records, her critics say, it is impossible to know whether Federcasalinghe leaders are really providing a service or simply lining their own pockets. And, as Carol Beebe Tarantelli notes, Gasparrini has never shown the organization's records to anyone. Tarantelli believes that the purpose of Federcasalinghe is simply to bring power and wealth to its officers. Federation officials defend their initiatives, saying that the credit card and SME investment were intended to give housewives the economic clout to achieve their political goals.[11]

Federcasalinghe's primary goal has been clear-cut since the organization's creation: full recognition for the multiple roles that Italian mothers play as cooks, child rearers, household managers, caregivers to the elderly, and amateur psychologists to their families. Housewives offer incalculable service to the state, federation leaders insist. By soothing troubled husbands, raising well-adjusted children, and generally keeping things running they prevent social upheaval. Conscientious mothers save the government untold sums that it would otherwise have to be spent on caring for young people, stressed-out working-men and the infirm elderly. In other words, though housewives seem to work only for their individual families, they should actually be seen as employees of the state.[12]

Federcasalinghe wants the government to acknowledge the value of that work in the same way that other kinds of work are compensated: with economic remuneration. For more than a decade, it has sought legislation granting state-funded salaries to mothers who work in the home. Its members demand that mothers receive the same workers' injury compensation that other Italian workers get. By the early 1990s, the federation, supported by allies on both the left and right, had won retirement pensions for housewives in their own right, not as dependent spouses. That is only their due, Gasparrini argued, challenging housewives and politicians alike to broaden their vision of workers and productivity. "A woman who is a full-time mother," Gasparrini argues, "is also a manager with legitimate needs and desires, a part-time worker, and devoted to the old people of the home." What this mother needs, says Gasparrini, is "government allotments, pensions and insurance equal to her role in this society."[13]

But in December of 1992, Parliament passed a law that, in practice, granted higher pensions to women who worked for wages than to women who chose to stay home. In the spring of 1993, tens of thousands of housewives took to the streets to protest what they called "the pension massacre." Setting up tables on streetcorners in cities across Italy, they collected 60,000 signatures for a referendum to overturn the law. Calling themselves *Sindacato Donna*, the Women's Union, supporters of the referendum said that "the state of Italy is ungrateful." Gasparrini added that "the woman is being seen again like a subject, something between a disabled worker and a concubine. This law penalizes marriage and reaffirms the principle of the subalternation of women, violating her right to parity and social dignity."[14]

Citing the need for "a political movement for a new Italy where women are more than an appendage of men," Federcasalinghe announced the formation of a women's party to run "against the men who have taken bribes . . . We are citizens who have to have a voice in everything: privatization, nominations, governing, even undersecretaries." The federation planned to use its numerous local chapters as bases from which to launch the party. It is not clear what happened to this idea. But, after a series of headline-grabbing demonstrations that prompted the newspapers to announce that "Housewives in the Piazzas Declare War," nothing further was heard about a women's party. Within a few months, Federcasalinghe had promised its full electoral support to Silvio Berlusconi.[15]

Berlusconi, who was no stranger to corruption charges even then, seemed an unlikely choice for a women's organization that had railed continually during the previous year against the venality of politicians. But Berlusconi had made brilliant use of his media empire to expertly package himself as an "anti-politician," a departure from the old Italian system that had nurtured his business triumphs. This image make-over may have had a particularly strong impact on women who worked at home and thus were able to watch Berlusconi's TV stations all through the day. Knowing his audience, Berlusconi made a clear pitch to housewives. Or, as one Italian political wit observed, "the cavalier put his stockings on the right way to please housewives."[16]

Berlusconi promised to bring only "new men" into government to remake Italy. He pointedly included women among those "new men," offering candidacies and cabinet posts to several well-known progressive women politicians whom he convinced to join his right-wing alliance. But more important to Federcasalinghe, Berlusconi promised to work for state-funded housewives' allotments. He also publicly honored the contributions made by mothers. "I know what toil it requires from the housewife to care for everyone in the home," he boasted to crowds of cheering wives and mothers, "to create a climate of serenity when the husband returns home from work, to keep the family equilibrium."[17]

Federcasalinghe rewarded Berlusconi with absolute political fealty, putting its local organizations at his service. Members rang doorbells and got out the vote. Housewives claimed partial credit for Berlusconi's resounding victories in both the national and European Parliament elections in 1994. And then they waited for him to act on their legislative goals. By the end of 1994, when Berlusconi's government fell under a hail of indictments and corruption accusations, the housewives' movement had gotten none of the legislation they had hoped for. Gasparrini had gotten little more than Berlusconi's support in her race for European Parliament, and a leadership position in the Italian delegation sent to the planning meeting for the 1995 International Women's Conference in Beijing. It was beginning to look as though the housewives' alliance with Berlusconi was little more than Italian politics as usual. Gasparrini quickly recovered. Early in 1995, she announced the formation of a national housewives' labor union, which would provide mutual credit and health care insurance and would reserve the power to call strikes. It remains unclear whether she can pull this off, whether the powerful men with whom she has repeatedly aligned her movement are once again using her, or whether she and her housewives are instead making strategic use of them.

MOTHERHOOD AND POST-WORLD WAR II ITALIAN POLITICS

Italian mothers have served as favored political footballs for the better part of the twentieth century. From Mussolini to Berlusconi, Italy's male politicians have frequently solicited the support of wives and mothers in times of crisis by sounding alarms about the decline of the family. Since World War II, elected officials, particularly in the Christian Democratic Party, have campaigned hard among women voters, promising legislation that in one vague way or another was supposed to benefit the family. That strategy has been highly successful. The DC enjoyed a solid base of support among traditional housewives.

This latest courting of mothers by conservative politicians is reminiscent of the era following the Second World War, when Christian Democrats attempted to scare women voters away from the Communist Party. It also evokes the backlash years following the radical upheavals of the 1960s, when the DC warned mothers that legalizing divorce would bring about the imminent demise of the family.[18] The 1990s have also been a time of tremendous political uncertainty in Italy, and conservative politicians have recycled the old verities for lack of any new ideas. But there are also several important reasons why all of the attention that has recently been lavished on mothers suggests a realignment rather than a simple rehashing of Italian politics.

One result of the 1970s Italian women's movement is that women's voices now dominate all sides of the motherhood debate. The number of women in Italy's Parliament doubled in the 1994 election. Interestingly, more than half of the newly elected women represent right-wing parties. And mothers are organized as never before. Having not only survived but flourished after the demise of the once omnipotent Christian Democratic Party, Federcasalinghe may well represent a permanent new fixture in Italian politics—traditional wives and mothers organized not simply to serve the interests of established male power brokers but rather to promote their own ideas and goals.[19]

Described by one Milan newspaper as "potentissima" (extremely powerful), Federcasalinghe has deep structural and ideological roots in modern Italian political culture that make the idea of a housewives' political union less strange to the Italian electorate than it might be in the United States. Federcasalinghe's success at developing a disciplined national organization can be attributed in part to the strong tradition of women-only religious and political auxiliaries in a country that was, until very recently, a sex-segregated society. Italian women's auxiliaries have been cultivated since the Second World War by male clergy and politicians on both the right and the left who saw them as vehicles for controlling housewives' money and votes. As has often been the case with women's auxiliaries, from labor unions to religious organizations, these groups became something more. Despite their conservative orientation, Catholic and Christian Democratic women's auxiliaries fueled housewives' organizing around family issues. Boasting a national base, these women's groups pushed the Church and its political arm, the DC, to take public stands on women's issues. In a similar evolution, the women's wing of the Italian Communist Party, the Union of Italian Women, developed into an institutional base for feminist action during the 1960s and 1970s, eventually becoming an autonomous movement.[20]

Twentieth-century Italian mothers' and housewives' movements have staked out positions all along the political spectrum. During the 1930s, Mussolini promoted the fascist Rural Housewives' Organization that created women's artisan collectives and encouraged the planting of cash-crop household gardens. These right-wing organizations provide one model for the economic autonomy arguments of more recent housewives groups. But the fascist programs sought to harness women's economic output for the state war machine, not to promote housewives' economic independence. And the Mussolini dictatorship was far more interested in women's production of children rather than in any other aspect of women's household labor. Mussolini sought to modernize childbearing as a way of generating human fodder for his war machine. Fascist Mother's Day ceremonies illustrated this vividly. Rather than celebrating the human bond between real mothers and their children, the dictatorship celebrated mothers' fertility. Each year, Mussolini assembled each province's most prolific breeders for a rally in Rome. Not a single woman's name was ever mentioned. Instead authorities read aloud the number of their live births, always more than a dozen and sometimes as many as twenty.[21]

A more recent influence on the current housewives' movement can be found in the Christian Democratic women's associations organized in the 1950s and 1960s. These groups served a social control function, imbuing members with the Church's patriarchal teachings and mobilizing Catholic housewives against the Communist Party and against legislation to legalize divorce and abortion. However, they also galvanized Catholic housewives in ways that the DC may not have intended. Based in the Church's teaching that the state had a responsibility to protect and preserve the family, such groups led conservative housewives to believe that they had a right to claim entitlements from elected officials on behalf of their children.[22]

Although, in the U.S. context, federal funding of wages for housework would be seen as a liberal-left idea, in Italy that demand has been associated with the right as well as the left. Both of the core groups in conservative politics, the neo-fascists and the Church, have argued a strong link between the family and the state. Where they have differed is in the equation between rights and responsibilities. Neo-fascist politicians placed families at the service of the state, whereas Catholic political theorists have emphasized the responsibilities of the state to families.[23]

But motherist politics have not been the sole province of the Italian right. Housewives and mothers' groups have also participated in subsistence protests about the price of rent, land and food, protests that have been traditionally associated with the left. After World War II women played a leading role in peasant mobilizations to demand land. In the 1960s and 1970s, some of the country's poorest urban mothers from Turin to Palermo staged illegal occupations of public and private buildings to demand improved housing and services for poor families.[24]

In an attempt to reach out to poor women, feminist groups in the 1970s first raised the issue of wages for housework. Marxist feminists saw wages for housework as an issue that could enhance women's solidarity across class lines and raise feminist consciousness among women who might not share their beliefs on other issues. Interestingly, Catholic women's groups affiliated with the DC were quick to support the idea, as was the pope. In 1979, the Christian Democrats, once again claiming a "crisis in the family," sponsored a resolution calling on the state to pay allotments to mothers. But because their bill focused on the role of mothers as "the first and unsubstitutable educators of the next generation" and authorized payments only to mothers who did no paid labor outside the home, many feminists and Communist party women condemned it as an attempt to push women back into the home. Women on the left similarly opposed a 1994 call by Pope John Paul II for family allotments, which was supported by the Duce's granddaughter Alessandra Mussolini, a member of Italy's lower House, and by her neo-fascist National Alliance Party. The pope's proposal is similar to those of Federcasalinghe with one important difference. It emphasizes a return to traditional gender roles rather than women's choice.[25]

Motherist rhetoric and the Italian Catholic women's groups that have long espoused it got a big boost during the early 1990s when the massive scandal known as Tangentopoli resulted in the investigation of virtually every well-known politician in the country. Desperately fleeing the taint of corruption, political figures of all stripes fought to be associated with that icon of selflessness, the Italian mama. By 1994, many leading figures in Italian politics, particularly those on the right, were enthusiastically talking about mothers.

That resulted in some frightening echoes. Half a century after his death, Benito Mussolini, the ultimate promoter of Italian masculinity, was suddenly resuscitated as the champion of women and children. During 1994, his name, policies and pronouncements dominated the national discourse on motherhood. "The most important measures in favor of women and the family were taken by Mussolini," announced arch-conservative Irene Pivetti shortly after she was elected Speaker of the Italian House in May 1994. "After Fascism, nothing more was done." Pivetti and other right-wing women politicians lauded Mussolini's creation of publicly funded prenatal and infant care, tax breaks to large families and public homages to mothers in order to score points in the revived debate over what the state owes mothers.[26]

Parliamentary Deputy Alessandra Mussolini and Berlusconi's Agriculture Minister Adriana Poli Bortone—the leading women in the neo-fascist National Alliance Party—frequently cited Il Duce's initiatives on behalf of mothers and children, in hopes of attracting women's votes to their newly powerful party. Claiming the high ground in the battle over who cares most about mothers, Alessandra Mussolini became one of the loudest voices in the Italian House calling for state allotments to women who stay home to raise their children. Poli Bortone led a campaign for the creation of a cabinet-level Ministry of the Family. Its purpose, Bortone said, was to shift the focus of political discussion from "a mother's right to work" to "a mother's right to stay home." Echoing her party's alarmist language about national moral decline, Poli Bortone insisted that legislative support for families is not just a women's issue. "We are . . . interested in sorting out society . . . And when you begin talking about the family, you are talking about everything."[27]

It may seem ironic that so many Italian women in the 1990s are waving the flag for Benito Mussolini, given that his regime denied women the vote, banned them from most jobs, and created an insatiable war machine that claimed the lives of countless Italian men and women. But even during the dictator's reign, many of his policies on behalf of women and children were embraced by feminists. It is precisely this kind of ideological slipperiness that makes so many people uncomfortable with Federcasalinghe's motherist politics.[28]

Is Federcasalinghe, consciously or not, reviving and legitimizing fascist ideas about the relationship between the family and the Italian state? Gasparrini says no. Her organization is not fascist, she has repeatedly insisted, and is in fact anti-fascist. "It is true that Mussolini tried to defend the family, and that he defended maternity," she said recently. "But he did it so that he could send the young to war, to the army. If we say today that we want to defend maternity, it is an act of love, for children, for the country. It is truly very different logic."[29] Nevertheless, the language used by both Gasparrini and Berlusconi—citing a child's "right to a serene mother," and mothers' "service" to the state in calming the troubled spirits of working husbands—is directly evocative of fascist homilies on the family. And the fact is that, despite Gasparrini's rejections of the neofascist National Alliance, she and her movement joined Berlusconi in a political alliance with the neo-fascists.

That, says Carol Beebe Tarantelli, is typical of Gasparrini's opportunism. "There were a lot of people who were on the Christian Democratic bandwagon who jumped off when it became clear that the DC was going to crash and there was only going to be a little bit left," says Tarantelli. "I don't know what to say finally about Gasparrini except that she's right wing. She's up for sale. She makes a lot of noise and she has done, as far as I can see, nothing."[30]

Whether one agrees with that assessment or not, it is not a simple matter to assign either to Federcasalinghe or to Gasparrini a clear position on the political spectrum. Federcasalinghe has always asserted strong Catholic allegiances, not surprising given that its members are Italians with roots in the Christian Democratic Party. Yet the organization is not explicitly anti-abortion, and its attempts to provide divorce insurance for members suggest a realistic assessment of the number of marriages that fail. Instead of taking up the more conventional right-wing position on morality and family, Federcasalinghe officers instead describe themselves as leaders of a women's rights organization. They propose no restrictions on who should be paid wages for housework, seeing government allotments as an entitlement of all who do unpaid labor in the home. And they have called on women who work outside the home to abandon what they see as a false distinction between housewives and workers, and to join together "to solve all of our problems more easily."[31] At the same time, their talk of serene motherhood and of a return to fundamental values strongly echoes the rhetoric of right-wing movements throughout Europe and the United States.

Italy's current crop of women politicians—on the right as well as the left—is moving away from what they see as the old-fashioned idea of organizing women separately. Livia Turco, the leading woman in the Democratic Party of the Left (the former Communist Party), disbanded the party's Women's Commission in 1994, saying that its time had past. And Irene Pivetti has argued that conservative women "don't think of segregating ourselves." In this political context, Federcasalinghe appears both reactionary and forward-looking when its leaders promise hope for change in an autonomous political movement of housewives and women workers.[32]

In the final analysis, the 1990s Italian housewives' movement could be a true amalgam, leaning right in its alliances and its religious orientation but open to influences from the left and from feminism, or it could be just following the wind. The complicated politics of the Italian housewives' federation sets off alarms for those analysts who believe that mothers' movements are dangerous precisely because they can be pulled right as easily as left, and manipulated by opportunists on either side. But, as traditional party formations around the world have begun to wither and to seem increasingly irrelevant, it is worth taking a second look at movements like Federcasalinghe. For the success of such groups suggests that politically organized mothers, operating outside of existing ideological boundaries, may represent an important political phenomenon. Both the danger and the promise are real. It remains to be seen which will prove stronger.

NOTES

1. *La Repubblica*, June 10, 1994.
2. *Il Messagero*, June 10, 1994. See too Victoria De Grazia, *How Fascism Ruled Women: Italy, 1922–1945* (Berkeley: University of California Press, 1992), p. 164.
3. *La Stampa*, February 20, 1994; Reuters, April 3, 1994.
4. Patricia Thomas, interview with Federica Rossi Gasparrini, Rome, June 28, 1994; *La Stampa*, April 29, 1993.
5. *La Stampa*, March 28, 1993; Patricia Thomas, interview with Federica Rossi Gasparrini, November 10, 1994.
6. *La Stampa*, March 28, 1993; *La Repubblica*, June 10, 1994.
7. *La Repubblica*, June 10, 1994.
8. *La Stampa*, March 28, 1993; Thomas interview with Gasparrini, Rome, June 28, 1994.
9. *Il Sole*, November 25, 1991.
10. *Il Sole*, February 20, 1992; *La Stampa*, January 17, 1993.
11. Author's telephone interview with Carol Beebe Tarantelli, December 23, 1994.
12. *La Stampa*, May 22, 23, 1992.
13. *La Repubblica*, June 10, 1994.
14. *La Stampa*, April 29, May 1, 12, 1993.
15. Ibid.
16. *La Stampa*, February 20, 1994.
17. *La Repubblica*, June 10, 1994; *Il Messagero*, June 10, 1994.
18. See Ginsborg, *A History of Contemporary Italy: Society and Politics, 1943–1988* (London: Penguin Books, 1990), chapters 5 and 10.
19. For a more complete analysis of the rise of conservative women politicians in 1990s Italy, see Alexis Jetter, "Turning Right," *Vogue*, November 1994.

20. See Lucia Chiavola Birnbaum, *Liberazione della Donna: Feminism in Italy* (Middletown, Conn.: Wesleyan University Press, 1986), pp. 65–75, 111–143; and Paul Ginsborg, *A History of Contemporary Italy: Society and Politics, 1943–1988* (London: Penguin Books, 1990), pp. 141–185, 348–403.

21. See De Grazia, *How Fascism Ruled Women*, pp. 71–72, 107–110. As De Grazia illustrates, many Italian women revolted against the broodmare image so central to the fascist politics of motherhood.

22. See Ginsborg, *A History of Contemporary Italy*, pp. 171–176; Birnbaum, *Liberazione della Donna*, pp. 111–132.

23. Ginsborg, *A History of Contemporary Italy*, pp. 173–176.

24. See Ginsborg, *A History of Contemporary Italy*, pp. 366–367.

25. Birnbaum, *Liberazione della Donna*, pp. 135–141; *La Repubblica*, March 26, 1994.

26. Miria Novella de Luca, "Femminismo 'Stagione Finita,'" *La Repubblica*, May 28, 1994; Miriam Mafai and Lee Marshall, "The March of Italy's Women," *The European*, May 6–12, 1994.

27. Poli Bortone quote in Mafai and Marshall, "The March of Italy's Women." For a complete analysis of Benito Mussolini's initiatives on behalf of, and to extend control over, the Italian family, see De Grazia, *How Fascism Ruled Women*, pp. 41–116. For Alessandra Mussolini's views on wages for mothers, see "Donne, non solo Mamme," *La Repubblica*, March 26, 1994.

28. De Grazia argues this effectively in *How Fascism Ruled Women*. For a summary of her argument, see pp. 1–17.

29. Thomas interview with Gasparrini.

30. Telephone interview with Tarantelli.

31. *La Stampa*, January 6, 1992.

32. Patricia Thomas inverview with Livia Turco, Rome, June 11, 1994; *La Stampa*, March 28, 1993.

REDEFINING MOTHERHOOD

Technologies and Sexualities

Overview

Redefining Motherhood Through Technologies and Sexualities

Diana Taylor

This section provides a spectrum of perspectives on the changing nature and politics of motherhood in an age of rapidly advancing reproductive technology. Technological and social progress, many people hoped, would offer women more choices. Technology could free women from the biological limitations of age and compulsory heterosexuality, while revamped social institutions could extend child care and educational services to all children. Cherríe Moraga's personal narrative on lesbian pregnancy and motherhood shows how this Chicana, already a renowned activist, playwright, poet and essayist, became a "radical" mother as well. She writes: "I imagine most people would consider it radical to finally decide at forty to have a baby, to take it upon one's lesbian self to say to her partner, 'I'm going to do this, I hope you'll go there with me.'" Moraga's earlier efforts to make the 1970s white feminist movement more open to women of color, and to make the Chicano movement address feminist issues, relied on the same personal philosophy: "to make *familia* from scratch, [. . .] with strangers if I must, if I must, I will."

Linda Mulley's "Lesbian Motherhood and Other Small Acts of Resistance" illustrates that the process of radicalization begins, rather than ends, when a lesbian becomes a mother. Mulley, a Vermont teacher who works with children who are developmentally disabled, was used to exerting "quiet, personal advocacy" in her work and personal life. But she soon realized that she had to take more dramatic action to protect her children from the homophobic barbs they experienced in school and in their community. "I felt caught," she confesses. "I wanted to protect [them] by taking bolder steps involving the entire school community, but feared that such an action might place [them] at risk for discrimination and rejection." Mulley's desire to protect her children soon forced her into the same quandary faced by women in environmental or military struggles. Each mother's activism, initiated to protect her children, threatens to expose that child to greater ostracism or danger.

These two accounts by lesbian mothers demonstrate that motherhood is, by definition, political. The question of who gets to be a mother, and the struggles awaiting any woman who chooses a nontraditional path, indicate just how political that choice is. In the best of all possible worlds, reproductive technology would be feminist technology, enabling lesbians, older women, and infertile women to have the children they'd otherwise never have. This technology might enable us to move beyond the stereotype of mothers as young, heterosexual women.

However, instead of liberating women, reproductive technology has in many ways extended the reach and power of patriarchy and misogynistic medical establishments. Reproductive technologies such as ultrasound and amniocentesis are often used to identify the sex of an unborn child, leading to the abortion of female fetuses. Madhu Kishwar, editor of the Indian journal *Manushi*, which is dedicated to the study of women and social justice, explores India's sex-selection practices. Although these practices are outlawed, they have not only continued but increased. A 1971 study showed 93.0 females for every 100 men in India, while a 1981 study showed that there were only 92.9 females per hundred males.[1] A 1991 study shows that 100 million females are "missing" worldwide, largely as a result of abortions performed on female fetuses after their sex had been determined.[2] Sexual technology has also been actively used against poor and politically underrepresented women. U.S. women from Native American, Puerto Rican and other marginalized communities have found themselves unwitting victims of sterilization programs.

In an age of reproductive technology and surrogate motherhood, scholar Rita Arditti argues, we can no longer think of "mothers" as simply those women who gave birth to or adopted children. As technology changes the biological processes that have historically grounded our understanding of motherhood, women—and the law courts—have had to grapple with fundamental conceptual shifts. Now, clarifications have become necessary: Are we talking about a "mother" in biological terms, or as the person who cares for the child, who assumes responsibility for the child's spiritual, mental, physical, and emotional development, and who, in so doing, assures the continuity of life? The traditional role of "mother," which includes the biological aspects of pregnancy and birthing as well as the nurturing mother–child relationship, has been split up into functions, into several compartmentalized and commercialized parts: egg, womb, caretaker.

These issues grow even more complicated when we consider which birthing mothers actually get to keep their children. "Surrogate" mothers may give birth, but their contractual arrangement prohibits them from establishing a relationship with their offspring. In most cases, the term "mother" is even denied them. They are known as "host wombs," "fetal containers," "alternative reproduction vehicles," or "gestational surrogates." Poor women and women of color are prime targets for what has come to be known as "pure" surrogacy, an arrangement in which the woman does not provide the egg, but "only" the womb. Women from the Third World are also targeted as a cheap labor force for well-to-do couples.[3] The question of who gets to be a mother, and who gets considered a mother, has as much to do with economics as with biology.

This compartmentalization of motherhood has hindered women's rights on several fronts—including, some argue, on the abortion issue.[4] So while technology may have destabilized our definition of "mothers," it does not appear to be protecting either the rights or lives of females, or liberating them from biological limitations.

NOTES

1. "Stark Data on Women: 100 Million are Missing," *New York Times*, Nov. 5, 1991.
2. Ibid.
3. See "Women as Wombs: International Traffic in Reproduction," Janice G. Raymond, *Ms.*, 1, no. 6 (May/June 1991):29–33.
4. Prioritizing the right of the sperm and the egg over the birth-mother of "pure" surrogacy further legitimates the independent status of the fetus.

Waiting in the Wings

Reflections on a Radical Motherhood

Cherríe Moraga

PRÓLOGO

Lesbians don't make babies with our lovers. We make babies with strangers in one-night stands or on the doctor's insemination table, with friends in a friendly fuck or loveless mason jar, with enemies who at the time were husbands or boyfriends, or ex-husbands and boyfriends whom our children call *"papi"* and we may still consider family. We cannot make babies with one another. Our blood doesn't mix into the creation of a third entity with an equal split of DNA. Sure, we can co-adopt, we can coparent, we can be *comadres*, but blood *mami* and *papi* we ain't.

I know the stories that we only admit to one another in private, our children's hunger for "normalcy" (that *mami* and *papi* business) no matter how much they love us. A brilliant butch lover I had years ago told me about a boy she raised for many years with his mother. One night her heart broke when, as she was tucking in the bespectacled boy of ten, he wrapped his arms around her neck and called her "Daddy," with everything he had in him. When I finally met the boy, I saw that he shared Maria's poor eyesight, wit, and brainy humor. Most of all, he learned how to be a boy from Maria. He learned masculinity from Maria, and she was a wonderful male role model, the best of fathers with a woman's compassion.

I want to write here of love, the love of lesbians, the love of lesbian mothers in spite of all the odds against it. I have been the lesbian lover of a mother. I know what it is to live with that uncertainty as the "nonbiological parent" (such a cold American term), knowing that your love may have no other reward than the act of loving in the here and now. Not enough for most of us. But we lesbians learn to live with the uncertainties. Maybe that's what I love about us.

In a way, I asked the same of Ellen on a deeper level, not to be a mother, but only a lover of my child, a lover of me. Probably that's the most noble of gestures, more noble than offering sperm and having the privilege of knowing your bones' memory lives on in another being, without obligation.

I imagine most people would consider it radical to finally decide at forty to have a baby, to take it upon one's lesbian self to say to her partner, "I'm going to do this, I hope you'll go there with me." To ask a young gay man, eighteen years her junior, "I'm going to do this, will you help me?" Without question in another era, in another geographical region outside of San Francisco, another cultural point of reference, my having a baby as an avowed lesbian would have been a radical phenomenon indeed. And in most circles I imagine it still is. But not in my own circle, not in the circle where I have constructed *familia*, not with a woman partner as firm as the steady and changing earth, not among the women I call *comrades*, the donor I call *"manito,"* nor among my blood *familia*. Having Rafael Angel was in a way the most natural evolution of two lives—his and my own—the most logical next step on a road whose mysterious twists and turns daily make me marvel.

I tell friends, I almost missed Rafaelito, that he had been there waiting in the wings, and I could hear his voice in the most remote corners of my dreams and in the raising of other women's children. That is how I account for his precipitous birth at only twenty-eight weeks of gestation. He was a spirit who, for some time, was waiting to get here, through me. He was in a hurry. And when I finally opened my heart and listened, he took hold of me right away. I was pregnant with the first insemination, and six months later, he was born, weighing only 2 pounds, 6 ounces.

As a child and a tomboy, I never fantasized about having children, no more than most little boys do, dreaming about a brood of five sons, enough to make up a basketball team. When I came out as a lesbian at the age of twenty-two, I simply assumed since I would never be married to a man, I would never have children. So while my sister was busily making babies every three or four years, I was busily making lovers (yes, about every three or four years). Then at the age of thirty, it hit me. I was a woman, and, therefore, potentially capable of having children.

This may sound strange, a statement of the blatantly obvious, but buried deep inside me, regardless of the empirical evidence to the contrary, I had maintained the rigid conviction that lesbians (that is, those of us on the more butch side of the spectrum) weren't really women. We were women-lovers, a kind of "third sex" and most definitely not men. So having babies was something real women did, not butch lesbians, not girls who knew they were queer since grade school. We were the defenders of women and children, children we could never fully call our own.

In many ways, I lived out that fantasy. In my mid-thirties, I was involved with a wonderful artist and her young child, whom I will call here Joel. In the three years of our relationship, I had grown to think of Joel—whether sanctioned or not—as my own. Then one day, I lost them both without warning and with great wrenching, not so much from the woman, but from the child. This was the baby I had watched become a boy, whom I had walked to kindergarten, taught how to ride a two-wheeler and build sand castles on the beach. We had hiked in the foothills together, I pointing out leaf and *flor*. I had explained the meaning of morning frost to him, the metamorphosis of polliwogs to frogs, of caterpillar to marvelous *mariposa*. And I had also made his morning breakfast, bathed him in the evening, picked him up from day care, and given him medicine in the middle of the night. I didn't do these things equally to his mother, but I was a partner to her and a parent to him to the degree I was allowed. Simply, I knew Joel with a kind of heart's knowledge that I have never been able to completely erase.

I remember once, just before the "official" break-up, Joel and I had been separated from his mother and each other for many weeks. He had been staying with his father, and after some urging, his dad let me have Joel overnight. The first thing I did was give him a much-needed bath. Pulling Joel out of the tub I wrapped him in a huge cotton towel and took to grooming him, tenderly cleaning his ears with a Q-tip, clipping his finger- and toenails, rubbing his smooth *cafecito* skin with sweet oil. Suddenly, he looked up at me and blurted out, "You're my Mom." We were both missing her badly. And at that moment, I could already taste their forever-absence from my life.

The dreams where Joel appears, always in crisis, have gradually dissipated with the birth of my Rafaelito. Still I think of him often . . . kindly, sadly. I remember one incident recently, when after shopping I was putting Rafael into his car seat, I called him "Joel." It shocked me, for although I have almost called Rafael that name so many times, I usually catch the word before it slips into the air, never to be retrieved. I felt guilty, I'm not sure why, and I assured my son, *tú eres el único, hijo*, the way we must reassure our lovers when we, by accident, call them by a past lover's name. When this happens between lovers, we are mortified. What does it mean? We always fear that she—that other named one—was the greater love. And sometimes she was. But, sometimes she was merely a profound touching, an awakening that will always be remembered by that name, even when the same place is touched by another.

That is who Joel is to me. My first real son and the mother he called forth in me made my hunger for Rafael Angel all the more urgent: a child that would never be taken from me, a child to raise from scratch.

One thing Joel's presence in my life taught me was that, without realizing, I had grown up woman enough to mother a child. The child grew inside me, the loss of the child, the discovery of the mother, the recognition that I had nursed dozens of hungry women throughout my life—as I had my own mother—from the time I could remember, and in that resided my lesbian conviction, my lesbian loving. I am a daughter and have always loved the daughters in all our beauty and brokenness. But what of children . . . ?

When I was five months pregnant, I wrote: "*What is sex or prayer (I don't know which) is the spring's sunlight descending into the cooling golden rod hills. I watch it retreat, starting my bath in the evening light, finishing in darkness. I watch my womb grow, watch the sudden transformation of my body like some holy miracle. I try to reach somewhere wounded and or-phaned inside of me and bring this sudden image of my queer womanhood into its view: I, the object of my own desirous lesbian woman-hungry eyes. I, a mama, too, like all the mamas I have longed for and loved.*"

The pages that follow are my own queer story of pregnancy, birth, and the first year of mothering.[1] It is a story of one small human being's survival, of life, of thriving in the age of death, the age of AIDS. These are mostly journal entries, interspersed with reflections I wrote later because at the time I was too immersed in the living to speak of it.[2] It is a poet's journal (I see now in retrospect), for even giving birth does not satisfy the artist's hunger. Finally, this is the story of faithfulness between two lesbian lovers (mothers) and the family that sustained us.

EL 6 DE ENERO

The feast of the epiphany, a good day to start a life.

When Ellen and Pablo[3] sat around me on my bed after the insemination, a comforter covering me, my legs propped up in the air with pillows, I felt "made love to." That's the expression I used and that was the feeling exactly. The way I always imagined becoming pregnant would feel like, in the best of scenarios. But the insemination had nothing to do with sex or orgasm or excitement, except our three-way titillated embarrassment over the proce-dure. Pablo stood in the bathroom, trying to think about *anything* sexier than the mouth of a mason jar. And Ellen and I waited nervously in the bedroom together, Ellen practicing pumping water in and out of the syringe. Probably the best lovin' I'd ever known, I can say unequivocally. I am still awed by the fact that these two people loved me enough to go through whatever embarrassment to help me conceive. "That's all there was to it?" Ellen's mom would ask us months later. "Yes." "But it's so simple." "Yeah," I answer, "one way or another that sperm has just got to get inside you." Very simple . . . and unromantic. Still, I felt "made love to." And whether pregnant or not, I knew I would never forget what that softness felt like, my legs up and open to receive whatever destiny had decided for me. I close my eyes and dream Pablo as a sweet twin lover. I put my mouth and nose into the hollow of Ellen's neck, breathe her in, and I am sustained. Momentarily, there is *tranquilidad*.

28 ENERO 1993

Today I feel my hormones acting up, blowing me up, sitting heavy on my chest. I wonder if this is all just a bad case of PMS. I wonder if I am pregnant. I feel my body a stranger. I am without desire. What happened to desire? Or is it that my desire is so great and lies muted somewhere inside me.

I wish I knew how to pray. I am at times filled with joy as the sun spills into my bedroom window. I clasp my hands before my altar, light a vela, *study* la virgen's *impassive expression, wave the scent and heat of copal over all my openings and long for* una respuesta *. . . a word, an image, a vision. Does the journeying I must make right now involve miles of physical territory or is it an interior map I need to explore through reading, reflection, conversation . . . ?*

I proceed with the plan of having a baby because I have only myself the kindness of friends, the cosmos to trust. I experience pain often in my womb, my vagina. I don't understand the signs. I ignore them, go on. I do know having this baby demands all my attention. Demands diet, exercise, counsel, prayer, apoyo, hogar, fuerza y visión. *I am always on the verge of tears in this writing. I keep getting flashes, mental glimpses of my parents waiting for me at the Hollywood/Burbank airport. With each visit, they seem a bit smaller, physically, a bit older, slightly more vulnerable. Standing at the gate, they greet me with expectant, anxious eyes, my Dad always noticing me a few seconds after my Mom. I am filled with emotion. This family means so much to me, this family slipping away. I grow to comprehend, somewhere in my heart, how transitory this physical life is.*

I miss L.A. In a way, I miss how I am essentially L.A. born-and-bred, but my spirit resides elsewhere.

JANUARY 29

Returning from the play reading in Los Angeles, I ignore what is most evident, my desire for this child. I give it a half-hearted attention, not being able to fully believe it could happen to me. In the deepest places I am afraid of the commitment, I am afraid of the disappointment. I am afraid to want her and be unable to have her. My sister and Ellen both try to convince me to take a "home pregnancy test," but I am superstitious. If I want it too bad, it won't happen.

Finally, coming back from L.A., I promise Ellen that if she buys the test, I'll take it. She does. In seconds after I put the required few drops of urine onto the test paper, two pink lines appear indicating I'm pregnant. There is no ambivalence in those lines: they are a dark solid unwavering pink and there are clearly two of them. Ellen and I both look at each other, dumbfounded. I still can't believe it. How could two tiny lines, such insignificant markings, pronounce something as irrevocable as a human life? Ellen can't believe my resistance. She volunteers to take the test. If hers turns up with only one line, then will I be convinced? Yes, I promise. Sure enough, one line and a faint one at that. We stare at each other in the bathroom, looking back and forth at her test and mine. Ellen's eyes are dancing with excitement, but I can't fully take it in and make a silent agreement not to count on any babies until I get a blood test from the doctor. It isn't denial exactly, more like *this is too good to be true.*

30 ENERO

It is nearly February and I realize in weeks I am to take off to Guatemala for "The Popol Vuh Project,"[4] but I have made no plans. And I grow tired at the thought of it. I don't know. For some reason, I think of staying home. Reading all I can on The Popol Vuh, *beginning to work on "Medea,"[5] slowing down. For some reason, I think of visiting Angelina, seeking her consejo about this baby, improving my diet, my exercising. For some reason I want to take care of myself.*

3 FEBRERO

Just got a call from the doctor. Bona fide pregnant. First try.

I haven't written of my days with the reproductive sciences, the fertility experts, the sonograms of my fetus-sized fibroids—all benign and thoroughly unproductive. I had all the tests, in advance, to make sure everything was in working order "down-there," the tubes clear, the hormones balanced, in short—a healthy habitat. In spite of my good health, the fertility specialist had given me the odds, bad even for forty-year-old heterosexuals who are "doing it all the time," he said. Still, I'd give it a shot. *How?* He wanted to know, but didn't ask. When I came in with the news of my pregnancy, whispering to the nurses, "I did it the home-grown way," they all cracked up, teasing the doc . . . *So much for science.* He took it in good stride and would even come to see my baby months later in the ICN, telling me he had never seen me look so happy.

7 FEBRERO

Sueño. *There are two paths. One high, one low, leading to the same destination. The lower path runs along the shoreline. Cathy and I follow it. The scene is breathtaking. A turquoise water lapping against a bleached Mexican desert sand. There are deer in the distance. They, too, are turquoise, the color of Indian precious stone.*

15 FEBRERO

Sueño. *Two images of my baby. One where the baby is born already a grown boy. So beautiful, so sensual. I touch him all over. I can't believe he is mine, although I am so disappointed that he was born a boy. I touch his penis inside his pants. I know I have gone too far, but I am delighting so much in his beauty. Then my baby is born again. This time a tiny beautiful dark-haired Mexican girl. I am in heaven. The joy is endless, although throughout both parts of the dream I wonder how it is my baby was born so fast when she was just nothing more than a seed inside of me. I remember looking at the baby girl's genitalia, thinking at first the swollen round vagina is balls, then realizing, no, it is a vagina. She is transparent. Her skin a see-through casing holding in muscle and bone. I know in the dream, the skin will take on the appearance of flesh later.*

19 FEBRERO

This baby settles into me. If I were to write about being a writer I would say it has something to do with the contemplative life, the life of standing at the end of a pier, the sun an hour into the horizon of black bay waters. The skyscraper reflections make me believe that at forty my life is barely beginning. I know it is this life I carry within me that causes me to imagine a future, a future I could never dream in any lover, only in family, only in my sister with whom I shared a bedroom and a dream-life for twenty years. As girls we believed we would never be parted. Not really.

I stare into the black sea and know my eyes mirror that same endless dark depth and I float out under the Golden Gate Bridge and into the Pacific, knowing with complete clarity that my life will take me (us) to many lands, to many languages. How is it that travel seems more possible now, thinking of this life . . . this barely-formed being? I walk back to my car at a brisk pace. Driving home the radio announces the Senate passage of a bill outlawing the entrance of HIV-infected immigrants. One reporter speaks of 270 Haitians imprisoned in camps, "a living hell," he calls it. And a prayer rises up to my lips. We all deserve a future.

I return home to cook catfish. Full of gratitude, the barriers between Ellen and me dissolve. And I believe we will never be parted. Not really.

28 FEBRERO

Sueño. *It is barely past midnight when I awaken, trembling from the nightmare. I only remember Ellen's face, like my sister's, and her bottomless rage. My entire body fills with the fire of first fear, then despair. I do everything in my power to calm her down. It is too late, all I can do is escape the dream. I will myself awaken. My body bounds with adrenaline. I feel the new life inside me stir. Does this baby feel the hot rush of passion, does she feel my burning blood? And I think of how this small smudge of life knows me like no other, how once I knew my mother the same way and was born with the knowledge of her pain and fears. This is not the legacy I wish to pass onto my baby.*
More dreams. *I am bleeding, not heavily, but not exactly spotting either. I try to call the Nurse. It is late when I arrive at the hospital. The day is done. She is irritated. "Are you really bleeding or just spotting?" she asks. I feel guilty, embarrassed that I am not sure, that I may be overly worried.*

2 MARZO

My skin has broken out in a desperate rash. This morning I awaken to a narrow band of pain just below my ribcage. I feel my uterus expanding. I know the baby is larger now. Its presence is irrevocable and the gravity of this change hits a deeper level. I go back to bed hoping the pain will subside. It does. I awaken to the sound of the boiling kettle. Ellen is up.

The results of the CVS test are in. Ellen and I are on extension phones, we hear the genetic specialist tell us, the baby is a boy. "That's good news, isn't it!" she asks. I smile weakly. "Yes, of course. Yes, thank you." We hang up. Speechless.

The day before, the specialist had left word on the answering machine that the test had shown the baby to be perfectly normal genetically. I hadn't realized how worried I had been until I replayed the recording and burst into tears. I hadn't known I had been holding my breath for those first twelve weeks, fearing to tell anyone (outside of my closest circle of *comadres*) in the event that the baby would not be healthy. After all, I was forty years old and pregnant for the first time in my life. So, the question of the baby's sex came later, as an afterthought, when one has the luxury to ruminate over such things.

I confess the news of a baby boy came as a shock . . . to both of us, probably even more so to Ellen, who—having grown up the only girl among four brothers, worked as a firefighter, and raised a gender-bending male teenager for a time—feels her "male karma" has been thoroughly fulfilled. (Well, I guess not.) Naive as it may seem, we believed we were getting a girl, if for no other reason than that we did the insemination early (too early really) for me to get pregnant. The reasoning was, I was rushing off for a week in New York, during the end of which I would be ovulating. Rather than waiting another month, Ellen, Pablo and I just decided to "break the ice" (so to speak) and get the "virgin voyage" (so to speak) over with. When I learned I was pregnant, I figured all the Y-chromosomes had long ago taken their leave since they are the fast swimmers of short duration. I figured wrong. In the end, I realize science has nothing to do with it. This baby boy is a soul wanting to get here. *Punto final.* Later Ellen asks, "What will you name him?" "Rafael," I answer, no doubt in my mind. I have always loved the name.

We go to the local bookstore—Ellen and I. I look up the name Rafael to see what message it brings. In a book of Saints, I find "Rafael" listed among the other Archangels. "The healing power of god," it states. Patron of musicians and travelers. "Perfect," I say. And I am more reconciled as I see at the bottom of the listing that Rafael Angel's feast day falls on my expected delivery date. September 29. Okay, I say to myself. I get it. Es el destino.

18 MARZO

Ellen calls from work and tells me Tede is sick with AIDS. It is news I have been resisting for three days. A rumor, I told myself. But today it is confirmed and I think only of the other news, of the boy I am to birth. This birth, I think, may be for them, this male birth for so many dying brothers. Why else are so many lesbians giving birth to boys? I imagine such thoughts bring no succor to the men dying. But there is meaning in the fact that my fetus has formed itself into a male, a meaning I must excavate from the most buried places in myself as well as from this city/this era of the dying into which my baby will be born. I understood the female, the daughter. The son holds a message I will learn to decipher with my heart.

I don't understand dying. I don't understand Tede's dying. My first thought, so selfish, I can't bear to endure another AIDS death. My brief acquaintance with it with Rodrigo left me mute, horrified. It is not the death that frightens so, it is the slow humiliating dissolution of the body. I fear the face of death. I am ashamed of my fear.

The sun passes through my bedroom window and I find hope in its afternoon warmth. I pray my baby feels it too upon his face and frail chest of pale skin. All day today I have been unable to write. The days draw nearer to The Last Generation[6] *deadline, but the news of my son came as a deep shock to me, that sent me to bed to recover. These are not the words I seek, but as the* I Ching *oracled, "God has manifested himself:" The destiny that is joining this boy-child and me and Ellen together is out of my hands and I open my heart to receive him. I name him Rafael Angel . . . for life.*

19 MARZO

Three months into my pregnancy and I begin to write more thoroughly. I awaken this morning to thoughts of the baby sleeping inside me. Last night amid sweating sleeplessness, I feared my baby was leaving me. I feared the fevers were burning him out. I feared there was no place for my shock at this maleness. I spoke with him all night last night. I spoke to him for understanding amid aching joints and a low-grade fever and a steady dampness between my thighs. I spoke to him and asked that he not abandon me, that he hold fast to me, that this sickness is a baptism, as I sweat out my disappointment in order to discover and embrace the innocence of my son beating within me.

I tossed and turned last night with images of "Mexican Medea." I still know that this is the play I must write, although I fear it. How is it I can be pregnant and write of killing a child? La llorona. I believe that my son can forgive his mother's relentless need to describe the source of our female deformation. It is not mere feminist rhetoric that makes a woman stop dumbfounded in the face of a life of raising a son. It is the living woman-wound that we have spent our lives trying to heal. I tell Pablo, "I wanted a female to love." He answers, "You've done that your entire life as a lesbian." Yes.

I awaken, rested, cooled. It is an overcast morning and I hear the little neighbor-girl, Morgan, descend the steps from upstairs, chatting endlessly to her mother as she does every morning on her way to school. This morning I hear her voice as a small boy's voice and it is equally tender.

22 MARZO

Last night, a miserable night without sleep, unable to breathe. Spring has arrived, along with my allergies. My body is thick with fatigue. Ellen and our neighbor, Ski, dig up the garden, stir up new life after months of rain. I wait for this wave of illness to pass so I can return to work, so I can give my attention to my growing child inside me.

At times I fear he has fallen asleep for good inside me. I worry my own fears will turn him bitter against me. I do not feel Rafael Angel as some formless entity that I will shape with my own hands and love. He enters this planet, a soul intact. Who is this being? Some days I imagine him a bitter old man, un juez, severe and authoritative. I imagine him judging my harshness, my moods, my mean ways. At other times, I feel him a young sage-spirit, as delicate as his angelic name.

I ABRIL

New York City. *This morning as I am thoroughly alone, I put my fingers to that nostalgia (my New York days, my New York lovers) and remember, but it is no past woman I discover there, but more the eruption of the older me. How do I describe that at the moment of orgasm, I feel the infant inside me curl up into a hard fist, no violence, but a hard ball of intensity swelling in my womb? And I cry for this life, this miracle. This sexuality that is happening to me unlike any I have experienced. The slightest contact evokes a response . . . touching my self touching Ellen touching me. I am female essence relieved of all burden, but this stirring, this kicking up of life between my legs . . . inside my belly . . . I make love to it, the life.*

> *My body is not in this room. It is in a cave somewhere, somewhere dark, somewhere fecund. There is plenty of dirt around me, between my toes. The animal kicks inside me and that's all the sign of life I need. There is nothing else required of me, but to dwell here, pregnant.*

8 ABRIL

Back in San Francisco. *I don't know what makes me cry, except the weight of all this change. Sueños where my baby turns out whiter than I expected, but beautiful still and talking too soon. I never got to hear his first word. Was it* "mami, "papi," "flor?" *Was it truth? No, this baby is already walking and talking full sentences and I lament that I have missed something in his growing.*

Now, I am putting the laundry into sorted piles. I go to the washroom to discover that there is no detergent and Ellen is to blame. No one is to blame, but I must blame someone, for some one thing not going as planned. We fight. Ridiculous. She leaves for work and I barely let pass the sound of her tires on the gravel driveway before I am buried face into the pillow and weeping. My womb pressed up against the stiff mattress. I feel a slight fluttering and I know the tears are only about this, this overwhelming pending change in our lives. I would never want to go back now, childless. But I wonder of our future. I make room for the baby and am overwhelmed by every box of baby hand-me-downs consuming the space necessary for his arrival. There is no detergent when I need to wash the clothes. I cry.

9 ABRIL

7 A.M. Sueño. *A small cup-sized baby has erupted from my womb. It has dark hair and what seems like painted black lines for emerging features. The tiny sack of baby hangs by a cord between my legs and I keep trying to push it back inside, knowing it is not yet ready to emerge.*
When I dream again, *someone old has passed on. It is not a tragic death because the age is ripe for dying. Upon hearing the news, I receive long green-stemmed flowers of some kind. They will soon blossom yellow and creative. I know it is my baby.*

Upon wakening, I go to the bathroom and find myself spotting more heavily than I have since the beginning of my pregnancy. It is a thick earth-brown color. I panic, then try to calm myself: I lay here in bed and ask my baby to give me a sign of life, a fluttering so I know all is well.

12 ABRIL

I am the moon's keeper. Vigilant, at 4 A.M. the moon rises, I dawn nocturnal. She appears in trinity, each reflection a bit more ephemeral. I rise, search out her light in people-less bedrooms, through half-open shades. The garden is afternoon-illuminated and the vegetables grow too like babies. In the distance there is the baby-morning cry of a backyard cat, a city rooster's complaint. It is already dawning in San Cristóbal. I remember, walking at 5 A.M. to the bus station in that sleeping town. I remember an aloneness more pro-

found for the loss of a child. I am not now as I once was that orphaned woman walking the cobblestone in the pre-dawn silence. I am she who rises en busca de la luna, seeking mother/daughter, seeking light. Moon keeper, I divine.

13 ABRIL

I can't get to the heart of my feeling here. I watch my body change daily and know I am not fully resided in it. These miserable allergies are dragging me down into a fog of anxiety, depression. The days are gorgeous and I cannot fully appreciate them, the winds stirring up the pollen, the seeds of life. Pregnancy happening everywhere and ironically my body is reacting against it. I cling to Ellen in a way I never imagined.

14 ABRIL

It is impossible to concentrate on anything but this sudden exposure. I an-nounce my pregnancy to my "Indígena as Scribe" writing class and immedi-ately I am surrounded by shock and excitement and consejo: "You must get your water filtered." "You have to be smudged in the delivery room. It freaks the hospital staff out cuz the smoke alarms can go off." "Call my mother, la partera, *she'll deliver your baby." All good women, concerned women, all thoroughly Indian women in their response to me.*

I wonder why it is during these times that I am drawn to myth over and over again; possibly it is this work on "The Heart of the Earth . . ." In the Indígena *class I write, "On the first day of mourning, the men whose hairiness I inherited arrived in canoes with houses built upon them ('floating* palacios') *in search of the 'sun's excrement.'" I guess this low-grade headache, low-grade fever has something to do with knowing my giving birth involves me in this trajectory, this continuing history . . . of conquests and culture clashes, of the regeneration of* raza *and the creation of new* razas.

Nation. Nationality. I am the mother of a Mexican baby. I am the worst and best of the Chicano *nacionalistas*, I picked a man for his brains and dark beauty. And the race continues. But mostly I picked him because I knew he loved me without wanting me. A gay man. A queer contract. And I gotta whitegirl lover with lovely cullud girl curls and a butt to match and Spanish that don't make a fool outta her. This is my home. For now. I don't know what the future will bring. We try to get what we can on paper, to protect ourselves against pain, against loss, but the papers don't protect us.

17 ABRIL

Sueño. *I recall the image of a nun who refuses to wear the modern habit. She insists on wearing the traditional kind, but adds that if she cuts a hole into her chest and places a mirror there, everyone will be able to see into her. She will be hiding nothing.*

Since the bleeding—how to describe it—I am homebound and read daily of Maya ritual bloodletting, of shamans and diviners. I remain ever-awed by the fragility of the life inside of me or maybe it is only I who am fragile. At each threat to my pregnancy, the baby remains sólido, intacto. His heartbeat growing in resonance, conviction, full human-beingness. What relief to hear it beating without disturbance next to my frantically beating heart, as Nurse Eileen put the heart monitor to my womb. Bleeding buckets between my legs on the way to the hospital, my future without this child rushes before me. I try to stop it, how familiar childlessness is to me, how much simpler it would be, how every corpuscle in my body resists a return to that state.

When I get to clinic, I go straight into the staff area, looking for Eileen. "She's gone for the day," they say. "But I'm bleeding," I respond. And then I hear her voice. "Cherríe, is that you?" She enters the room, her round freckled face wrinkling into a frown. When I see her, I am no head, no future, no thought. I am all girl-child with baby and I cry to her, "I'm bleeding." She rushes me into an examination room and feels for the baby with groping hands. At that point of contact, I feel my baby move up into the round shape of her hold. I know my baby is whole and complete inside. No miscarriage.[7]

I have no control over this vulnerability. It is so hard to want something so bad and to feel this destiny of mother and child is truly out of my hands, truly a gift from the cosmos. I am here to receive it, but I cannot cling to it any more than I can predict the nature of the son I will have. I keep thinking he is his own soul.

25 ABRIL

I return from The Ceremony at Bear Camp. I return to my bed, the afternoon sun spilling over the bedspread and I nap after thirty hours without sleep. Ellen is taking a bath, then is off to rehearsal, now in the last stages of her play.[8] I feel momentarily guilty that she has endured the hardships of the weekend on account of me and now is unable to even sleep it off, recuperate as I am. But I am too exhausted to hold the guilt and fall into a deep sleep. When I awaken, I am convinced that there is some ritual of closing I still need to perform, since we had to leave the camp earlier than the rest. I rise, wash all my clothes, clean my car of the earth and mud and clean my hair and body of fire, smoke and fatigue.

Now there is this writing and the "medicine" continues to do its work in its deeply peculiar, unromantic, and specific way. I have moved outside to a spot in the sun. The bay breezes never fully allow for a steady warming heat. There is always a slight chill in the air. This writing is part of that closing, that opening, that continuance of what touched me somehow, unwittingly, in these last days of pure offering. Not that my spirit was pure, only there was no other way to understand the weekend, except to see it as an offering. All was discomfort, working when what I was needing was rest, waiting on men (which I found distasteful), the intensity of the heat from the sweat lodge (this I wanted), the endless hours of sitting in ceremony, unable to stretch my cramped legs and spasming back, fighting back a constant call to sleep.

But there were gifts given minute-by-minute and I return home and experience a change I had not anticipated. There was the presence of my child inside of me throughout. I may never feel this "unalone" again, I thought. Months from now, even as he sucks at my breast, he will be apart physically. But not now. Now we are siamese twins, his body and spirit residing solidly inside me. During the ceremonia, as others suffered separation around me, I did not feel alone. Holding my womb, I rocked and rocked, and my son and I spoke secrets to each other in the circle of the fire. I prayed and dosed off into mundane dreams of steak dinners and other small cravings, then would awaken and pray some more.

I prayed that I would learn how to raise a male child well, that the wounds men have inflicted on me, even in their absence, will not poison me against my son. At times, I could barely stomach the preference given to males throughout la ceremonia: they, the firekeepers, the pipecarriers, the jefes. So, I look for an opening of understanding in all this. I did not have the biographies so many of the folks present at the ceremony claimed: drug abuse, poverty, violent relationships, "skid-row." My battles, challenges, have always been more invisible. But it is with that biography and this baby inside that I proceed. Adelante. I ask for light. I thank the spirit for what has already been freely given.

Son to his mother at the Ceremony:
   "You can lead a horse to water.
   You have led me to the river,
   It's up to me if I'm gonna drink."

There is no closure, only this beginning, my return to "Heart of the Earth" with new eyes, my return to Ellen with renewed love, understanding. I have this life inside me to thank for the generosity his presence has brought to our relationship. Seeing Ellen's goodness to me in my pregnancy has opened my heart to her in a way I know cannot be reversed. She has allowed me to depend on her. For the first time in my life.

28 MAYO

Sueño. *Ellen and I are at a* botánica. *The walls are lined with jars of herbs and medicines from floor board to ceiling. I don't know what our illness is or the remedy. I do not feel ill. At one point, a beautiful boy of about nine approaches. He is the son of Ellen's friend. We say her name in greeting him. He is the essence of life itself. A beautiful brown face, huge eyes, thick dark hair. He exudes a genuine kindness. Upon waking, I wonder . . . is he my son?*

30 MAYO

I can't write sitting up in bed anymore. My belly's too big. The baby moves around constantly now, especially when I am resting or sitting still. He is a fish inside me, flapping his tail, gulping down the waters of my womb. He is pure animal, nothing human about these sensations. They are the animal I am when I make love, am hungry, move my bowels, fall into a deep unconscious sleep.

Hours ago, Dorothy was here with her nine-month-old baby and her lover. We ate well, conversed lightly, the baby drawing most of our attention. Mostly we spoke of the business of writing and the idea of writing a novel came back to me. Suddenly this baby is due and I realize the vulnerability I feel with my writing career as a playwright and poet. How little money it earns, how hard it is to promote the work. But beyond the money, I long for that kind of extended involvement in a work. I think, what pleasure to immerse oneself in one story for a long long time. I always have the sense that my writing is incomplete somehow—the poems, the plays, the essays—always striving at something not wholly realized. Maybe the novel would allow me that space to explore the deepest concerns. Thoroughly. I don't know. I write theoretically here when the urge is to create.

My body now taking on the full shape of creation does not lessen my need for art.

11 JUNIO

New York City. *Here again, to work on yet another draft of "Heart of the Earth." I can't write now because I need to keep my feet up because they have swollen into flintstone feet in this New York heat and my hands grow quickly numb holding up this book and pen in the air over my belly. All I am waiting for is to escape this heat, to be rejoined with Ellen on the Cape, to rest. . . .*

18 JUNIO

Cape Cod. *Ellen's mom's house. I awaken this morning as an expectant mother, worrying over the amount of Vitamin C I am taking. Is it all right for the baby? The baby greets me with bolder movements each day. I feel him now just right of my navel. I dream his future face nightly. I feel a slight muscle spasm in the left side of my neck and imagine my baby has traveled up there, stirring everywhere throughout my body.*

Hormones. I cry freely and without will or censor. Last night I go to bed, weepy-eyed when Ellen comes in. We have just seen a show about transsexuals. Since the featured male-to-female started out heterosexual, I suggest her sexuality (attraction to women) might remain the same after her operation and she will become a lesbian. Alice, Ellen's mother, is mind-boggled. "But they made her a vagina with feeling. After all that, how could she still want to be with a woman?" I respond, "I have a vagina with feeling and I want to be with a woman." She goes silent. Ellen comes back into the room and we argue about numbers—what percentage of transsexuals become straight, what relationship sexuality has to transsexualism. The "debate" is not the point. I am hurt by Alice's response. She is not being mean; my mother would unwittingly have done the same. But I wonder how it is that everyday we are in her face—nice girls—and at night we make a purposeful and impassioned love, and still, in her mind, sex has to be with a penis. Ellen misunderstands my sadness—my hormone-induced tears. She complains of my man-hating, my dick-centered resentment (envy). I go to sleep wallowing in my queer sense of isolation/alienation even from my lesbian lover. She's a femme, I think. She doesn't really understand.

Ellen tells me daily how much more feminine I look. I see it, too, my hair longer than it's been in fifteen years, my hips and thighs and breasts rounding from this pregnancy, the softening taking place throughout my body, the tears. I like it and yet in bed feel a strong urge to reassert my butchness, my self as a love-maker.

I tell her, the stakes are higher now. As I feel myself enlarging in openheartedness, in body, I feel closer to her than ever. I tell her the sex has got to meet that heart place. I tell her how frightening that can be for me, that nakedness. "We are so different," she responds. It is a statement of faithfulness, I know. And I have faith too, although I cry. I cry because I know this is another step into a deepening between us, the terrain of which is as unfamiliar as this baby. After four years, how does one continue loving? What does it look like?

I think a lot about writing these days. These journal entries are my meager attempts to grease the tool again, discover the next step en la jornada. *What must be written next! My road is now open, with "Heart of the Earth: A Popol Vuh Story" on tour in upstate New York, and the play collection[9] and* The Last Generation *off to their publishers. I tell Ellen the old feeling returns. Can I ever produce anything again! I feel empty of stories, empty of ideas, words, images, impulses. But the creative juices used to fuel this baby's development make my hunger for writing no less. I shape these letters onto the page as a dance circling circling circling until I arrive at the heartbeat, a pulse, a place from which the writing stirs new life.*

20 JUNIO

I don't know if it is the pregnancy or allergies again that cause me to want so much sleep. I take 2–3-hour naps, stay up till midnight, sleep again till 10 A.M. **Sueño.** *I have a vague sense that last night I dreamed I had given birth prematurely. He is barely seven months and I worry that his lungs are not yet fully developed enough to survive on his own. I love to feel Rafaelito move. At those moments I am not alone. He stirs and I am, for a few moments, filled with concentration, connection, purpose.*

21 JUNIO

Summer solstice found the Cape a heavy hot grey cloud pressing down upon its grey citizens. But there is an unparalleled beauty here. It lies in the waveless sea.

22 JUNIO

"But after you hear the story, you and the others prepare by the new moon to rise up against the slave masters."
    I lose the thread, the purpose of the writing until I am reminded by Leslie Marmon Silko's words—that a story can cause revolt. That is my sole purpose (arrogant as it may seem) to write those kinds of stories, stories to agitate, stories to remind us what has been forgotten. These days I doubt my capacity to do that. I doubt I can even write again. I wonder if that feeling ever goes away in the life of the writer. There in the realm of my doubt, the world becomes unbearably small, as small as my pitiful ego. But when I imagine I can speak with the voice of others—that others can speak through me—how wide and hopeful the project of writing becomes again.

Kaiser Hospital, Hollywood. *I watch the heart monitor obsessively. It is everything to me. Like religion. All that matters is the stress-free beating of my baby's heart, his kicking signs of life, the steady unwavering pattern of the monitor print-out, indicating no contractions. But I am awakened at 2 A.M., a routine check and am told contractions are 7–8 minutes apart and my world shrinks to the parameter of my thirsty womb as I beg my baby to stay put there, hold on, cling to me incubating as long as possible. Twenty-seven weeks is so damn young.*

My water broke the day before I was due to return to San Francisco. After my stay in Cape Cod, I had flown to Los Angeles for a brief visit with my family, knowing I probably wouldn't see them again until after the baby's birth in late September. It was a Monday morning and suddenly feeling overwhelmingly tired, I excuse myself from the breakfast table, my parents both turning their faces up to me and away from their morning eggs. I had to go back to bed, I told them, just for an hour or so. And they agree rest is what I needed. The exhaustion was so sudden, so bottomless and I drag myself off to the small room that was once my brother's bedroom. The phone rings, just as I feel the rush of warm water bathe my thighs. I know it is Ellen, I reach over to the phone lift up the receiver. "My water just broke," I cry. She catches the first flight out of Boston.

The ambulance drive to Hollywood Kaiser is interminable. I try to "read" the route from the shape of streetlights overhead, the curve of freeway interchanges, the palm and sycamore trees overhead lining the backstreets we travel. My mother is in the front seat with the driver, my father will meet us there in his own car. I make idle chit-chat with the central *americano* ambulance assistant but my mouth has dropped somewhere into my womb and I sing only one song: *Hang on,* mijito. *Stay inside me, please stay inside me.*

I am flat on my back as I am rolled on a gurney into the labor room. If the baby doesn't come in twenty-four hours, the doctors tell me, he can stay in my womb for weeks, maybe months, even without the fluid. The object is to keep the baby inside me for as long as possible. I am to remain flat on my back and in the hospital until the baby is born. The next day, Ellen arrives. I didn't realize how I was needing her, how I was holding my breath back, until our eyes meet. Her face is the mirror of tenderness, recognition I have been waiting for. She rushes to me. My parents graciously leave us alone and I cry with everything I've got in me.

After the initial crisis, it appears that Rafael has decided to hold on for a while. I have had no contractions for twenty-four hours, so I am moved into the maternity ward to homestead. At twenty-seven weeks gestation, they tell us that the baby's lungs are not strong enough to breathe on their own. Ellen has already found two books on premature birth. She studies them. She explains the risks to me, editing out the worst potential parts of the scenario. Thirty-two weeks is our goal. At thirty-two weeks gestation, the baby can breathe well on his own, the heart duct which is connected to the lungs has closed and the baby will be small, but quite whole and out of danger.

Thirty-two weeks never come, nor do a full twenty-eight. In the next six days the baby remains inside me, my family visits me with vigilance, Ellen ever-faithfully at my bedside. With every change in my body temperature, every increase or decrease in contractions, I am taken from the maternity ward to delivery and back again, I am visited by neonatalists, and a revolving door of residents, interns, nurses and nurses' aids. But no one seems to be able to clearly answer my questions: *How did this happen?* I had no infection, no trauma to my womb. And, what are my baby's chances for survival and a healthy life?

3 JULIO

11 P.M. Rafael Angel is born 3:05 P.M. Full moon. I am speechless, my child somehow exactly as I had imagined him. This gift, this messenger, this child who could not wait to enter me, to enter this world. I sleep now to dream of him, dreaming down the hall, a 2 pound, 6-ounce milagrito, mi bebé.

The intensive part of the labor was short: four hours. I have the nurses call Ellen that morning of the third, somehow knowing today would be the day. The doctors still have given me no clear sense of what a twenty-eight week birth means for my baby's health. I try to push that worry out of my mind. I think only of a safe delivery.

The night before, Ellen had stayed with me in the labor room until the early hours of the morning. The contractions were strong enough to feel, but not so strong that I couldn't fall asleep. I finally send her home (my parents' home) for some rest. At 7 A.M. I am awake, the contractions are stronger now, still not severe enough to be concerned, I think. I have the nurses call Ellen. A few hours later, Ellen and my sister arrive, independent of one another. That's all I need. Once my sister and lover are here, I know I'm in good hands.

Needless to say, Ellen and I had never gotten to the natural childbirth classes. Those were to be reserved for those lazy August months when I'd have nothing better to do. My sister, however, was a virtual pro at Lamaze, having given birth to four healthy babies with that method. So, minutes after JoAnn arrives, she is grilling me with questions about my symptoms. Where do you feel the pain? How far apart are the contractions? And Ellen is flipping frantically through childbirth books, trying to read about what's going to happen minutes before it's happening. But they make a marvelous delivery team. As the pains increase in intensity, Ellen (per JoAnn's instructions) pushes on my lower back to relieve some of the pain. I have never appreciated Ellen's physical strength as I have that day. No lightweight lover for me. The girl is pure power.

This was my first baby and for a full week of being taken in and out of the labor room, I had heard my neighbor-laborers screaming at the top of their lungs. *"Ay Mamacita!"* "Give me some damn drugs!" "No! No! No!" So, I figure whatever pain I got going, which was the most fierce physical pain I had ever experienced, it had to get worse and I was trying to conserve what energy I had for the long haul. My sister kept assuring me that a big mouth didn't necessarily mean bigger pain. Still, I hung on, politely breathing as JoAnn instructed, pushing out air in long drags, then short rhythmic puffs. All the while, Ellen kept pressing on my back for a moment of blessed relief, then rushed back to her birthing books. In the meantime, JoAnn jotted down in a little note pad how close the contractions were coming. Now the contractions were one on top of the other and virtually unbearable. My sisters suggests I get up on all fours to relieve the pressure on my lower back where the pain is the most severe. The moment I do, I feel the revolution occur inside my womb, the pain taking a somersault inside of me, dropping down into what feels like my bowels. (Thinking back, that one move may have saved me hours of labor.) I fall back onto my back, feel the urge to defecate, tell them so. JoAnn says, "That's the baby." Ellen rushes out to get a doctor. The staff has virtually ignored us for the last three hours since every time they checked, the monitor wasn't reading the contractions as intensely as I was experiencing them. (When in doubt trust machines not pregnant women.)

Now, the doctor wastes no time in coming. Since the time my water broke, seven days earlier, I had not been examined vaginally, for fear of infection. No one, therefore, had checked the dilation of my cervix throughout the labor. Now the young Asian-American resident is opening my legs. I glance at the clock above her head. Three o'clock. Her hand moves up inside me. "I can feel the head," she says. "Get her into the delivery room."

Now I know what that statement means for a premature baby. Within five minutes, the on-call staff at the Intensive Care Nursery—the neonatalist, the respiratory therapist, the ICN nurse—will meet us in delivery. Ellen and JoAnn have disappeared. Next time I see them, they are standing on each side of me, wearing pale pink surgical gowns and masks. The doctor tells me to push. And I do. Grabbing my sister's hand on my left side, my lover on the right, I push with everything I've got. I hear them prompting me on, everybody approving. Good, good, good. I push. That's it, he's coming. Go on. I push. There he is, one more . . . Ellen telling me she can see him . . . Then the doctor's voice is urgent. Stop. Don't push. Hold back. I don't know why. My vagina is pure fire, a horrible burning when everything in me wants to push him all they way out they tell me to stop. But it is the cord, the cord is wrapped around his neck. The doctor remains very calm, cuts Rafaelito free, then I let him spill out of me.

Relief, my body is engulfed in a pleasure . . . an animal pleasure, a pulsing, an aliveness like nothing I've ever known. I am a girl and a woman and an animal and *estoy temblando* like the best of sex, the best of being thoroughly entered and spent. They don't bring the baby to my belly as they do in the movies. I see, out of the corner of my eye, a circle of masked strangers around him. They, too, are dressed in pink. I am afraid to look, afraid to know how my baby looks. Is he well? Is he breathing? A final push and the afterbirth spills out of me. I want to keep the cord, bury it somewhere, somewhere far away from this hospital. How is my baby?

Then Ellen finally ventures over to him. I hear her from the distance (a mere distance of five or so feet) that seems so far away from me, she says, "He has an *indio* nose." And I cry from relief now, I cry and laugh and tremble with the joy of his birthing. It was the best thing to say. I know he is okay, or else she would have said something else. He is okay, alive, whole, born. They rush him out of the delivery room into Intensive Care. I still haven't seen his face.

After a few hours of recovery, Ellen and my sister take me over to the ICN. I must admit, I am afraid to go, afraid to see this being whose face my lover has seen but not I, not yet. But when I do see him, he is a miniature of all I understand of beauty. He is the tiniest creature I have ever seen. His skin hangs off of him *como un viejito* and there is a thin veil of dark hair coating his body. He is the most beautiful little monkey in the world. I am not shocked to see him. He looks just as I had imagined him, but his fragility is almost unfathomable. How do I protect him from so far away?

That night, after Ellen leaves, I consider what has brought me (now us) to this place in time. In a way, the most natural thing in the world was to give birth here in Los Angeles, among my blood *familia*. I knew as I held my lover and my sister's hand in the grip of labor, that this was what I knew as *hogar*, sustenance, that this is how a woman should always give birth, surrounded by women and how lucky I was to be a lesbian, to have it all: mother, sister, lover—that family of women to see me into motherhood. I couldn't help but think, I had willed it in some way, to give birth to Rafael Angel in the City of the Angels.

NOTES

1. For the purposes of this publication, I have excerpted those writings leading up to and culiminating in Rafael Angel's birth.

2. Original journal entries are italicized.

3. A pseudonym.

4. During the time of this writing I was working on an adaptation of *The Popol Vuh*, the Quiche Maya Creation and Heroes' Story. The adaptation entitled "Heart of the Earth" is produced by INTAR Theatre of New York.

5. "Mexican Medea" is a play based on the Greek tragedy and the Mexican myth of La Llorona. I had begun the play two years earlier and returned to it when Berkeley Repertory Theatre commissioned it during this period.

6. *The Last Generation* is a book of poems and essays published by South End Press of Boston in the fall of 1993.

7. The heavy bleeding occurred when polyps that had formed on my cervix fell off.

8. "The Roof's on Fire."

9. *Heroes & Saints and Other Plays*, published by West End Press of Albuquerque in winter 1994.

Lesbian Motherhood and Other Small Acts of Resistance

Linda Mulley

About five years ago, my daughter returned home in tears from her seventh-grade class trip, an event that she had hoped would mark all the accomplishments and hard work of her first year in middle school. Instead, on the way home from that beach trip, Laura had sat trapped in a hot, overcrowded school bus while several of her classmates taunted her about her mother, the Dyke.

Their words were cutting: "Hey, Laura, why don't you invite your mother to eat with mine? I mean, you know, *eat* mine? Come on, Laura, we all know your mother's a dyke." And other comments about fags, queers, dykes, lezzies, and weirdos. As painful moments do, this half hour of teasing seemed interminable to her, and annihilated the entire day of celebration and fun. It also destroyed what last bit of self-esteem she had managed to hoard away and hide from the attention of the cliques who took adolescent pleasure in ignoring and deriding her because she was different.

After that miserable day, and throughout the year that followed, I watched Laura's natural sociability, athletic prowess, taste and talent for music and drama evaporate. She began to display hidden talents for brooding, moodiness, passivity, and blame. She requested that I not be seen with her in town, that I not eat at restaurants with any women friends, that I essentially disappear with her into some asocial space where no one could accuse us of anything because we were no longer visible. Always a quick study, my thirteen-year-old daughter believed she had to annihilate what she loved most in order to survive.

Reflecting on what single event pulled me through the corridor of peaceful isolation into "kitchen table activism," I suppose that experience was it.

Although I had taken stances before, picketing Mafia-run gay bars, marching for Gay Pride, and participating in the aftermath of the Stonewall uprising,[1] nothing compared to the anger and outrage I felt looking into my daughter's innocent eyes that day.

I felt at the same time helpless and powerful, like an animal needing to pounce but restrained by my own fear that nothing I could do would matter—and by Laura's insistence that I do nothing, or worse would befall her. In fact, I did next to nothing, meeting once with the principal and guidance counselor, and worse did befall her. What passed as childhood taunting in seventh grade escalated into open harassment in eighth grade, and despite her school's well-intentioned but fruitless efforts to protect her, Laura eventually chose to leave Vermont and live in California with her other mother—my ex-partner—and her respectable nuclear family.

Laura's experience jolted me into the realization that providing her with solid values in a stable home surrounded by a community of strong women and men friends was not enough. Not only was I unable to protect her from the prejudice and cruelty the world would deal her, but I had contributed, however unintentionally, to the pain she experienced. That made me rethink my position of quiet, personal advocacy, which until that point had consisted of carefully selecting Laura's schools and teachers and voicing my concerns about the exclusive portrayal of traditional families in class readings and discussions.

In the meantime, my four-year-old son, Gabriel, was putting on weight and height like a garment he was entitled to, stretching toward kindergarten and oblivious to the issues and fears generated by his sister. I found myself in a state of intermittent disturbance as he moved through the grades, wondering how and when the teasing would begin, how he would respond to it. I armed him with karate lessons as if he could block and kick any insult that would come his way. Each year, I would take his carefully chosen teacher aside and fill him or her in on our life-style and my concerns. These conversations were variably met with interest, disbelief, compassion and some degree of discomfort. Yet I had done the same with Laura's teachers—many of whom were now teaching Gabriel—and still the kids had targeted her.

By the time Gabriel entered fourth grade, some things had changed for the better. He was one of several children of lesbian parents in a small public school that prided itself on its forward thinking, nurturance and commitment to quality education. Still, I felt caught: I wanted to protect him by taking bolder steps involving the entire school community, but feared that such an action might place him at greater risk of discrimination and rejection.

I was forced to take a hard look at my time-honored strategies of thinking a lot, doing a little, keeping a low profile, hoping for the best, and letting things take their own course. I now knew that course was full of potholes that weren't healthy for Laura, Gabriel or any child. I thought hard and long about the chances of my son's self-esteem surviving the kind of onslaught Laura's went through, and I thought them slim. In a class of twenty-two white, mostly upper-middle-class fourth graders, he was the only child with a single parent, the only child without an identifiable father, and the only child of a lesbian. I no longer felt we could afford the luxury of silence.

Throughout my life, I've faced this dilemma of silent invisibility versus vocal visibility. For a very long time, invisibility served me well; to some extent, it still does. Whether by nature or nurture, I am a mostly shy person who will seek the cover of trees rather than face the exposure of an open field. As a result, it has taken me many years to understand the high price of invisibility—the costs associated with assuming it, maintaining it and finally shedding it.

For me, coming out has been an ongoing process. Now forty-nine, I came out to myself first, probably at eighteen; to the lesbian community, at twenty-four; and to my family at twenty-six. But coming out as a lesbian—as an adult, for myself—was a world removed from coming out as the lesbian mother of my children. It was only when I understood that, to paraphrase Audre Lorde, my silence would not protect them, that I was able to come out as a lesbian mother activist.

Few of us who came of age before Stonewall had the support of others in breaking our silence. Like many other lesbians and gays who grew up during the 1950s and 1960s, I learned to pass as a budding heterosexual. I pretended interest in my boyfriends, developed "understandings" with some, and even maneuvered double dates with the girls I secretly loved. My heightened interest in my girlfriends gave rise to many arguments with my mother. I can well recall her shouting at me from our front door, "Better you should come home pregnant than a homosexual!" (And getting pregnant out of wedlock in 1956 won no model daughter prizes.) In my twelve-year-old body and mind, I understood that my family would never understand me. I was one of the people they outwardly derided and detested, and I knew for my own protection that I had to keep silent under all circumstances.

Silence alone wasn't enough. I had to hide any outward sign—no matter how innocent—of my sexual difference. When I was fifteen, my mother discovered a pack of cigarillos in my night table drawer. I remember buying them after seeing a "Can a gentleman offer a lady a Tiparrillo?" commercial. She presented them as evidence of my perversity to my father, who, waving them in one hand, screamed obscenities to me about sick homosexuals, and with his belt in the other hand, accused me of being one.

I became hysterical, ran to my room and slammed the door. Both parents followed me upstairs, and while my father held me down on the floor, my mother attempted to force tranquilizers down my throat. She was trying to calm me down, but to me, it felt as though I were being choked. From that moment on, I realized that my family could truly hurt me, not only emotionally but physically, by their ignorance and fear about my sexuality.

The lessons I learned at home I applied at school. Hiding my sexual preference from even my closest friends was my tool for belonging. I went nowhere without my cloak, and for many years, lived a very private and troubled inner life while ostensibly popular and well liked by my classmates. I developed a deep sense of shame about my feelings toward women, and eventually, the shame turned to self-hatred and thoughts of suicide. Even when I finally became lovers with a woman in college, we didn't identify ourselves as lesbians—at least, not right away. Our relationship was serendipitous, a chance meeting of souls that had more to do with our attraction as "people," not women.

I never actually came out to my family. My mother outed me by discovering a love letter in an old jacket when I was twenty-six. Her reaction and that of my father was precisely what I feared as an adolescent. They threw me out of the house and told me not to return until I was cured. In retrospect, their rejection was a blessing. It moved me by necessity out into the world, and more importantly, removed the constraints of conditioning that kept me from coming out to myself and others.

By the late 1960s, I had moved to New York, discovered the lesbian bar scene and a new identity as a lesbian. Within a year, I was picketing the same Mafia-controlled gay bar that I frequented, the only social haven I had ever known, urging women to follow me to a loft dance sponsored by the new Gay Liberation Front. These alternative dances were the emerging gay movement's answer to increasingly oppressive conditions in gay bars throughout the city. In this particular bar, we were forced to pay to check our coats (even if we weren't wearing one), to buy alcohol at inflated prices and regular intervals (even if we didn't drink), and to provide entertainment for the owner's leering friends. Raids were common, but if the owner had paid off the police, we would be warned so we could leave before they arrived.

In that short walk from 6th Avenue to the Gay Liberation Front dance in the Village, I could actually feel myself taking form, becoming visible. That sense of visibility and presence grew with every action, pride march, and meeting until I knew with absolute assurance that I was a lesbian who belonged to a community of other lesbians and gays, and that, at least within some circles, I no longer had to hide.

I also no longer wanted the city. Saying good-bye to New York, which had been my safety for six years, was not difficult. My consciousness had been stretched to its limits, and, having been raised a country girl, I longed for days without fear and nights without sirens and screams. When I first traveled to

Vermont in 1970, I knew immediately that I wanted to live there, for I loved the beauty of the land. I found work as an educator of children with disabilities, and met a woman who would be my lover for many years. And for the first time, I felt an ache to have a child in my life.

"Motherhood marks the precise moment when you lose your freedom," the sister of a famous feminist stated casually in an avant-garde movie I saw at least twenty years ago. Her statement gave me pause, because I was seriously contemplating motherhood—a new idea to one raised when the term lesbian mother was an oxymoron.

Up to this point in my life, I had no image, no thought form, certainly no role models for a woman who could be a lesbian and a mother simultaneously. Even though I was intellectually aware that all women could have children, I never imagined that I or any other lesbian would or even could have children. If lesbians were fortunate, we would find and have each other. Children lived in the Land of Married Couples. In the city, I had met children of lesbians, but they were products of failed marriages, not of advanced technology—which, in those days, was reserved solely for lactating farm animals. Lesbians and single mothers were generally not permitted to adopt children through mainstream agencies in the 1960s and 1970s. And though I'd heard rumors of lesbians and gay men who married for the purpose of having children, that option held little appeal for me.

As I grappled for a way to satisfy my need for a child, I could imagine only one option: to find a woman, preferably a lesbian, with a baby or young child in need of adoption. Looking back now, twenty years later, that wish seems astonishingly starry-eyed. How could I have imagined that, among the few lesbians then living in Vermont, a lesbian mother would materialize who wanted to place her two-year-old daughter in a woman-identified home? But, against all odds, just such a mother existed—and just as remarkably, through a network of friends, she found us. We quickly made arrangements for a private adoption.

But there was a catch. All legal adoptions required the approval of state welfare agencies. And, back in 1978, no "out" lesbian had ever succeeded in adopting a child in Vermont. My lover, Barbara, and I decided that I would apply as a single woman to circumvent the issue of sexual orientation. Our attorney assured us that the interview with the state investigator would be routine, a blip on the screen, a shoe-in for a prospective parent with my credentials. But that prediction soured with the first get-acquainted question posed by the investigator: "Are you," she asked, "a lesbian?"

Staring at her across the kitchen table, I knew my answer would determine our destiny as parents. In the seconds that pounded between her question and my response, I had to formulate an answer that would be either a lie or an indictment. Somehow, the words that came out were neither. I gulped. "Some people think so," I heard myself say. The investigator sighed with relief, telling me in a confidential tone that Laura's mother was a lesbian and thought I was one also. She counseled me not to tell the mother anything different, because otherwise she might block the adoption. That was the end of it: I became Laura's legal parent six months later with her mother's blessing, the state's sanction, and my integrity shaken but (more or less) intact.

A year after the adoption went through, however, Barbara and I separated, and though I hadn't intended it, I ended up raising Laura largely by myself. In the years that followed, I became involved with a married woman and her husband, a relationship that lasted four years.

I had never given pregnancy serious thought, but Gabriel came to me in a dream. I was stationed atop a mountain with a small group of people whose task was to count the souls leaving the earth. I was assigned to the tower room with another woman. As we counted those who left, I noticed a small sphere of grey-blue light forming in the sky. Its brilliance grew as it hurtled toward the tower. In seconds, it metamorphized into human form, and latched onto my chest where it clung tenaciously. Unable to extricate myself from this "thing," I screamed for help. No one could remove it. Someone suggested I yell, "I'm not your mother!" which I did repeatedly, with no results. I awoke gasping and shaking. Not long after, I found out I was pregnant, and gave birth to Gabriel in 1984.

There have been a few times in my life that have required a complete paradigm shift. Becoming pregnant and giving birth were two such life passages. As difficult as it was for me to accept my fertility—and my baby—it was even more difficult for many of my lesbian friends, who viewed me as a traitor and assumed I would abort. Some even offered to pay for the procedure. I found far more support among my straight friends, particularly those who were mothers, and leaned on them through my pregnancy and Gabriel's birth. I knew of no other mothers who, as lesbians, had decided to become pregnant. And I knew of only a few who had become lesbians while their children were growing or grown. In Vermont, anyway, we were still an exotic species.

And we were certainly no less exotic in Peabody, Massachusetts, my hometown. But the experience of giving birth transformed my relationship to my family. Originally shocked by and opposed to my pregnancy, my parents softened once Gabriel was born. Of their six grandchildren, he is the only grandson. (It's amusing to me, and to them, that of their three daughters, the queer one produced the boy they had always wanted.) The passage of time, and my becoming a mother, gradually prodded my parents into a stance of resigned acceptance and then unconditional love. They may not agree with what they view as my choice of life-style, but they are no longer waiting expectantly or insistently for me to change.

Becoming a mother also radicalized *me*. It has made me feel not only for my own children, but for all children and mothers everywhere. Becoming and being a mother universalized the experience of becoming and being a mother. And yet, in the real world, there are differences between being a mother and being a lesbian mother. One of the differences is obvious: how we conceive and reproduce. Another difference, perhaps not so obvious, is the need for the lesbian mother to educate her children about the hate that exists in the world, and how that hate can affect them.

That difference is shared by mothers of other minority groups. What is unique about the lesbian mother's situation is the awareness that she, unlike a black or Asian or Latina mother, can hide out in her body and life-style for the sake of her children, and pass for a heterosexual or asexual single mother. That is a choice for every lesbian mother who is not partnered.

But as with every choice, it also contains a sacrifice: in this case, her identity as a woman and her integrity as a mother. In lying to her community, she also lies to her children and passes on to them a message of shame and victimization. However, if she claims her sexual identity, she invites the intolerances and prejudices of her community into her child's life, and makes her children vulnerable.

For it is still open season on lesbians and gays on playgrounds across America. In many communities, and certainly in mine, children have learned not to use racist or ethnic slurs. But the game, "smear the queer," and references to fags, dykes, queers and fairies are commonplace. In elementary school, these words may not have the full sexual meaning they develop later; bullies simply use them to taunt and control other children. But kids learn quickly what is and is not tolerable. And children of lesbian and gay parents are as vulnerable as children who are questioning their own sexual identity. At the elementary and middle-school levels, they often suffer rejection and taunting from their classmates—or silence themselves as protection from harassment.

As children grow older, words like "faggot" and "queer" take on more specific and more personal meanings—and become more lethal. In high school, gay and lesbian youths are three times more likely than heterosexual students to attempt suicide. And they are at greater risk for school failure and substance abuse.

Sadly, few gay teachers offer themselves as positive role models. I know of no public school educator in Vermont who feels safe enough to be "out" in his or her school district. At a recent Vermont chapter meeting of the National Education Association, I sat with 14 public school teachers, none of whom felt safe enough, despite Vermont's gay rights law, to discuss their gay life-style publicly or to offer support to students struggling with gay and lesbian issues in their schools.

Yet many of these teachers, with the support of heterosexual allies, are working behind the scenes to establish safe discussion and hang-out spaces for gay, lesbian and bisexual students. This small but powerful message of acceptance from their schools can make an enormous difference to kids who feel left out of the social scene, or worse, harassed by those who are in it. The bad news is that lesbian and gay teachers remain closeted and invisible, projecting a silent message of shame and fear that cannot be missed by the students who most need them.

Into the breach has jumped, to my own amazement, the Amazon Lesbian Mother. It's been said that mothers don't make children; children make mothers. In my case, my children have turned someone who simply wanted to be an ordinary get-your-backpack-and-don't-forget-your-lunch mother into an amazon warrior mother. I stumbled on that identity during the 1993 Gay and Lesbian March in Washington. A good friend suggested over the phone prior to the march that several of us meet for dinner at a well-known café on Amazon Mother's Street. I never questioned her, but quietly thought, "Wow! They've even changed the names of the streets in Washington, D.C., for this march." When we finally did find the café but no street of that name, I asked another friend where Amazon Mother's Street was. She laughed, and said, "I think she said '*M as in* mother Street!'"

However unconsciously conceived, the image of Amazon Mothers appeals mightily to me: a band of plain old moms with flour on our jeans and a schedule book in our hands, showing up at staff meetings, organizing workshops, sitting on panels, telling our stories and the stories of our families. To our children, we're just moms, acting funny again. But we simply won't quit until the schools are safe for our kids, for all kids.

I consider my choice of work, helping children with disabilities learn to communicate, no accident. In rural states like Vermont, where there is little ethnic or racial diversity, our tolerance issues arise around class, ability and sexual difference. Although people with disabilities do not have a choice about remaining invisible, they usually lack mirrors or reflections in their families much as gays and lesbians do. They often grow up with a sense of isolation and nonbelonging. In the field of disabilities, we bring children and adults home from institutions to live in their local communities.

In Vermont, this movement is called Homecoming. The children, even those with the most severe disabilities, are being educated in public schools, and part of my work is to help integrate them into regular classrooms and into their communities. This isn't always easy to accomplish because many people have fears about people who don't speak, who look and act differently from them.

A few months ago, another lesbian parent and I took a shaky first step toward a Homecoming of another sort: With the help of Outright, an organization that provides support to gay and lesbian youth, we conducted a training workshop for teachers and administrators on issues facing gay and lesbian students, and the children of gay and lesbian parents. We decided to begin at the elementary school where both of us have children enrolled.

Now, elementary school may strike some people as a bit too early to start talking about sexual difference. But it is our belief that lack of awareness and information in the early grades lays the groundwork for harassment in the later grades. Children are taught about racial and ethnic differences from the earliest grades, and attitudes of tolerance and respect for this kind of diversity are cultivated. However, homosexuality isn't discussed until sixth grade—and then, for only twenty minutes in health class. And the health instructors confess that they're unsure what to say about it.

In fact, teachers and administrators at my son's school said they really needed some help from us in figuring out how to talk with children about gay and lesbian issues and respond to their questions about it. To our amazement, the school, nestled in a beautiful river valley near the New Hampshire border, became the first elementary school in the state to require full attendance of its staff in training of this kind. That was brave, for Senator Jesse Helms (R-N.C.) had just introduced an odious amendment that would place any school's federal funding in jeopardy for allowing open discussions like this on school grounds.

After months of preparation, the day of the workshop finally arrived. I could feel the air in the room: a mixture of tension, exhaustion and relief. We didn't know what to expect or what the response would be. Some faces reflected discomfort; others, anticipation and curiosity; still others, disinterest and boredom.

But the faces in the audience were as familiar as many in my own family. Teachers, some of whom I've known for fifteen years, were struggling with new information about homophobia and its effects on students and families. They'd just viewed a video documentary about gay and lesbian teen suicide, and there were few dry eyes looking back at me as I took my place on the panel.

I began to read a letter that Laura, now eighteen, wrote to her middle school principal last year. I found myself crying, overwhelmed by the feelings that came up during the video and by the sense of community and support I felt in that room. Eventually, I composed myself and read Laura's words:

When I attended the middle school a few years back, I experienced harassment on an hourly basis. I thought there was something wrong with me because I was a girl and because my family was gay. I didn't like myself . . . I was always paranoid and I would cry and fight with my mom . . . It wasn't until I moved away from here to a more urban and diverse area that I realized it wasn't me or my family that had a problem. It was the people I had to go to school with. The image that Hanover projects is one of a semi-rural, heterosexual, upper-middle-class WASP community. And what I learned in school was that if you, or anyone you knew, didn't fit into that image, you were teased and harassed for it.

I glanced at Laura's third- and fourth-grade teachers. They were half-smiling, proud of her for speaking out so strongly. Laura's seventh-grade guidance counselor caught up with me at the door, and explained that he didn't know what else he could have done about the relentless harassment she had faced in school. I urged him: "Just start like this. Bring this training to your school."

The workshop has already started to make waves in our small community. In its aftermath, a group of gay and lesbian educators in our Vermont river valley recently formed G/LEARN: The Gay/Lesbian Education and Resource Network. The goal of our group is to train teachers, establish rap sessions for young people who want to talk about gay and lesbian issues, and support the children of gay and lesbian parents. We hope to provide a resource for schools and communities in central Vermont in the form of information, training, videos and workshops.

Most kids seem to be ready—even though their parents may not be. A recent concert by a gay male singing group at a local elementary school prompted howls of protest by some parents. But one particularly articulate fifth grader, who wrote a letter to the editor of the local paper, said that children are ready to talk honestly about these issues:

I have . . . heard that parents are complaining that their kids have suddenly started using the words "faggot" and "queer" to put down other people, but those are the very same words the students at [my school] have been using all the six years I've been here . . . It seems that people are making a big deal about a little thing. A gay a capella group came to the school. So what? It's time children know gay people exist in society, even if it isn't a very welcome society, and I think the reason for this senseless discrimination is fear.[2]

One irate reader sent an anonymous piece of hate mail to the boy's father, saying that the letter was clearly written not by his son but by his wife—"a known radical"—whom he should "mussel" (muzzle) in the future.

So we still have a long way to go. For lesbians and gays—and their children—the journey outward continues to be a lonely one, with all the attendant fears and worries that years of social battering and negative conditioning bring. But we hope to make a positive statement to gay and lesbian students, and to children of same-sex parents, that they do indeed belong to a community rich with its own history, tradition, courage and talent.

Most important, we will work to sheathe the double-edged knife that keeps gay and lesbian parents from taking action on behalf of their children: the dilemma of wanting to protect their children by taking bolder steps involving the entire school community, but fearing that such an action might place them at greater risk for discrimination and rejection than they already face through silence.

And in the process of fighting for our children, we have witnessed the birth of something quite special: the Amazon Lesbian Mother. She is a social construct in the making, and she is remaking me and many other lesbian mothers in this country.

NOTES

1. The modern gay rights movement is generally considered to have begun in June 1969, when a group of gay men and lesbians at the Mafia-run Stonewall Bar in New York's Greenwich Village decided to resist a routine police raid, beatings, and roundup. A three-day riot followed. Out of that emerged the first "Gay Liberation" organizations.

2. Jack Nelson, letter to the editor, *Valley News*, West Lebanon, N.H., February 22, 1995.

Commercializing Motherhood

Rita Arditti

We fear a future that combines Margaret Atwood's *A Handmaid's Tale*, in which lower-class women are employed as breeders for a more privileged class, and Aldous Huxley's *Brave New World* of manufactured made-to-order people.
—The National Action Committee on the Status of Women (Canada), October 1990

In the last fifteen years the power to control and intervene in the human reproductive process has enormously increased. New technologies have been developed that allow all kinds of recombinations to occur with eggs, embryos and sperm. In vitro fertilization (IVF), contract pregnancy (so-called surrogacy), freezing of embryos, screening of genetic characteristics and many other related procedures have become common, everyday occurrences.[1]

The central metaphor that dominates the technological approach to reproduction is that of "separation." Although we have had sexuality without procreation in practically all cultures from the beginning of time, we can now have reproduction without intercourse. The unity and wholeness of the reproductive process have been divided into a number of discrete steps, each one amendable to intervention and manipulation, each one subject to eugenic principles of selection and elimination. The technologies separate not only procreation from sexuality, but more significantly they separate motherhood into different components that used to be part of a whole process. We are now at the point where biological motherhood is in question and in need of explicit definition, just like fatherhood used to be.[2]

The high degree of social acceptance that the reproductive technologies encounter is, in great part, linked to the positive images presented by the media, by an ever-growing infertility industry and by scientists working in the field. This image promotes the new reproductive technologies by portraying them as benefitting infertile women by increasing the number of procedures they may now choose from, in their quest for biological motherhood.[3]

What is not immediately clear is that the "infertile women" they are speaking about are mostly white, middle- or upper-class, able-bodied, heterosexual women who can pay for expensive interventions or who have the health insurance coverage that will allow them to try these procedures. These are the "infertile women" our society is concerned about. This is ironic, since black women, for instance, have an infertility rate one and one-half times higher than that of white women, and childlessness, for sociocultural reasons, can be a particularly devastating experience to a poor woman or a woman of color.[4]

A veritable infertility industry has arisen to promote and market the new reproductive technologies: IVF clinics; sperm banks; surrogacy companies; drug companies; and scientific instrumentation companies specializing in the instruments used in the procedures.[5] This industry determines the definition of "appropriate" research based on what will be most profitable to sell. Medical entrepreneurs have become more and more interested as insurance companies, often pressured by consumer groups, start to pick up the costs. And, as happens in other areas of the health care establishment, the industry is not interested in the prevention of infertility, but rather in finding a "technological fix" to deal with it.

IN VITRO FERTILIZATION

IVF is a sophisticated technological procedure where women's bodies are subjected to intensive testing and highly interventionist manipulations: hormonal treatments to produce several eggs (superovulation), ultrasound monitoring, egg retrieval through surgery under general anesthesia or through a ultrasound guided needle that will puncture the ovaries (requiring local anesthesia), and implantation of embryos with more hormonal treatments. If pregnancy ensues, amniocentesis and Caesarian section are most often part of the picture.

Each step of the IVF process presents risks for the physical and mental health of women.[6] At least five women have died while going through IVF procedures,[7] and there is increasing evidence that the hormonal treatments used to produce superovulation may augment the risk of ovarian cancer.[8]

IVF came to public attention in 1978 when the first "test-tube baby," Louise Brown, was born in England. Since then, the use of the technology has grown exponentially: there are currently over 270 centers in the United States performing IVF and other related procedures, like gamete intra-fallopian transfer (GIFT) and zygote intra-fallopian transfer (ZIFT).[9] It is estimated that in the next few years the IVF industry will be a $6 million annual business. "Infertility is a huge market," asserts James Twerdahl, marketing director of Fertility & Genetics Research Company. And with about three to four million American couples having difficulty having a baby, the infertility business will *probably* continue to grow.[10]

In vitro fertilization was originally developed to help women with blocked oviducts, a condition that prevents the meeting of the sperm with the egg. It is now being used with couples where the woman is perfectly fertile and it is the male partner that has a fertility problem. The original focus on infertile women has shifted to the current one on "infertile couples" (heterosexual couples), which makes possible a redefinition of IVF as a therapy for male infertility and legitimizes the exclusion of lesbian and single women from the application of this technology. The problems of childless single, lesbian and heterosexual women in "nontraditional" family situations are not even considered by current clinic practices. Reflecting a very conventional view of families, the literature of the clinics is directed solely toward "infertile couples."[11]

It is also used for couples where the infertility is of unknown origin and it may indeed become, in the future, a preferred mode of reproduction, not just for the infertile. Carl Wood, one of the researchers in Australia who has pioneered IVF, claims that conception by reproductive technology is superior to natural conception because of "quality control" issues: "Natural conception compares less favorably than artificial conception as it includes unwanted children, parents incapable of parenting, poverty-stricken parents, and women with medical diseases or habits likely to adversely affect the child."[12]

The reporting of success rates by the IVF clinics is one of the few areas where the infertility industry has been challenged by the media and by consumers. The claims that the clinics have made about their results have been highly inflated.[13] Dr. J. Benjamin Younger, president of the American Fertility Society, admitted, "Figures were given out that were technically correct, but figures can lie" if taken out of context. "It was exploitation," he said, referring to the way that some clinics presented their statistics.[14] And Dr. Geoffrey Sher, of the Northern Nevada Family Fertility Clinic in Reno, Nevada, one of the largest independent clinics, candidly stated: "The whole thing in IVF is numbers. You need to be above a certain threshold to make a lot of money."[15] Finally, in 1992, a U.S. congressional subcommittee chaired by Representative Ron Wyden introduced legislation to protect the public and to establish accountability in the infertility treatment business.[16]

Because of the low success rate of the procedure, many women go through it not just once, but a number of times, increasing even more their health risks and ending, not uncommonly, with a bill of $30,000 to $40,000 (at $3,000 to

$10,000 per attempt) and no baby. The message is that if a woman does not get pregnant it is because she is not doing enough, as a sign in an in vitro clinic claims: "You never fail until you stop trying."[17]

International drug companies like Oregon and Serono Laboratories that produce the drugs used in the IVF procedure have been active in promoting IVF. These two companies were the prime sponsors of the 1986 conference of the European Society of Human Reproduction and Embryology in Brussels, which attracted participants from all over the world and where more than fifty companies exhibit their products. Annette Burfoot reports that "Organon offered free videotapes on how to perform IVF to the medical practitioner participants."[18]

Contributing to the commercialization of IVF is the marketing of the techniques from Monash University in Melbourne, Australia, one of the centers where IVF has been developed. IVF Australia, the company that handled the transaction, has changed its name to IVF-America and is currently the largest for-profit IVF corporation in the United States. At its six branches it offers free seminars on infertility and reproductive technology, opportunities to hear from couples that have gone through the procedures and information about "New Financial Options" (from a full page ad in the New York Times, November 9, 1992). The founder of the company, Vicky Baldwin, knows that promotion pays as she states, "We invest heavily in public relations."[19]

Interestingly enough, and in spite of all the hype regarding IVF, a 1990 Report from the World Health Organization stated that "IVF and related technologies have not been adequately evaluated. Published results of randomized clinical trials to determine the true effectiveness of IVF are not yet available. Moreover, there has not been adequate research on the short-term and long-term risks associated with IVF and other medical treatments." The report stresses that IVF and related technologies have created many public health, legal and ethical problems, and that there is need for research on the preventable causes of infertility, including "the role of environmental factors, workplace hazards, contraceptives, iatrogenic causes, sexually transmitted diseases and emotional factors."[20]

CONTRACT PREGNANCY

Contract pregnancy (also called "surrogate" motherhood) is, unquestionably, one of the leading bioethical issues confronting our society. "Surrogate" motherhood is a misnomer, clearly reflecting the male perspective on the issue. There is nothing "surrogate" about the woman who carries new life in her body, nourishes it with her own blood and gives birth to a baby.[21]

The "surrogacy" industry provides men with the opportunity to have babies who carry their own genes. This is not a minor detail, as anybody who reads *The Surrogate Mother* by Noel P. Keane and Dennis L. Breo will find out. They are quite open about it: "There is a simple reason why people prefer finding a surrogate mother to adopting: the child will bear the genetic imprint of the man."[22]

For-profit "surrogate" companies advertise using the language of the market: "Its first product is due for delivery today. Twelve others are on the way and an additional twenty have been ordered. The company is 'Surrogate Mothering Ltd.' and the 'product' is babies."[23]

Mary Beth Whitehead, whose case finally put the issue of contract pregnancy in the public eye, was called a "surrogate" in the contract drafted between the Whiteheads and William Stern, the sperm donor, who was called the "natural father." As detailed in the contract, she had to agree not to smoke, drink or use any drugs during pregnancy, to obey all medical instructions of the physicians involved in the case, to undergo amniocentesis and ultrasound, although she was not in the age bracket where this is usually recommended, and to agree to an abortion if the baby was in a some way not "perfect." Moreover, if the baby was born dead or she had a miscarriage, she would be paid $1000 instead of the $10,000 regular fee.

In other words, the contract transferred the control of her body to W. Stern, reinforcing the western patriarchal view that the woman is the passive incubator of the man's sperm, merely a container for the development of his progeny. "Surrogacy" contracts create, from the beginning, a family arrangement in which motherhood is split (one is the biological mother, the other the social) while the father is one, both genetic and social.[24]

Though the "Baby M" case was the only one widely covered by the media, many other "surrogate mothers" have also tried to reclaim their children.[25] A case in point was that of Alejandra Muñoz, a twenty-year-old Mexican woman brought illegally to the United States to be inseminated by her cousin's husband. She had a second-grade education, did not speak English and could not read handwritten writing. She was asked by a member of her family to "help" her infertile cousin by agreeing to an "ovum" transfer. After the insemination and one month into the pregnancy, Alejandra Muñoz was told that the embryo transfer could not be done and that she would have to carry the pregnancy to term. At that point, she signed an agreement by which she would have received $1500 to continue the pregnancy. After she signed the agreement, the phrase "I will give up my rights to the baby" was added to it by the infertile couple. In this case, the judge decided that the two sides should share joint custody and that Alejandra Muñoz could see her child four times a week.

This case clearly raised the issue of the exploitation of poor and immigrant women, through the use of their bodies, to an unprecedented degree.[26] In practice, commercial "surrogacy" can thrive because of class differences and the exploitation of poor women. Contracts are drawn mainly between upper-middle-class couples and working-class or lower-middle-class women. As Ellen Goodman pointedly writes, "The whole sorry business of surrogate motherhood is riddled with economic bias. It's rife with messages about buying and selling children, about who can 'afford' to have them."[27]

A recent case highlights some of the perils of commercial surrogacy. In January 1995, James Alan Austin, a twenty-six-year-old bank analyst from Pennsylvania, was charged with beating to death his five-week-old son born to a surrogate mother. Police said Austin told them he had beaten the baby with his fists and with a plastic coat hanger. Austin, who is single, had paid $30,000 to the Infertility Center of America for arranging the contract. While most centers screen the surrogate mothers, only a few do a psychological screening of those who will get the baby. Pennsylvania has no legislation dealing with surrogacy.[28]

More recently, a new twist has been added to the already problematic "surrogate" contracts. Up until now, women used as "surrogates" always furnished the ovum for the creation of the embryo. Now, IVF technology and "surrogacy" companies have joined forces and created what is known as "total surrogacy." Because IVF allows for an egg fertilized in the lab to be implanted in the womb of a woman different from the one who donated the egg, it is now possible for a child to be born from a woman and to be genetically unrelated to her or his birthmother. And so, now we have a new term, "gestational surrogacy," for a new phenomenon: a woman who carries the embryo of a couple with whom she has no genetic connection.

How absurd can it get? In 1990, a judge in California denied parental rights to Anna L. Johnson, a black woman who had been hired as a "gestational surrogate" by a couple (an Asian-American woman and a white man). The judge declared that Anna L. Johnson was a "genetic stranger" to the baby she had given birth to and was nursing. Anna L. Johnson argued, to no avail, that although the child did not grow from one of her eggs, she had bonded with him during pregnancy, and because she had given birth to the child, she was entitled to be recognized as a parent. The case was appealed and the California Supreme Court recently upheld the lower court's decision. Johnson's lawyer has vowed to appeal to the U.S. Supreme Court.[29]

The decision of the judge is an attempt to establish the primacy of genetics in the definition of motherhood. This should not come as a surprise. The mainstream scientific establishment, the media and the biotechnology industry steadily put forward their belief in the supremacy of genetics. Stressing the role of genetics in reproduction, they reinforce a mechanistic and distant view of the procreative process, a view that obliterates the intimate, nurturing relationship that develops when a child grows inside a woman's body. The supremacy of the genetic egg donor parallels the supremacy of the sperm. Men cannot give birth, but they can donate sperm, and so their experience of reproduction is either as donor or as social fathers. Motherhood now equals fatherhood.

The old and, until now, unchallenged definition of motherhood has become questionable. As "gestational surrogacy" increases, at the cost of $40,000 for the procedure, and couples who donated their sperm and eggs are allowed to put their names on birth certificates as real parents, we will see other cases like the Anna Johnson's case. "Gestational surrogacy" is good business, since it expands the clientele to women with ovaries and no uterus, and it is especially attractive to the industry because women who are not genetically connected to the child will, supposedly, feel less of a temptation to challenge the "surrogacy" contract. Couples may feel that the child is more "truly theirs" if the child carries their genetic makeup, and, as shown in the Johnson case, eventual claims for custody from the "surrogate" are less likely to succeed.

Furthermore, and of great importance to the industry, it increases the pool of possible "surrogates," because genetic considerations lose importance, since the woman will now be used exclusively as the "environment" for the growth of the fetus. This means that women of races and ethnic groups that were previously left out of the potential pool of candidates will now become included. Given the dire economic circumstances of women in Third World countries and of most women of color in this country, "gestational surrogacy" becomes another tool to the exploitation of poor women's procreative power.[30]

Some businessmen, like John Stehura from the Bionetics Foundation, speculate that one-tenth the current fee could be paid to such women, as in the Alejandra Munoz case. When he was asked what countries he had in mind, Stehura replied, "Central America would be fine." A woman from the Third World who fulfilled this function could even have a serious health problem; he added, "However if her diet is good and other aspects of her life are OK, she should become a viable mother for a genuine embryo transfer."[31]

So, it may seem that genetics is where it's at. The rest of biology and the full range of human experience disappear in the shadow of DNA. But not really; it is not as simple as it seems. It turns out, interestingly, that the infertility industry plays it both ways. There is now a new market, postmenopausal women who want to become mothers. It seems that what makes pregnancy impossible in older women is the fact that their eggs are "deteriorating," and that they have "poor quality" eggs (these are the terms used by the industry). Using egg donors circumvents this problem and older women can now become pregnant.[32] So, will these women also be considered "genetic strangers" as Anna L. Johnson? And if the egg donors decide to ask for custody, will the courts award them custody? Not likely. It seems that the primacy of genetics disappears by simply paying the egg donors $1,500.[33] Infertility clinics advertise to attract egg donors. Ads appear in women's journals looking for "Anonymous Egg Donors."[34] The infertility industry compares egg donation with sperm donation, even though sperm donation involves only masturbation and ejaculation of seminal fluid and egg donation involves hormonal treatments to stimulate the ovaries to produce several eggs, daily ultrasound monitoring of the ovaries, an operation under general anesthesia to remove the eggs, or ultrasound-guided retrieval of eggs through the vagina using local anesthesia.

The brave new world of egg donation is moving rapidly ahead, while the moral, ethical and legal questions that this procedure raises remain unanswered.[35] Particularly worrisome are the cases being reported to women being pressured by their families to donate eggs to an infertile family member. The ethics of consent and the politics of coercion around contract motherhood and egg donation are barely beginning to be explored.[36] Raymond's work on "altruism" and the conditioning that has rendered women's altruism practically obligatory throws light on the complex and suble range of factors that affect women's "choices." Raymond discusses noncommercial "surrogacy" but, as she points out, altruism has also been used to rationalize commercial "surrogacy" and egg donation.[37]

We cannot overestimate the interests of the infertility industry in shaping the direction in which the reproductive technologies are going. The clinics are now adding "pre-implantation diagnosis" services to their menu of options: they plan to use recent advances in genetic technology to identify embryos that contain genetic abnormalities and to implant only those with desired genetic characteristics. Commercial "surrogate" matching services use advertising or direct mail solicitation to find potential "surrogates." One service has run advertisements in a student newspaper whose readership is largely between the ages of sixteen and twenty-three.[38] The Infertility Center of America, the latest creation of Noel Keane, the primary "surrogate" broker in the United States, advertises for an international clientele, in English and Japanese, in the Northwest Airlines *World Traveler Magazine* in popular magazines, such as *People*, in the United States.[39]

What all this boils down to is that people who have the money to pay—for "surrogacy" agency fees, for IVF, and for other related procedures—will be the ones who get the babies, the ones who get recognized as "mothers." For the postmemopausal and older women who have children with donated eggs, the genetic contribution is now downgraded. For the couples who go through IVF using their genetic material and having the embryo implanted in another woman, the genetic connection is deemed paramount. It truly all depends on who can pay the fees of the clinics that provide these services.

FEMINIST RESISTANCE TO THE TECHNOLOGIES

At the 1989 international conference on Reproductive Engineering and Women's Reproductive Health held in Bangladesh, participants noted that while women in the west are being offered pronatalist reproductive technologies, women in the Third World are offered hormonal contraception and sterilization to curtail their fertility.[40] Both practices reflect the attempt to control women's fertility and to use women as experimental subjects. The declaration from the conference called attention to the ideology of eugenics that permeates much of reproductive engineering and expressed opposition to the medicalization and commercialization of the desire of women for motherhood.[41]

More recently, an Australian National Conference held in Melbourne in 1991, with approximately two hundred participants from a wide range of backgrounds, reached consensus in stating that surrogacy, in whatever form, should not be permitted, because it is contrary to public policy as: (1) It treats children as commodities; (2) It uses women's bodies as a means to an end; (3) It exploits women; and (4) It is destructive to the family of the woman who acts as a surrogate. The statement also supports legislation that discourages "surrogacy" arrangements whether commercial or noncommercial and that prohibits certain practices involved in "surrogacy" arrangements.[42]

The most encouraging sign of opposition to the commercialization of motherhood has come from Canada, where the National Action Committee on the Status of Women (NAC), the largest feminist organization, representing over five hundred member groups, released their report, "The New Reproductive Technologies: A Technological Handmaid's Tale," in October 1990. The report states that the "NAC believes that these technologies represent the wrong direction in society's attempt to solve the problems of infertility. We believe, that, on balance, the new reproductive technologies are oppressive to women. They are not effective in preventing or curing infertility or disability but will contribute to economic and social trends that erode women's overall rights, well-being and social standing. We fear a future that combines Margaret Atwood's *A Handmaid's Tale*, in which lower-class women are employed as breeders for a more privileged class, and Aldous Huxley's *Brave New World* of manufactured made-to-order people."[43]

Regarding the definition of biological motherhood, the moment clearly has come to take a strong stand: the woman in whose body a child is gestated and from whom it is born makes a greater biological contribution to the child than the genetic donor. The risks that she takes, her physical involvement and the process of childbirth should be the parameters on which the definition of biological motherhood is based. As Barbara Katz Rothman cogently puts it: "Every child has one identifiable parent at the moment of birth: the person from whose body it emerged."[44] As for "surrogacy," we should be following the examples of other countries (Germany, Australia) that have enacted vigorous anti-surrogacy legislation.[45]

The commercialization and medicalization of pregnancy are striving to eliminate women as full beings in the procreative process. The dynamics of for-profit business have entered directly into one of the few realms of our lives that had, up to now, resisted that intrusion. The rules of the capitalist market, when applied to women's bodies and reproductive power, institutionalize women as breeders and devalue motherhood. "Surrogacy" turns children into commodities—objects that can be bought, sold and returned if defective. The commercialization of women's procreative power promotes the exploitation of women, especially low-income women, and constitutes an attack on the dignity of all human beings. It should not be allowed to continue.

NOTES

1. Rita Arditti, Renate Duelli Klein and Shelley Minden, ed., *Test-Tube Woman: What Future For Motherhood?* (London: Pandora Press, 1984); Gena Corea, *The Mother Machine: From Artificial Insemination to Artificial Wombs* (New York: Harper & Row, 1985); Patricia Spallone and Deborah Lynn Steinberg, ed., *Made to Order: The Myth of Reproductive and Genetic Progress* (New York: Pergamom Press, 1987); Patricia Spallone, *Beyond Conception: The New Politics Of Reproduction* (Granby, Mass.: Bergin & Garvey, 1989); Robyn Rowland *Living Laboratories: Women and Reproductive Technologies* (Bloomington and Indianapolis: Indiana University Press, 1992).

2. Barbara Katz Rothman, *Recreating Motherhood: Ideology and Technology in a Patriarchal Society* (New York: Norton, 1989); Maria Mies, "From the Individual to the Dividual: In the Supermarket of 'Reporductive Alternatives,'" *Reproductive and Genetic Engineering* 1, no. 3 (1988):225–237.

3. Janice G. Raymond, "The Marketing of the New Reproductive Technologies: Medicine, the Media and the Idea of Progress," *Issues in Reproductive and Genetic Engineering* 3, no. 3 (1990):253–261.

4. Laurie Nsiah-Jefferson, "Reproductive Laws, Women of Color, and Low-Income Women," in *Reproductive Laws for the 1990s*, ed. Sherrill Cohen and Nadine Taub, (Clifton, N.J.: Humana Press, 1989) pp. 23–67.

5. Office of Technological Assessment, Congress of the United States, *Infertility—Medical and Social Choices* May 1988, GPO stock number 052–003–01091–7; Sandra Blakeslee, "Trying to Make Money Making 'Test Tube' Babies," *New York Times*, Sunday, May 17, 1987.

6. Corea, *The Mother Machine* p. 144; Helen Bequaert Holmes, "Hepatitis—Yet Another Risk of In Vitro Fertilization?," *Reproductive and Genetic Engineering* 2, 1 (1989):29–37; Renate D. Klein, *Infertility—Women Speak Out About Their Experiences of Reproductive Medicine* (London: Pandora Press, 1989); Spallone, *Beyond Conception*, p. 56.

7. Gena Corea, Work-In-Progress On The Deaths of Women Resulting From IVF Treatment, Institute on Women & Technology, Box 338, N. Amherst, Mass. 01059.

8. J. Raloff, "Ovarian Cancer: Homing in on the True Risks," *Science News* 143 (January 23, 1993), p. 54.

9. GIFT: gamete intra-fallopian transfer. In this procedure, the egg is removed via laparoscopy and immediately mixed with sperm. The sperm–egg mixture is transferred into the fallopian tube where fertilization may take place. ZIFT: zygote

intra-fallopian transfer. Here the fertilized egg (zygote) is transferred into a fallo-pian tube.

10. Blakeslee, Sandra, "Trying to Make Money", Office of Technological Assessment, *Infertility—Medical and Social Choices.*

11. Marta Kirejcyk and Irma Van Der Ploeg, "Pregnant Couples: Medical Technology and Social Constructions Around Fertility and Reproduction," in *Issues in Reproductive and Genetic Engineering* 5, no. 2 (1992):113–125. For instance, Lynne Millican, a psychiatric nurse in the New England area, is now pursuing legal charges against a clinic for refusing to perform a scheduled IVF on her because she was not in a "traditional family situation." She was not yet divorced from her husband when she tried to get pregnant with another partner. Maureen Dezell, "Uncertain Miracle," *Boston Phoenix*, April 15, 1994, pp. 20–26.

12. Dan McDonnell, "IVF Professor Blasts Critics," *The Sun*, June 8, 1988. Quoted in Gena Corea and Cynthia de Wit, "Current Developments and Issues: A Summary," *Reproductive and Genetic Engineering* 2, no. 1 (1989):63–90.

13. Gena Corea and Susan Ince, "Report of a Survey of IVF Clinics in the USA," in *Made to Order: The Myth of Reporductive and Genetic Progress*, ed. Patricia Spallone and Deborah Lynn Steinberg (New York: Pergamon Press, 1987) pp. 133–145; Warren E. Leary, "In Vitro Fertilization Clinics Vary Widely in Success Rates," *New York Times*, March 10, 1989, p. A16.

14. Richard Saltus, "Fertility Clinics Plan to Disclose Results," *Boston Globe*, November 20, 1989.

15. Blakeslee, "Trying to Make Money."

16. The Fertility Clinic Success Rate and Certificate Act of 1992 (HR 4773) requires each infertility clinic that performs IVF to report annually to the Secretary of Health and Human Services (HHS) on its pregnancy success rates and on the identity of each embryo laboratory working in association with the clinic. The law also directs the secretary of HHS to develop a model program for state certification of embryo laboratory accreditation programs, and to publish and disseminate information concerning infertility clinic pregnancy success rates and other related data.

17. Judith D. Schwartz, *The Mother Puzzle: A New Generation Reckons With Motherhood* (New York: Simon & Schuster, 1993).

18. Annette Burfoot, "The Normalisation of a New Reproductive Technology," in *The New Reproductive Technologies*, eds. Maureen McNeil, Ian Varcoe and Steven Yearley (London: Macmillan Press, 1990), pp. 58–73.

19. Blakeslee, "Trying to Make Money."

20. World Health Organization, Summary Report, "Consultation on the Place of *In Vitro* Fertilization in Infertility Care," Copenhagen, June 1990, pp. 18–22.

21. Arditti, Rita, "Wombs for Rent, Babies for Sale," *Sojourner*, March 1987 pp. 10–11; Katha Pollitt, "The Strange Case of Baby M," *The Nation*, May 23, 1987 pp. 681–688.

22. Noel P. Keane with Dennis L. Breo, *The Surrogate Mother* (New York: Everest House, 1981), p. 1.

23. Robyn Rowland, *Living Laboratories: Women and Reproductive Technologies* (Bloomington and Indianapolis: Indiana University Press, 1992), p. 4.

24. Phyllis Chesler, *Sacred Bond—The Legacy of Baby M* (New York: Times Books, 1988); Mary Beth Whitehead with Loretta Schwartz-Nobel, *A Mother's Story* (New York: St. Martin's Press, 1989).

25. Surrogacy Information Packet, n.d., The Foundation on Economic Trends, 1130 17th Street, N.W., Suite 630. Washington, D.C. 20036; C-Span Congressional

Hearings on Commercial Surrogacy, Committee on Transportation, Tourism and Hazardous Materials, October 15, 1987.

26. Arditti, "Wombs for Rent."

27. Ellen Goodman, "The Word That's Not Mentioned in the Baby M Case," *Boston Globe*, February 17, 1987.

28. Tamar Lewin, "Man Accused of Killing Son Borne by a Surrogate Mother," *New York Times*, January 19, 1995, p. 16.

29. Reuters, "Surrogate Mother Has No Rights As Parent, California Court Rules," *Boston Globe*, May 21, 1993, p. 3.

30. R. Arditti, "Who's the Mother? Ask the Infertility Industry!" *Sojourner*, December 1990, pp. 10–11; Katha Pollitt, "Mother Not a Mother?," *The Nation*, December 31, 1990, pp. 839–846.

31. Corea, *The Mother Machine*, p. 215.

32. Gina Kolata, "Menopause Is Found No Bar to Pregnancy," *New York Times*, October 25, 1990; Richard Saltus, "When the Biological Clock Pauses," *Boston Globe*, October 30, 1990.

33. Kolata, "Menapause Is Found No Bar."

34. *Soujourner: The Women's Forum*, December 1995, p. 46.

35. Nadine Brozan, "Babies from Donated Eggs: Growing Use Stirs Questions," *New York Times*, January 18, 1988.

36. Jocelynne A. Scutt, "The Politics of Infertility Counselling," *Issues in Reproductive and Genetic Engineering*, 4, no. 3 (1991):251–256; Jocelynne A. Scutt "A Question of Choice? IVF & the Politics of Coercion," *Issues in Reproductive and Genetic Engineering*, 5, no. 3 (1992):265–273; Anne C. Thacker, "Social Implications of Developing Medical Knowledge in the Field of Human Reproduction. A Case of Ignoring Some Human Rights," *Issues In Reproductive and Genetic Engineering*, 5, no. 2 (1992):127–135.

37. Janice G. Raymond, *Women as Wombs: Reproductive Technologies and the Battle Over Women's Freedom* (New York: HarperCollins, 1993).

38. Office of Technological Assessment, *Infertility—Medical and Social Choices* p. 271.

39. Northwest Airlines *World Traveler*, international edition, XXV, no. 5 (May 1993); *People*, April 5, 1993.

40. Christine Ewing and Renate Klein, "Joint Resistance: Women Oppose the Technological Take-Over of Life," *Reproductive and Genetic Engineering* 2, no. 3 (1989):279–287.

41. Declaration of Comilla, *Issues in Reproductive and Genetic Engineering* 4, no. 1 (1991):73–74.

42. Jo Salomone, Report on Australian National Conference, "Surrogacy: In Whose Interest?" *Issues in Reproductive and Genetic Engineering* 5, no. 1 (1992):79–94.

43. National Action Committee on the Status of Women (Canada), "The New Reproductive Technologies: A Technological Handmaid's Tale," *Issues in Reproductive and Genetic Engineering* 4, no. 3 (1991):279–296.

44. Rothman, *Recreating Motherhood*, p. 256.

45. Martha A. Field, *Surrogate Motherhood—The Legal and Human Issues* (Cambridge and London: Harvard University Press, 1990), p. 177; Raymond, *Women as Wombs*, p. 56.

Mothers and Disappearing Daughters

Sex Determination Tests in India

Madhu Kishwar

Is there any truth in the argument that the killing of unwanted girls will ulti-mately help make life better for those daughters that are allowed to live? Is scar-city of women likely to lead to their lives becoming more valued? [Yet] why ob-ject to sex-selective abortion, especially if the women themselves are averse to producing more than one or two daughters? If we do not want to have the right to prevent women from aborting unwanted children, how can we support the State when it tries to prevent women from aborting unwanted daughters?

Technologies like amniocentesis and ultrasound, used in most of the world for detecting fetal abnormalities, have come to be used in large parts of India almost exclusively for determining the sex of the fetus, so that the mother can have an abortion if the baby happens to be female. These sex determination tests are perceived to have genocidal potential, for the rapid spread of these tests has resulted in sex-selective abortions of hun-dreds of thousands of female fetuses.

The magnitude of the problem can be gauged by noting that Dr. Sunil Kothari of Delhi, during an interview on the BBC, admitted to having per-formed sixty thousand of these tests, and declared with total conviction, "This is the best way of population control for India."[1] There are thousands of doctors all over India who are engaged in the same type of medical practice. Some operate openly, some in a clandestine manner.

India has a low sex ratio; that is, the population of females in the overall population is noticeably lower than males, and is continuing to decline. By 1991, the sex ratio was 929 females to 1000 males, with 30 million fewer women than men overall. Many people attributed that ratio to underreporting because of traditions like purdah.[2] But slowly the realization dawned: The problem was not undercounting of females. They simply did not exist.

This was not because Indian women are genetically more fragile and prone to dying faster, but because of the culture of son preference. So strong is the desire for sons that the birth of daughters is dreaded in many homes, especially if the family already has one or two daughters. Consequently, these daughters are often neglected, suffer discrimination in food allocation and medical attention in case of illness, and even lack the basic love and care that often is the key to survival or death. These baby girls are more likely to be undernourished and neglected, and are allowed to die when they fall ill.

In some communities, daughters are straight away killed as soon as they are born, because they are perceived as an economic and social burden. For many women, this pattern of neglect and discrimination continues throughout their lives—so much so, that by the time they reach adulthood, these women begin to practice it on themselves as well as on their own daughters.

It is important to remember that virulent forms of son preference and devaluation of daughters are not historically an all-India phenomenon. Sex ratios have been far more imbalanced in some landowning communities than among the landless poor, or even among artisanal groups. The most alarming aspect of this situation is that, over the last few decades, low sex ratios are slowly becoming the norm across India. In addition, lower status groups that not long ago had favorable sex ratios are beginning to emulate higher status groups in rural areas, and are recording a decline in the proportion of their female populations. Thus, the culture of overvaluing male lives at the cost of female lives is not a mere hangover of traditional norms, as is often believed, but is also a modern phenomenon.

For instance, when amniocentesis first became available at Delhi's All India Institute of Medical Sciences in 1975, only one of the thousands of tests performed that year was performed for a purpose other than discovering the fetus's gender. And almost all of the women who found out they were carrying a female fetus aborted her. Protests against use of the procedure led to the decision to discontinue use of the test at all government hospitals. However, that did not stop private hospitals, clinics and doctors from providing this service on a large scale.

Many women's organizations and other concerned citizens have responded to the epidemic of abortions of female fetuses by demanding a ban on sex determination tests. The western state of Maharashtra, in which Bombay is located, was the first to outlaw these tests, after a government-sponsored study found that 85 percent of gynecologists were performing amniocenteses solely for sex determination. Only a tiny proportion were done to detect genetic disorders. Most disturbing was the finding that nearly every one of the 15,914 abortions performed during 1984–1985 at a single abortion clinic in Bombay was undertaken after sex determination tests. It was estimated that 40,000 to 50,000 sex determination tests were being conducted per year at the time of the study. Similar clinics had sprung up in most small towns, as well as in the big villages of Maharashtra.

Three other states—Punjab, Haryana and Gujarat—soon also banned these tests, because clinics were indulging in aggressive campaigns to abort female fetuses. Billboards with such messages as "Pay 500 rupees now and save Rs 5 lakhs later"—playing on the anxieties of parents about having daughters—had become a common sight in these states.

However, the law remained a dead letter and the clinics continued to mushroom and thrive in all of these states. The only difference the new law made was that huge billboards that had earlier read *"Ladka Ya Ladki Jaanch karaiye"* ("Find Out If It's a Girl") were replaced by barely veiled messages such as *"Swasth ladka ya ladki?"* ("Healthy boy or girl?") or *"Garbh mein bacchhe ki har prakar ki jankari"* ("Everything you always wanted to know about the child in your womb").

Doctor-client complicity ensured that the clinics flourished despite the ban. A magazine reported that in a small town like Sirsa in Haryana, at least one hundred tests were being performed every day. Doctors in the town declared openly: "Earlier we used to give our findings in writing. Now we will simply tell them the sex of their child verbally. Who can stop us from doing that?"[3] Despite the dismal failure of the law, some women's organizations continued to demand comprehensive country-wide legislation and even more stringent provisions to deal with the problem.

In 1994, the Parliament enacted another law, called the Prenatal Diagnostics Techniques Act. This law prohibits any genetic counseling center, laboratory or clinic from performing any prenatal diagnostic technique unless the pregnant woman is more than thirty-five years of age, she has undergone two or more spontaneous abortions or miscarriages, she has been exposed during her pregnancy to substances potentially harmful to the fetus, or she has a family history of mental retardation or physical deformities.

Attempting to ensure that the results of these tests are not used in deciding to abort a female fetus, the law states: "No person conducting prenatal diagnostic procedures shall communicate to the pregnant woman concerned or her relatives the sex of the fetus by words, signs or in any other manner." Likewise, the law bans advertising in any manner whatsoever the availability of prenatal diagnostic procedures as a means of determining the sex of the fetus. Any person violating the law can be imprisoned for up to three years, and fined up to 10,000 rupees (roughly equivalent to $285 in U.S. dollars).

The Maharashtra Act had exempted from punishment any pregnant woman who underwent the test. The parliamentary act of 1994 does not take such a lenient view. Any woman found guilty of using the tests to determine the sex of her child is punishable with imprisonment for up to three years, and a fine of up to 10,000 rupees, unless she can prove that she acted under duress. If found guilty of a second offense, the term of imprisonment can extend to five years, and the fine up to 50,000 rupees (roughly equivalent to $1,430 in U.S. dollars).

With a law as draconian as this, one would imagine that people would be too frightened to conduct or undergo such tests. This is far from the case. Delhi, the seat of India's central government, is reported to have two thousand clinics with facilities for carrying out prenatal sex determination tests, which are available for a fairly reasonable amount. It has, no doubt, become more expensive than before the new law. However, it remains within the financial capacities of the majority of families.

Several women's organizations protested and demanded that the law be made even more stringent. They want genetic tests to be permitted only in government hospitals. But government doctors can be bribed just as easily as private ones into providing the test.

It is time that we face the fact that such a law cannot work in India, or in countries governed in ways similar to India. This is not to suggest that India is uniquely lawless. In fact, what is true for India applies equally to many societies that have had the misfortune of undergoing a long spell of western colonial rule. They inherit a tyrannical state machinery totally unaccountable to the people they rule over, because these governments were developed as an instrument of subjugation rather than for providing service. Since, in most postcolonial societies, the ruling elites failed to overhaul the machinery of governance when they took over to make it more responsive to people's needs, the government machinery continues mainly to be used to harass people and extort bribes out of them.

The more stringent a law, the greater the likelihood of it being used for making money by state officials. (The law imposing several years of jail on convicted prostitutes, for example, has meant only that brothels pay bribes to police for protection, and that police "raids" serve only to keep the prostitutes fearful, captive and willing to pay up.)

In addition, if the clinics go underground, it will become impossible to monitor clinic functioning and safety, exposing pregnant women to even greater risks. Moreover, the technology for performing these tests is easily available and relatively inexpensive; just about anyone can set up such a lab. There is no way to police these mushrooming clinics, especially since many doctors have begun to use portable ultrasound machines that they carry in their cars to perform tests in people's homes. And technology has quickly outstripped the legislation, which covers only amniocentesis. Ultrasound has become the new method of choice for sex determination tests—but it is impossible to ban because it is used for a whole range of diagnoses of diseases.

But most important of all, if parents do not want a girl child, getting rid of her does not require much outside help. Simple neglect and underfeeding does the job as effectively as the best of technologies. Under current conditions, there is no way we can legislate that families provide adequate nourishment to girls.

Finally, there are too many people who feel that sex-selective foeticide is an important part of India's answer to overpopulation. Most families in India keep producing children until they feel they have the required number of sons. In the process, several daughters are born before the needed number of sons arrive. Therefore, if families could ensure the birth of a son or two without risking the birth of too many unwanted daughters, they would have more of an interest in smaller families.

Many people have even argued that as women become scarcer their lives would become more valued. One reason why India's Medical Association has failed to take a stand against these tests is that most doctors involved in the business argue that they are doing "noble work." One pioneer in the field has stated, "Happy and wanted children is what we desire . . . Unwanted babies must be aborted." Another woman doctor, Sudha Limaye, head of the obstetric and gynecology department of Bokaro General Hospital in Bihar, is reported to have said, "Our priority is population control by any means. Amniocentesis should be used as a method of family planning and be made available to everyone at a minimum cost or even free."[4]

Some studies have revealed that most parents go in for sex determination tests only after the birth of one child—usually a daughter. These families do want at least one daughter, but do not want to risk a second, and certainly not a third. Instead, they want to ensure that they raise at least one son who will live into adulthood, which means, given high mortality rates, that the woman must bear at least two sons. One study shows that the two-child norm, now prevalent among urban middle-class educated parents, causes anxiety for parents whose firstborn is female.

Now, many will argue: What is wrong with helping people to achieve their desired family size? The question is particularly thorny for feminists, who tend to support a woman's right to abortion. Why object to sex-selective abortion, especially if the women themselves are averse to producing more than one or two daughters? If we do not want to have the right to prevent women from aborting unwanted children, how can we support the State when it tries to prevent women from aborting unwanted daughters?

Most of those supporting the laws against sex determination tests respond by saying women are being socially coerced into getting rid of daughters, that they are not free agents. Therefore, they argue, banning sex-selective abortions does not amount to encroaching on a woman's right to decide how many children she should have. However, several studies have revealed that in large parts of the country, mothers' aversion to having more than one daughter is no less strong than that of male family members. Investigations have shown that many women go for these tests on their own initiative and that they are not mere victims of coercion.

A recent study, entitled "The Silent Deaths: A Study of Female Foeticide in Delhi," found that most of the women clients were highly educated and from well-off families. Several of the interviewed women actually suggested that sex-determination tests should be legalized since this technology is a gift of scientific advances and optimum use should be made of it. Some talked about the social pressure to have a son. Others pointed out the need to "balance" their families since they already had a daughter. Though the doctors performing the tests and subsequent abortions claimed that they provided this service only to those women who already had two daughters, the researcher found that several of the women who opted for the test already had a son.[5]

Why is a family considered incomplete or imbalanced without sons? Is there any truth in the argument that killing unwanted girls will ultimately help make the lives of those daughters that are allowed to live any better? Is scarcity of women likely to lead to their lives becoming more valued?

From what we know about the regions with low female-to-male sex ratios, it appears that the market law of supply and demand does not operate in this case. Communities with low sex ratios tend to be more misogynistic than those with high sex ratios, which tend to allow for more female autonomy and dignity. A culture of seclusion and purdah, disinheritance of women from property, low female literacy rates, poor health, and low employment rates are all characteristic of low sex ratio regions. The incidence of domestic violence is also higher in these regions.

If women's own lives are so negatively affected by discrimination, why then are women so wrapped up in the culture of son preference? Aversion to having daughters is a culturally conditioned choice rooted in certain economic and political power relations within the family and community.

One study done in a Punjab village found that both peasant women and landless agricultural laborers displayed an overwhelming preference for boys and a serious dread of having daughters. Some women wanted no daughters at all. Even those who mentioned that daughters provide support to their mothers, sharing their problems and easing the burden of domestic work, still did not want any daughters. Two of the fifteen peasant women interviewed got sterilized after they gave birth to two sons because neither they nor their families wanted a daughter. One said that, because she had eight sisters and had suffered so much as a result, she never wanted to give birth to a girl. One reported that her own mother had died within days after the birth of her fifth daughter because her husband had become very unhappy at the birth of yet another daughter.[6]

Why then do women dread having daughters? Their own lives as women, and what they saw of their mothers' lives, give them an aversion to producing another sufferer like them. In addition, their own status in the family is downgraded, and they become vulnerable to more abuse every time an unwanted daughter is born, or if they fail to produce a son. Occasionally a woman whose place in the family is already insecure seems to become incapable of breastfeeding her infant girl. If the birth of the girl child makes her life more miserable, there is reason for her to hate that child—and even to want it dead.

There are other reasons that women don't want baby girls. Most women do not see their daughters having a chance at a better life than they themselves have experienced. And families see these daughters as a future burden, due to the dowry system and limited employment opportunities for women.

In a culture where both men and women are expected to subordinate their individual interests to that of the family, it is to be expected that ultimately women themselves see their own interests as indistinguishable from the family's interests, and consequently become actively involved in favoring male children at the cost of daughters, just as they ignore their own health and nutritional needs but seldom those of their husband.

In a very moving letter, one of *Manushi's*[7] readers and friends, Rajbala, gave an account of how women have themselves internalized the aversion to giving birth to daughters. Rajbala comes from a politically progressive peasant family in Haryana. She married a man from a similarly oriented family; his father is a Communist living in Punjab.

When Rajbala gave birth to her first child, she named her Manushi, after the magazine, because she felt it connected very closely with her life. She wrote to the magazine:

All members of our family were very happy I gave birth to a girl. She was born in a hospital in Hissar. We distributed sweets to the nurses and other hospital staff. All of them reacted as if we were doing something strange and laughable . . . We are acquainted with two families of doctors in that town. My husband visited them and gave them boxes of sweets. They did not even listen carefully to his announcement that a girl had been born. They merely assumed that since sweets were being distributed, a boy must have been born. They rang up their parents and told them to visit to congratulate us on the birth of a son. When their parents came to see us, bringing a present of money for the child, and heard that we had a girl child, they were terribly embarrassed and began to justify their visit by saying that they had assumed, because of our distributing sweets, that we had a son . . . They felt this was some sort of ill omen and thought we would perhaps be annoyed by their having come to congratulate us on a girl's birth, so they hurriedly left without giving anything to our daughter.

Several months later, a female relative of ours came to visit us. While talking to my mother-in-law, she remarked: "Nani, could I ever imagine that one day, I too would have children? When, the first two times I gave birth to stones, I wept day and night, wishing that I had been fortunate enough to have a child." I felt very sorry for her and asked how she had given birth to stones and whether she had got herself checked up. She replied angrily: "I had stones just as you had a stone." When I understood her meaning, I felt as if a heavy stone had fallen on my head. My face grew red with anger, astonishment and sorrow that she could call my daughter a stone. Tears came to my eyes at the thought that in our society, a woman, a mother, can call her daughter a stone. Ignoring my reaction, she ended her story by saying that her second daughter was a blessing in disguise because she died and after her death two children (sons) were born.

One day, when my daughter was one and a half years old, she fell ill. My father-in-law took her to the doctor and pleaded with him, saying: "Please cure this child. She is as good as a grandson to me." The doctor replied: "Comrade *saheb*, don't worry. Even if you fling a girl into a bramble bush, she will survive. It is boys who are not only hard to get but who die of the slightest sickness." However, he began to treat our daughter, but that very night our very dear daughter, our much loved daughter, left us and went away. Our daughter who used to dance to the tunes on the transistor, who used to run to show us the picture of a cow in her book as soon as a calf entered the field, who used to run to embrace her grandfather's legs, went away. Our feelings on losing her were unbearable, inexpressible.

But when our fellow villagers came to condole with us, their words, which still resound in my ears, were: "Stop crying now, she was a worm from hell and has gone back to hell." Another woman said: "Don't sorrow so much, she was a tempest. After the tempest comes the rain (a son)." A third said: "How unkind of god. This was not so precious a thing that he needed to take it away." Yet another said: "You must have committed some sin in your former birth. First you gave birth to a girl and then the god called her away." A man who saw my father-in-law grieving was surprised and said: "Comrade, a peasant is freed from the weight of seven births and goes straight to heaven if his daughter dies a virgin in her father's house."

Every day, every moment, I remember my daughter and I also remember all the bitter words I heard, from her birth to the time of my separation from her, which renew my strength to fight against this society in which to give birth to a girl is considered the punishment for sins of a previous birth, and a girl's death equivalent to paradise for her parents.

Such strong misogynist attitudes are in some ways peculiar to Punjab and the neighboring northwest plains, because Punjab, in particular, has been a frontier area for centuries. It witnessed constant warfare: when not facing outside invaders, the diverse groups inhabiting this area have frequently been at war with each other. The peoples of this area came to pride themselves on their martial traditions. This area is also most influenced by the culture of the Muslim invaders and rulers from the northwest, and from central Asia. As a result, the native peoples adopted more stringent forms of female seclusion and purdah that went far beyond those practiced in other parts of India.

Ownership of land was the hallmark of higher status; however, no family could take its continuous possession of land for granted for very long. Therefore, there was a constant drive toward acquiring more and more land. And the landowning communities in the northwest came to value physical strength, skills in wielding weaponry, and related "manly" qualities such as aggressiveness and virility far more than is healthy for any society.

In such a situation women came to be valued primarily as the bearers of sons, and were seen as liabilities in most other contexts, even when economically productive, because they need more physical protection from enemies. The fiercely patrilineal family and kinship structure mandated that daughters be sent away to the husband's family after marriage. Rights over her were transferred to the marital family. Not only were daughters a constant source of anxiety because of their assumed need for greater protection against an outside world full of enemies; they were also an economic drain because they had to be provided with a dowry.

The establishment of British rule brought an end to internecine warfare as well as to external invasions. But British rule only exacerbated land hunger and unleashed new forces that further strengthened the power of men over women. This led to further devaluations of women's lives and to the spread of this misogynist culture to other parts of the country. The most important and far-reaching of the changes introduced by the British was their imposition of new land ownership patterns, which created the basis for the near total alienation of women from the land—even though it was women, in many areas of the country, who were the primary cultivators of the land.

In conformity with Victorian norms, land entitlements were given by the colonial rulers to "male heads of family," bypassing the customary laws that allowed various categories of entitlements to women. This concentrated property in the hands of men in an unprecedented way and paved the way for the disinheritance of women. The culture of dowry is a by-product of this modern trend. (It is noteworthy that there is little mention of exorbitant dowries causing the ruin of families in the literature of pre-British India.)

As women were increasingly disinherited, daughters began to appear as liabilities. *Kanyadan*, the gift of a daughter, became not so much a matter of earning *dharmic* merit (merit from doing one's appropriate duty) so much as getting rid of an unwanted burden. It is in this context that dowry payments began to assume the form of offerings to a groom's family so that they would take a burden from the bride's family.

Why should women be considered an economic liability? As land becomes scarce and population pressure increases, possession of land becomes the all-important asset. If, in such a situation, ownership of land is vested exclusively in the hands of men, women begin to be treated like mere dependents and considered as liabilities rather than assets. Therefore, bringing a bride into the house is seen as adding to the economic burden of the family, except in those peasant households where women's labor is the mainstay of agricultural operations.

But even in these communities, modernization is tilting the scales against women—and, as a result, is cultivating a strong preference for sons. As a result of British law, which confers upon men exclusive rights to land ownership, only daughters who remain unmarried have the right to work on and live off their father's land. But daughters do not inherit as sons do. And if an unmarried daughter is raped or has a brief affair with a man, she loses her right to live off the family land in the same way she would if she had married.

A widow cannot claim a share in her husband's land even if she is the one cultivating it. She can claim a right to the land only through her son, if she has one. As a result, rural widows who produce only daughters have a very precarious position. Those with only daughters or infant sons tend to be relatively powerless. The land of such widows is often snatched away from them through force or fraud. Thus, women are forced into a position of both needing and preferring sons. Another reason for son preference is that the outside world of education and employment is extremely male oriented and male dominated. Therefore, if tribals have to seek a foothold in the mainstream economy, they can do so only through sons.

In addition, growing disparities in male–female earning capacities have made families view their traditional expenses in a new light. Apart from the pressure of dowries, some communities like the Kallars in southern India are now beginning to see traditional ceremonies associated with women—at puberty, pregnancy, childbirth and a host of other rituals—as burdensome. They have begun to argue that their economic survival requires restricting themselves to no more than one daughter, because more daughters mean increasing indebtedness and economic ruin. This community has recently become notorious for female infanticide.

If we want to stop the killing and neglect of women, it is not enough to simply pass a law and hope that it will succeed in countering all those social and economic forces that make women's lives appear expendable. The few government attempts to prevent the destruction of girls have been total failures. In October of 1992, the chief minister of Tamil Nadu in southern India launched a program hailed as a "Revolutionary Leader's Scheme to Save the Female Child."[8] Mothers were encouraged to leave their unwanted baby girls in special cradles set up in public health centers throughout Tamil Nadu. No questions were to be asked of a parent who left a child there.

Fully 51 infant girls were deposited in the cradles during that year. Many were either handicapped or illegitimate. Of the total, 39 were handed over to voluntary organizations to bring up. But of the remaining twelve left in the government's care, eleven died of neglect, and one was taken back by her parents, who feared that she too would die in the same manner. One reporter commented: "The scheme went the way of the female child. It did not survive to celebrate its first birthday."[9]

The government announced a monetary reward to anyone providing information about cases of female infanticide. Not a single person came forward in the year following the announcement to claim the award, according to a newspaper report.[10]

Another Tamil Nadu government initiative to save infant girls fared no better. Officials offered to provide financial assistance to impoverished parents to help them meet the costs of educating and marrying off their daughters. The parents had to have an income below the poverty line, have no male heirs, and one of the parents had to have been sterilized. But the scheme failed, largely because it was based on the mistaken assumption that it is only among the poor that girl babies are killed. This is far from the truth. Even in Tamil Nadu, the problem of female infanticide is confined to the economically mobile, land-owning castes. It is among these relatively prosperous people, who now demand high dowries, that female infanticide is becoming more prevalent. Among the Vellala Goundars, for example, a well-off, land-owning group, the going dowry is one lakh in cash, one kilo in gold, and a car—together with a wide variety of household goods.

In contrast, poorer landless castes, whether in the north or in the south, rarely practice female infanticide. Therefore, targeting the entire "save the girl" scheme at India's poorest families makes the whole program absurdly off target.

CONCLUSION

When I argue that a legal ban on female foeticide won't work, I do not mean to imply that we should leave things as they are, nor that the resultant scarcity of females will inevitably raise the value of female lives. What I am suggesting is that we stop looking for quick fixes and instead face the problem squarely: There is no way to ensure the healthy survival of baby girls unless families find them worth nurturing. Thus, our interventions must enhance the value of daughters in the eyes of their family, rather than hand over their upbringing to charity organizations or condemn them to a life of neglect and discrimination.

We must address the economic, educational and vocational needs of young women so that they appear as assets, rather than as drains, on the family's economic base. To accomplish this, we must push for the following advances.

First, we must make it legally impossible for families to disinherit daughters. Dowry, after all, is an offshoot of the practice of denying women an inheritance in parental property. This could be done through legislation that deems invalid any will that does not include a daughter's name as an inheritor.

We must provide high-quality education to girls from an early age, and provide them with vocational skills that can assist them in finding employment in something other than the lowest-paid unskilled and futureless manual labor—where most of the few who find jobs now end up. Loans for women are also critical, to enable them to start and expand new businesses. Some needed changes are cultural, and therefore they will be harder to accomplish. We must, for example, launch a cultural campaign to eradicate the widely held prejudice against accepting monetary support from daughters.

But a relatively easy place to start this process of change—toward ensuring a dignified life for women—is within the health-care system. For the desire for sons is not the only reason that women feel compelled to produce so many children. A more important reason is the high infant death rate. Families are never sure how many of their children will survive to adulthood. Hence there is great pressure to produce more children than the family thinks are needed, taking a heavy toll on women's health and energy. The high birth rate and the shamelessly high infant and maternal mortality rate are due to the lack of elementary health care in large parts of the country. Basic survival needs, such as safe water and accessible fuel for cooking, are often lacking as well.

We need to build a responsible birth planning program on the strong edifice of a sensitive primary health-care system that improves the nutritional and health status of women and girls. A healthy woman, freed of needless drudgery, such as traveling long distances for water and fuel, is more likely to have the strength to improve her earning capacity and acquire the skills to negotiate with the outside world more successfully. This in turn should strengthen her bargaining power within the family.

These are all long-term measures. This does not mean that, in the meantime, we should keep quiet and let these sex-determination tests continue without registering our protests. We should picket outside clinics that perform these tests, attempt to persuade medical societies to take a stand against such tests, and write articles to convince people of the harm such tests pose to our society.

In short, we must spare no occasion to mobilize public opinion against the culture of son preference and the practice of sex-selective abortion that follows from it. We must keep making people who have anything to do with it feel guilty, allow them no peace of mind until they are willing to recognize the harm they are doing—and stop. Only then can we protect the future of our daughters, and end this madness that is costing them their lives.

NOTES

1. BBC program, broadcast on Indian television in early 1990s, focused on India's problem with sex determination tests and female foeticide (no exact date available).
2. Source: *Census of India, 1991 Provisional Population Tables* (New Delhi,

India, 1991). Purdah is a practice inaugurated by Muslims and later adopted by various Hindus; it is found especially in India. Under purdah, women are removed from public observation by means of concealing clothing such as a veil, and by the use of high-walled enclosures, screens and curtains within the home.

3. Minu Jain and Harry Singh, "Foetal Divide," in *Sunday* Magazine, July 24–30, 1994.

4. Ibid.

5. Reported by Sharmila Chandra in *Indian Express Magazine*, October 28, 1990.

6. Berny Horowitz and Madhu Kishwar, "Family Life: The Unequal Deal," in *In Search of Answers* (London: Zed Press, 1984).

7. *Manushi* is a feminist magazine published in India. The author is the magazine's founder, editor, and publisher. This account first appeared in *Manushi* 33 (1986): "They Called Her a Stone."

8. Sam Rajappa, writing for *The Statesman*, October 17, 1993.

9. See *Statesman*, October 17, 1993.

10. Ibid.

REFLECTIONS ON FEMINISM

AND MOTHERHOOD

Overview

The Uneasy Relationship Between Motherhood and Feminism

Diana Taylor

"Reflections" brings together two themes that run through this collection: the uneasy relationship between feminism and motherhood, and the potential for using "maternal thinking" to develop a feminist politics of peace. Marianne Hirsch, author of *The Mother/Daughter Plot* and co-editor of *Conflicts in Feminism*, offers a "diary" of her trajectory as a feminist mother working for more than twenty years to overcome the resistance—by both nonfeminist mothers and feminists who are not mothers—to a feminist politics that embraces motherhood.

In some ways, these resistances are understandable. As Hirsch outlines, for many feminists writing in the 1970s, everything surrounding the "mother" question seemed to be a product of patriarchy—from the false choices that made a woman choose between a family and a career, to the assumption that she was the sole or main child-care provider, to the economic dependency that resulted from this skewed situation. Motherhood, as a social arrangement of roles and responsibilities, has been viewed as a trap by many women. It excluded and devalued the existence of women without children, even as it locked mothers into restrictive and often humiliating and disempowering relationships with their partners or with government agencies, sometimes both. And given the brutality with which poor mothers are treated in the United States—from the slave days in which African-American women's children were taken from them and sold, to the current welfare wars that threaten to remove children from poor mothers—it is little wonder that many feminists, then and now, would want to distance themselves as far as possible from the mother problem.

Who would want to identify with such an embattled role? Why couldn't mothers just think of themselves as professional women who happened to have children? Through this "Diary," Hirsch maps out the debates as she has experienced them, from the time she was a college student in the 1970s until the present. Hirsch articulates what many of the voices resounding through this collection seem to suggest: Mothers need feminism just as urgently as feminism needs to think about the many social problems that face mothers.

Sara Ruddick, author of the important book, *Maternal Thinking: Towards a Politics of Peace*, also offers a reflection on her career as a scholar committed to theorizing about maternal thinking. After a professional lifetime dedicated to delineating a "politics of peace" informed by maternal practice, she admits feeling pessimistic and disheartened. Maternal political practice, she acknowledges, covers "war mothers as well as peace mothers, racist as well as anti-racist mothers." She recognizes the difficulties of categorizing an identifiable activity such as "mothering." How would this be distinct from other women's roles such as *daughtering, wifeing, friending*? Are loving, caring and protecting gendered activities? Doesn't the fact that they have been gendered (*mothering*, as opposed to *fathering* or *parenting*) reflect and reaffirm patriarchal assumptions of the mother's role as somehow separate from other aspects of the woman's private, professional and political life?

Ruddick's essay shows that attempts to define "maternal practice" are as complicated as defining "mother" or "mothering." Mothers, as subjects, often become conflated with *mothering* as a maternal *practice*. Maternal thinking, similarly, derives from the "work" traditionally associated with mothers: conflict resolution, caretaking, and so forth. Clearly, however, neither the thinking nor the praxis is gendered. And while this volume attests to the fact that many mothers undertake courageous, extreme, exhilarating, self-sacrificing and at times even hateful acts for their children, it is impossible to conclude that mothers (already an unstable category) *act* in any one way, or that their *actions* have enough in common to constitute a *practice*.

Even the most basic assumptions that one might make about maternal practice—that it valorizes or works for the continued existence of the offspring above all else—cannot be made about all mothers. Take, for example, groups such as the Palestinian "mothers of the martyrs" or religious fundamentalists who resist medical treatment that would save their children. Ruddick notes that some women who work tirelessly for what they feel is the protection or advancement of their children (such as the mothers in the KKK) do not necessarily defend children's rights; they defend their own children's rights at the expense of other children. The contrary also happens: The Mothers of the Plaza de Mayo became one of the most effective and visible human rights group on the international scene when they decided they were not just demonstrating for their children, but for everyone's disappeared children.

In spite of the many difficulties and contradictions that Ruddick has encountered in her work on maternal politics, she reminds us that "it is perverse to fix on the worst cases of righteous tribalism when we can look attentively and with hope at the many remarkable kinds of cross-cultural appreciation of which political mothers are capable." Nevertheless, some of the voices included in this volume are profoundly disturbing to those who hope to link feminist and maternal praxis to shape a more caring and egalitarian society. Some of the skinhead and KKK mothers, for example, call themselves feminists. But Ruddick proposes a model that might lead the way out of this painful contradiction: "Maternal politics, just because it issues out of particular and familiar allegiances, can inspire a move from one's 'own' to 'other,' from local to more general without denying, indeed by continually remembering, irreplaceable and specific loyalties and love." Grace Paley offers this typically succinct assessment of the importance of maternal politics: "If you don't want children, that's fine. If you don't care about children, that's bad." The lesson to be learned from this is fundamental to the discussions in this volume. We have to care not just about "our" rights but all women's rights, not just about "our" children, but about all children.

Feminism at the Maternal Divide

A Diary

Marianne Hirsch

*F*eminist movement, feminist theory and motherhood have maintained uneasy affiliations since the beginnings of the second wave of feminism in the 1960s. Throughout the late 1970s and 1980s, as a feminist in the United States working on motherhood, and arguing for the inclusion of maternal perspectives within feminist perspectives, I have often found myself, theoretically and ideologically, in a difficult position. On numerous occasions, in conversations and conferences as well as in my own writing, I was acting out, painfully and even tearfully, some of the most cruel tensions and contradictions between feminism and motherhood.

In the spring of 1993, I attended a conference on motherhood and activism, bringing together scholars, writers and activists who have developed a politics of social resistance from their roles as wives and/or mothers. A conference on radical motherhood promised a way out of the seemingly irresolvable divisions between mother-inclusive feminists and those who see work on maternity as a return to oppressive and exclusionary mythologies.

Thinking about women who have defined themselves as political actors within their very maternal identities inevitably led me to think and talk, at the conference, about feminism and its difficulties with motherhood. As I was talking, however, and as I listened to the other presentations, I realized that this audience, interested in such a "motherist" politics, was very different from the audience I had assumed, that is, those feminists who have had *difficulty including maternal perspectives in their work. I had resisted seeing that feminists and mother-activists were, in fact, separate groups, with their own issues and concerns. In working so hard to get feminists to take mothers seriously, I had neglected to take into account that even radical mothers and mother-activists do not necessarily identify as feminists, or take feminism seriously. At the conference, feminism rarely came up. Yet for me, it was and remains centrally important. Unlike many of the other participants, I came to the conference out of second-wave feminism, academia, feminist theory, and a deep interest in the perspectives and the practices of mothering, not, like many others, out of an interest in the institution of motherhood, and how it could be deployed for political ends. These sites have shaped my conviction that feminists need to listen to the experiences of mother and that mothers, in turn, need feminism.*

The following diary, inspired by Ann Snitow's 1990 "Gender Diary," [in Conflicts in Feminism, *ed. Marianne Hirsch and Evelyn Fox Keller (New York: Routledge, 1991)] attempts both to outline my path to this certitude and to justify it. I am grateful to Mary Childers, Jane Coppock, Alexis Jetter, Temma Kaplan, Margo Kasdan, Annelise Orleck, Sara Ruddick, Ivy Schweitzer, Leo Spitzer and Diana Taylor for their skeptical readings of this diary and for their inspiration.*

1970

I am a senior in college, working on a thesis on two male writers and the female characters they offer up to fantasies and projections of their male protagonists. Vladimir Nabokov's Lolita and Robert Musil's Tonka never grow up: one a nymphet and the other a saint, they both die prematurely and immaturely of their lovers' idealization of an eternal feminine. I am fascinated by the imaginative force that makes a living women into an aesthetic figure and refuses to see her or to listen to her voice. I don't know how to recognize or analyze the gendered basis of this transaction.

It's hard to concentrate on the thesis as Kent State and the invasion of Cambodia erupt, as a new curriculum that does away with grades and requirements gets under way, and as we begin serious talks about opening the university to the community. I hand in the thesis the day before we declare a strike protesting the invasion—classes are called off for the rest of the semester and we engage in serious anti-war organizing, staging several large demonstrations.

Graduation is a muted affair: we cancel the campus dance and ban all music, we wear white armbands and no caps, we stage street-theater performances alongside the academic processions to show our parents and teachers that we mean our protest—not only against a war that has shaped the consciousness of our generation, but against everything that their lives represent: capitalism, militarism, elitism, the bourgeois family. When my father expresses some doubt that the university will become the open campus we envision as early as the next fall, I cannot forgive his skepticism.

A week after graduation I get married to my college boyfriend. It's no contradiction: our life is meant to be different indeed—idealistic, devoted to social change, egalitarian. We travel through Western and Eastern Europe for the summer, eagerly searching for alternative social structures. In the fall, I start graduate school, set up house with my husband, who teaches high school—a job that, before the draft lottery was instituted, might have offered a draft deferment. I see myself as a graduate student first, though part of me enjoys playing house as well. It's not just an engagement in domesticity; it's a project to invent new gender relations, to reverse stereotypes and preconceived habits. We take turns doing everything domestic and I even consider taking an auto mechanics course to eradicate one of the last barriers to gender equality.

I don't know how the idea of a women's consciousness-raising group first comes up. Perhaps it is during one of my first conversations with a fellow graduate student who asks, in the midst of a discussion of our academic interests, whether I have orgasms. I had never seen the political dimensions of sexuality. We join together with some other students and some neighbors to form our women's group and by January we meet regularly in each other's apartments, asking husband and boyfriends to leave for the evening, unable to assure them that we will not be discussing intimate details about them and our lives with them. As the anti-war and the civil rights movements lose their energy and promise, we come to see this as our day, envisioning far-reaching political and personal changes.

There are eight of us. We don't focus on the fact that we are all white, all middle-class, all heterosexual: we are singularly and deeply concerned with our gender identity before anything else. We discuss our histories, our sexuality, our various relationships with men, our socialization and social definition as women; we read the outrageous SCUM ("Society for Cutting Up Men") Manifesto and Anne Koedt's "Myth of the Vaginal Orgasm"; we follow the suggested consciousness-raising topics of New York Redstockings; and we find astonishing strength and revelation in our commonalities. Amazingly, we don't focus on the fact that two of us have children. It's more difficult for them to find time to meet and we try to accommodate their fractured schedules, but neither their children nor their maternal identity ever become points of discussion among us. Instead, we talk endlessly about sex and about our relationships with our mothers. Energized by the frustrations we share, we determine, again and again, that we will not be victimized as our mothers are, that we will not subordinate our lives to men or to prevalent ideologies of femininity, that we will insist on equal pay and equal treatment for all women, and that we will avoid their depressions, frustrations and unacceptable compromises as they could not. Our mothers become the emblems of a womanhood we need to reject, and the children in our two sisters' lives do not make any of us any more sympathetic to the maternal project. It never occurs to us that our feminist bonding could include our mothers or ourselves as mothers. I don't know how the two mothers in the group live that contradiction, or whether it even feels like a contradiction to them.

1971–1974

In identifying our newly formulated feminist consciousness with a rejection of maternity, we find ourselves echoing larger trends. In 1974, Shulamith Firestone publishes *The Dialectic of Sex*. Following the classic critiques of woman's maternity by Simone de Beauvoir in *The Second Sex* (1949) and Betty Friedan in *The Feminine Mystique* (1963), Firestone identifies motherhood as the prime barrier to women's equality. If only the species could reproduce itself differently, these writings boldly suggest, if only women would resist the social and psychological pull toward maternity, we could enjoy some of the freedoms and the achievements of men. Reproductive technologies could liberate women from pregnancy and birth, and thus from the repressive structures of the nuclear family. Women's interests can only be advanced outside the family, and if it were not for pregnancy, birth, and the institution of motherhood, alternative, perhaps communal, living arrangements and extrafamilial, anti-oedipal forms of relationship might be envisioned.

Following these suggestions, "equality feminists" of the 1970s, like the women in my consciousness-raising group, identify themselves as "daughters" celebrating "sisterhood" and breaking away from our mothers' lives. Robin Morgan later wrote of her own discomfort with her maternal identity in the feminism of the 1970s, which identified motherhood with the reproduction of patriarchy: "Since the patriarchy commanded women to be mothers (the thesis), we had to rebel with our own polarity and declare motherhood a reactionary cabal (antithesis). Today a new synthesis has emerged; the concept of mother-right, affirmation of a woman's childbearing and/or childrearing when it is a woman's *choice* . . . It is refreshing at last to be able to come out of my mother-closet and yell to the world that I love my dear, wonderful, delicious child" (Robin Morgan, *Going Too Far: The Personal Chronicle of a Feminist* [New York: Vintage, 1978], p. 8). But in the feminism of the 1970s, Morgan, like the two mothers in my group, is unable to combine her own maternal identity with her feminist commitments.

Offering an alternative to motherhood or daughterhood, "sisterhood," we feel, can provide the possibility of mutuality and reciprocity. The metaphor of sisterhood, though still familial, can describe a feminine model of relation, an ideal and an alternative within patriarchy. It could help women to envision a life and a set of affiliations outside of the paradigm of mother/child relations and the compromises with men that motherhood seems to necessitate. It can liberate feminist women from our anatomy and from the difficult stories of our own mothers, stories of accommodation, adjustment and resignation. "Sisterhood" can free us, as we are fond of saying, to "give birth to ourselves." In the demoralizing Nixon and Ford years, sisterhood takes up all of our political energies. I know that we need to transform ourselves and our homes even as we try to raise consciousness about women's oppression on larger institutional fronts. But I find it difficult to speak with and draw into feminism women who identify themselves primarily as mothers and homemakers. I see why they perceive my feminism as elitist, exclusive and threatening, but I don't know how to confront either my discomfort or theirs. As much as I try not to, I often end up, at social gatherings, in conversations with men. Along with other feminists, I work hard to bond with women across the barriers of class, race and culture, to do serious personal and political coalition work, but we cannot bond across the barrier of generation and across the maternal divide.

1974–1978

I start my first teaching job at a newly coeducational institution in 1974. Consciousness raising quickly takes on an institutional urgency, and a long struggle against sexism on behalf of women students, faculty and staff begins. I join with other feminists to fight for equal access and equal representation of women at all levels of the institution. We no longer have time to raise our own consciousness—a serious mistake, for there are so many unexamined assumptions that lead to so many crucial mistakes—but instead get busy educating department heads, deans, provosts and presidents about the subtle differences between men and women that need to be accommodated in the institution and about the complexities of gender equity. At our insistence, the university adopts an affirmative action plan and a maternity leave policy. As feminist activists, not as mothers, we begin to agitate for day care, determined that women not be disadvantaged by their maternity. We make sure that there is child care for every meeting, lecture or concert, that meetings get out by 5:30 P.M. the time day-care centers close. When we start a faculty and community "Feminist Inquiry Seminar" we use some of our funds to reimburse mothers for child care. We try to insist that other seminars do the same, for both mothers and fathers. We do all this as feminists, out of conviction, not as mothers, out of experience. We start a study group, reading Freud and Marx to find the roots of women's oppression in the very paradigms of our own education and struggle.

The job market in the humanities is as bad as it has ever been. Nevertheless, my husband and I both get jobs, but a thousand miles apart. I cannot follow him and there is no question of his adjusting his life to mine. We begin a long-distance commute in 1975. In 1977, still hoping to fulfill my dreams of gender equity in my own life and in the lives of my peers, I get pregnant. Personally, though not yet theoretically, I know that I can be a feminist and a mother: shared parenting, maternity leave policies and day care will free me to carry on with my professional and political aspirations. It feels important for committed feminists to be raising the feminist men and women of the next generation. But mostly, with or without this self-reflection, I just know I want a child. It all turns out to be too difficult for a two-career couple in an economy of scarcity and I soon discover the many severe personal costs: in my case, a temporary shift off the tenure track, divorce, the return to my old job, a period of single motherhood.

I'm lucky to have time to read during my pregnancy and while nursing my infant son. The first book I pick up in my new identity is Adrienne Rich's recently published *Of Women Born: Motherhood as Experience and Institution*. In her distinction between experience and institution, Rich gives me the first sympathetic feminist reading of motherhood. In her analysis of the way the "institution" of motherhood is shaped by patriarchal social and ideological structures, she defines motherhood precisely as the intersection between these delimiting constructions and each woman's own personal "experience." I begin to see mothers as subjects in their own right, and thus as sisters in feminism.

Rich decries what she called the feminist "matrophobia" in which I have so unthinkingly participated: not the fear of our mothers, but the fear of becoming like our mothers. In our desire to "become individuated and free," she says, we "perform radical surgery," removing an essential part of ourselves. "We are none of us 'either' mothers or daughters; to our amazement, confusion, and great complexity, we are both." I find here the feminist project for which I have been searching. Recognizing how intertwined daughters are with mothers is essential to feminist progress. "This cathexis between mothers and daughters—essential, distorted, misused—is the great unwritten story." Certain shifts in feminist analysis and, less obviously, my own maternity give me the tools with which to try to write the "unwritten story" of mother-daughter relations. This is the project I take on.

1978–1984

I'm not sure when I acknowledge my shift from "equality feminism" to "difference feminism." Our institutional struggles for equity and access reveal that what we have been asking for will not be enough. It is not enough to make space for women among existing structures: we have to transform the institution to accommodate the needs and lives of women. The project of transformation looms large and challenging: it reaches into our very psyches and bodies, the basic structure of our thinking and being. It promises to radicalize every aspect of our lives. The "difference feminists" or "cultural feminists" of the late seventies and early eighties seek the specificities of women's voices, of women's ways of knowing and writing by returning to motherhood, and especially to mother/daughter relationships. Here is where we try to find the sources of what we perceive as feminine tendencies toward relationality and affiliation, as opposed to what we identify as primarily masculine values of autonomy and separation. Here we can explore the implications of these gender-divergences, not only for women's psychology, but also for women's and men's ways of thinking, for the connection between gender and power, for our attitudes toward the world around us and our prevalent models of scientific knowledge. Classic feminist texts of the late 1970s, relying on psychoanalytic theories radically revised, analyze women's mothering as an important source and crucible of gender difference: I'm thinking or Rich's *Of Woman Born*, Dorothy Dinnerstein's *The Mermaid and the Minotaur*, Nancy Chodorow's *The Reproduction of Mothering*, Jane Flax's "The Conflict Between Nurturance and Autonomy within Mother/Daughter Relations and Within Feminism," Jessica Benjamin's *The Bonds of Love*, Evelyn Fox Keller's *Reflections on Gender and Science*, Carol Gilligan's *In a Different Voice*, Helene Cixous's *The Newly Born Woman*, Luce Irigaray's *This Sex Which Is Not One* and *And the One Doesn't Stir Without the Other*. These writers, influenced by object-relations psychoanalytic theory or by poststructuralism, point to an alternative to patriarchy and the logos, to a world of knowledge and experience in which subject-object dualism, separation, autonomy, and power relations might be reenvisioned.

Rich herself writes her book in a maternal voice, expressing the joys and pleasures, as well as the pain and frustrations, of maternal experience. But some of the other cultural feminist writing of this period, including my own, is located in the perspectives of daughters and is structured by mixed emotions about maternity. Although we all posit the centrality of maternity, we write from the child's view of mother/child relationships. With few exceptions, the field of feminist writing and theorizing has not yet created a space for the life and the thoughts and work of the mother, for a maternal subjectivity. Nor has it fully been able to take motherhood out of the realm of feeling and being, to politicize and contextualize it. The object-relations models that have in part inspired it are primarily focused on the child, seeing the mother as a silent and holding background to the child's development.

There are exceptions to this focus on the child, for example, Jane Lazarre's *The Mother Knot*, published in 1976, an account of her personal and experiential struggle with her maternal identity and with the work of mothering biracial children in a racist culture. I read Lazarre in the late seventies; I think of including it in my first course on "Mothers and Daughters" in 1980. I don't, ostensibly because it is written by a mother of sons, but I suspect it is really because I am still unable to listen to the honest description of the pain and frustration of maternal experience.

In 1978, I am the divorced single mother of an infant boy, and an assistant professor working tirelessly and anxiously for tenure. Getting tenure becomes a prime area of struggle for academic women: it becomes clear that we can best transform the academy by advancing through its ranks in large numbers. Some of us join together in collaborative research and writing projects to fight the competitive structures of tenure. We need each other's support and we need the institutional base of Women's Studies, which we work together to create and in which we design an administrative structure that challenges the institutional norm: we have rotating cochairs, and a steering committee, and we make decisions by group consensus. Women's Studies provides the academic space for our feminist scholarly inquiry and our experiments with feminist pedagogies. It becomes the space of personal and political community and coalition, the space where we need to deal with our commonalities as well as our differences, where some of us must confront our white, middle-class, heterosexual positions of privilege.

With a few colleagues who remember, as I do, the energies created in our consciousness-raising groups of almost a decade ago, I start a support group dedicated to analyzing our place as adult women in the institutions in which we work and the lives we wish to lead. Each of us certainly needs support and advice; we need a sense of community in a hostile environment; we need to draw strength from one another as we question our own assumptions and those of the institution. Much of our scholarly work has taken a feminist cast and we worry whether it will be acceptable for tenure.

There are eight of us and, again, we don't fully see how the fact that we are all white, middle-class and heterosexual might limit our perspective and discovery. We realize, immediately and painfully, however, that three of us are mothers of small infants: one of us is divorced, one is separated, and one is married and is living with the father of her child. Although we are all friends and share so many institutional and personal concerns, the group meets only for a few months. The breakup is painful and leaves many scars. We have different agendas: some of us are more interested in personal discovery, others need more professional support. It is significant, however, that the primary cause for the break seems to derive from the now much-discussed issue of motherhood, although that fact is masked by a professional misunderstanding that serves as an alibi for our split-up.

To my utter shock, my sisters and I find ourselves on opposite sides of what appears to be an unbridgeable divide. Those of us who are mothers have made an irreversible choice. We find ourselves inundated by the dailiness of our maternal work, silenced by our angers and even by pleasures we cannot articulate, except perhaps in some unreconstructed and ideologically suspect clichés about the superiority of our life course. Those who are not mothers feel equally powerless, overwhelmed by social and familial pressures, by their complicated ambivalences about the subject, by the presence or absence of a partner and potential father. The discussion starts to take a turn I have never experienced among feminist sisters to that degree—we seem no longer to be able to talk to each other. This one difference takes over everything else, evacuating our powerful points of connection. Each of us has so much invested in the choice she has made, or is in the process of making, that we simply cannot bear to contemplate the alternative. Every word is heard as pressure or competition. The discourse of mothers sounds either abject and unbearable, or celebratory and clichéd. There is simply no middle ground. Unexplored and unspeakable jealousies make the "childless" life too painful to contemplate for those of us with babies, especially for me, a single mother, struggling with tenure, with loneliness, fear and inadequacy. Our/my envy masquerades as pity or contempt. Many of us remain friends, but our feminism cannot accommodate the maternal divide. We can fight together institutionally for better child care and better maternity leave policies, but personally and theoretically we remain divided.

In the meantime, I make sure my dissertation gets published so that I might have the freedom to write the book I really want to write—the book on mothers and daughters, a book I then see as providing the groundwork for an analysis of femininity within patriarchy. "There can be no systematic study of woman in patriarchal culture," I write in the late seventies, "no theory of woman's oppression, that does not take into account woman's role as a daughter of mothers and as a mother of daughters, that does not study female identity in relation to previous and subsequent generations of women, and that does not study that relationship in the wider context in which it takes place: the emotional, economic and symbolic structures of family and society." As I talk with feminist colleagues and start presenting my work at conferences and in seminars, I begin to notice how exclusive this rhetoric sounds to many. In no way do I mean to imply that mothers are better or closer to what women are supposed to be, but that is how people hear me. The divided face of my support group begins to haunt me at other feminist gatherings and conferences. At the same time, I still read and write much more as a daughter than a mother; I conceive of the book as a study of daughters' relations with their mothers, and not at all as a study of motherhood.

We live in a culture that romanticizes motherhood and idealizes children, a culture dominated by fantasies of maternal omnipotence and by fears of maternal power, anger and violence. It is difficult to speak dispassionately of mothers, and even more difficult to speak in a maternal voice. Nancy Chodorow and Susan Contratto show in their article "The Fantasy of the Perfect Mother" (1982) that to a very large degree, feminist writing is often itself determined by primary process fears of maternal power and anger at maternal powerlessness. This formulates so much of what I have been experiencing. I see additional sources for the hesitations feminists have shown in adopting a maternal voice or perspective: the perception of mothering as a patriarchal construction, or a form of collusion with patriarchy; the discomfort with the vulnerability and lack of control attributed to maternity; the fear and discomfort with the body and the relentless feminist policing of anything that could be seen as arguing for essential or biological gender differences; the ambivalence about power, authority and anger—all qualities identified with motherhood; the heavy feminist reliance on psychoanalysis, which sees only the child and makes the mother a holding and silent, enabling, background to the child. These ambivalences and reliances have largely isolated feminist thinking from the experience of mothers, from maternal subjectivity, though, as Robin Morgan quite rightly announces, through the 1980s, feminists are becoming more ready and able to hear maternal stories.

Toward the middle and certainly by the late 1980s, however, just as far-reaching and balanced studies of maternity—Sara Ruddick's *Maternal Thinking*, for example—begin to shape feminist theory, many feminist critics attack "difference feminism" or cultural feminism. They decry much feminist writing about maternity for contributing to an essentializing of women's experience—for returning women to the destiny of their anatomy. Cultural feminism seems to some to exclude from the ranks of feminism those women who eschew motherhood. Even worse, critics claim that "difference feminism" is unable to envision a meaningful life for women separate from motherhood. Discussions about maternity in which I participate at feminist conferences and seminars are inevitably interrupted by the emotional voices of those who feel excluded by a mother-inclusive feminist discourse, however nuanced— by a discourse they experience as alienating and even "violent" in its exclusionary power. More than that, they see feminist attention to motherhood and to mother-daughter relations as a turn to the private: to a form of introspection and psychologizing that could never effect lasting social change. These feminist critics identify motherhood with "individual" concerns, forever depoliticized. They see it as perpetuating heterosexuality and patriarchy.

1985

Now, remarried and the mother of two sons and a stepson, I have the great fortune to spend a year working on mothers and daughters at an all-female research institute. The first week, a few of us begin a study group in feminist theory to discuss what is emerging as the crucial issue in the feminism of the eighties and as a dividing line in our group—race. "Difference feminism," eager to explore and to value the specificity of women's experience and expression, has so focused on gender as to ignore other important spaces of difference, namely, race and class. Finding commonalities among women has meant establishing an exclusive and biased vision of a feminine largely defined by a white middle-class norm. As I read, with more urgency than ever, the work of women of color and as I engage in painful discussions within a diverse study group, I begin to recognize the power of these unseen assumptions in my own thinking. I see how monolithic my thinking about women and about mothers and daughters has been. I see how my desires for commonality, and the psychoanalytic perspectives I have adopted, have made me resistant to acknowledging important differences among women. I begin to work on inflecting my gender analysis with the categories of class, race and sexual orientation.

As "differences feminists" caution against any general notion of "woman" or even "women," certainly against any decontextualized and dehistoricized notion of "motherhood," I see that my analysis of mother-daughter relations needs to be built on divergences as much as on commalities. It needs to be suspicious of notions like "motherhood" or "the mother-daughter relationship" for fear of generalizing or universalizing. It needs to take into account radical differences among mothers caused by race, class, economic status, sexual orientation; it needs to be based on all the localized studies on lesbian mothers, African-American mothers, and mothers mothering in a variety of specific and time-bound cultural contexts that are beginning to come out. It needs to see that the mother-exclusive feminism in which I have been writing has been a white, heterosexual, middle-class feminism and that African-American feminist writing, for example, has not excluded the maternal in the same way at all.

Thus Alice Walker, for example, begins *In Search of Our Mothers' Gardens* in the voice of the daughter who wants to come to terms with the conflicting legacies of many mothers—of black "mothers," like the writers Phyllis

Wheatley and Zora Neale Hurston, and all those mothers and grandmothers whose creativity was stifled by the institution of slavery, as well as of white "mothers" like Virginia Woolf who understood gender but neglected to take into account the added oppression of race. Writing as the daughter of all these mothers, and of her own, Walker places women's maternity at the source not only of sexism but also of the particular racism encountered by women of color. But, in "One Child of One's Own," she writes as a mother combining a maternal with a daughterly perspective to find, however ambivalently, a site of resistance in maternity and in mother/daughter bonding: "It is not my child who has purged my face from history and herstory and left mystory just that, a mystery; my child loves my face and would have it on every page, if she could, as I have loved my own parents' faces above all the others, and have refused to let them be denied, or maybe to let them go" (p. 382). This type of subversive and resistant mother/daughter collusion is characteristic of Walker's "womanism," and I come to see in the writings of women of color in Walker's generation the most contradictory, complex and nuanced, the most richly ambivalent perceptions of motherhood and daughterhood.

Instead of a general theory, I realize at this point, in the mid-eighties, that what I need are such local and multivocal analyses as well as the painstaking work of crossing boundaries and building coalitions. But even this work is open to the critique of supporting what is still being represented as an essentially conservative social institution that ties women to their homes and their bodies. It still seems as coming dangerously close to privileging a biological dimension of female experience, and it still feels exclusionary to those women who either are unable or have chosen not to experience pregnancy, birth or parenting. In spite of the recent concentration on single mothers and lesbian mothers, the very mention of "motherhood" still seems to promote the oppressive nuclear family.

While race most radically divides the women scholars and artists at the institute where I am working in 1985, another important split emerges between women who are mothers and those who are not. In the many discussions at colloquia, lunches and study groups, this division seems to me to grow to inform the perspectives and reference points of the participants in ways I had not expected and around topics that do not obviously lend themselves to distinctions based on motherhood. As we discuss the implications of certain theoretical formulations, as we formulate strategies of social change, as we focus on political commitments, those of us who have children seem to take them and their future as an important point of reference. Others find this rhetoric exclusionary as well as conservative and familial, private, narrow and politically suspect, radically limiting for all women.

By now, of course, we are in the Reagan/Bush era, working in and against the context of the culture's fierce pronatalism and the resulting violent attacks on abortion rights. To claim motherhood becomes more and more difficult in the era of "family values" and the family agenda of the right. Ann Snitow's version of this history presents 1980s feminism as succumbing almost completely to the culture's pronatalism and celebrating the voice of the mother as *the* primary, the only feminist voice, and thereby edging out other voices. Mapping mid-1980s feminism, Snitow selects as its most influential books and issues Phyllis Chesler's *The Sacred Bond*, the debate about the "mommy track," Betty Friedan's *The Second Stage*, Arlie Hochschild's *The Second Shift*, and Silvia Ann Hewlett's *A Lesser Life*, insisting that their attention to motherhood backtracks and reverses an earlier desire to divorce women from a necessary association with maternity. I cannot agree with this view. As someone who spent the 1980s trying to write about mothers and feeling myself fall into all the pitfalls I have just outlined, I see a different history of hesitations, cautions, fears, conflicts, defensiveness, revisions, modulations of voice and argument. What I see as still missing is a "mother-inclusive" feminism that does not elevate motherhood as the only goal for women; a feminism that would resist projection and idealization on the one hand, and devaluation of mothers, on the other—a feminism that recognizes the vast differences among mothers who mother in vastly different social, economic and cultural conditions. We need to conceive a feminism that includes maternal voices without either sentimentalizing or blaming mothers. We need a feminism respectful of mothers that would resist the trap of pronatalism—that commits itself to speaking *positively* of and to *women* who are (and here our language betrays us) "childless," or "not mothers."

With these goals in mind, a few of us form a discussion group composed of mothers who are also feminist theorists, scholars whose work touches on mothering in various ways. It's exhilarating: we are now among ourselves, we can speak freely. We devote ourselves to formulating a language in which to discuss maternal *experience*—what is left out of everything we are reading—and to theorize, though not of course naively, from that experience. Here is a chance to take some risks, to depart from the accepted 1980s feminist study group model, and to come back to a revised and yet-to-be formulated model of feminist consciousness raising. Unfortunately the group's class and racial homogeneity impose serious limits on the discoveries we will be able to make. Still, this is not our major stumbling block. The most difficult aspect of our discussion is the tone we use to describe our experiences as mothers and the limited range of voices culturally available for this task. Some of us are bothered when others sound too celebratory about their maternal feelings and accuse them of idealizing these and fitting them into narrow cultural stereotypes; others sound much too negative and despairing, incapable of expressing maternal pleasure along with the pain, and again the pain comes too close to cultural stereotypes. More serious still is a disturbing set of divisions that emerge between the discourse of mothers and that of daughters, opposing voices we each in various ways contain and cannot combine. We find, as we reflect on this, that when we speak *as mothers*, the group's members are respectful, awed, helpful in the difficulties of formulating maternal experiences. However, the tone and affect change when we speak *as daughters* about our own mothers, and we all giggle knowingly, reverting back to old stereotyped patterns of discussing a shared problem—our "impossible mothers"— much as I had done in the consciousness-raising group fifteen years ago. The sympathy we must muster for ourselves and each other *as mothers*, we cannot quite transfer to our own mothers. Although, as mothers, we are eager to tell our stories, as daughters we cannot fully listen to our mothers' stories. This tragic asymmetry between our own two voices is so pervasive as to be extremely difficult to discuss. It reveals the depth and the extent of the "matrophobia" that exists not only in the culture at large, but also within feminism, and within women who are mothers, ourselves, who have spent a good part of our careers thinking about motherhood. We each seem to be wearing two different colored lenses, making it impossible for us to see anything but a blur when we look out of both eyes at once. For me this is the most poignant discovery of the group, a discovery that increases my determination to concentrate in some detail in my work on the perspectives of mothers and on the difficulties feminists have in sympathizing with those perspectives. I write a chapter on maternal anger that clarifies for me what it is that is so difficult to confront in maternal stories. I concentrate on the mother in Alice Walker's "Everyday Use" and on Toni Morrison's Eva in *Sula*, looking particularly at Walker and Morrison's courage in positing an angry mother at the core of their daughterly texts, and thus in confronting an anger directed, in some sense, at them as daughter-writers. I try, through anger, to circumscribe the contours of maternal subjectivity and to look at what might be so difficult to hear in maternal stories. Again, I go to the texts of women of color, finding models of specificity there.

1987

I am almost finished with *The Mother/Daughter Plot*. The book has shifted from being about mothers and daughters written from the perspective of the daughter, to being about the missing maternal voice, about the shapes of maternal subjectivity and the difficulty of articulating it. I am wondering what to say in my introduction when Tony Morrison comes to my campus to read a chapter of her as yet unpublished novel. It is the first chapter of *Beloved* and I realize that she has written the maternal story for which I had been looking throughout my own work. I realize that Morrison's Sethe, damaged, wounded, broken, sad, bereft as she is, can provide a model for the encounter between feminism and motherhood: she can show us why as feminists we cannot afford to leave motherhood behind, and why maternal agency, and perhaps also motherist political action, builds on the consciousness, the awareness and commitment that feminism offers.

It has become a predictable move for feminist theorists of all backgrounds to go to the texts of women of color for exemplary models of embodiment, for historicized or contextualized feminine practices. In looking at Sethe, I am aware of following this trend. At the same time, doing so, I hope to cut across the divergent familial ideologies (black and white) that the novel reveals without, however, erasing the differences between them. A feminist discussion of maternity, as I see it, is precisely a discussion that needs to take differences due to race, class, ethnicity, sexuality and historical specificity into account, even while allowing points of convergence to emerge. The slave mother, in particular, demands a most rigorously discriminating analysis of difference, while at the same time enabling the most far-reaching perception of relationship. Sethe invents a model of mother-love she herself never encountered.

When I first read the novel, I read it through the lens of generational and political change, and I wonder why Morrison chose to tell the story through Sethe's perspective rather than Denver's, for example. Denver is someone with whom the readers can identify: she is born on the threshold between slavery and freedom, she is born into freedom in a mythic scene of renewal and rebirth. Her access to the memory of slavery is mediated and therefore much more like ours, as readers: Denver is the child of survivors. She is of the new generation, free to start a new life, the one who needs to be the keeper of the memory but who need not be destroyed by the pain. I see her as an emblem for the young feminist who must leave her mother's pain behind if she is ever going to design a new life. But no, Morrison chose Sethe, the survivor, the mother. In doing so, Morrison does what I have suggested feminism needs to do—she has claimed maternal experience, adopted a maternal voice, looked at the configurations and shapes of maternal subjectivity.

And what has she found? The conversations between Sethe and Denver, Sethe and Beloved, some of them conversations from beyond the grave, are the kinds of conversations feminists need to be having: they are conversations exploring the divergent experiences of women within the oppressive institutions of patriarchy, slavery, and capitalism, of women whose unique experiences shape their psyches but who still need to talk with one another across their differences.

Morrison has cast the black mother as the holder of meaning and memory whose self extends across generations in the service of her community's self-recognition. She becomes the voice of resistance in a society that managed to find a way to survive through repression, displacement, forgetting. At its best, I begin to see, a maternal perspective and voice can create and inspire the broad sympathy that allows for the recognition of affiliations as well as the awareness of particularity and distinction that are necessary for a transformative politics. At its most threatened, however, a maternal perspective cannot look beyond the danger posed to one's own child and is willing to sacrifice the children of other mothers, one's own children, oneself. Morrison explores those stakes unsentimentally. She reveals the politically transformative dimension of a motherhood that is not afraid to question its own most basic assumptions, and thus she reclaims motherhood for feminism.

1993–1995

Two colleagues are organizing a conference on "Redefining Motherhood." It will not be on mothers and children, or on maternal subjectivity, but on maternal agency—on radical mothers! Theorists and activists will be talking to one another about their work and their experiences. Studying, as the papers and presentations at the conference do, mothers who are political agents, who have appropriated and redefined their maternity as an instrument of political engagement, therefore, can offer a way out of the debilitating conflict between feminism and motherhood. But I fear that a "motherist" politics, however radical, will still be seen by feminists as exclusionary, potentially conservative, essentialist, sentimental.

As I prepare for the conference, I reflect on how, as feminists, we need to politicize motherhood and to recognize the political work that mothers do—we need to claim that work for feminism, to learn its strategies, so that we might convince mothers that as much as feminism needs motherhood, mothers also need feminism. We need it to connect our maternally based political work to a larger feminist transformative cause that might well alter the very bases of our work. Activist mothers need to understand the power and gender relations that have made the mother's voice so politically effective, but that nevertheless need to be changed.

Listening to the papers at the conference, meeting activists who struggle for welfare rights, environmental safety, human rights *as mothers*, I feel energized by the representation of maternal activism and motherist politics. At the same time, I see a remarkable hesitation on the part of both scholars and activists to invoke the term "feminism" to describe their activism or to articulate the relationship between "motherist" politics and feminist politics. A politics based on motherhood, I realize with some discomfort, can be invoked in the service of any political agenda. The strategies used by Nazi mothers or by the mothers of the Klan may not be identical to those deployed by the mothers at Love Canal, but the tenets of a politics of motherhood—the care and nurture of children and the health of their physical and social environments—can serve divergent and contradictory political causes. Precisely because of the power of maternal voices, mothers' activist work can be appropriated for any political goal, from the most progressive to the most reactionary. It seems to me that only an explicit feminist consciousness, an explicit commitment not just to children, but to women, can insure against such appropriation and can inspire a more fundamental commitment to radical and fundamental social and ideological change. I'm not saying that feminist activism is more fundamental than the fight for human rights, peace or environmental safety—such comparisons cannot be productive. Yet if we are to fight for human rights, for peace, or for environmental safety *as mothers*, we can gain a strategy of coalition and an instrument of politicization from feminism that might help us to divert the debilitating appropriations that are the risk of assuming a maternal position. We can benefit from the transformative structures—consciousness raising, group study and coalition building—that feminists have forged to effect both political and psychic change and we can try to see how personal transformation might be at the core of political change.

This articulation between feminist politics and "motherist" politics is most needed now if, as women committed to social change, we are to renew our hopes and regain our energies. It is difficult to remain hopeful in the mid-nineties, as so many hard-won gains are subject to hateful backlash, as feminists themselves have given in to debilitating conflicts and divisions, as we fear losing a basic sense of commonality and coalition. But feminism struggles to affirm its commitment to women, however contested. It continues to refine its methods of analysis. Even in its strategies of conflict, however flawed, in its difficulties with its own successes, in its hesitant acknowledgements of power, in its efforts to renew its agendas, it has much to offer the political struggles of mothers, even as it can be renewed and inspired by the political activism of mothers. To envision a mother-inclusive feminism and a feminist "motherist" politics still remains the task of feminists and of mother-activists at the end of this remarkable century.

Rethinking "Maternal" Politics

Sara Ruddick

I came to the Dartmouth conference on motherhood in a dispirited mood, ready to put mothers behind me. Many feminists had diagnosed maternal politics as symptom and cause of "backlash" against women. In their eyes, women acting as mothers, however good their cause, and whatever increased skills and authority they gained from their actions, reinforced traditional stereotypes of femininity. Many progressives of various allegiances were scornful of the effect of mothers on politics. They saw maternal politics as, at best, a spectacle that diverted attention from the real plays of power; at worst it was an irrational, unpredictable force that could be used as quickly for evil as for good.

The doubters reinforced my own pessimism. In an evidently violent and neglectful world and country, mothers as a group seemed to be barely discernable, let alone effective, as agents of care or justice. When mothers were visible, in the past or present, they have sometimes been painful to witness. Klan mothers in Indiana in the 1920s, patriotic Nazi mothers in Hitler's Germany, and homophobic mothers in today's United States remind anyone who still needs reminding that mothers can be moved to act "as mothers" in support of sexual bigotry, totalitarian governments, racist policies, and patriotic militarism. Mothers *do* act against many kinds of violence; do act for a respectful, caring, lively peace. The Argentinean Madres, the Green Belt movement in Kenya, and Women Strike for Peace in the United States are only three of many examples. But there are war mothers as well as peace mothers, racist as well as anti-racist mothers. Maternal roles, identities and symbols serve them all.[1]

Yet despite these reasonable grounds for pessimism, I continued to find the idea of political motherhood seductive. And I knew I was not alone. Over the last decade, many women and some men have spoken to me about ways that daily care and responsibility for children transform their thinking and their lives. They were seeking, and in some cases had created, a more evidently public forum where they could enact values which they struggled to achieve in their daily work: protectiveness, nonviolence, respect for spiritual complexity, the treasuring of individual life, whatever values they believed that their particular transformative experience of mothering had provoked. The Dartmouth Motherhood conference itself lent credence to my hopes and theirs. Mothers in the United States and around the world had organized against racist policies, environmental destruction, abusive labor practices, and many other forms of neglect and violence. These mothers spoke not only of cruelties that beset them but also of their resilience and success.

I left Dartmouth reconnected to the idea of political motherhood and inspired to explore the promise of a particular kind of maternal politics, one that challenges rather than serves dominant official policies. But the conference also reminded me of certain obstacles that stand in the way of understanding or developing effective maternal protests. Two such obstacles concern initial responses to the very idea of the "maternal." Doubts about the trivial insignificance of maternal politics on the one hand and its dangers on the other are imbued with less conscious anxiety. This makes it hard, at the present moment in the United States, even to discuss political motherhood. Second, there is a tension, emotional and conceptual, in the relation of political motherhood to the mothering of ordinary women and men. The conference also raised for me two interesting and fundamental questions about maternal politics: How is it possible for mothers to translate particular passionate loyalties to children and kin into political actions on behalf of the well-being of "other" children and their mothers? How can displays of maternal suffering lead to effective action and elicit aid from distant mothers and others who live in relative safety?

I

To begin at the beginning, it often seems difficult, at this time in the United States, even to discuss "maternal" politics. A hot emotional atmosphere surrounds the "mother" whenever she appears on a feminist, academic, or political stage. Allegedly adult and public discussions become suffused with passions of childhood: love, hate, blissful and wretched dependency; grievances no mother can assuage, longings no mother can satisfy. Some of us also bring to our talk about mothers passionate fantasies provoked by our own experiences of mothering: for example, compelling desires to order our children's lives and their world, an illusion of ultimate responsibility for children's well-being, and, correlatively, exaggerated shame for our "failures."

In partly conscious thrall to childhood and maternal passions, it is easy to idealize powerful or suffering mothers, to expect too much and suffer disappointment too quickly. It is as if mother(s) must do everything or have done nothing; that with mothers in the room there is no need, or worse, no space for anyone else. Hard-earned lessons of childhood and motherhood have to be learned again in political contexts. The strength of the strongest mother(s) is never sufficient to satisfy political, any more than personal, need; nor is maternal will exhaustive of political, any more than personal, agency. Maternal politics, like *any* politics, is partial. Like any politics, maternal politics is always limited by context, incomplete and imperfect.

Personal fantasies of maternal omnipotence and failure are exacerbated by more public attitudes toward politicized motherhood. The alleged failures — or alleged pretensions — of maternal politics tend to be described in matrophobic and misogynist ways. A vocabulary of abuse — crazy, naive, self-indulgent, sentimental — comes readily to hand for political mothers as it does for child-rearing mothers. More specific charges also often have a matrophobic ring. Thus the Argentinean Madres were "*locas*" when they were most endangered by, and dangerous to, a brutal military tyranny. Now when they refuse to engage in "normal" politics and thereby, according to their critics, become irrelevant — perhaps even a danger — to Argentinean democracy, they are called stubborn, apolitical, unable to change with changing times. This alleged intransigence could be interpreted as principled adherence to accountability instead of naive stubbornness. Alternatively, the Madres' determinedly "abnormal" politics could be assessed for the distinctive contribution it makes, *along with other politics*, to Argentina and to human rights generally.

Another example, this one from the United States: When mothers oppose the organized violence of their state or cadre, as many mothers in the United States opposed the impending Gulf War, they (like men and women pacifists generally) are dismissed as sentimental apoliticos. When, war underway, these same mothers tie yellow ribbons around any symbolically likely object at hand, they seemed besotted with loyalty to (leader, military) Fathers, fickle, and, again, sentimental. Yet fickle ribbon-tying mothers could be seen as consistently protective, first protesting war and its dangers, then, battle underway, rallying for the safety of "their/our" children. This is not to excuse the patriotism of wifely mothers, which I found furiously disheartening. Rather it is to consider realistically but generously the complex motives and worldly limits of mothers who act politically.

The atmosphere will never be cool when mothers come on the scene. Indeed, the power of maternal politics depends on the emotions it generates in people who have had or have been mothers. But it might be possible to look at maternal politics as we might look at any other politics—feminist, socialist, or anti-militarist, for example—that also engage less-than-conscious passion. We could then ask what limited but distinctive contribution a politics of motherhood might make in a particular political context.

II

I spoke earlier of women and men who believe that their lives have been transformed by caring for children and who want to put this transformative experience to public use. They may act "maternally" in many kinds of political groups, including ones that do not highlight maternal or parental rhetoric and ideology. Nonetheless, they believe that when they organize against drugs, work for curricular changes or after-school programs, organize a protest to preserve their neighborhoods or lands or to ban the sale of guns, they are extending ways of thinking and acting that originated in responsibility, care and love for children.

While almost any movement could draw upon some women's maternal loyalties, there are some protests and projects that enact a "politics of attachment" appropriate but not limited to mothers. To cite one example: in September 1994, in the United States, there was a protest against the sale, ownership, and proliferation of guns and for gun control. The great majority of participants had lost someone to gunshot wounds: children, parents, lovers, husbands, friends. A few mourned victims personally unknown to them. Each of the marchers brought a pair of "empty shoes" worn by the people—children and adults—who had been killed. These empty shoes symbolized the ruptures of attachment. It is foolish, politically or conceptually, to distinguish sharply between kinds of attachment: maternal, paternal; filial, parental; ties of marriage or friendship.[2]

There is a more familiar, narrower meaning of "maternal politics" in which women present themselves as "mothers." While men may support these "mothers" in various ways, this version of maternal politics relies on its culture's ideology of female mothering. Although most women participants are mothers in a conventional sense, some may not be legal or biological mothers of particular children; progressive reformer Jane Addams is an example. Nor need participants allude to or reflect upon their actual mothering work. Rather, they deploy a maternal identity and celebrate maternal relationships, exploiting the symbols of motherhood evocative in their particular culture. They may create groups that are explicitly maternal by name: Mothers Against Drunk Driving, Mothers Against Nuclear Madness, and the Argentinean Madres are examples. Or they may participate in *women's* movements that include, but do not limit themselves to, maternal rhetoric and identity. Women's Strike for Peace, the Women of Greenham Common, Women in Black, Chilean Women for Life (under Pinochet), and the Women's Association of Bosnia and Herzegovina serve as examples.[3]

"Ordinary" women/mothers (but not usually ordinary maternal men) often participate in mother-identified politics or in mother-inclusive women's groups. But, judging from conversations over the years, they also sometimes feel that in these groups their experience is swallowed up in, or used by, the politics that speaks in their name. Some advocates of maternal politics seem to trivialize the work and experience of mothers. They may, for example, claim that "maternal" is only a metaphor that serves wider political aims or insist defensively that a woman (or a man) need not be a mother to engage in maternal politics. A few, not mothers themselves, actively resent attempts to connect political motherhood to a maternal experience and identity they do not share. To be sure, many explicitly political mothers do respect the work and experiences of "ordinary" mothers. But in the midst of organizing, they are confronted with demanding political tasks; they deploy motherhood but may have little time to reflect upon it. Even when they are distant from crises and action, attending conferences like the one at Dartmouth, for example, they may talk almost entirely of their political struggles. A person who comes to a conference on motherhood hoping to talk about the political relevance of her own maternal experience may then feel as if the importance of mothering is once again dismissed.

The disquiet of "ordinary" mothers with political motherhood may be exacerbated by the relation of "maternal" politics to biological sex or socially constructed gender. Mothering is a kind of work in which men as well as women can fully engage; yet in a world that distinguishes mothers and fathers, neither women nor men easily think of men as mothers. "Ordinary" mothers may feel that women's or mother's groups exclude men or, when they are inclusive, require both women and men to relinquish a cherished masculine fatherhood. On the other hand, gender-neutral "parenthood" obscures the distinctive responsibilities of mothering that are still, so often, borne by women. It also circumvents possibly fruitful connections between mothers and (other) women acting on a variety of causes in "women's" groups.

Whatever the tensions between frankly political and "ordinary" mothers, maternal politics as a whole depends upon each. Maternal politics is effective because it appeals to the ordinary passions of women and men who are, or who identify with, mothers. Moreover, ordinary maternal thinking is a resource for reimagining political processes and articulating political goals. Mothers are, for example, preoccupied with the limits of control, the necessity for and abuse of obedience, conflicts between hope and truth-telling, principles and techniques of nonviolent fighting—to mention only a few recurrent themes with which I am familiar and that are redolent of political import. Indeed, it often seems as if maternal reflection on these issues lacks only one organizing step or sentence to emerge into "politics."

Yet in the absence of an explicitly maternal politics, many reflective mothers fail to see *any* political meaning in maternal work or to extend their richest, most illuminating maternal conversations to larger, public issues. Confronted with the idea that mothering is a sociopolitical project, such "apolitical" mothers could be prompted to translate their maternal experience into more public terms, even, perhaps especially, if they took exception to the particular political agenda that galvanized their attention. At the same time, "ordinary mothers" who have been longing to act politically can find that their desires are fortified and focused by publicly political motherhood even if they choose to work only in gender-neutral groups that avoid maternal rhetoric. Of course, "Mothers and Children" are already everywhere evoked and recruited in support of official public policies. But a politics of *protest* originated and controlled by "mothers," jars accepted sensibilities in ways I will shortly suggest, and transforms maternal status from emblem to agent.

III

Political motherhood almost always begins with and represents a mother's commitment to her "own" children and family. Mothers organize against the conscription of *their* sons, the disappearance of *their* children, the pollution of *their* lands. The first and most likely extension is to children of the group or "people" with whom a mother identifies and to the community on which she depends. Given this particularity, how is it possible for mothers to appreciate the suffering or act on behalf of "other" children and their mothers?

Evidently the movement from one's own to others is difficult and fragile. Mothers often organize only for goods their own children require, remaining indifferent or, where competition is involved, hostile to the claims that "other" mothers and children make on community resources. At its most dangerously tribal, maternal politics actively sets itself against the alien and the "other"; its agenda becomes frankly racist, patriotically militarist, fearful of whoever is sick, homeless, or foreign. It is therefore crucial to learn whether and how it is possible to create, out of the particular loyalties and loves of mothers, cross-cultural respect for, even appreciation of the pleasure, pains, and loves of "others."

Fortunately, maternal parochialism is only one strand and liability of maternal politics. There is also ample evidence of the capacity of mothers to create extensive commitments to distant and different children and mothers. Mothers who act in their own town or country may, without conscious effort, inspire recognizable variants of their protests elsewhere. The Madres of Argentina and Women in Black in Jerusalem have inspired distant but mimetic "local" actions; two international conferences under their auspices attest to this possible propitious consequence of contagious coalitions.[4] Some groups, amidst outrage and cries of betrayal, make it their defining purpose to forge alliances with the "enemy." Women in Black or the mothers of Northern Ireland are two of many examples. Perhaps most astounding, some mothers create out of their particular suffering connections to peoples whose suffering, and whose cultural context, are radically different from their own. The Madres offer a wonderfully heartening example of the cross-cultural extension of sympathy for distant sufferers and righteous protest on their behalf. Although they endured brutal assault against their own children, the Madres came in the course of protest to identify first with all disappeared children, then with anyone disappeared in their country, then with any children across the globe who suffered violence or abusive neglect.

It would be worse than presumptuous to measure the moral achievement of mothers who construct alliances with "enemies" or who, out of their own suffering, create cross-cultural political commitments. We can only listen carefully for hints in the stories they tell. Nor should we ignore the malign effects of some maternalist parochial passion. But it is perverse to fix on the worst cases of righteous tribalism when we might look attentively and with hope at the many and remarkable kinds of cross-cultural appreciation of which political mothers are capable.

Even in the midst of cross-cultural connection, maternal politics remain passionate and particular. This passionate partiality is often seen as a limit of maternal politics. "Real" politics should organize against all injustices; its causes are meant to be transpersonal and transcendent. I, however, see the partiality of maternal politics as part of its promise. People are passionate and local. What looks like the ability to transcend particular attachment is often defensive, self-deceived, or a luxury of the strong and safe. Most political relationships have to be created in the midst of passionate particularity, not outside of it. Maternal politics, because it issues out of particular and familiar allegiances, can inspire a move from one's "own" to "other," from local to more general without ever denying, indeed by continually remembering, irreplaceable and specific loyalties and love.

IV

Political mothers often come together out of shared pain; they appeal to mothers and others who live in relative safety by making their pain visible. Thus, to cite a paradigmatic example, the Madres literally paraded their suffering, wearing photographs of their lost children around their necks. Sometimes pain is only anticipated; mothers then come together out of fear and try to evoke similar fears in others. Thus protesters have tried to represent in advance the suffering that would follow upon war, ecological disaster, or nuclear "exchange" or accident. The presentation of suffering to achieve political ends is widely suspect. Suffering is thought to be self-preoccupying, even addictive, to those who experience and express it. In some current feminist discussions in particular, "the victim"—as she is often called—is thought to be so identified with her suffering that she cannot assert her*self*, cannot take or enjoy power or relish the pleasures that come her way. Mothers in particular have been designated as "ladies of sorrow," personal mourners or martyrs of the nation who weep over suffering they cannot change and for which they take no responsibility.

In ordinary mothering as well as in politics, there are risks in the attempt to sway others by displaying one's own pain. But whatever the liability of public expressions of suffering, there seems to me a greater danger in ignorance, indifference, or denial. Often people fail to recognize, or to admit publicly, their own victimization; they must be brought to appreciate present and future harms to themselves of, for example, weapons testing, environmental policies, employer practices, or medical experiments. Typically, people do not apprehend the suffering of "others" whose lives are distant or different from their own. Even to begin to elicit their sympathy, it is necessary to represent graphically real and potential injuries the "others" suffer.

While it is politically necessary to present suffering, it is difficult to predict or control the effect of the presentation on its audience. Witnesses may respond to suffering with sympathy and help. But suffering also evokes fear and denial, passive and sentimental pity, sadomasochistic excitement or disgust. It becomes a political task to present suffering in ways that hearten sufferers and encourage spectators to sympathetic action. What then can we learn from effective maternal actions about ways of presenting suffering?

One feature of maternal politics may seem too obvious to mention. In maternal suffering, the self who suffers is preoccupied not with her*self* but with another. The suffering that mothers present is not only shared, but is also often centrally located in children who are hurt, families that cannot be fed or held together, communities destroyed by violence. Mothers call us to witness a pain that they bear but that originates in the violation of the beloved, in the disruption of attachments. We are meant to act alongside them, to protest and protect on their behalf even as they protect and protest the violation of others; we are meant to reach out to those who are, in ordinary and extraordinary ways, already, as always, reaching out.

This intrinsically extensive feature of maternal suffering complicates the idea of "self" absorption. It also, I think, encourages an extensiveness in respondents who are led to think about their children and others who they care for. It is these already outward-reaching, protective activities that are imaginatively extended to include some sort of aid to distant mothers and children.[5] This imaginative translation across cultures is facilitated by the intimacy and familiarity of the injuries mothers present. Children are "lost," temporarily or permanently, in ordinary times. To have a child "disappeared" forever is a terrifying enactment of a recognizable terror. Officials and teachers, snobs and bigots, bullies and domestic tyrants routinely hurt children. Systematic lethal abuse by those who govern activates rage already in waiting.

When pain is familiar, it is more easily evocative, but familiarity may also fail to rivet attention or, alternatively, may arouse self-preoccupied fears. Typically, however, effective maternal politics creates a disruption within the familiar by violating, even as it expresses, assumptions of ordinary love and fear. Political mothers occupy a public space, appearing decidedly *as mothers*, but in a place where neither they nor the evidence of their love, fear and loss is expected to appear. The women of Greenham Common tacked familiar paraphernalia of British domestic life—pillow cases, diapers and drawings— against the wire gate of a nuclear base. The Madres carry photographs that belong in a bedroom or living room into the central government square. Tokens of childhood, photographs intended to capture events and stages of ordinary life, are "typical"; they present children meant to appear, to live. Yet this appearance in public official space is a threat and sign of disappearance; records of life are suffused with policies of death.

Presentations of pain tend to include other, less-expected emotions. Protesting political mothers are visibly and audibly angry. Rather than accepting their suffering or bearing it nobly, as mothers of sorrow are meant to do, they denounce its perpetrators. Yet, remarkably, political mothers are also sometimes playful or sexually provocative. Called before the fearsome House Un-American Activities Committee, members of Women Strike for Peace staged a parody of a women's luncheon meeting. Covering themselves with honey before penetrating the fence of the missile base, Women of Greenham Common invited soldiers to a "Teddy Bear Picnic." Temma Kaplan has told of several instances, particularly in Africa, where women challenged authority by using their own bodies—their nakedness, menstrual blood and sexuality— to ridicule and provoke.[6] When women sport with images of femininity and propriety, they mock the authorities mothers are meant to serve, the customs they are meant to preserve.

The violation of spatial expectations, intermingling of presence and absence, the simultaneous expression of love and its destruction, the joining of suffering with anger, sport and sex, all these disruptive conjunctions are often heightened by danger. Many participants in mother's movements are subject not only to arrest but also to physical and sexual abuse, long jail sentences and torture, or murder. To be sure, not all maternal protests risk physical danger.

However, for women to appear in public angry, loving and rebellious, standing against, rather than in support of, church or state, risks ridicule and ostracism. Maternal protests that express great courage in circumstances of extraordinary physical danger defy whatever connections an individual or culture might make between the maternal and the sweet or the passive. Mothers who overcome far lesser fear and self-doubt also begin to invent a politics of responsible, active motherhood.

v

I've never used the word "evil" in all my years in Washington, but what's going on down here is really quite evil . . . It is very clear to me that we will never, ever get done what needs to be done unless we build a movement . . . We're going to have a march. We're going to mobilize as many people and groups as we can to come to Washington in the spring. It's time for mothers, frankly, and fathers if they want to come along, and grandmothers and grandfathers and nurturers and caregivers and religious leaders to come and say to these people in an election year that hurting children is morally and politically unacceptable.
—Marion Wright Edelman, Children's Defense Fund[7]

People gather at conferences like the one at Dartmouth for many reasons: to record the failures and successes of maternal politics, to warn of the dangers of maternalism,[8] to deflate unjustified claims for maternal virtue or power, to celebrate heroic and creative maternal projects and resistances. Presumably, some participants also hope to galvanize support for mothers' movements already underway, perhaps even to invent new maternal politics suitable to their particular political context. I at least, who came to the Dartmouth conference dispirited, left with a new question: could maternal politics, today in the United States, make a distinctive contribution to a politics of justice and care?

Admittedly it is difficult to imagine maternal voices effectively piercing the din of sentimental and reactionary motherhood on the one hand, cynicism, self-absorption, racism, greed and fear on the other. Yet I know that many mothers feel driven to put their maternal experiences to more public use. And many of them want to preserve or create a society which nourishes and respects all of its children. I am neither strategist nor optimist. In far better times, the idea of *organizing* a protest, rather than gratefully participating in one, strikes me dumb. But I see and hear from activists and potential organizers in the United States and around the world who seem resilient and ready to engage the forces that would destroy children's lives.

A distinctly maternal politics would be only one element in myriad efforts to mobilize maternal passions. Fathers would join with mothers, grand-mothers and grandfathers with their children, "nurterers and caregivers" of all sorts could come along. Religious communities, unions, teachers, nurses and doctors—anyone committed to children would be urged to participate. This politics would be unified by its message: whether or not it is an election year, "hurting children is morally and politically unacceptable."

Although its constituency would be diverse, this politics would recognize "private," "domestic" passions and enact them in public. It would thereby challenge, as more specifically maternal protest does, not only the policies but also the procedures, the politesse, of public discourse. There would be more movements, like the "empty shoes" protest against guns, that galvanize but are not limited to maternal passion. Some would protest against direct assault. But it is equally crucial, and perhaps more difficult, to imagine sharply fo-cussed protests against the brutal, but increasingly normalized social *neglect* of many children and against the destruction of the *institutions* indispensable to their well being. As I said, the very idea of organizing a protest short-circuits my computer. But I have a longing for what I would like to see others produce.

Within the myriad politics that evoke maternal images and galvanize ma-ternal passion, it seems to me that there may be a place for distinctly maternal politics, "for mothers, frankly." Mothers as objects—symbolic and real—are at the center of agitated discussion. If, as subjects, we speak and act "as mothers," people will already be listening. Women who present themselves as mothers may be especially able to counter dominant cultural images of tame and sentimental motherhood through publicly expressing a clear-sighted, an-gry determination to hold leaders accountable for children.

But there are angry active mothers already on the political stage, some-times "as mothers," sometimes along with other angry people. And some of these mothers are fully engaged in a politics of neglect, racial dominance and sexual bigotry. The mothers I imagine would be determined to create an alternative disruptive, transfamilial and transcultural *maternal* identity. This identity could express publicly, in its symbols and actions, a sexual ethic that visibly repudiated the compulsory heterosexuality and limited, patriarchal family forms in which the idea of motherhood has been embedded. It would express, by the presence of its constituents and through its rhetoric and sym-bols, a determination to root out and destroy racist assault and neglect that destroys children and vitiates maternal efforts of protection.

"Real" mothers, as we know, are—and will remain—passionately divided on crucial issues affecting children, such as immigrant rights, "welfare," sexual mores and education, and gun control. Deeply felt division should neither surprise or discourage us. Our social circumstances differ radically; passion for our children makes injustice to them that much more painful; maternal work and love do not flatten but often intensify our oddities of temperament and aspiration; the issues we face do not admit of simple resolution. But it is profoundly disheartening to see mothers turning against each other, casting some of us out as "bad"—lazy, lustful, greedy, mean, addicted; superstitious, reactionary, radical, foreign, dull or flighty—not meant to be mothers, perhaps not meant to be here at all.

In presenting themselves as "mothers," women who *do* share some political aims might create an ideal of maternal solidarity by *demonstrating* it; by marching together. They would not be like each other, might not even like each other. But they would stand with each other—single and coupled mothers, healthy and ill mothers, drug-free mothers and mothers fighting addiction, lesbian and heterosexual mothers, "welfare mothers" and career mothers, teenage mothers and elderly grandmothers, illegal, legal, "alien" and citizen mothers. They would stand in "maternal solidarity" with any mothers and any children under siege.

Mothers have, at best, very limited power; we will neither save nor destroy the peace and well-being of our states and communities. But we have some power, many allies, many kinds of organization we can join. There is no natural mother love, let alone a maternal love waiting to be politicized for peace, or care, or justice. Maternal politics will have to be invented. Yet it is also true that the materials of invention are at hand, drawn from creative protests of the last decades and the lively imaginations of the youngest parents and lovers. Marion Wright Edelman is not hallucinating when she sees "evil" in official plans and private callousness. Yet, as I hear across the country voices of maternal anger, fear and desperate love, it seems to me that there is also reason for hope.

NOTES

1. At the conference, Kathleen Blee's talk on the Klan was particularly insistent and incisive about the racist potentialities of mothers' groups, even those that were feminist.

2. *New York Times*, Sept. 20, 1994.

3. Within "women's groups" there is often tension between women who exploit or express maternal feelings and women, often feminist, who do not want in any way to associate themselves with motherliness. The explicit celebration of lesbian sexuality also causes tension within women's groups, although lesbians, of course, find themselves among mothers and nonmothers. These tensions seem to be useful and productive because they shake up misleading connections between motherliness and wifeliness or heterosexuality. And I personally, partly because of these tensions, am more at ease in women's than in mothers' groups.

4. The Argentinean Madres convened a "Gathering of Mothers in Struggle" in Paris, spring 1994. Women in Black held an international conference of women's peace groups in Jerusalem, Dec. 1994.

5. Very few people will respond to sufferers with the degree or intensity of protectiveness they offer to their own children or "people." But there are many kinds of lesser aid—for example, letter writing, mimetic protests of solidarity, rallies or various kinds of publicity, lobbying or protests—designed to elicit one's own government's support for the sufferer's cause, financial aid for each of these efforts or direct financial aid. If a display of suffering is to be effective, witnesses must be told how to "do something" that requires the kinds of sacrifice or courage available to them. Or they must be able to invent appropriate actions for themselves. Otherwise, awareness of others' suffering can lead witnesses to despair or guilt and then indifference.

6. Amy Swerdlow, *Women Strike for Peace: Traditional Motherhood and Radical Politics in the 1960s* (Chicago: University of Chicago, 1993). On Greenham Common see Ann Snitow in *Mother Jones*, Feb./March 1985. For Temma Kaplan's paper see this volume.

7. *The New Yorker*, Jan. 15, 1996.

8. For a discussion of the class arrogance to which maternalism is liable, see Linda Gordon, *Pitied but Not Entitled* (New York: Free Press, 1994).

Contributors

RITA ARDITTI is a member of the graduate faculty of the Union Institute. She has co-edited two anthologies, including *Test Tube Women: What Future for Motherhood?* and is at work on a book about the Grandmothers of the Plaza de Mayo in Argentina. She is one of the founders of the New Words women's bookstore, and of the Women's Community Cancer Project, both in Cambridge, Mass.

XIAOLAN BAO is assistant professor of history at California State University, Long Beach, where she teaches Chinese and women's history. She is revising her dissertation, entitled "Holding Up More Than Half the Sky: A History of Women Garment Workers in New York's Chinatown, 1948–1991," and has published widely on working-class women's history in China and in the United States.

CAROL BARDENSTEIN is assistant professor of Arabic and comparative literature at Dartmouth College. She has written on transculturation in Arabic literature, underground Arabic literature, and dynamics between canonical and noncanonical Arabic literary forms. She is currently writing a book entitled "Trees, Oranges, and the Prickly-Pear Cactus: Palestinian and Israeli Discourses of Indigenousness."

KATHLEEN BLEE is professor of sociology at the University of Kentucky and author of *Women of the Klan: Racism and Gender in the 1920s*. She is writing a book on the role of women in contemporary racist groups in the United States, and has just co-written a book on the origin of chronic poverty in Appalachia.

DOLLIE BURWELL gained national recognition in 1982 when she led five hundred Warren County, North Carolina, mothers who laid their bodies down in front of PCB-laden trucks to protest the state's decision to create a PCB dump in their community. Now the Register of Deeds in Warren County, Burwell was an organizer of the first annual People of Color Environmental Summit in Washington, D.C.

MARY CHILDERS is the director of equal opportunity and affirmative action at Dartmouth College. She is the author of "A Conversation About Race and Class" with bell hooks, and other articles.

KATHY DOBIE is an investigative journalist whose work has appeared in *Mother Jones, Ms., Vibe, The Village Voice, The Progressive, Vogue,* and many other publications. She is an associate editor for Pacific News Service, and a writer at large for *Vibe.*

RUBY DUNCAN is the founder of Operation Life and was for twenty years the leader of the Las Vegas welfare mothers' movement. She was recently featured in a documentary profiling ten leading women in Nevada politics, produced by public television station KNPB-TV in cooperation with the Nevada Women's History Project. Duncan is also the recipient of an honorary degree from the University and Community College System of Nevada.

LOIS GIBBS, the former Niagara Falls, N.Y., housewife who galvanized the grassroots movement to combat toxic waste in New York's Love Canal, is founder and executive director of the Citizens' Clearinghouse for Hazardous Wastes. Among her honors are the 1990 Goldman Environmental Prize, *Outside* magazine's "Top Ten Who Made A Difference" award for 1991, and an honorary degree from the State University of New York, Cortland College.

REMA HAMMAMI, a Palestinian scholar and activist, is the former director of the Women's Affairs Center in the Gaza Strip. She is currently a member of the faculty of the Women's Studies Program at Bir Zeit University in Palestine.

MARIANNE HIRSCH is professor of French and comparative literature at Dartmouth College, where she is Distinguished Professor in the Humanities. She is the author of *The Mother/Daughter Plot: Narratives, Psychoanalysis, Feminism,* and *Beyond the Single Vision,* as well as the co-editor of *Conflicts in Feminism* and *The Voyage In: Fictions of Female Development.* She is currently at work on a new book, *Family Frames: Photography and Narrative in the Post-Modern.*

ALEXIS JETTER, a former metropolitan reporter at *New York Newsday,* is a widely published journalist, a Pulitzer finalist, and an adjunct assistant professor at Dartmouth College. Her articles have appeared in the *New York Times Magazine, The Manchester Guardian, Vogue, The Village Voice, The Nation, Mother Jones,* and many other publications.

TEMMA KAPLAN is a critic, activist, and professor of history and women's studies at the State University of New York, Stony Brook. She is the author of *Anarchists of Andalusia, 1868–1903,* which won the 1977 Berkshire Prize for best book by a woman historian; *Red City, Blue Period: Social Movements in Picasso's Barcelona;* and *Crazy for Democracy: Women in Grassroots Movements.*

MADHU KISHWAR is the founder, editor, and publisher of *Manushi,* a magazine published in New Delhi that is devoted to social justice and women's rights. Kishwar is actively involved in human rights and civil liberties in India and teaches at the New Delhi Centre for the Study of Developing Societies. She is co-editor of *In Search of Answers: Indian Women's Voices from Manushi,* and the author of a forthcoming collection of essays, *A Horror of Isms and Other Essays.* She has published widely in academic journals and the mainstream press.

CLAUDIA KOONZ is professor of history at Duke University, author of *Mothers in the Fatherland: Women, the Family and Nazi Politics* and co-editor of *Becoming Visible: Women in European History*. She is deeply involved in refugee relief work in the former Yugoslavia. Her writings have appeared in *The New York Times Book Review, The Voice Literary Supplement,* and *Women's Review of Books.*

WINONA LADUKE directs the White Earth Land Recovery Project in White Earth, Minnesota, which is working to reclaim the Anishinabe people's original lands from federal, state, and county governments. An Anishinabe, she co-chairs the Indigenous Women's Network and is a board member of Greenpeace. She is also program director for the environment program of the Seventh Generation Fund, a Native foundation supporting grassroots Native initiatives in environmental justice and community restoration.

WANGARI MAATHAI is an internationally known environmentalist, human rights activist, and opposition leader in her native Kenya. One of the first women professors in East and Central Africa, she founded the Green Belt movement, which has trained more than 50,000 Kenyan women to reforest a once-lush land desertified by clearcutting and soil erosion. The Green Belt movement has spread to countries across Africa. Maathai is the recipient of the Goldman Environmental Prize, the United Nations Environmental Program Global 500 Award, and a Woman of the World award from the Princess of Wales.

CHERRÍE MORAGA is a poet, playwright, and essayist, and the co-editor of *This Bridge Called My Back: Writings by Radical Women of Color*. She is the author of numerous plays including *Shadow of a Man*, winner of the 1990 Fund for New American Plays Award, and *Heroes and Saints*, winner of the 1992 Pen West Award. Her most recent book is a collection of poems and essays entitled *The Last Generation*. Her most recent play, *Watsonville*, won the 1995 Fund for New American Plays Award.

LINDA MULLEY, an adjunct professor of education at Dartmouth College, works for children with developmental disabilities and their families. A pre- and post-Stonewall lesbian activist, she has also been a lesbian mother for seventeen years. She is a founder of the Gay/Lesbian Research and Education Network (G/LEARN), a Vermont-based organization that works with local schools to create safe environments for gay and lesbian youth and for children of gay and lesbian parents.

PATSY RUTH OLIVER was a leader in Friends United For a Safe Environment in Texarkana, Texas. She alerted her African-American community of Carver Terrace, once a creosote dump and now a Superfund site, to the danger of toxic poisoning in their homes, and led a successful crusade to force the U.S. government to move them to safety. Oliver, one of the first two black women to sit on the board of the Friends of the Earth, was a fiery voice inside the environmental justice movement.

ANNELISE ORLECK is associate professor of history at Dartmouth College and author of *Common Sense and a Little Fire: Women and Working-Class Politics in the United States,*

1900–1965. She is currently working on a book about the welfare rights movement in Las Vegas, Nevada, entitled *Gambling With Human Lives: Women, Children and Welfare*. She is also writing a short volume on Soviet Jewish immigrants in the United States.

GRACE PALEY is one of the world's foremost short-story writers and a life-long fighter for social justice. Her major publications include: *New and Collected Poems, Later the Same Day, Enormous Changes at the Last Minute, The Little Disturbances of Man, Leaning Forward*, and *Long Walks and Intimate Talks*. Paley taught for twenty years at Sarah Lawrence College. Since retirement, she has taught at Stanford, Johns Hopkins, and Dartmouth.

ALICIA PARTNOY is one of the few "disappeared" victims of the military dictatorship during Argentina's so-called Dirty War (1976–1983) to "reappear." Partnoy is a writer and activist who serves on the board of Amnesty International. She has published a book of stories, *The Little School: Tales of Disappearance and Survival in Argentina*, and a bilingual collection of poems, *Revenge of the Apple*. She is also the editor of *You Can't Drown the Fire: Latin American Women Writing in Exile*. Partnoy has three daughters.

SARA RUDDICK teaches philosophy and feminist studies at the New School for Social Research. She is the author of *Maternal Thinking: Toward a Politics of Peace*, and co-editor of *Working It Out* and *Between Women*. She is currently co-editing a collection of essays by political theorists, legal theorists, and theologians entitled *Ordinary Mothers' Work: Moral Struggles in Bearing and Raising Children*. She is also completing a book on feminist ethics entitled *Clinging to Lives*.

SIMONA SHARONI is an Israeli feminist and peace activist who is currently assistant professor of peace and conflict resolution at the American University in Washington, D.C. She is the author of *Gender and the Israeli-Palestinian Conflict: The Politics of Women's Resistance*. Her current research, which compares the dynamics of change in Palestine-Israel, Northern Ireland, and South Africa, explores people's sense of identity after peace agreements are signed. The essay in this book was supported by a grant from the John D. and Catherine T. MacArthur Foundation.

DIANA TAYLOR is professor of Spanish and comparative literature at Dartmouth College. Author of *Theatre of Crisis: Drama and Politics in Latin America*, she has recently co-edited *Negotiating Performance in Latin/o America*. She is the author of the forthcoming *Disappearing Acts: Spectacles of Gender and Nationalism in Argentina's 'Dirty War.'*

UNIVERSITY PRESS OF NEW ENGLAND
publishes books under its own imprint and is the publisher for Brandeis University
Press, Dartmouth College, Middlebury College Press, University of New Hampshire,
Tufts University, Wesleyan University Press, and Salzburg Seminar.

Library of Congress Cataloging-in-Publication Data
The politics of motherhood : activist voices from left to right /
    edited by Alexis Jetter, Annelise Orleck, and Diana Taylor.
        p.   cm.
    ISBN 0–87451–779–6 (cloth : alk. paper). — ISBN 0–87451–780–X
(pbk. : alk. paper)
    1. Mothers—Political activity.   2. Women in politics.   3. Women
political activists.   I. Jetter, Alexis.   II. Orleck, Annelise.
III. Taylor, Diana.
HQ1236.P64   1997
306.874'3—dc20   96–26125